MW01277912

DUTCH COLONIALISM, MIGRATION AND CULTURAL HERITAGE

Cover: Tile picture of the 'Oost en West' Association, which in the first half of the twentieth century popularized knowledge about the Dutch colonies in the East and West Indies. Design Jan Toorop.

KONINKLIJK   INSTITUUT
VOOR TAAL-, LAND- EN VOLKENKUNDE

DUTCH COLONIALISM, MIGRATION AND CULTURAL HERITAGE

Edited by

GERT OOSTINDIE

KITLV Press
Leiden
2008

Published by:
KITLV Press
Koninklijk Instituut voor Taal-, Land- en Volkenkunde
(Royal Netherlands Institute of Southeast Asian and Caribbean Studies)
P.O. Box 9515
2300 RA Leiden
The Netherlands
website: www.kitlv.nl
e-mail: kitlvpress@kitlv.nl

KITLV is an institute of the Royal Netherlands Academy of Arts and Sciences
(KNAW)

Cover: Creja ontwerpen, Leiderdorp.

ISBN 90 6718 317 8

© 2008 Koninklijk Instituut voor Taal-, Land- en Volkenkunde

Contents

GERT OOSTINDIE

Preface

This is an unusual book. A few words of explanation may serve to explain its origins and the logic behind it, without doing away with the obvious fact that there are two very distinct parts to this volume. The main intent of this preface is simply to clarify the ideas and work leading to the present, two-tier book.

Cultural heritage is one of the many legacies left by colonialism world-wide. Over the past few years, we have witnessed an increasing interest in this heritage, often in highly contesting terms. It is now widely accepted that the concept of cultural heritage includes both tangible and intangible herit-age. The former, more conventional dimension refers to material 'things', legacies ranging from colonial landscaping and built environment through artefacts to archives – tangibles presenting themselves prima facie and often screaming for concerted efforts to be made in order to rescue and/or preserve them. Tangible heritage has long been the near-exclusive forte of archaeolo-gists, art historians and archivists. Intangible heritage refers to the realm of the immaterial and includes languages, oral and musical traditions on and from the colonial period, mental legacies and the like. The uncovering, recording and interpretation of this intangible heritage requires the expertise and effort of another community of specialists, particularly anthropologists, historians and musicologists.

Experts working in the field of cultural heritage have increasingly come to appreciate the need and the opportunities to combine the practices and insights of these once rather discrete traditions. Today it is conventional wisdom – expressed by UNESCO and many other prestigious institutions – to emphasize that the two can and should benefit from one another. No colonial fortress without its contemporary stories and interpretations, no collective remembrance which does not invite research in old archives or art collections.

The contested nature of cultural heritage from the colonial period is obvious. The recourse policy makers take to adjectives such as 'common', 'mutual' or 'shared' only underlines the awareness that this past and its lega-cies arouse divergent and at times strongly confrontational memories and interpretations. The sensible approach to cultural heritage policies departs from this understanding while attempting to provide a forum where divergent approaches to the past and its legacies may engage in a constructive and fruitful manner.

The Netherlands has a long colonial history; the days when this past was unconditionally celebrated are gone. In recent years quite some effort and means have been invested in developing a policy for cultural heritage cooperation with the various nations affected by Dutch colonialism. A succinct comparative analysis of Dutch policies may be found in the second chapter of this book. Suffice it to say at this point that cooperation in this field has been predominantly of a bilateral nature; occasionally, attempts have been made to forge supranational networks limited to the orbit of either the former Dutch East Indies Company or its West Indies counterpart. No programmes exist involving the 'entire' former Dutch 'colonial orbit'.

There are evident explanations for this, beyond contemporary politics and orientations – colonialism, by nature, had widely divergent characteristics and consequences, and the same can be said for contemporary legacies. Moreover, the various academic disciplines involved tend to work mainly in their own secluded realms. Started in 2007 with funding by the Netherlands Ministry of Education, Culture and Science, the KITLV research programme 'Migration and culture in the Dutch colonial world' aims to broaden our perspective and to help reflect on a comprehensive and comparative approach to the field of shared cultural heritage. This is both timely and feasible. Timely, as an awareness of today's global interconnectivity should compel us to think about the early modern roots of globalization; and timely also as there is a growing interest in comparative approaches in the field of common cultural heritage based on an awareness of the rich historical knowledge rooted in these migration experiences. Feasible, as our present understanding of local and regional histories enables us to move on to more ambitious comparisons.

Migration has been a primary focus of this programme and is central to the present book. Since large-scale movements of labour forces are a pivotal dimension in Dutch colonial history, we propose to make this a central concern in cultural heritage policies. As will become clear from this book, colonialism sparked migrations with crucial but uneven demographic, social and cultural consequences in the various Dutch colonial settlements and colonies as well as 'back home'. Colonial migrations and the ensuing tangible and intangible heritage and specific categorizations defined what we came to regard as cultural heritage today, and why. For this reason experts from *all* countries involved in this programme share a common interest in migration.

Early on, migration flows created an intricate web connecting the Netherlands to Africa, Asia and the Americas; Africa to the Americas and to Asia; in the nineteenth century also Asia to the Americas, with ultimately, in the post-World War Two period, the direction of migrations shifting to the Netherlands. In colonial times, this migration was usually 'free' when coming from the Netherlands and forced when directed from Africa to the Americas. Between Asia and Africa, and at a later stage between Asia and the Americas, migration flows covered the entire spectrum from free to coerced. The 'free' postcolonial migrations to the Netherlands are a separate matter altogether, with uneven combinations of push and pull factors.

These various migration flows helped to create colonial societies that were never typically Dutch, but that did demonstrate specific Dutch characteristics as compared to the cultural impact of other European powers on their colonial settlements. Power imbalance, ethnic differences and creolization characterized the cultural configuration of these colonial societies. Today this history is distinctly visible in cities such as Paramaribo or Willemstad – in other cities once part of the Dutch colonial realm, such as Colombo, Recife, Jakarta, Cape Town, Elmina, Georgetown and even New York, one has to dig much deeper. In some places history reveals itself in the built environment and even in oral traditions and language usage; in other places images of days long gone are evoked mainly through archival records.

Comparative research into this colonial history and its legacies is relevant for the countries involved but no less for the Netherlands, where public history is widely debated. In this process the erstwhile metropolis – partly in response to large-scale postcolonial migrations – increasingly accepts that those roots also stem from colonial history. The contours of a comparative programme are very broad: the relevant period spans centuries, the geographical scope is enormous, the nature of the research may vary from (maritime) archeology and art history via the management of archives and actual archival research to historical-anthropological investigations focusing on retrieving intangible cultural heritage. Hence our focus on migration as a pivotal dimension in colonial history.

As for the contents of this book, its second, and largest part offers extensive surveys of the extant literature and quantitative data available on the movements of people under colonialism. The three chapters discuss European migration to the colonies (Gijs Kruijtzer); slave trades and slavery (Rik van Welie); and indentured labour migrations (Thio Termorshuizen), respectively. As such, this second part represents a unique attempt to synthesize and compare the work of specialists usually only focusing on one country or region. It is concluded with a quantitative appendix compiled by Hanneke Lommerse.

The first part provides a broader perspective. My opening chapter sum-
marizes the crucial importance of migration in Dutch colonial and post-
colonial history as well as the uneven effects of the various migrations in
the Dutch orbit. In the second chapter, Anouk Fienieg, Robert Parthesius,
Brittany Groot, Rivke Jaffe, Sjoerd van der Linde and Pauline van Roosmalen
discuss Dutch policies for cultural heritage and past and present cooperation
with partner countries, as well as offering a comparison of the Dutch tenets,
objectives and practices with policies enacted by other former European colonial powers. In the third chapter, I offer some reflections on the highly divergent ways colonial history is remembered (or not) in the various countries
involved, with some suggestions for possible future projects linking research
and cultural heritage policies.

It should be pointed out that *Dutch colonialism, migration and cultural heritage* does not even attempt to present a serious analysis of the cultural impact
of the various migrations in the various societies involved. While most chapters deal in one way or another with the very uneven cultural impact of the
movements of people, we have refrained from a systematic and comparative
analysis to this end. The obvious is stated – lesser demographic significance
tends to translate into lesser cultural importance and present-day legacies,
and vice versa – but this does not answer important questions of cultural
genesis, including the significance of colonial hierarchies and distribution of
power. It is here that we simply make the case for the crucial significance of
migration to colonial history and the resulting cultural heritage, as an invitation for further work.

This volume provides a modest prelude to a wider debate between scholars and cultural heritage specialists from all countries touched by Dutch
colonization – including, of course, the Netherlands itself. Draft versions
of these chapters were discussed in a highly stimulating workshop held at
the University of Stellenbosch, South Africa, from 25 to 27 March 2008. This
workshop was in itself a rare occasion. Expertise on 'Dutch' Asian, African
and Atlantic history and cultural heritage may be widely available, but serious mutual comparisons are scarce and a truly international debate is in its
infancy at best.

The Stellenbosch workshop, the research for this book and its publication were
financed by the Netherlands Ministry of Education, Culture and Science. I
acknowledge with sincere appreciation this financial support and in particular the unwavering commitment of Vladimir Bina, Sabine Gimbrère and Kees
Somer to this project. It has been a pleasure to work with this Ministry and
its representatives – their contributions reflect an open mind and a genuine
awareness that Dutch funding alone is not enough to make things work and
that 'sharing' cultural heritage demands an open, non-chauvinistic attitude.

Valuable advice was also provided by professors Femme Gaastra (Leiden University) and Susan Legêne (VU Free University Amsterdam).

Many thanks to the participants of the workshop at Stellenbosch University, superbly co-organized by Siegfried Huygen: Rose Mary Allen (the Netherlands Antilles); Aspha Bijnaar (National Slavery Institute NiNsee, the Netherlands); Fernando Rosa Ribeiro (Unicamp, Brazil); Maurits Hassankhan (Minister of Internal Affairs, Suriname); H.D.S. Hettipathirana (Sri-Lanka-Netherlands Heritage programme, Sri Lanka); Hui Kian Kwee (University of Toronto, Canada); Susan Legêne (VU Free University Amsterdam, the Netherlands); Wim Manuhutu (Museum Maluku, Utrecht, the Netherlands); Badri Narayan Tiwari (University of Allahabad, India); Robert Parthesius (Centre for International Heritage Activities, the Netherlands); Akosua Perbi (University of Accra, Ghana); Bambang Purwanto (Gadjah Mada University, Indonesia); Arminda Ruiz (Museum of Archeology of Aruba); Henk Schulte Nordholt (KITLV and VU Free University Amsterdam, the Netherlands); Nick Southey (University of South Africa in Pretoria, South Africa); Alex van Stipriaan Luïscius (KIT and Erasmus University Rotterdam, the Netherlands); Astrid Weij (Erfgoed Nederland, the Netherlands); and Leslie Witz (University of the Western Cape, South Africa).

Apart from those participating in the workshop, a large group of historians commented on draft versions of various chapters. Their contributions are acknowledged in the relevant chapters. It must suffice here to thank them collectively for their time and the generous sharing of their expertise.

In the final phase of text editing, I received much-appreciated help from Kirsten van Immersum and particularly Inge Klinkers. I gratefully acknowledge Hanneke Lommerse's dedicated and cheerful assistance to the entire project from its very beginning.

The illustrations in this book document in very diverse ways the Dutch presence in the eastern and western hemisphere. As they are all of KITLV provenance they also attest to the richness of the Institute's collections.

Finally, an accolade to the research team at my institute, KITLV/Royal Netherlands Institute of Southeast Asian and Caribbean Studies in Leiden: Gijs Kruijtzer, Hanneke Lommerse, Niels and Erik Sitton, Thio Termorshuizen, Rik van Welie and Esther Zwinkels. At the time of this project, this small team consisted of BA, MA and PhD students. You all contributed more than I could and perhaps should have asked for. *Chapeau.*

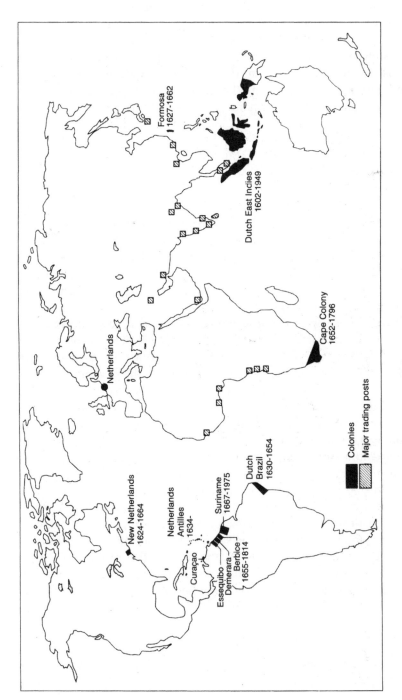

Main areas of the 'Dutch empire'

Formosa
1627-1662

Dutch East Indies
1602-1949

Netherlands

Cape Colony
1652-1796

New Netherlands
1624-1664

Netherlands
Antilles
1634-

Curaçao

Essequibo
Demerara

Suriname
1667-1975

Berbice
1655-1814

Dutch
Brazil
1630-1654

Colonies

Major trading posts

GERT OOSTINDIE

Migration and its legacies in the Dutch colonial world

The fragmentation of memory is one of the many legacies of Dutch colonialism in Asia, Africa, the Americas and ultimately in the Netherlands itself. The historiography of Dutch colonialism can be neatly divided into geographic branches, with each of these subdivided into smaller entities. This book aims to broaden the perspective by presenting a comparative approach to colonial migrations in the Dutch orbit. This introductory chapter provides a bird's eye view of relevant colonial history as well as a succinct discussion of the major types of migration sparked by Dutch colonial rule and some preliminary observations on the resultant cultural legacies.[1]

An exceedingly brief history of Dutch colonialism

To provide some context, a few words on the general outlines of Dutch colonial history are requisite. While Dutch ships were engaged in incidental explorations and commercial pursuits all over the tropics by the late sixteenth century, the scale and organization of overseas expansion was greatly enhanced with the establishment of the Dutch East Indies Company (VOC, 1602-1799) and the Dutch West Indies Company (WIC, 1621-1792). This would lead to the establishment of a series of trading posts along with a number of genuine colonies mainly administered by these companies.

A glance at the superbly rendered digital *Atlas of mutual heritage*[2] illustrates the enormous expanse of area once covered by the VOC and the vast number of former settlements, fortifications, trading posts and the like, reflecting this history. From the Cape Colony in South Africa, this string of

---

[1] I thank those participating in the workshop held at the University of Stellenbosch, 25-27 March 2008, as well as Peter Boomgaard, Pieter Emmer, Henk den Heijer and Gijs Kruijtzer for their critical comments on an earlier version of this paper.
[2] www.atlasofmutualheritage.nl

historical settlements ran through eastern Africa, the Middle East, South and Southeast Asia to China and Japan. These settlements tended to be short-term and comprised very few Europeans. In a few other places, such as Cochin in present-day India, the Dutch presence lasted longer. Nonetheless, few traces remain. Of more significance were the brief Dutch colonization of Formosa/ Taiwan (1624-1662) and the unique opportunity offered by the Japanese rulers to Dutch officials and traders to settle the small island of Dejima in the harbour of Nagasaki (1641-1859).

The VOC only achieved genuine long-term colonization and permanent settlement in the Cape Colony in South Africa, Sri Lanka and contemporary Indonesia. Most issues pertaining to common cultural heritage therefore centre on these states. The direct impact of the Dutch in the other territories was of modest significance outside the realm of commerce. Only a few of the present-day Asian states that are heirs to the latter category of territories have a distinct interest in early encounters with the Dutch.

For much of the period during the French Revolution and the Napoleonic wars the Dutch colonies were occupied by the British. After the Peace of Vienna (1815), the colonial empire in Asia was reduced to its prize possession, the Indonesian archipelago ('Nederlandsch-Indië'). The Dutch state – by now a Kingdom – assumed full imperial powers itself. The 'pacification' of the entire archipelago was only completed by the early twentieth century. By then, Indonesia had become of crucial importance to the Netherlands. The country would remain a Dutch colony until the declaration of independence in 1945, even if effective control ended in 1942 with the Japanese occupation and the official transfer of sovereignty was only finalized in 1949, or even as late as 1962 with the cession of New Guinea (Papua).

Despite auspicious beginnings, the Dutch empire was eventually less successful in the Atlantic. In West Africa settlements tended to survive for only short periods, with just a few, in present-day Ghana, becoming long-standing Dutch trading posts. Elmina (1637-1872) was the most notable and endured the longest. The first two Dutch colonies in the Americas, New Netherland (1609-1664) and Dutch Brazil (1630-1654), were lost fairly quickly to the British or reconquered by the Portuguese, respectively. The focus then moved to the Caribbean and the adjacent Guyanas on the northern coast of South America. Eventually the Dutch held on to six Antillean islands as well as four plantation colonies in the Guyanas.

The Napoleonic wars again ushered in a wave of British occupations. Afterwards, Berbice, Essequibo and Demerara – present-day Guyana – were ceded to Britain. Suriname and the islands returned to the Dutch realm. Suriname became an independent republic in 1975, while the Antillean islands still form part of the Kingdom and have no interest in changing this post-colonial status.

A paradox underlies Dutch colonial history. For the Netherlands, colonial expansion in Asia, particularly in the Indonesian archipelago, was of great importance, economically, geopolitically and culturally. The lasting Dutch legacy in Asia, however, is very limited beyond the fact that colonialism created the geographic contours of what is now the Republic of Indonesia. The reverse applies to transatlantic expansion, which ultimately proved to be of lesser importance and interest to the Dutch but would nevertheless leave a lasting impact in their former colonies. In Africa, the former Cape Colony defies this paradox. Relations between the Netherlands and Cape Town would remain significant in many areas, even long after the British takeover.

The key to understanding this paradox – and the unique model of the Cape Colony – lies in demography and in the migration histories that are central to this book. Dutch colonialism implied large-scale human migrations for all continents involved: mainly on a voluntary basis for Europeans, overwhelmingly forced for Africans, and in a variety of arrangements for Asians. In all cases, climate and pre-colonial demography were crucial in the triggering of these migrations. Only colonies with a moderate climate attracted large numbers of Europeans – hence only the short-lived New Netherland colony and particularly the Cape became genuine settlers' colonies. Migration to tropical areas typically involved bonded and semi-bonded labour organized under colonial auspices.

The crucial importance of the African slave trade and Asian indentured labour migration to the Dutch Atlantic is well-known. While the two chapters in this book on slavery and indentured labour confirm this, they also indicate that the trade in and use of enslaved and subsequently indentured human beings ran at a similar level in Asia. The contrast lies in the ethnic characteristics and relative numerical importance of these migrations. In the Indonesian archipelago, the majority of the bonded and semi-bonded migrants were ethnically akin to the local population and, with the partial exception of Chinese migrants, integrated with the local population fairly quickly or, to a lesser extent, with the European colonists. Of even more significance, in most areas and episodes the numbers of these 'colonial' slaves and indentured labourers were dwarfed by the native population.

The contrast with the Dutch colonies in the Americas is enormous. Pre-Columbian native populations were of importance in New Netherland and in Dutch Brazil, but in the Caribbean the number of Amerindians was low and declining. Hence, next to peripheral Amerindians and modest numbers of European colonists, enslaved Africans, and subsequently in Suriname Asian indentured labourers, came to constitute the massive majorities of the local populations. In other words, and in stark contrast to the Dutch East Indies, colonial migrations reshaped the Dutch Caribbean. It is evident that these demographic contrasts resulted in strongly diverging contemporary legacies, not in the least pertaining to common cultural heritage.

Post-colonialism is not just a matter of periodization and academic paradigms. The concept also applies to the last migratory movement connected to colonialism, or rather the ending of it. As in so many other cases, decolonization in the Dutch orbit resulted in new migrations. The volume of post-colonial migrations to the metropolis from the East and from the West is roughly comparable in absolute numbers. The number of Dutch citizens with roots in Indonesia is now estimated at just over half a million, while the metropolitan Dutch Caribbean community falls just below that figure.

Here again, the contrast lies in the proportional significance. In relation to an Indonesian population now at 235 million, the number of Dutch with Indonesian antecedents is insignificant and, moreover, ethnically not at all representative. The Dutch Caribbean communities, in contrast, are representative of the sending communities, are not much smaller than the populations in the Dutch Caribbean and maintain strong transnational ties. As we will see, this has all sorts of contrasting implications for the way colonial history is remembered – and thus probably also for future cultural heritage policies.

Colonization and colonists

In most places where the Dutch founded colonies, other powers had preceded them. Dutch colonialism therefore also implied both learning and deviating from previous European practices, in administration, the military, landscaping and architecture, social and cultural life. This simple observation raises a series of questions of obvious relevance to debates on cultural heritage which, for practical reasons, cannot be dealt with here.

Next, there is the issue of the 'national' character of Dutch colonialism. To a greater extent than any other colonial power – with the possible exception of Denmark, a minor player – the Netherlands encouraged Europeans of other nationalities and even religions to establish themselves in its colonies. One may safely assume that this had consequences for the development of a Dutch variant of colonialism. Another key question is how the 'Dutch' colonists, very much in the minority in most of their new habitats, related to the wider society.

The chapter by Gijs Kruijtzer on 'free' European migration in the Dutch orbit does not attempt to address, much less fully answer the last two questions, but it does present indispensable ground work from which to depart, particularly for the earlier colonial period.[3] For more detail, it must suffice

---

[3]   Obviously free Chinese migration was extremely important within the Dutch Asian sphere, but this topic is not discussed in this book.

here to refer to his contribution and to the quantitative appendix at the end of this book. But what is the general picture?

A first conclusion evident from Kruijtzer's data, but perhaps forgotten in living memory, is that a considerable number of the 'Dutch' forming the backbone of Dutch colonialism were born outside the Netherlands; they would adopt the Dutch ways – in language, religion and so on – only along the way, if at all. Whether on the company fleets, in Africa, the Americas or Asia, 'Dutch' sailors and colonists were often of other European stock (and, increasingly, non-European too). There were Germans, but also Southern Netherlanders, French, Scandinavians, Swiss, even some British. In the Dutch Americas, Portuguese Jews (Sephardim) and later Ashkenazim formed a considerable part of the European population.

The great majority of these Europeans arrived at Dutch colonies of their own volition. There was no enslavement of Europeans and only a fraction of all Europeans crossed the oceans as indentured labourers. Yet there are obvious qualifications to the issue of European volition. Specific European groups, in particular Jews, opted to settle in the Dutch colonies in order to escape religious repression. The great majority of European migrants chose to leave due to economic forces, probably with the elusive goal of returning better-off within a few years. In practice, up until the nineteenth century, return rates were as modest as spectacular economic successes were sporadic and premature death was ubiquitous.

As even the European segment of Dutch colonial societies was heterogeneous, it comes as no surprise that in most Dutch colonial settlements, 'European' culture was by no means only a tropical variant of the Dutch ways. Perhaps something like a genuine Dutch colonial variant developed in government. After all, metropolitan instructions were sent by the ruling Dutch elites and were followed – to an extent – by a colonial officialdom dominated at the top levels by Dutchmen. Social life was an altogether different matter.

During the times of the VOC and WIC, the size of the European communities was small in all Dutch colonies, with the exception of the Cape Colony, with some 20,000 Europeans at the time of the British takeover during the Napoleonic wars. This figure provides a massive contrast with all other colonial cities of the Dutch empire prior to 1800. Whether in Batavia, Kota Ambon or Ceylon in the East or in Recife, Paramaribo or Willemstad in the West, the total European population in these places ranged between a mere couple of hundred to a few thousand. Only in Batavia and a handful of other Indonesian cities did the European population rapidly accelerate after the mid-nineteenth century, adding up to a total of some 210,000 by 1930.

The European segment was therefore tiny in most Dutch colonial settlements throughout the seventeenth and eighteenth centuries. Intermediate groups of Eurasians or Eurafricans did emerge in most places, in spite of early Dutch regulations issued to counter racial mixing. Initially the greater number of births in these communities derived from relations between European men and Asian or African female slaves. Manumission was an established practice in Asia, more so than in the Americas. But even in the Dutch Caribbean a non-slave status would ultimately come to characterize the majority of Eurafricans. Fairly soon these mixed segments were of considerable numerical importance both in Asia and in the Caribbean. In Elmina, Paramaribo and Willemstad, Eurafricans outnumbered the European segment by the late eighteenth century. In Batavia and Galle (Sri Lanka), Europeans officially slightly outnumbered Eurasian mestizos – but then again, contemporaries wondered about the 'purity' of these Europeans.

The ethnic, colour and class segmentation of Dutch colonial cities was further complicated by the emergence of a group of free men and women of local origin in Asia, and of African origin in the Caribbean. Like the majority of Eurasians and Eurafricans mentioned above, these groups were legally free during the times when slavery still functioned and they were more or less assimilated into European colonial culture – always bearing in mind that 'European' increasingly implied a thoroughly creolized variety of Dutch culture.

In all of this, and bearing in mind the unique character of the Cape Colony, one finds strong parallels in the various parts of the Dutch empire up until 1800. But there are important contrasts as well. In the Americas, the Dutch, like all other European powers, virtually created new societies – taking advantage, that is, of the genes and labour of enslaved Africans. Apart from a small number of marginalized Native Americans, the populations of these Dutch American colonies were made up of Old World immigrants. With the short-lived exception of New Netherland, Europeans formed tiny minorities in these societies.[4] The starkest example of this is Suriname, where the population of African origins made up over 95 per cent of the population until the abolition of slavery in 1863. On the Antillean islands the imbalance was less stark, but again the 'African' population vastly outnumbered the European.

In Asia, of course, the great majority of the populations in and around the 'Dutch' settlements predated European colonization. Beyond the new colonial centres, European immigration had no major demographic consequences. The one caveat that comes with this observation relates not to European migrants, but to the considerable number of Chinese living in and around Batavia, the result of a steady stream of immigration tolerated if not actively encouraged by the Dutch. Their numbers quickly increased, to the

[4]   Of course, the Dutch demographic and cultural impact on former New Netherland would outlive the formal Dutch colonial period by many decades, arguably even centuries.

point that eighteenth-century Batavia has been described as a Chinese town. But of course, once one draws a wider circle around Batavia or once one focuses on all of Java, let alone on the entire Indonesian archipelago, one cannot escape the conclusion that demographically, the mass of 'locals' dwarfed the immigrant communities, whether of European, Eurasian or *peranakan* (native) Chinese stock.

The picture of proportional insignificance of the European and Eurasian segments of the Indonesian population does not fundamentally alter after 1800. Many more Europeans emigrated to the booming colony from the mid-nineteenth century onwards, whether for business, government or as enlisted soldiers in the colonial army. In the early 1890s, the size of the European and Eurasian population taken together stood at 60,000 and by 1934 at 240,000. Europeans and Eurasians nonetheless remained a fraction of the overall Indonesian population, which increased from less than 15 million in the mid-nineteenth century to 35 million around 1900 and nearly 60 million by 1930.

In Africa, Elmina would remain a Dutch colonial enclave until 1872, but both the absolute and the proportional number of Europeans living there remained small. Serious Dutch migration to Africa focused on South Africa well into the twentieth century, over time bequeathing the British colony and next sovereign republic with a strong white Afrikaner community – but as much as this is Dutch history, it does not formally pertain to Dutch *colonial* history anymore.

In the post-Napoleonic Caribbean, only Suriname and the six Antillean islands remained within the Dutch orbit. Dutch immigration to Suriname was transient and insignificant with respect to numbers. By the mid-twentieth century the colony's local 'European' population had all but disappeared through creolization and (r)emigration to the Netherlands. A firmly rooted, creolized European segment did perpetuate its centuries-old existence in the Antilles, particularly on Curaçao. Over the past century, successive immigration waves have even strengthened the European proportion of the population – but descendants of enslaved Africans remain the vast majority on all islands except for Aruba and Saba.

What are the implications of these data on migrations and settlements for the theme of 'common' cultural heritage between the Netherlands and its former spheres of influence? What reasons do we have to think of commonality in the first place? Three general observations are in order here. First, more than any of its European counterparts, Dutch colonialism depended on Europeans from other nationalities. There were simply insufficient Dutch men willing to leave their native country, much less Dutch women. While by definition *all* overseas European communities creolized both demographically and culturally, this creolization had an extraordinary dimension in the Dutch orbit. Thus, well into the nineteenth century, the Dutch language was not even dominant among the European segment of the Dutch colonial populations. Neither was the Dutch Reformed Church in religious matters. The parameters of colonial rule were set in the Netherlands and to an extent executed by Dutch officials – but only in the highest ranks were these officials generally Dutch themselves.

What does this imply for our understanding of the commonality of cultural heritage? To start with, the simple observation that we cannot narrow down our understanding of the *colonial* input to *Dutch* culture. While tourist brochures may highlight the 'typical Amsterdam canal houses' on Willemstad's Handelskade, we should be aware that the typical 'European' musical genres of the island that developed over time speak of Iberian rather than Dutch legacies (not to mention the new creole dimension). Likewise, the Afro-European creole languages of the Dutch Caribbean derive their vocabularies primarily from Portuguese (Papiamentu, Saramaccan) or English (Sranantongo) rather than Dutch. In the Asian settlements, Dutch was only one among many languages spoken within the European communities; colonial architecture adhered to a generalized European style. In other words, even the commonality between Dutch culture at home and 'Dutch' colonial culture cannot be taken for granted.

Second and possibly of more interest, the numerical insignificance of the 'Dutch' European segment had profound consequences. It has often been observed that the Dutch colonial legacy pales in comparison to legacies left by other European colonies. Language is the most striking case in point. Dutch was only spoken by tiny minorities in Asia and left only a few traces, even in Indonesia, although a great number of Dutch words made their way as loanwords into Indonesian. In the Caribbean colonies, Dutch likewise was a minority language all through the colonial period. It only became widely spoken in Suriname during the twentieth century, in a specific context of educational reform, ethnic competition and growing orientation and migration towards the Netherlands. Ironically, in the Antilles Dutch is an unpopular second language only, in spite of the islanders' choice to remain within the Kingdom.

Finally, a similar observation may be made regarding the religious legacy left by Dutch colonialism. Christianity remained marginal in the Dutch Asian colonies. Christianization was limited to scattered regions in the Dutch Asian colonies (though the roughly ten per cent Christians among the contemporary Indonesian population still amount to some twenty millions). In a broader Asian perspective, there is nothing particularly remarkable here: of all European colonial powers only Spain, in the Philippines, left a lasting religious heritage. But in the Caribbean too, there was little Dutch religious zeal. In the Antilles, the European elites clung to their own Protestant or Jewish convictions, leaving the christening of the African majorities to Spanish and Spanish American Catholic missionaries. In Suriname, the hesitant late eighteenth-century decision to allow for christianization of the free non-Europeans and, only from the 1820s onwards, of the slave populations, led to the invitation of German Moravians and later also Dutch Catholic missionaries. Asian immigration implied the reconfiguration of the colony's religious landscape; little concerted effort was made to convert Hindus and Muslims to Christianity and the results were predictably limited.

The most significant linguistic legacy of Dutch colonialism is therefore found in South Africa; the major religious legacies are located in South Africa and to a lesser extent in the Caribbean. Thus, even if the Cape Colony was Dutch only up until the late eighteenth century, it arguably remained the most European of all Dutch colonial settlements long after. And of course, even if subsequent European migration to South Africa was no less heterogeneous under British rule than before, the early Dutch legacy survived into the present, for better or for worse.

Slave trades and slavery

In common with European colonial practice and with pre-colonial customs in most colonized areas, the Netherlands engaged in slave trade and slavery. Although for the Atlantic region much research has been undertaken on this subject, this is not the case for the operational sphere of the VOC. Slave trades and slavery in 'East' and 'West' were two circuits that, as far as we know, were virtually independent of one another; they do, however, lend themselves very well to mutual comparison. This includes the scale and organization of the slave trade, the number and origin of the slaves, their economic importance to the colonies, contrasts between indigenous and foreign slavery, slavery regimes, inter-ethnic relations, creolization and local cultural formation and, finally, the abolition of the slave trade and ultimately of slavery itself ('Emancipation'). As colonial slavery is at the core of the matter, this theme spans the period from circa 1600 until 1863.

Several conclusions may be drawn from the chapter on Dutch slave trades and colonial slavery presented by Rik van Welie and the supporting data in the Appendix. First, the numbers game. The Dutch role in the Atlantic slave trade has long been established. Over the centuries, Dutch slavers were minor players, embarking some 555,000 or five per cent of the 12.5 million enslaved Africans destined for the 'middle passage' across the Atlantic. In the seventeenth and early eighteenth century, however, the Dutch share was more prominent and the Dutch were also instrumental in exporting the sugar-and-slavery model from Brazil to the Caribbean.

Whereas the Dutch slave trade is mostly thought of as an Atlantic phe-

St. George d'Elmina Castle

nomenon, historians have long known that the VOC also engaged in slave trading. In a pioneering article, Marcus Vink (2003) has suggested that the Dutch Indian Ocean slave trade was actually more voluminous than it was in the Atlantic. Van Welie's discussion of the literature and evidence makes it clear that the methodological and conceptual issues are far more complicated for the Asian slave trades than for the Atlantic area. Even short of satisfactory quantitative series, we may confidently say that the Dutch were active slavers in Asia themselves and equally unscrupulous buyers of Asian and to a lesser degree African slaves supplied by other traders, most of these Africans and Asians, particularly Chinese.

Up until the abolition of slavery, slave labour formed the backbone of the colonies in the Americas – slave-produced tropical crops were actually the raison d'être of these colonies. Dutch Brazil and the Guyanas were typical plantation economies, with enslaved Africans making up the vast majority of the population. Conversely, in most of the Asian settlements and colonies, slave labour was mainly urban and incidental to other forms of locally procured labour, whether bonded or not. Slaves formed a tiny minority of the overall population in the Asian colonies. Only in places such as Batavia, Banda and Ambon did they make up half of the population by the late seventeenth century and would hence have a more significant cultural impact.

Much has been written on the absence of a serious abolitionist movement in the Netherlands regarding the Atlantic slave trade and slavery. Clearly the lack of abolitionist fervour contrasts with ideas about Dutch progressiveness and humanitarianism. Studies on slave owners' attitudes in the Dutch Caribbean only confirm this sobering observation. Again, the study of Dutch attitudes to enslavement in Asia is only in its infancy. There is no indication, however, that Dutch colonialism has a more commendable record here. Perhaps it was even easier to conceive of slavery as self-evident in Asia than in the Americas. In Asia, the Dutch, like other Europeans, simply participated in pre-colonial networks of slave trading and were not alone in their deployment of slaves.[5]

Historians tend to be weary of generalizations regarding 'mild' versus 'harsh' variants of slavery, even more so when such variations are explained by referring to factors such as the national or cultural backgrounds of slave owners. Wherever there is slavery, abuse is endemic; and so is slave resistance. Nonetheless, we may possibly discern some contrasts between the practice of slavery in the Dutch Atlantic and in Dutch Asia. For all we know, for most enslaved, slavery in Asia would imply urban and domestic rather than agro-industrial labour; it was more gender-balanced and implied lesser racial and ethnic distinctions. As a consequence, manumission was far more com-

---

[5]   See Oostindie 1995 for a comparative perspective on Dutch abolition and emancipation.

mon, as was the likeliness that the descendants of manumitted slaves would be fully integrated into the wider society, not always in the lower classes. For most Asian slaves, there was no such thing as the dreaded middle passage, probably lesser racial stigmatization and, perhaps, lesser alienation.

While this hypothesis awaits scholarly scrutiny, for present purposes it is useful to highlight another dimension of the history of slavery. Throughout the Americas as well as in the Afro-Caribbean diaspora in Europe, the Atlantic slave trade and New World slavery are crucial to the way descendants of these enslaved Africans think of themselves, how they view colonial history and how they deal with present-day issues ranging from racism to social achievement. Their visible African ancestry moreover makes them victims of this history identifiable to all. Slavery, in a sense, has remained, or has become, a central feature in Afro-American identity.

Nothing of this sort applies to the former Dutch colonies in Asia. Remember that slavery was not nearly as dominant in the Asian territories as it was in the Americas. Moreover, it is difficult to point at legacies of slavery or at descendants of slaves – and where this *is* possible, in Indonesia, one will more likely be dealing with traces of the indigenous slavery both preceding and outlasting colonial slavery. In other words, while colonial history itself does not have the contemporary weight in Asia that it has in the Caribbean, slavery evokes even less living memories.

The implications for debates about common cultural heritage are evident. Slavery is a central concern in any debate on heritage legacies between Dutch and Caribbean specialists, politicians or the general public (Van Stipriaan et al. 2007; Oostindie 2008). So far, it has no place whatsoever in discussions between Indonesian and Dutch participants, and while scholars will certainly pick up this issue, it is unlikely that this will spark much of a change in general awareness. An open question is what place specialists in the field of cultural heritage will allot to colonial slavery.

This observation leads to the wider issue of the cultural legacies of the Atlantic slave trade in the Americas. Centuries and perhaps even decades ago, the 'Eurafrican' cultures of the Americas were easily denigrated as corrupted forms of European civilization. Afro-American emancipation as well as scholarly debates have forwarded more nuanced interpretations. 'Creolization' today has become the leading paradigm on cultural formation in the history and anthropology of 'plantation America', emphasizing mutual cultural affects in conditions of systemic power asymmetry (Price 2001). The result of centuries of creolization has been a series of new syncretic cultural forms, each presenting a cultural continuum between ideal-typical 'European' and 'African' poles. Yet most scholars would add that this continuum actually functions as a hierarchy, with most of the prestige and certainly the best chances for upward social mobility at the European end. This then suggests that these mixed cultures have developed a strong affinity with a generalized 'Western' culture. It is hard to seriously discuss 'common' cultural heritage in the Americas without touching on this debate.

And then, of course, we have the delicate question of slave trading and slavery in Africa. While Elmina was merely one out of many European fortresses dotting the West African coast, it was Dutch for over two centuries and as such served as a hub for Dutch slave trading. Most African slaves were brought from other places though; the great majority of enslaved Africans embarking at Elmina came from far afield and were supplied by Africans from various ethnic groups now sharing citizenship with those once traded as slaves. There is no clear-cut story of European or Dutch villains and African or Ghanaian victims, as also the Ghanaian government is making abundantly clear.

We do see a concerted effort though, to incorporate this painful history into the bilateral relations of Ghana and the Netherlands. Some criticize the commoditization of the slave trade, others argue that projects such as the restoration and conversion into an open-air museum of Elmina are laudable healing and reconciliatory initiatives while at the same time generating much-needed revenue through tourism. Either way, Elmina is a key location for the definition of what commonality means for people living on each side of the dreaded triangular trade – even if we take into account that the great majority of enslaved Africans taken to the Dutch Caribbean were embarked elsewhere.

Overseas slave trade, finally, has a long history in South Africa, and there is no doubt that Dutch colonialism left its mark in this respect as well. Estimated at 63,000, the total number of slaves disembarked at the Cape during the VOC period is not only relatively low but also remarkable for the wide spread of provenance areas, from Southeast Asia through South Asia and Madagascar to Southeast Africa. Slave labour was indispensable to the colonial economy and by the late eighteenth century, the Cape Colony deployed some 20,000 slaves, roughly the same number as the European segment of the population. But then again, suppression and bonded labour were also meted out to the local population, the Khoikhoi, who worked in serf-like conditions, and to other Asian immigrants.

As Nigel Worden (2001) has remarked, slave trade and slavery in the Cape Colony – after all, only a faraway regional episode in a large country with more recent and more widely shared drama's to remember – is only now becoming incorporated into the debates about South African history and cultural heritage. This issue will be addressed again in Chapter III, on historical memories and national canons.

Indentured labour migrations

Somewhere between the extremes of free labour and chattel slavery, we find various forms of indentured labour. Unlike the slave trades, this form of labour recruitment did eventually link Asia with the Americas, that is, between the mid-nineteenth century until the eve of World War Two. The major areas of recruitment for indentured labour were China, British India and Java. Both Chinese and British Indian labour migrations were primarily Asian affairs, although Chinese contract labourers also found their way all over the Americas, and British Indians to the Caribbean. Post-slavery Suriname was among the Caribbean plantation colonies at the receiving end. Initially, modest numbers of Chinese disembarked at this Dutch colony, followed by larger contingents of British Indians. In addition, Suriname was the only New World colony receiving Javanese indentured labourers.[6]

Asian indentured labour in the Caribbean has been dubbed 'a new system of slavery' (Tinker 1974). The rationale behind this indictment is clear. The need to make up for the abolition of the Atlantic slave trade and the diminishing supply of African-American labour was at the root of this new form of cross-oceanic labour recruitment. Volition of those recruited is a disputed dimension of the entire process from the recruitment in Asia to the rigid control enforced in their areas of employment. Thio Termorshuizen's review of indentured labour in the Dutch orbit confirms these rough beginnings, but also suggests a gradual amelioration of the system.

Bonded labour – not slavery exactly, but neither 'free' in the modern, capitalist sense – was nothing new to Asia. Pre-colonial systems of labour recruitment, often through warfare, had covered a broad range of bonded and semi-bonded arrangements, and the Indonesian archipelago was no exception to this rule. Migration had been one element in some of these systems, although most recruitment had been local. Initially, not that much changed with the advent of colonialism. Even the economically highly successful Dutch Cultivation System – semi-bonded labour recruitment organized and overseen by the Dutch colonial authorities in Java between 1830 and 1870 – did not involve migrations of any great distance.

Just as some lessons learned from Caribbean slavery found their way into the Cultivation System, so did experiences with the latter contribute to the systems of indentured labour recruitment subsequently deployed by the

---

[6]   For comparative reasons it would be useful to look at some minor indentured labour migrations. One such case is Malay and British Indian indentured labour in South Africa before, but particularly following the British takeover. Another form of indentured labour migration involves African contract labour to serve in the colonial army in the Dutch East Indies. However, quantitatively speaking these are only minor threads in the historical narrative.

Dutch colonial government. The new dimension was long-distance migration organized and/or supported by the colonial authorities. In Termorshuizen's review one easily detects the formal parallels between indentured labour migrations within the Indonesian archipelago and to Suriname. Perhaps more interesting, and certainly of more lasting consequence, are the contrasts.

What of the demographic and hence cultural impact of these various labour migrations sparked under the aegis of Dutch colonialism? Let us first consider the supply side, that is, mainland British India, China and Java. Over thirty million British Indians emigrated between 1840 and 1940, with as many as half of these repatriating later on. The overwhelming majority migrated within Asia, with only relatively small numbers moving to Africa or the Caribbean (Manning 2005:145-6). Even within the Caribbean, Suriname's share, some 35,000, pales in comparison to the number of Indian indentured labourers disembarking in Guyana and Trinidad. In other words, Suriname was a negligible destination in the overall history of British Indian migration – and yet, recent research has demonstrated that 'Suriname' does figure in Indian oral traditions. In present-day India there is a growing interest in the history of its diasporic communities. At the end of the day, however, even the tens of millions of former emigrants and their contemporary descendants are of modest significance to a one-billion-plus nation.

This similarly applies to the migration of Chinese. 'Chinese' – an anachronistic adjective in itself – migrants were all over Asia well before the advent of European colonialism and continued to migrate during the following centuries, both under regimes of indentured labour and as free labourers. Patrick Manning (2005:145-6) suggests that just over 50 million Chinese emigrated between 1840 and 1940, again with a return rate of just over half. The great majority migrated within Asia, particularly South and Southeast Asia. Some one million Chinese migrated to the Americas – the few thousand disembarking in the Dutch Caribbean are a mere footnote to this history. As in the case of British India, the demographic impact of these various migrations was of modest significance to China itself; the impact on Indonesia was more pronounced. It should be borne in mind however, that the indentured Chinese, somewhere around 200,000, moving to Sumatra, plus the 150-200,000 moving to the other Outer Islands between the 1880s and the 1920s, formed but two of a long series of Chinese migrations to the archipelago continuing to the present day.

Migrations within the archipelago of course antedated colonialism. One may conclude though that the organized recruitment of Javanese indentured labour for Sumatra did signal a new chapter. Again, the volume of indentured labour migrations within the archipelago dwarfs the Dutch Caribbean experience. The number of Javanese contract labourers and their families moving to northern Sumatra between the 1880s and 1920s probably came near to 700,000. If we add Javanese migration to the other Outer Islands and several lesser destinations, we come close to the one million mark. With some 33,000 arrivals, the figure of Javanese indentured labourers disembarking in Suriname again pales. Although the immediate demographic significance of these various migrations was scant for Java, one may say that these colonial beginnings did prefigure the more voluminous *transmigrasi* schemes of the post-independence era.

What of the impact of the colonial migrations at the receiving end, in the Dutch colonies? Both on Sumatra and the Outer Islands, Javanese and to a lesser extent Chinese indentured labourers had a lasting impact on the demographic make-up of the populations. Population figures soared once the indentured migration started, and a good proportion of the migrants chose to stay after the expiration of their contracts. Their descendants now form a significant part of the population of Sumatra, alongside post-war Javanese transmigrants.

But again, by far the most significant consequences of Asian migrant labour were felt in Suriname – not because the numbers involved were that high, but because their relative weight was enormous. At the time of the abolition of slavery, in 1863, inhabitants of predominantly African descent made up some 95 per cent of the Surinamese population. One full century later, this proportion was down to 47 per cent. This fall was entirely accounted for by the growth of the Asian communities, which stood at 35 per cent for the Hindustani and 14 per cent for the Javanese. The relative growth of this 'Asian' population has continued ever since.

As will be discussed later, these ethnic reconfigurations had lasting consequences for the way colonial history and its legacies are constituted in contemporary Suriname. Suffice it here to say that Asian migrations had immediate cultural implications for Suriname. 'Eurafrican' or Afro-Caribbean cultures are often characterized as creolized, new cultures but still fairly akin to European cultures. Massive immigration of Asians added an entirely new dimension to the creolized culture developing in Suriname. With the British Indians and Javanese came Hinduism and Islam, new conceptions of religion and kinship, aesthetic norms, musical styles, cuisine, et cetera. Certainly, Asian cultures too creolized in a New World setting – although ethnic distinction was strongly maintained.

This layering of African and Asian migration movements had all sorts of implications for ethnicity, identity politics and nation building. For present purposes, it is crucial that the Asian dimension in Surinamese culture has arguably had less exposure to Dutch culture and has demonstrated more resilience to overall westernization. And that, in comparison to Afro-Surinamese and Antilleans, Surinamese of Asian backgrounds seem less concerned with 'the West' and colonialism as tenets – or antagonisms – of their own cultures.

Post-colonial migrations

'Free' migrations of colonial subjects within the Dutch empire were to become more prominent in the twentieth century. Moluccan soldiers in the colonial army moved to Java, Surinamese professionals moved to the East Indies, where labour opportunities were better, Surinamese lower and middle class migrants found work in Aruba and Curaçao and so on. The one really significant and even dramatic new chapter in colonial migrations, however, was not connected to the further development of Dutch colonialism, but rather to its demise. For the first time in the history of Dutch colonialism, the metropolis became the recipient of large numbers of (post)-colonial migrants.

In the history of all European colonial empires one of the impulses to the emergence of anti-colonial struggles originated from the metropolitan sojourn of colonial subjects. Students of the various academic disciplines necessary to run a country became acquainted with like-minded people of their own and other colonies and developed a better grasp of the stark contrasts between colonial pretensions and practice. On returning home, demobilized soldiers experienced little of the appreciation they felt they were rightly owed by their metropolitan fellowmen. Working class colonial immigrants, while also exposed to overt racism, did have opportunities to join trade unions. In short, and in particular during the first half of the twentieth century, the metropolitan sojourn was a crucial *rite de passage* for many a later nationalist leader.

The Dutch colonial orbit is no exception to this rule. While there had been continuous but numerically insignificant and mainly temporary migration from the colonies all through the colonial period, this migration accelerated in the Interbellum. Of course, the immense Indonesian archipelago provided the greater number of colonial migrants. Most of these originated from the colony's traditional elites who were among the tiny minority passing through Dutch-language education and hence qualifying for metropolitan universities. In the Netherlands they became lawyers, medical doctors, engineers and so forth. They also developed ideas about an Indonesian nation that could do without the Dutch. In addition, there were scattered working class immigrants and, more importantly, revolutionary activists were welcomed into the political ranks of the Dutch left.

Migration from the Caribbean presents a similar picture, even if the numbers involved are scant. Pre-World War Two Caribbean students in the Netherlands, virtually all from the creolized elites, did form their own organizations and the like, but did not engage in political issues. From Suriname however, also came a small contingent of working class migrants, one of whom (Anton de Kom) would provide critical inspiration to his country's post-war nationalist movement.

World War Two marked the beginning of the dismantlement of the Dutch colonial empire.[7] The Japanese takeover of the Dutch East Indies in 1942 turned out to be the prelude to the full independence claimed by Indonesia on 17 August 1945, only to be accepted by the Dutch on 27 December 1949, after four years of strenuous negotiations and bitter warfare. The transfer of sovereignty to Indonesia sparked successive waves of 'repatriation', a dubious designation if we take into account that a great number of immigrants from Indonesia had never set foot in the Netherlands before and stemmed from families that had made the colony their home for generations, if not from time immemorial. In the aftermath of the 'loss' of Indonesia, some 300,000 Europeans, Eurasians and Moluccans 'repatriated' to the metropolis. This figure may be negligible in relation to an Indonesian population of roughly one hundred million in the late 1940s and 235 million today, but it involved the overwhelming majority from the Dutch colonial and Eurasian societies.

Whereas this first chapter of decolonization thus caused unrepresentative and proportionally modest migration, the 25 November 1975 transfer of sovereignty to Suriname sparked an exodus involving colonial citizens of all classes, ethnicities and generations, a cross-section of the entire population with some overrepresentation of the better educated. On the eve of the internally highly contested independence, 100,000 Surinamese out of a total population of less than 400,000 voted with their feet. Over the following decades, the demographic growth of the Surinamese community would mainly be a Dutch affair. Currently estimated at 350,000, the Surinamese community in the Netherlands is not that much smaller than the total population of Suriname.

Large-scale Antillean migration to the Netherlands, mainly from Curaçao, dates from the late 1980s, producing an 'expat' community of some 125,000. Again, the numerical significance of the migration relates primarily to the islands itself, whose total population is some 280,000. This Antillean migration is not representative by origins, as the overwhelming majority hail from Curaçao; the island's population decreased to 130,000 in the past decades. But again, with respect to social and economic characteristics the migrants form a cross section of the island's population.

Remigration figures for these three migrant communities have been insignificant for Indonesia and very low for Suriname, but substantial for the Antilles. For the latter, we may indeed speak of circular migration, even if the demographic growth of the Curaçaoan population has been heavily concentrated in the Netherlands.

---

[7]   See Oostindie and Klinkers 2003 for an overview of decolonization and post-colonial migrations.

Once more the question of cultural implications should be discussed. For Indonesia these were limited to the extent that the number of emigrants was proportionally insignificant. Bearing in mind the atypical composition of the emigrant population, we may assume that their departure hastened the marginalization of Dutch and also of the Eurasian culture in Indonesia.

Migration from Suriname and the Antilles did not fundamentally alter the ethnic, class or gender base of the sending communities. However, due to its large-scale character and the ensuing reconfiguration of the Surinamese and Antillean communities as truly transnational, the exodus has had a profound impact on these Caribbean cultures. It has become very difficult to think about these without taking the Dutch component into account.

Finally, there is the impact of this round of migrations on Dutch metropolitan culture. With the post-colonial migrations, colonialism has literally come home to the metropolis. The demographic consequences are obvious: today, out of a population of some 16.5 million, the number of Dutch citizens with colonial roots is estimated at roughly one million. In the Netherlands, as in other former metropolitan countries, the argument 'we are here because you were there!' therefore rings a familiar bell. The emergence of this post-colonial community has had a direct impact on the Dutch debates on national identity. And indeed, the colonial antecedents of Dutch history have been more strongly and critically incorporated into the national narrative than ever before.

Historical memory and national canons

There is a fundamental distinction in the demographic impact of Dutch colonialism around the globe. In contrast to the Cape Colony, with its moderate climate and significant European population, white communities in the Dutch tropical settlements constituted only a small segment of the total populations. But whereas the vast majority of the population in Asia were of native origin, the overwhelming non-European majorities in the Americas were brought there under the flag of Dutch colonialism.

This is crucial, also for an understanding of contemporary views on colonialism and its legacies. In Asia, the Dutch colonial period can be thought of as transitory, leaving only minor demographic or cultural traces.[8] This even applies to Indonesia, the Dutch prize 'possession' for 350 years. Perhaps only the memory of the episode of decolonization arouses strong feelings

---

[8] Taiwan is an exception here, not in the sense that Dutch rule lasted long, but because the Dutch period initiated massive Chinese migration to the island, that would eventually lead to its takeover in 1949 by Chiang Kai-shek's Republic of China.

Dwellings in a Khoikhoi village

in Indonesia – the rest seems forgotten by all but a few specialists. Dutch Caribbean societies by contrast are literally creations of Dutch colonialism, and as a consequence much of national history and culture is defined in one way or another in relation to colonialism. Hence, in Caribbean communities, cultural heritage policies are by definition debated and enacted in an ideologically charged atmosphere. This is only accentuated by the fact that contemporary relations remain intense and asymmetric, and by the transnational nature of today's Dutch Caribbean communities.

Again, South Africa must be considered separately, as a third model. Although Dutch colonialism ended two centuries ago, the Dutch demographic and cultural legacy would persist. It was the Dutch who in their time introduced not only their language and religion, but equally slavery and indentured labour – and it was primarily the white Afrikaners who were to embody and formulate the concept of apartheid in recent history. Talking about 'common' cultural legacies therefore is not devoid of political sensitivities.

Having said all of this, we still have a number of major comparative questions to address, ranging from Dutch attitudes towards the non-white populations and cultures, ideologies and practices surrounding interethnic relations, the organization of urban and plantation life, the emergence of creolized colonial populations and identities and so on. Much research has been undertaken into these issues, yet a truly comparative synthesis is left wanting. It does not require a great stretch of the imagination to envisage that a more rigid comparative approach to these issues would not only enable us to locate Dutch colonialism more firmly within a wider comparative framework, but would also stimulate the debate about the 'commonality' of cultural heritage *within* the former Dutch empire.

Colonialism, in short, impacted on the former colonies and metropolis in uneven degrees. There is tangible cultural heritage, partly visible to all, for example in colonial architecture, and partly hidden away in archives, museums, libraries and other collections. There is a wide spectrum of intangible cultural heritage, preserved in collective, conscious and unconscious memories and customs, which is increasingly recorded and interpreted by experts.

Between the former colonies and colonial settlements significant differences exist in the interest in cultural heritage from the colonial era. Not only does this reflect financial challenges to be met, but also variations in the appreciation of this past. Such contrasts have repercussions on both the formal and the informal canonization of colonial history. The broad comparison of the way various former colonies as well as the former metropolis now deal with this colonial past is still in its infancy. In the third chapter of this book, these issues will be taken up again. But first we will turn to a comparative discussion of cultural heritage and pertinent policies.

Bibliography

Manning, Patrick
2005   *Migration in world history.* New York: Routledge.
Oostindie, Gert
1995   (ed.) *Fifty years later; Antislavery, capitalism and modernity in the Dutch orbit.* Leiden: KITLV Press. [Caribbean Series 15.]
2008   'Slavernij, canon en trauma; Debatten en dilemma's', *Tijdschrift voor Geschiedenis* 121:4-21.
Oostindie, Gert and Inge Klinkers
2003   *Decolonising the Caribbean; Dutch policies in a comparative framework.* Amsterdam: Amsterdam University Press.
Price, Richard
2001   'The miracle of creolization; A retrospective', *New West Indian Guide* 75:35-64.
Stipriaan, Alex van, Waldo Heilbron, Aspha Bijnaar and Valika Smeulders
2007   *Op zoek naar de stilte; Sporen van het slavernijverleden in Nederland.* Leiden: KITLV Uitgeverij, Amsterdam: NiNsee.
Tinker, Hugh
1974   *A new system of slavery; The export of Indian labour overseas 1830-1920.* London: Oxford University Press.
Vink, Markus
2003   '"The world's oldest trade"; Dutch slavery and slave trade in the Indian Ocean in the seventeenth century', *Journal of World History* 14:131-77.
Worden, Nigel
2001   'The forgotton region; Commemorations of slavery in Mauritius and South Africa', in: Gert Oostindie (ed.), *Facing up to the past; Perspectives on the commemoration of slavery from Africa, the Americas and Europe,* pp. 48-54. Kingston: Ian Randle/The Hague: Prince Claus Fund.

ANOUK FIENIEG, ROBERT PARTHESIUS, BRITTANY GROOT,
RIVKE JAFFE, SJOERD VAN DER LINDE AND
PAULINE VAN ROOSMALEN*

Heritage trails
International cultural heritage policies in a European perspective

Almost a hundred years ago, in 1911, Jacob Cornelis van Overvoorde, an influential Dutch advocate of the preservation of old buildings, made a trip around the world to investigate the material remains of the glorious Dutch past overseas. Alarmed by the lack of awareness surrounding the material legacy of what he considered an extremely important period in Dutch history, Van Overvoorde issued an emergency call for the preservation of overseas monuments representing this period. Although these stone remains were unlike the monuments one finds in contemporary Europe, they were considered important because of their influence on indigenous art forms. Van Overvoorde (1910) was appalled by the lack of an inventory of overseas monuments, let alone an active preservation policy. According to him, the Dutch should follow the example of the British, who maintained the Dutch monuments in British India with more care than the Netherlands did its own in the Dutch East Indies.

A century later, managing the remains of the past is still a topical theme. In 2002 the Netherlands celebrated the 400th anniversary of the Vereenigde Oost-Indische Compagnie (VOC, East Indies Company). Various Asian coun-

*   The Centre for International Heritage Activities (CIE) in Amsterdam was requested by Gert Oostindie, director of the KITLV, to write a chapter on international heritage policies with regard to colonial heritage in a European perspective. For this purpose, the CIE established a working group chaired by Robert Parthesius. The participants come from different academic backgrounds but all are involved in international heritage policy. This chapter is the result of brainstorming and joint research by this group. We would like to thank all members for their input and comments, all respondents to our email questionnaire and of course Gert Oostindie for this assignment.

tries considered this decision unfortunate as, from their perspective, the anniversary should be commemorated rather than celebrated. From an Indonesian point of view, colonial oppression by the Dutch began in the seventeenth century, with the VOC, not with Dutch colonial administration in the nineteenth century. While for Indonesia this historic occasion was thus not an event to celebrate, for many in the Netherlands the VOC period represents the most successful century in national history.

The history of Dutch expansion is a story of wealth and power as well as war and repression. The resulting mix of pride and shame in discussing the colonial past is a recurrent theme, which is also evident in Dutch policies relating to colonial heritage, whether in the realm of the former VOC or in the Atlantic sphere once covered by the Dutch West-Indische Compagnie (WIC, West Indies Company). Since the mid-1990s, the Dutch government has created a political infrastructure intended to encourage and ensure funding for projects aimed at the preservation of Dutch colonial heritage overseas. For every partner country the Netherlands works with, different challenges and perspectives present themselves regarding colonial heritage and its management in the present.

The Dutch policy, which will be broadly discussed in this chapter, focuses on the concept of a *common* cultural heritage. Its purpose, as formulated by the government, is the joint conservation of this common cultural heritage. Cooperative efforts of this kind are utterly dependent on political goodwill and the commitment of all parties concerned. Within the policy framework, common cultural heritage is defined as overseas cultural heritage relating to the periods of the VOC, WIC and subsequent colonial rule.

This chapter aims to compare the Netherlands' active international cultural heritage policy with the policies of a selection of (former) European colonizing countries, thus providing a historical context, outlining when and how the concept of heritage was introduced and what the consequences are for the development, awareness and incorporation of heritage policies. It gives an initial overview of European international heritage policies, in an attempt to stimulate and contextualize the rethinking of Dutch heritage policy. Given the wide scope of this research, it is difficult to draw strong conclusions from this inventory. Therefore, it is presented as the first step towards further research on and awareness of this important topic. An introduction to Dutch common cultural heritage policy is followed by a discussion on the theoretical aspects of the concept of heritage, the roots of heritage management and the force field of heritage policy design, thus setting the stage for a European comparison.

Dutch common cultural heritage policy[1]

As a starting point for its Common Cultural Heritage Policy – one of the priorities within Dutch international cultural policy – the Netherlands chose the mutuality of colonial heritage.[2] In the definition used by the government, common cultural heritage refers to both the tangible and intangible remains of the former Dutch presence. This heritage dates back to an era when the Dutch sailed the seas as explorers or merchants and held control as rulers or colonial administrators. The policy framework divides common heritage into three categories:

1. Overseas cultural heritage: a collective term generally used for cultural heritage outside Europe, relating to the periods of the VOC, WIC and colonial rule.
2. Objects (including archives) the Dutch constructed in or transported to other countries, commissioned by third parties, for which they had no subsequent responsibility.
3. Objects currently in the Netherlands but originating in countries with which it once had a relationship of reciprocal cultural influence.

Generally, the deciding factor as to whether something is indicated as common cultural heritage is whether it is perceived as such in the country concerned. The priority countries for this policy as determined by the Dutch government are Russia, Indonesia, Sri Lanka, India, Ghana, South Africa, Suriname and Brazil.[3] With the exception of Russia, all of these have had some kind of colonial relationship with the Netherlands. However, not all countries once linked to the Netherlands by colonialism are included on the priority list, nor are the Netherlands Antilles and Aruba, former Caribbean colonies still forming part of the Kingdom of the Netherlands. Although Brazil was later added to the list, it has not been included in this overview because activities under the common heritage policy began only recently, making an analysis premature.

Since 1997 the concept of common cultural heritage has attracted political interest in the Netherlands and several projects were initiated under this policy, mostly financed by the Dutch Cultural Fund (Homogene Groep Internationale Samenwerking (HGIS) – Cultuur).[4] Political interest was ini-

[1]   This section is an abstract of Fienieg 2006.
[2]   Currently, the Netherlands uses the term 'common' for its cultural heritage overseas. During the past ten years the terms 'shared heritage', 'mutual heritage' and 'heritage overseas' were also frequently used in policy frameworks.
[3]   *Raamwerk gemeenschappelijk cultureel erfgoed*. Kamerstuk 27.032, no. 2, 26 April 2000.
[4]   This source of funding ended in 2007.

tiated by an appeal from the Dutch Member of Parliament Eimert van
Middelkoop, who thought colonial history and its remains were increasingly
regarded as nothing but a dark page in Dutch history. Feelings of guilt and
shame predominated. With the new policy, this heritage began to be reinter-
preted as a valuable tool for critical reflection on Dutch colonial history,
while simultaneously serving as a method to strengthen bilateral relations
with former colonies.[5] The policy aims to preserve common cultural heritage
and utilize it as an instrument for sharing expertise, building capacity for the
cultural field in the partner country, creating public awareness and increasing
knowledge of this heritage.

The partner country's political commitment is an important condition
for funding. Another condition is that the partner country must define a
selected heritage site as *common* heritage. However, a 2004 evaluation of the
policy and related projects revealed that in most cases the Dutch government
saw the concerned heritage as common, while the partner countries did not.
Often, their interest has been rather limited.[6] Policymakers may have overlooked the fact that the role of the Netherlands in the history of most of its
partner countries is a minor one. As was also argued in the previous chapter
by Gert Oostindie, Suriname and the Netherlands Antilles are an exception
in this respect, as the roots of the majority of their populations are connected
to the Dutch colonial history of slavery and indentured labour.

The concept of common cultural heritage is complex. The mutuality
in this definition assumes a shared view of the concerned heritage on the part
of the Dutch and the partner country. Heritage, the 'silent' remains of history,
resonates with the echo of many voices in the contemporary interpretation
and presentation of a site. The stories selected in this process determine the
site's character and consequently its meaning for society. However, such stories differ depending on the storyteller. A quick scan of the partner countries
demonstrates that their perspectives can differ from the Dutch interpretation
of a common heritage site. The tension between pride and shame and the
conflicting interpretations of history through heritage are clearly visible.

The overview presented here demonstrates that different countries have
their own way of dealing with this type of heritage and that as a result of
this diversity Dutch policy practices have become very pragmatic. Naturally,
there is not one perspective on heritage and history within the nation state,
given that national populations are not homogeneous entities and may be
divided, for instance along ethnic lines. This multivocality and the pluralism of interpretation are well illustrated in the following case studies, which

5   *Verstrooid verleden*. Kamerstukken 1996-1997, no. 25.320, Den Haag, April 1997.
6   *Verslag consultatie internationaal cultuurbeleid; De plaats van cultureel erfgoed binnen het internationaal cultuurbeleid*. Ministry of Foreign Affairs, Den Haag, 28 May 2004.

briefly describe the reality of cultural heritage policy and its implementation and development between the Netherlands and six of the related priority countries.

Since interpretations of common heritage differ from country to country, we also see that the Dutch and the partner country's interpretations may be at odds. Sometimes this is due to societal changes or to differences in the dominant perspectives on a heritage site. In some cases sites were not even designated as monuments prior to Dutch involvement. In countries such as Suriname the shared history is obvious, while in others, such as Indonesia and Sri Lanka, it may be more appropriate to speak of a synchronous history as the local and colonial populations shared a geographical location but their descendants have very different views on the history of these sites.

Asia

Indonesia

Indonesia, the former Dutch East Indies – originally the central point of the VOC emporium – became the Netherlands' most important overseas possession in the nineteenth and twentieth century. From a Dutch point of view Indonesia plays a major role in its national history. In Indonesia, concern for the colonial heritage is slowly developing. This heritage is appreciated more as an economic resource in processes of urban revitalization than as a cultural resource or part of national history.

In the first decades following Indonesia's independence in 1945 most Indonesians did not consider Dutch heritage important. Amongst younger generations, however, a small group is currently demonstrating a growing awareness. While it labels heritage from the Dutch colonial period as Indonesian, and not as Dutch or common, this group feels that it is important to preserve it. Sometimes heritage marked as common by the Dutch government is not considered heritage at all by this new generation; at other times it no longer regards this as the heritage of the oppressor, but as Indonesian. The growing historical distance might explain these differences.

The increased interest in colonial heritage is also functional, given the financial possibilities of designating monuments as common heritage. Despite the new awareness, remaining administrative problems have precluded the signing of a joint policy framework for common heritage collaboration with Indonesia.

Sri Lanka

Sri Lanka, formerly Ceylon, was an important VOC trading post. Dutch influences are still visible in many coastal towns, especially in the city of Galle, a
UNESCO World Heritage Site. The Dutch period has received much attention
on Sri Lanka, accompanied by political commitment to the preservation of its
heritage. The Dutch occupy a relatively safe position in Sri Lankan history,
being neither the first European conquerors nor the last colonial rulers.

The Dutch and Sri Lankan narratives of the heritage sites have much in
common. They recount the same histories, both of which focus on the Dutch
population in Ceylon and not on influences on and consequences for the local
population. In this, the mutuality of this shared history is open to challenge:
although formal interpretations do not disagree, the absence of a local Sri
Lankan voice and perspective is evidence of exclusionary historiography and
historical practice.

India

With only a few exceptions, Dutch heritage is not defined as heritage at all
in India. The Indian agency responsible for monuments, the Archaeological
Survey of India (ASI), originates from the period of British rule, when a
number of Dutch-period monuments were listed as such, albeit with limited concern or attention. There is a lack of public awareness and almost no
political commitment to further Dutch-Indian collaboration on these common
heritage sites; and it is impossible to develop a policy of common heritage
without recognition by the partner country. Yet several sites are closely linked
to the Dutch period, especially in the south, where the VOC established many
trading posts.

A few projects have recently begun in this region, upon the insistence
of the Dutch. India has many monuments with a more obvious – often religious – relation to present-day society and the Dutch presence has almost
completely been forgotten. Although India is a priority country for the
Netherlands, it would appear that there is no common heritage to preserve.
In this case, the development of a Dutch common heritage policy takes a back
seat with regard to themes and priorities concerning the more recent British
colonial influence and ongoing debates about religious heritage.

Africa

Ghana

The most important common material heritage shared by Ghana and the Netherlands are the castles and forts along Africa's Gold Coast, a primary hub of the Atlantic slave trade. Nowadays, as heritage sites, these fortifications form a major tourist attraction for African Americans and other members of the African diaspora in search of the consolidation of their identity and the symbolic affirmation of a territorial location for a common past. In this regard, the castles are extremely important to Ghana. They are registered as architectural monuments and thus are government-owned rather than local collective property. The local community of Elmina (the former Dutch headquarters on the Gold Coast) is not involved in the management of this heritage and receives limited benefits from the tourist flow to the castle.

But the Dutch period also has positive connotations. Dutch surnames engender pride and every January Elmina celebrates the Dutch Christmas. This is perhaps less surprising when taking into account that Elmina flourished in the Dutch period, but suffered poverty and destruction during British rule (Doortmont 2005:36-7). The common heritage of Ghana and the Netherlands may have a future because of the positive economic spin-off, although as yet there is no sense of common heritage as such.

South Africa

South Africa and the Netherlands share a history dating back to the first settlement established by the VOC in 1652 and continuing to the present day. Much of it and the resulting common heritage now have contested meanings. An example is Cape Castle in Cape Town, a monument reflecting Dutch rule over the region. The castle served as the starting point of South Africa's colonization but is also a landmark for the apartheid period. Substantial Dutch financial support was available for this monument, but ultimately the South Africans rejected the funding. Debates surrounding the castle's use and its ownership by the Ministry of Defence resulted in the project being cancelled.

For the Netherlands, Cape Castle is a perfect example of common heritage. The building originates from the VOC period and was established by the entrepreneurial maritime merchant Jan van Riebeeck. South Africans, however, do not only associate the castle with the Dutch period, but also with apartheid. It was a symbol of repression; its silhouette was even used as an emblem on military uniforms.

In contrast to other VOC countries, the Dutch-descendant population in

Tomb of Sheikh Yusuf, Islamic mystic from Makassar, and four followers at
Cape of Good Hope

South Africa (Boers and later Afrikaners) remained in power long after the departure of the Dutch colonial authorities, through the repressive white supremacist system of apartheid that lasted until the 1990s. The Dutch common heritage factor plays a minor role in Cape Castle's image, compared with interpretations of the castle as a symbolic reminder of apartheid, the most salient period in contemporary South Africa.

The rewriting of history and its presentation to the public are important themes in most societies; this is particularly true with regard to the current rendering of the past in South Africa. The nation is engaged in a transition process of identifying and rewriting its collective memory. Its heritage policy increasingly recognizes the importance of intangible heritage in this process, including oral traditions. However, it may be too early for South Africa to embrace the concept of common cultural heritage. The close association of 'white' heritage from the Dutch colonial period with the recent history of apartheid makes the management of such monuments an extremely sensitive process.

South America

Suriname

In Suriname the temporal proximity of colonial history and historical memory poses a similar challenge to the concept of common heritage and the development of a policy in this field. Suriname became an independent republic in 1975, but remains strongly connected with the Netherlands. Does this mean that Suriname considers its heritage to be common with the Netherlands? Strong transnational ties make it difficult to differentiate between Dutch and Surinamese visions on common heritage. There are almost as many Surinamese living in the Netherlands as in Suriname. And, except for the small indigenous population, the majority of Surinamese have roots in the shared history of both countries: the Surinamese population is formed mainly by the descendants of African slaves and British Indian or Javanese indentured labourers.

Since this interrelated history and recent migration flows make it difficult to define two distinct visions on heritage, speaking of common heritage seems reasonable. From this perspective, almost everything originating before 1975 can be designated as common heritage of Suriname and the Netherlands. But, as Gert Oostindie will argue in the next chapter, there are contrasting interpretations and valuations of this past and its heritage. Suriname's HGIS projects have therefore been formulated with great care and contain almost no references to slavery or colonialism.

The Dutch government has financed projects such as the establishment of an art school in Fort Zeelandia, the transformation of Plantage Frederiksdorp into a hotel and collective management training for the Surinaams Museum. After the application for funding no reference was made to common heritage; common interpretations are hardly ever provided. In other words, the explicit implementation of a common heritage policy has found a politically more acceptable channel through implicit projects and contributions between both countries.

The historical context of cultural heritage management

The different perspectives on heritage sites and the tension between conflicting feelings of pride and guilt in the Netherlands where colonial heritage is concerned, are not surprising, particularly when considering the definitions and interpretations of heritage itself. Researching heritage policies first of all requires a working definition of heritage, or at least the awareness that 'heritage' is a complex term used for a wide spectrum of objects, monuments and traditions, tangible as well as intangible, moveable and immovable. It is important to realize that heritage does not just consist of static relics from the past; rather, it exists in the present and is shaped by continuous interpretation.

Old stones are not heritage – a building marked as an important example of medieval architecture is. Heritage, then, is always created. Yet it is not the same as history. Researching heritage involves asking questions such as: Who decides what is heritage and what is not? Whose heritage is it, who is included? Interpretation of any sort always leads to exclusion and as a result, heritage is always contested. Conflicting interpretations and the associated feelings of exclusion can lead to what is termed 'dissonant heritage' (Tunbridge and Ashworth 1996:21). In the context of a policy on colonial heritage, a significant issue is thus who is involved in the interpretation process. Marking heritage as colonial can be seen as a form of interpretation that directs, precludes and redirects subsequent interpretations.

The dissonant nature of heritage interpretation and the power relationships inherent in this are fundamental challenges in present intercultural heritage management collaboration. This is increasingly reflected in European attempts to deal with critiques of a perceived Western hegemony in heritage practices and policies. Understanding this, requires a more detailed look at the historical roots of heritage management in Europe itself. As this management is rooted in early attempts to study and preserve material remains as markers of the past, it is important to focus on the development of archaeological heritage management in particular, which can be traced back to the emergence of archaeology and its advancement as a discipline.

The roots of archaeological thought and concerns about how to deal with cultural remains have been traced back to the ideals of European Enlightenment in general and to the concept of 'cultural continuity' in particular (Cleere 1989b). However, archaeology as a discipline in the modern sense only developed in Europe in the eighteenth and nineteenth centuries, with the organization of archaeological societies and the institutionalization of archaeology through universities and museums. It was in this same period that it came to be exported globally as part of colonialism, either directly or indirectly through the favourable climate created by administrative and military contexts.[7]

The preservation of and research into archaeological remains during this period can be linked to concerns regarding (re-)establishing national identities in post-Napoleonic Europe (Willems 2002). They can also be connected to a colonial project that sought to explain – and justify – European dominance on the world stage in terms of an ongoing process of 'cultural evolution'. In these models Europe was commonly depicted as being at the 'civilized' pinnacle, whereas the 'savage' or 'barbarian' colonized peoples were usually seen through a culture-historical lens which interpreted their cultural innovations as a result of external diffusion rather than the product of indigenous development and initiation (Ucko 1995; Trigger 2006).

The first laws relating to the care of what is now termed 'archaeological heritage' appeared at roughly the same time as the archaeological discipline developed in Europe. Concerns relating to the preservation of material remains of the past were often developed within nationalist frameworks of collection and documentation for educational, ideological, financial or religious purposes (Díaz-Andreu 2007; Eickhoff 2007). From the late nineteenth century onwards, concerns about the destruction of historical landscapes and the survival of scientific data played an additional role.

Interestingly, heritage laws dealing with archaeological remains sometimes emerged earlier in overseas contexts than in the colonial metropole itself, as was the case in the Dutch East Indies with the passing of a Monuments Preservation Act in the early twentieth century, a direct reaction to the British example in Indo-China and India (Soejono 1984; Toebosch 2003). By and large, such efforts were aimed at selecting and interpreting indigenous heritage within 'Western' frameworks of understanding and categorization (Tanudirjo 1995; Ucko 1995). Moreover, they focused mostly on preserving or restoring monuments for the educational or scientific benefit of a public at home in Europe,[8] with little regard for the monuments' real and potential local significance.

---

[7] Byrne 1991; Trigger 2006. Some authors have in this sense even spoken of imperialist archaeology (see Trigger 2006).

[8] At this time, the first cautious calls for managing former Dutch colonial heritage in Indonesia could also be heard (see Van Overvoorde 1919).

The above outlines the start of heritage management in Europe, which became institutionalized in political discourses and legal frameworks in the second half of the twentieth century. Gaining impetus within the environmental debates in the 1960s and 1970s, followed by the emerging awareness in the 1980s and 1990s that destruction must be prevented through interdisciplinary, integrated and proactive regulated systems, heritage management developed as a profession in its own right. But while 'academic' archaeology increasingly incorporated self-reflexive critiques of its socio-political implications for 'non-Western' contexts and communities, this was arguably less the case for the field of heritage management. Practical and financial constraints played a role in this, as did positivist beliefs in terms of dealing with heritage concerns and political demands. The result was that by the end of the 1980s, there was a mounting critique of the 'remarkably coherent style of archaeological heritage management practiced throughout the world with almost no discussion of how it came about' (Byrne 1991:272).

Such discussions did appear soon after, with the rise of indigenous movements and postmodern theoretical critiques, as was reflected in international conferences such as the World Archaeological Congress in Southampton in 1989. This greater attention to regionally distinctive variations of archaeological research and approaches to heritage management led to international criticism of the unquestioned conservation ethic that was apparent in 'Western' heritage management discourses and embedded within international heritage policies and institutions (Ucko 1995; Cleere 1989a; Trigger 1989). In short, these dominant approaches linked a conservation ethic to state agencies and policies, and were based upon what were seen as objective valuations, selections and surveys of 'heritage' sites deemed worthy of preservation, to save them through integrated planning, salvage excavations, restoration and/or public education programmes (Byrne 1991:271).

While most professionals agreed that material markers of the past were non-renewable and under threat of disappearing globally, they did not agree on the obvious 'need' to preserve them.[9] Such a need, so apparent in 'Western' societies, was questioned increasingly as it became clear that not all societies and cultures recognized this as a problem nor would they approach its management in the same way. Indeed, there appeared to be many different opinions about what constituted 'heritage' in the first place.

From the 1980s onwards it became increasingly clear that the idea of 'cultural continuity', central to the conservation ethic regarding material markers of the past, sometimes contrasted sharply with the notion of 'spiritual continuity' apparent in many contexts across the world (Cleere 1989b). In

---

[9]   More recently, the idea of the past as a non-renewable resource has been criticized as well, see for example Holtorf 2002.

these contexts, heritage tended to be valuated in connection with the 'spirit of place' and social or religious meanings, while the preservation of the actual material remains was not necessarily considered a priority. Still, in many post-colonial states European forms of heritage legislation had meanwhile been adopted, while the legacy of culture-historical approaches to interpreting the past was often evident as well. In many cases this led to the preservation of pre-colonial as well as colonial cultural heritage within frameworks of post-colonial national identity (Byrne 1991; Ucko 1995).

Given that these forms of heritage legislation and theoretical backgrounds to disciplines were adopted in an unchanged form by post-colonial states, it was recognized that 'Western' approaches to heritage preservation might not have been directly imposed following decolonization. Rather, they could be seen as the result of what some development theorists have termed 'inappropriate ideology transfer' through subsequent political, scientific and financial international frameworks (Byrne 1991:274).

In these contexts discrepancies between 'Western' concepts of heritage management and endogenous socio-cultural systems and values presumably contributed to conflicts regarding heritage preservation, ownership and development. Added to this, was the awareness that governments had used archaeological interpretations and heritage legislation to establish policies that delineated and mobilized specific histories and identity groups (Smith 2004) and that this tended to disempower indigenous communities in particular. It was recognized, then, that heritage management was ultimately not only about archaeological and architectural remains, but even more so about the values attributed to them.

According to this new awareness, an exclusive focus on heritage preservation of material remains is often inappropriate when taking into account local views on cultural heritage related to, for instance, intangible values, traditions, ethnicity, livelihoods and/or the need for development and poverty reduction (Lopes Bastos and Kanan 2003; Pwiti 1996; Seif 2006). Coupled with concerns about expanding cultural tourism and globalization, declining cultural diversity and the impact of short-term economic strategies, attempts to accommodate different approaches to heritage management took shape in the 1990s with the adoption of international guidelines such as the Nara Declaration on Authenticity in 1994 of the International Council on Monuments and Sites (ICOMOS), which explicitly recognized the existence of cultural and heritage diversity. Besides this, the idea of implementing integrated and holistic heritage management approaches became popular (Mason and Avrami 2002).

Of these approaches, the model that emerged through the Australian Burra Charter (1998) has gained widest currency, mainly because of its emphasis on community participation and the ideological concept of valuing the resource. This model does not see the preservation of the material remains of a heritage site as the fundamental objective, but rather argues for managing its 'cultural significance', which is seen as the multitude of sometimes conflicting 'values' (including aesthetic, economic, social, religious and historical values) that can be ascribed to the site by a range of stakeholders. Although international organizations and policymakers such as ICOMOS and UNESCO have adopted these value-based approaches in recent years, and although such models call for more community participation in decision making, the question remains which values receive priority in policymaking or, in other words, which stakeholders actually perform the 'valuing' of the heritage resource.

The policy context

In addition to taking into account critiques of ethnocentric views on heritage management, it is important to understand that policy is not created in a social vacuum. Policies in general, and heritage policies in this specific context, are formulated within a broader force field. These forces can manifest themselves within the bureaucratic policymaking body, but they can also be external, either in the form of local and national lobby groups or as national and international 'epistemological communities'.

National cultural policy, and heritage policy as a subcategory, is subject to the efforts of lobby groups. Recent years have seen the emergence of post-colonial migrant groups making an impact on the heritage scene. The recent focus on diversity in European cultural policy emphasizes the multicultural nature of heritage and the role of migrant or minority organizations in formulating and executing national or municipal heritage policy. Examples are the Mayor's Commission on African and Asian Heritage in London (MCAAH 2005) which recommended, among other things, the infrastructure development of African and Asian community-based organizations engaged in heritage work.

Such a lobby-driven focus on diversity and inclusion within European nations[10] reflects discourses of multiculturalism present at national and international levels of epistemological communities of heritage experts. These communities are knowledge-based networks whose members are linked by specific technical expertise (on culture heritage), but who will also share a set of normative and principled beliefs, causal beliefs, discursive practices and a 'policy project'. They influence local, national and international policy through the diffusion of technical knowledge and related norms, values and specific terminology (Haas 1992). In the Netherlands, heritage professionals

[10]   Van Gorp and Renes 2007. This national-level trend towards 'shared' or 'mutual' heritage initiatives is balanced by the search for a shared European cultural heritage, emphasizing convergence rather than diversity at the level of the continent.

within governmental and non-governmental organizations may themselves be part of such heritage-based epistemic communities, or at least be influenced by the values, attitudes, discourse and policy strategies they disseminate nationally and internationally.

In the case of cultural heritage policy such communities might consist of, at a national level, actors in academia and the museum world, including archaeologists, anthropologists and museum studies specialists. International bodies concerned with cultural heritage represent these communities at the international level. These could include 'global governance institutions' such as UNESCO and other United Nations (UN) institutions, along with international non-governmental organizations and professional networks such as ICOMOS and the International Council on Museums (ICOM). It is within this 'global public sphere' (Kirshenblatt-Gimblett 2006), through these networks and the discourses circulating within them, that concepts such as 'mutual' and 'shared' heritage are introduced and can come to gain policy salience.

Since 1997 the Netherlands has adopted an approach to cultural heritage reflecting a concern for both the colonial past and contemporary multiculturalism. This approach is evident in many Dutch policy documents.[11] It reflects the influence of specific interest groups and broader expert networks on negotiations, within heritage policy, regarding colonialism and diversity. Similar negotiations have been taking place within other European countries, with a wide range of policy outcomes.

Dutch common cultural heritage policy in a European perspective

So far we have discussed the concept of common cultural heritage and the global-historical trends and regulatory guidelines – local, national and international, public and private – which have directed the development of heritage management in general and policy implementation and implications in particular. As our focus on the Netherlands and its partner countries has illustrated, heritage is something that is created. The practical realization of any cultural heritage policy thus involves the ethical issue of finding a balance between different interpretations by different actors, who often have different goals and whose operations are shaped by changing socio-historical realities and geopolitical agendas.

'Colonial' heritage and the presentation of the period of European expansion and colonization remain the subject of continuous negotiations and potential dissonance within many countries. In the Netherlands, these issues have been

---

[11]   See *Raamwerk gemeenschappelijk cultureel erfgoed* (2000), *Ruim baan voor culturele diversiteit* (1999), *Koers kiezen; Meer samenhang in het internationaal cultuurbeleid* (2006).

approached in part through the development of an official policy of 'Common Cultural Heritage'. However, as was demonstrated in the case studies above, this issue is relevant beyond the specific Dutch context. This raises the question of how other European countries are dealing with similar issues.

The following section will give an overview of the international cultural heritage policies of European countries that were selected due to their former involvement in colonialism. The comparative perspective this inventory adopts aims to stimulate the active rethinking of Dutch heritage policy. While colonization worldwide has not been restricted to European expansion, it is this period and its influences on European policy with which this chapter is concerned. Accordingly, this overview limits itself to a comparison between the Netherlands and the following European countries: Portugal, Spain, the United Kingdom, Germany, France, Italy and Belgium. This examination of cultural heritage policy in relation to former colonies is concerned specifically with 'official' aspects; that is, policy development and the awareness of it in the respective European governments as is evident from official policy and state-led projects. There is only brief consideration of the implementation of these policies and their reception within the former colonies.

As stated above, the 'commonality' of heritage is often open to debate. With the previous themes as a theoretical framework, a questionnaire was formulated for the seven aforementioned European countries. Policymakers, heritage experts and scientists from these countries were asked to introduce and comment upon their policies concerning colonial heritage. Interviews and further discussions with other stakeholders as well as a review of secondary literature complemented the results of this questionnaire,[12] resulting in a preliminary overview of European colonial heritage policy. The first question posed within this comparative research was whether a concept of common heritage, similar to that in the Netherlands, exists in the selected countries and whether specific policies have been developed to facilitate cooperative efforts towards conserving this heritage.

The following is a brief outline of different state and non-state organizations and administrative bodies involved in the development and concerns of international cultural heritage policy and associated projects. These cases are all framed through a comparative lens that is also looking at the theoretical and practical realities of policies that offer an alternative or complementary approach to the Dutch framework of 'common heritage'. The order in which they are presented reflects the level of similarity to Dutch policy.

---

[12]   Much of the general data in the cases presented here is derived from the following sources: The Council of Europe/ERI Carts 'Compendium of cultural policies and trends in Europe', ninth edition, 2008 (http://culturalpolicies.net/web/index.php; European Heritage Network: National heritage policies (http://european-heritage.net/sdx/herein/national_heritage

Portugal

Of the researched countries, Portuguese policy regarding the heritage of European expansion is most comparable with the Dutch common heritage policy. Like the Netherlands, Portugal emphasizes the European features of its heritage in the former colonies and its policy started with a focus on common language and common history. While it appears to refer more explicitly to the colonial past than Dutch policy, in both cases, whether the term 'colonial heritage' or 'common heritage' is used, the former colonizing country is still claiming some form of ownership of the heritage concerned.

In addition to official institutions, a number of private foundations are engaged in intercultural programmes. The two primary public actors are the International Cultural Relations Office of the Ministry of Culture and the Institute Camões, now under the authority of the Ministries of Culture and of Foreign Affairs. The main private actors are the Fundação Oriente (Orient Foundation) and the Calouste Gulbenkian Foundation.

Within Portuguese national heritage legislation cultural heritage incorporates all assets that merit special protection and enhancement, to the extent that they reflect relevant cultural interest or bear witness to a social or cultural value. The Portuguese language is seen as the basis of the country's sovereignty and as an essential constituent of Portuguese cultural heritage. Interestingly, this element is almost completely absent in Dutch policy.

Within the framework of bilateral and multilateral relations with Portuguese-speaking (lusophone) nations, for instance through the Community of Portuguese Language Countries (CPLP), Portugal contributes to the preservation and enhancement of cultural heritage that is testimony to chapters of its common history, located within or outside the national territory. Its policy includes strong cultural agreements, for instance with the African Countries of Portuguese Official Language (PALOP countries), including the former colonies of Angola, Cabo Verde, Guinea-Bissau, Mozambique and São Tomé and Príncipe. These cooperative efforts are concerned with safeguarding material and non-material heritage, referring especially to common language but also specifying support for initiatives from the PALOP countries relating to built heritage, the Portuguese language, books, libraries and the safeguarding of joint archives and intellectual property. One of the most important aspects is the training of local technical experts in these fields.[13]

The Portuguese state also contributes to the preservation and protection of any cultural heritage located beyond the Portuguese-speaking sphere, provided that it bears special relevance to Portuguese 'civilization and culture'. Cultural heritage policy is specifically aimed at the conservation and protec-

---

[13]   www.gpeari.pt/english/acordos.asp?zona=relacoes_bilaterais

GEZIGT OP SURATTE

View of Surat

tion of first, cultural heritage of European importance and second, cultural heritage with an outstanding universal value, particularly regarding cultural assets incorporating or showing significant connections with Portuguese cultural heritage.[14]

In addition to national policy frameworks, Portugal has, since 2006, supported significant projects through UNESCO and ICOMOS with regard to World Heritage of Portuguese Origin (WHPO). The first international meeting on this subject was held in April 2006 in Coimbra, Portugal. Its main purpose was to pave the way towards the creation of an international cooperation network of experts from all countries containing heritage of Portuguese origin.[15] This network will be charged with developing identification systems and tools, gathering knowledge, safeguarding and fostering each country's heritage and providing technical support for the preparation of the corresponding Tentative Lists. This will involve, specifically, drawing-up applications for serial nominations of World Heritage Sites of Portuguese Origin.[16] In accordance with the overall UNESCO strategy to promote less well-represented categories and improve the geographical distribution of World Heritage Sites, Portugal and countries identified as possessing cultural heritage of Portuguese origin,[17] have pledged to work towards these goals.

Portugal also coordinates meetings and publications relating to the UNESCO Slave Route Project as part of 2008 European Year of Intercultural Dialogue. In addition, in March 2006, Angola, Brazil, Mozambique and Portugal participated in a joint conference on world heritage and the Portuguese language.[18] In April 2008 the Portuguese Minister of Foreign Affairs announced, during a visit to the Sultanate of Oman, that Portugal would launch a programme for the international inventory, conservation and rehabilitation of heritage of Portuguese origin. He also presented the nomination of World Heritage Sites of Portuguese Origin dispersed throughout the world as contributing towards improving the balance of World Heritage Sites with positive developmental and equitable consequences.

In addition, important international cooperation takes place privately through the Fundação Oriente, with headquarters in Lisbon and delegations in Macao, India and East Timor. This foundation pursues activities of a cul-

---

[14]   Fundamental Law of the Portuguese Cultural Heritage (English translation), 8-9-2001, no. 209/01 Series I-A, Statue/Act Law no. 107.01, pp. 5808-29.
[15]   See UNESCO Cultural Heritage Laws database (http://www1.ci.uc.pt/whpo/home.html, for 'World heritage of Portuguese origin') and news report at http://whc.unesco.org/en/events/282/
[16]   WHPO conclusions Coimbra, 29-4-2006, at http://www1.ci.uc.pt/whpo/home_en.html
[17]   These are: Angola, Bahrain, Benin, Brazil, Cabo Verde, East Timor, Ghana, Guinea-Bissau, India, Kenya, Morocco, Mozambique, Nigeria, Paraguay, São Tomé and Príncipe, Tanzania, Uruguay and the Administrative Region of Macao (China).
[18]   http://whc.unesco.org/fr/actualites/239

tural, educational, artistic, scientific, social and philanthropic nature, mainly in Portugal and Macao, aimed at developing and continuing historical and cultural ties between Portugal and the Far East, specifically China, and at cooperation with the migrant Macanese community worldwide. Although main exchanges relate to the arts and music, the foundation also emphasizes its work in the recovery of architectural and cultural heritage, with a geographical concentration in Macao, India and Portugal and a thematic focus on 'state monuments'.[19]

The International Department of the Calouste Gulbenkian Foundation supports restoration work on Portuguese-built heritage across the world, with projects submitted by the authorities in the relevant countries. Part of the costs must be met locally, while the foundation may send technical experts and other specialists for an *in situ* study of the condition of the heritage proposed for restoration. It may also intervene directly in these projects and in the definition of guidelines for project execution.[20]

As these few examples demonstrate, Portugal is an active player in the international heritage field, contributing through official state directives which are complemented with private projects and initiatives. Common language and common history form the basis of its heritage policy. There is a wide range of activities but it is not clear how, for instance, PALOP countries are involved in decisions regarding which project to finance, or how they value the monuments of the common past without Portuguese intervention.

United Kingdom

In contrast to Portugal and the Netherlands, the United Kingdom's (UK) cultural heritage projects relating to former colonies focus on development issues and cultural diversity rather than on common heritage and common history.[21] However, the heritage activities funded by the British government are quite similar to those initiated by Portugal and the Netherlands.

The Commonwealth is a key institution for the United Kingdom, connecting 53 nations formerly part of the British Empire, much larger but somewhat similar to the Portuguese CPLP. The projects and aims of international cultural cooperation focus on sustainable economic and humanitarian development

---

[19] Fundação Oriente annual report 2006:29 (a full list of activities by the Fundação Oriente can be downloaded from http://www.foriente.pt/159/activity-report.htm)
[20] http://www.gulbenkian.org/english/serv_internacional_1.asp
[21] Sources for this policy summary include: http://www.thecommonwealth.org/; http://www.britishcouncil.org/; http://www.culture.gov.uk/; http://www.lottery.culture.gov.uk/; http://ctc.britishcouncil.org.cn/welcome.html; *DCMS International Strategy* 2006, downloaded from http://www.culture.gov.uk/NR/rdonlyres/F26AE9B0-90D0-472B-8E43-8AC92F534549/0/internatonal_strategy_revisedOct06.pdf

as well as environmental issues. At first glance the United Kingdom does not appear to have a specific policy regarding heritage in its former colonies. However, awareness and funding of international cultural heritage is evident in various national governmental bodies, such as English Heritage, the British Council, the Foreign and Commonwealth Office (FCO) and the Building Monuments and Sites Division of the Department for Culture, Media and Sport (DCMS).

Many of these official bodies are regulated by policy that is concerned with various elements of heritage protection within the United Kingdom, thus not on an international level. For example, DCMS handles national heritage issues while the Secretary of State is responsible, with advice from English Heritage, for the scheduling of ancient monuments, the determining of applications for scheduled monument consent and the listing of buildings of special architectural or historic interest within England.[22]

But DCMS's international cultural policy also includes building and reinforcing relationships between British and overseas cultural organizations, thus improving the international position of the British cultural sector and its influence on public diplomacy. The United Kingdom's international strategy is aligned with goals presented by the FCO and often administered and co-supported by the British Council. In this regard it appears that international policy objectives are designed with an eye to international promotion and multilateral support of global developmental goals, rather than pursuing specific bilateral heritage partnerships.

English Heritage, established through the National Heritage Act of 1983, is active as both DCMS's and the government's statutory adviser on all matters concerning the conservation of the United Kingdom's built historic environment; similar to the DCMS it has a national focus.

The British Council, partly funded by the FCO, facilitates many international projects focused on sustainable development and culture for development initiated by individuals and independent organizations through business exchanges and networks. It has offices in 110 countries worldwide and is especially involved in arts and cultural initiatives for education and capacity building towards economic development. Its Creative Industries Unit promotes the United Kingdom's cultural heritage sector internationally through seminars and missions overseas.

Most state heritage policies focus on the built historic environment but are expanding towards cultural heritage institutions, including museums. International programmes through DCMS in cooperation with the British Council include 'Connections through Culture', a project relating to cross-cultural United Kingdom-China-Hong Kong partnerships in cultural devel-

---

[22] http://www.european-heritage.net (UK section 2.1.1).

opment.[23] Initiatives focus on art, theatre, dance, music and offer small-scale funding for travel, training and so forth, but also accommodate proposals relating to built heritage and funding, such as a photo exhibition of British architecture in Nanjing.

The majority of international heritage policies related to the British colonial expansion are framed in terms of cultural diversity or development cooperation. References to common, shared or colonial history appear to be absent in such strategies. An important goal of DCMS's international strategy, for instance, is sustainability, with international funding going to training and cultural heritage protection for priority regions with no specific or explicit historical connection to the United Kingdom. Another goal is diversity and within this strategy, key countries are those with a UK resident or descended population (for example Bangladesh, India, the West Indies and anglophone Africa). National educational and awareness-raising programmes within this focus may refer to the historical relations between the United Kingdom and these priority countries.

One such project is the recent opening of the International Slavery Museum in Liverpool marking the 200th anniversary of the abolition of the transatlantic slave trade (1807-2007). Another initiative was the British Museum Africa Programme, a joint British-African exchange and capacity building cooperative (2003-2006) aimed at including culture in development work in Africa and involving high-profile exchanges of staff, training initiatives and collection loans between the British Museum and partners across the continent. Any explicit references to historical colonial relations with the United Kingdom seemed to be absent in this programme.

These various priorities imply that while the United Kingdom may well be concerned with colonial heritage and its ongoing protection, international relationships in this regard are nurtured through broader (multiplayer) collaboration and projects initiated and implemented at the local rather than the state level. The explicit focus of official international cultural heritage policy is, in contrast to Portugal and the Netherlands, almost exclusively on development issues and cultural diversity, rather than on common heritage or shared history. This policy offers assistance and funding in relation to heritage in the former British colonies but does not claim ownership of this heritage by defining it as colonial or common.

Spain

Positioned more or less between the common heritage approach of Portugal and the Netherlands and the United Kingdom's emphasis on culture for

23   http://ctc.britishcouncil.org.cn/welcome.html

development and cultural diversity, Spain employs all these concepts in the management of its common Ibero-American heritage.[24] The Spanish state funds a range of related activities, mostly through the Organización de Estados Iberoamericanos (OEI, Organization of Ibero-American States for Education, Science and Culture). It provides international assistance regarding heritage through its contributions to UNESCO's World Heritage Fund, through financing foreign excavations by the Institute of Spanish Historical Heritage and through its convention with the World Heritage Centre for technical assistance in foreign countries. In addition, several training courses related to heritage have been carried out abroad.[25] Voluntary organizations focusing on culture and development also collaborate with UNESCO and Ibero-American associations.

Spain has been a member of the OEI since 1949 through the Directorate General of Cultural Cooperation and Communication, which coordinates the participation of the Ministry of Culture at the Ibero-American Conferences. The XV Ibero-American Summit in 2005 stressed the need to 'promote and protect the cultural diversity that underpins the Ibero-American Community of Nations, and to search for new mechanisms of cultural cooperation between Ibero-American countries able to strengthen the identities and the wealth of their cultural diversity and promote intercultural dialogue'.[26] At the same meeting, the heads of state and government were urged to work together on the production of a Cultural Charter for Ibero-America to reinforce the common cultural space that defines all Ibero-American countries. This document specifically recognizes a common culture and Spain's inclusion is evidence of a common heritage policy recognizing both the mutual aspects and diversity of the Ibero-American heritage.

In 1982 Spain signed the intergovernmental Andrés Bello Agreement promoting educational, scientific and cultural integration with the partner countries (Bolivia, Chile, Colombia, Cuba, Ecuador, Panama, Peru, Spain and Venezuela). The Andrés Bello Convention includes many Ibero-American cultural initiatives, notably 'Somos Patrimonio' (We are Heritage) with Spain and twelve Latin American countries as members. It offers a virtual space for

---

[24]   Sources for this policy summary include: The Council of Europe/ERI Carts 'Compendium of cultural policies and trends in Europe', ninth edition, 2008 (http://culturalpolicies.net/ especially section 2.4.3-2.4.6 on European and international cooperation and other relevant issues). The Council of Europe National Heritage Policies (http://www.european-heritage.net/, especially section 9.4 on international cooperation); http://www.convenioandresbello.org; http://www.aecid.es; http://www.aecid.es/03coop/4program_coop/Patrimonio/index.htm; Ministry of Culture at http://www.mcu.es/index.html; 'Somos Patrimonio'; http://www.micrositios.net/cab/index.php?idcategoria=1247

[25]   Source: http://european-heritage.net/

[26]   According to the summary in the Council of Europe/ERI Carts Spain section 2.4.3., http://culturalpolicies.net/

the development, sharing and discussion of cultural heritage and its management and use within sustainable development.

This emphasis on heritage for development is also furthered through the Agencia Española de Cooperación Internacional para el Desarollo (AECID, Spanish Agency for International Cooperation for Development), an autonomous body affiliated with the Ministry of Foreign Affairs and Cooperation through the Secretary of State for International Cooperation. This agency is responsible for the design, execution and management of cooperative projects and programmes for development, either directly, using its own resources, or via cooperation with other domestic or international bodies and non-governmental development organizations.

Among the agency's key cooperation programmes is Patrimonio para el Desarollo (Heritage for Development), the successor to the 1985-2005 Programa de Patrimonio de Cooperación Español (Heritage Programme of Spanish Cooperation). Heritage for Development focuses on Ibero-America, with projects involving the revitalization of historic centres, the restoration of monuments and the development of workshops in sites such as Cartagena (Colombia), Tikal (Guatemala) and Cuzco (Peru). The AECID supports this initiative technically and financially, by assisting local institutions in the development and execution of plans. The programme intends to contribute to the protection of identity, heritage and collective memory, improve the conditions of the urban liveability, generate economic activity and employment, and enhance governance aspects.

The Spanish heritage policy infrastructure, the OEI, is similar to the Portuguese CPLP and the British Commonwealth. All three countries are involved in heritage management in their former colonies, with each employing a different strategy. The major difference between the common heritage approach of Portugal and the Netherlands and the culture and development approach of the United Kingdom and Spain lies in the emphasis on development issues and the diversity of the heritage in the latter two countries.

Germany

Germany's Federal Foreign Office supports a programme promoting German cultural heritage abroad and the preservation of cultural heritage in developing countries.[27] Since its launch in 1981, 1,300 projects in 132 countries

---

[27]   Sources for this policy summary include country case studies and comparisons in Maass 2005 and the Council of Europe/ERI Carts 'Compendium of cultural policies and trends in Europe', ninth edition, 2008 (http://culturalpolicies.net/ especially section 2.4.3-2.4.6). For European and international cooperation and other relevant issues, see; http://www.european-heritage.net/sdx/herein; http://cms.ifa.de, www.windhuk.diplo.de, http://www.auswaertiges-amt.de/diplo/en/Aussenpolitik/Kulturpolitik/Kulturerhalt.html

have been facilitated. Its budget is to be used worldwide and is thus not solely restricted to priority countries. Currently, however, priority lies with projects relating to cultural dialogue between Europe and the Islamic world, in particular Afghanistan, including restoration and training programmes for moveable and immovable, tangible and intangible heritage.

A major recipient of funds within this cultural preservation programme is Namibia, a German colony between 1884 and 1915, for which, since 1985, circa € 900,000 have been made available for heritage projects. Bilateral cultural relations between Namibia and Germany are, according to the German embassy in Windhoek, rooted in their mutual history. In November 2007 the exhibition 'Namibia and Germany; A special relationship' opened in Swakopmund, after having been on show at the Goethe Centre in Windhoek. Activities similar in scope to those instigated under the Dutch cultural policy are 'Cultural preservation; Collection of oral history' and the 'Warmbad project', named after a town in the south of Namibia well known for its historic buildings dating back to the early twentieth century, including a German fort, officers' houses and a church. Funding was made available for the restoration of these buildings. The oral history project studied how different ethnic groups view the German colonial period, particularly the 1903-1908 colonial wars. This study resulted in the publication *What the elders used to say; Namibian perspectives on the last decade of German colonial rule* (2008).

International cultural policy is considered the third pillar of Germany's foreign affairs. In 2006 and 2007 major conferences were held to highlight the new political importance accorded to foreign cultural policies and to discuss future developments. The growing importance of these policies on the political agenda was underlined by changes in the federal budget. Counter to former trends, funding was increased in 2007 and 2008.

Primary areas of foreign cultural policies are cross-border cooperation in education and science, international cultural dialogue, promotion of the German language abroad and exchanges in the fields of art, music and literature. For the most part, these policies are implemented by intermediary organizations funded by the Federal Ministry of Foreign Affairs, such as the Goethe Institute, the German Academic Exchange Service, the Institute for Foreign Cultural Relations, the Alexander von Humboldt Foundation and the German UNESCO Commission. An important actor in transnational intercultural dialogue is the Federal Cultural Foundation (Bundeskulturstiftung).

Relevant bodies of the *Länder* (the states within the German Federation) cooperate closely with the Federal Government in the field of foreign cultural policy. Municipalities and civil society groups are also actively involved in cultural work abroad. One of the central cultural policy mandates is the protection and preservation of the built heritage: cultural monuments and manmade landscapes, including architectural, archaeological and paleontological monuments as well as parks.

The United Kingdom, Spain, Portugal, the Netherlands and (to a certain extent) Germany are the main actors in the field of European expansion heritage policy, but many other European countries are also concerned with this type of heritage without a specific national policy. France, Belgium and Italy support international cooperation at the project level through their embassies and international cultural institutions.

France

France does not have one policy framework but rather uses a system of various decentralized structures for international cultural heritage.[28] A major platform for international cultural cooperation is the Francophonie, a body that is comparable to the CPLP and the OEI, although it does not appear to be involved in (colonial) heritage programmes. France's central policy in international cultural cooperation is aimed at exporting expertise in the field of heritage and at achieving a balance between heritage and development so that the countries concerned will eventually become self-sufficient in this field. There is an emphasis on cultural diversity and on the promotion of French culture and language abroad.

Within the French Ministry of Culture and Communication, the Department of Architecture and Heritage has no explicit official policy regarding colonial heritage. However, in recent years a series of activities has taken place to identify, study and enhance this heritage, which for a long time was not considered interesting. Colonial heritage was, for instance, beyond the scope and attention of heritage activities funded by France in Vietnam or Algeria. However, a conference organized by l'Institut National du Patrimoine (National Heritage Institute) in 2006 followed a strategy of raising awareness and inventorying and sharing studies in former colonies and overseas territories.

Similar to many members of the European Union (EU), France is interested in representing cultural diversity or pluralism within its own multicultural society, influenced for instance by the EU. The worldwide promotion of the French language and culture is seen as a contribution towards this goal and official policy centres on the *rayonnement de la France*, the glorification of

---

[28]   Sources for this policy summary include country case studies and comparisons from Dodd, Lyklema and Dittrich-van Weringh 2006 and the following sites: the Council of Europe/ERI Carts 'Compendium of cultural policies and trends in Europe', ninth edition, 2008 (http://cultural-policies.net/web/index.php);The Council of Europe; National Heritage Policies, http://www. european-heritage.net/sdx/herein; http://www.culture.gouv.fr; http://www.diplomatie.gouv.fr (Personal contact from UNESCO, Marie Noel Tournoux); http://www.culture.gouv.fr/culture/ min/organigramme/index-organigrammes.htm; *Code patrimoine*, http://www.legifrance.gouv.fr/ affichCode.do?cidTexte=LEGITEXT000006074236&dateTexte=20080515

France. The principal objective of the Ministry of Culture and Communication is to link culture and new information technologies, to reach a greater number of French citizens, other Europeans and people throughout the world.

Italy

Italian awareness of the political and socio-economic relevance of international cultural cooperation has been growing since the early 2000s, along with the conviction that enhancing the international image of Italian culture would represent a valuable foreign policy tool.[29] There is acknowledgement of the need to rationalize the focus, by shifting the balance in foreign relations from Europe to other areas, such as the Middle East and Asia Pacific. Close cooperation in the conservation and re-appropriation of these countries' heritage is seen as the Italian way to contribute to the improvement of mutual understanding. Programmes have been developed with Latin America, Iran, Afghanistan, Iraq and China, but no reference is made to colonial cultural or common heritage in Italy's cultural policy.

The main institutional actor in this field is the Directorate General for Cultural Promotion and Cooperation (DGCPC) within the Ministry of Foreign Affairs. Together with the Directorate General for Cooperation and Development and with the technical and scientific assistance of the Ministry for Cultural Heritage and Activities, the DGCPC engages in cross-border cooperation in technical assistance and managerial and manpower training in the heritage field.

The Ministry of Foreign Affairs also includes various regional Directorates General (DGs), which in turn are responsible for Institutes such as the Instituto Latino-Americano and the Istituto per l'Africa e l'Oriente. Within the Ministry for Cultural Heritage and Activities there is no specific DG in charge of foreign relations. These are dealt with by the cabinet's Diplomatic Attaché and the heads of the various DGs involved, depending on the issue. Despite the lack of a specific DG for foreign relations, since 2000 the Ministry for Cultural Heritage and Activities has upgraded its role in terms of foreign cultural policy. The Ministry's strengthened international emphasis may be ascribed in part to the expansion of Italy's involvement in providing technical and financial support for heritage activities in developing countries.

Bilateral cultural cooperation is carried out through the Italian Cultural Institutes abroad, through bilateral cultural agreements and the joint organization of annual cultural events. The mission of the Institutes is the promotion

---

[29]   Sources for this policy summary include country case studies and comparisons in the Council of Europe/ERI Carts 'Compendium of cultural policies and trends in Europe', ninth edition, 2008 (http://culturalpolicies.net/), Instituto Italiano per l'Africa e l'Oriente: www.isiao.it

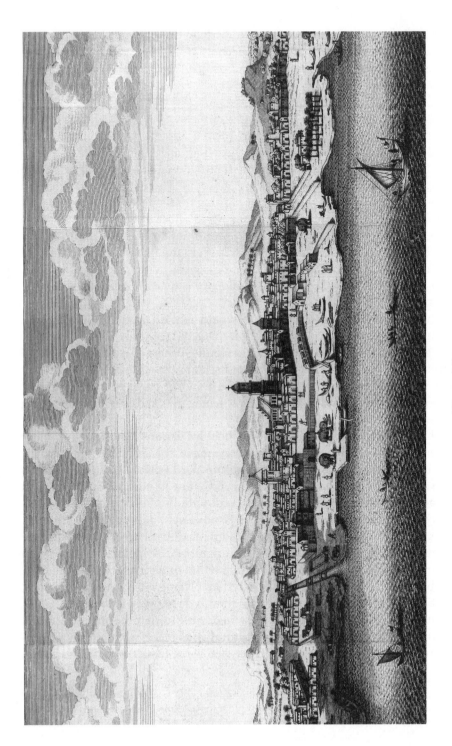

View of Goa

of Italian culture internationally. There are some Italian archaeological excavations taking place in former colonies (for example, Italian archaeologists
are involved in research in Leptis Magna, Libya), but there are few activities
with regard to Italian colonial architecture.

Recently, the Italian state has passed legislation pertaining to cultural
heritage and landscapes that includes references to the new interpretation
of heritage issues at the international level. For the first time, 'contemporary
architecture' has been marked as an important heritage category. This could
be an opportunity for colonial heritage cooperation, as most Italian colonial
heritage consists of modern architecture.

Belgium

Finally, cultural policy in Belgium – a federal state divided into three regions
(French-, Flemish- and German-speaking) – tends to be regionally focused.
Since 1993 the three regions have enjoyed self-government, allowing them
to enter into agreements not only with foreign states but also with foreign
regions or provinces. Belgian international cultural cooperation has been
transferred to the regional governments, which rotate in their participation
in international bodies. Cultural policies are governed by the subsidiary
principle, which means that in principle the state does not intervene directly
in cultural matters other than through general regulations and the awarding
of grants.

International cooperation for development is carried out by the Directorate
General for Development Cooperation under the supervision of the Federal
Ministries of Foreign Affairs, Commerce and Cooperation for Development.
A specific policy on international heritage cooperation or colonial heritage is
lacking but there are projects related to these topics that are funded by the
Belgian state. While there is no structural policy, at the level of projects and
within academia these matters do receive attention.

For instance, the francophone community has a cultural centre, Le Centre
Wallonie-Bruxelles, in Kinshasa, the capital of the Democratic Republic of
Congo (DRC), which finances projects relating to colonial heritage.[30] The
Flemish Minister of Culture has developed similar programmes, including a Flemish cultural centre in the DRC.[31] The Belgium-Africa connection finds strong support through many other channels, most significantly
through museums and university-based research collaborations, workshops
and foundations. For example, the Flemish Interuniversity Council's programme includes a special Congo project and cultural heritage initiatives

[30] www.wbri.be/cgi/bin3/render.cgi?id=0050484_matrice&ln=ln1&userid=&rubr=afrique
[31] www.kvs.be/index2.php?page=news

that fall within its development aid agenda.[32] In 2005 the Royal Flemish
Theatre in Brussels organized a major convention on colonial heritage in
Belgium and Central Africa. The initiative for this bilingual (Dutch-French)
event was taken by the Africa Museum in Tervuren and Ghent University.[33]
Additionally, in 2007 the Ghent Africa Platform within Ghent University
organized an international conference on heritage in Africa entitled 'Heritage
and/as reproduction in Africa; Outcomes and limits'.

Other university-based projects in Belgium include Avrug, a foundation
established within Ghent University organizing regular events pertaining to
colonial heritage and devoting special attention to the contestation of colonial
monuments in the public domain.[34] In addition, projects and workshops that
originally emphasized (the francophone) language have been expanded to
include attention to colonial monuments. The Flemish administration has
been working towards parallel initiatives and in 2007 the Vlaamse Vereniging
voor Bibliotheek-, Archief- en Documentatiewezen (VVBAD, Flemish Society
for Libraries, Archives and Documentation) organized the workshop 'Flemish
Heritage Abroad'.[35]

The largest research centre in Belgium focusing on Central Africa is the
Royal Museum for Central Africa in Tervuren, which in its master plan highlights the Congolese diaspora. Within the museum an advisory board is made
up of representatives of African associations in Belgium.[36] It was founded as a
colonial museum following the World Exhibition in 1897 and houses important colonial collections, both material and immaterial.[37]

The Belgian project-based approach backed up by funding, results in
increased awareness on the subject of colonial heritage, but such activities
take place without a comprehensive theoretical aim or policy framework.

Conclusion

From the results of the research described above it can be concluded that
all of the European countries surveyed are in some way concerned with the
cultural heritage of the European expansion and colonization. They do have
very different policies, practices and principles with regard to how this herit-

---

[32]   www.vliruos.be/index.php?navid=499&direct_to=Congoprogramma
[33]   http://cas1.elis.rug.ac.be/avrug/forum/bake.htm
[34]   http://cas1.elis.rug.ac.be/avrug/document.htm#gke
[35]   http://www.vvbad.be/node/1293/print
[36]   www.africamuseum.be/museum/about/comraf
[37]   http://cultuurweb.be/CNETPortal/DetailDossiers.aspx?id_dossiers=2C1A535F-C312-FED9-
FEBFC34746C17027&language=nl&locale=nl-NL

age should be defined, supported and approached. It is possible to make a distinction between those countries that focus on the colonial or common dimension of heritage and those that prioritize the development aspects of heritage cooperation.

Each country's policy has different levels, emphasizes different approaches, is based on a different infrastructure, starts from different premises and moves towards different aims. Broadly, we can distinguish between activities based on the notion of 'common heritage', preferred by Portugal and the Netherlands, and those focusing on cultural diversity, as favoured by the United Kingdom and Spain. For some countries, most activities are directed by an official policy or by policy guidelines, while others, such as Belgium and France, provide funding for projects outside a specific policy, working towards related or overlapping agendas that include heritage concerns. Sometimes the preservation of heritage is seen as the primary aim of an activity, in other cases it is rather a tool for development.

It is worth noting that the differences in policy directives and the comprehensiveness of policies are related to the different governmental structures, including forms of regional autonomy that result in different representative communities within a European country. For example, in Belgium the separation into three different linguistic regions complicates any all-encompassing policy. The individual linguistic and cultural concerns for each representative community are likely to emerge within the development of heritage projects both internally and in relation to the former colonial context.

Similarly, Germany is organized through a system of sixteen semi-autonomous federal states, an infrastructure which may partially be responsible for the absence of any federal policy in this field. In Spain a system of autonomous regions similarly reflects and articulates regional differences. In addition to such variations in government structure, it is important to note that the colonial history of some countries is very recent, as seen for example in the case of Macau, which only gained independence from the Portuguese in 1991.

Returning to this chapter's initial focus on the Netherlands, it is worth considering some of the implications of and potential tensions within Dutch (and Portuguese) appeals to 'commonality' through the concept of a common cultural heritage. This policy departs from the principle of similarity rather than cultural diversity. In the Dutch context, it can be argued that this has sometimes resulted in a practice of dissonant heritage, in which the perspectives of the Netherlands and its partner countries do not always match. In other words, the 'commonality' of common cultural heritage, by definition, will require a relationship of balance, which is never a given. Can a fortification in Indonesia be Indonesian and Dutch heritage simultaneously, and does this amount to common heritage? Does labelling a site as common entail the risk of silencing the voices of different communities and alternative interpretations?

Studying relations with the Dutch partner countries reveals that there is always some dissonance between the Dutch vision and the dominant interpretation held or presented by the partner country. Dutch policy does claim that common cultural heritage is not only part of Dutch history and identity, but of that of the partner country as well. This assertion has many ambiguous premises that remain unclear within the Dutch administration. Starting with definitions of heritage, it is necessary to underline that not all sites were considered 'common heritage' or even 'heritage' at all prior to Dutch involvement.

Heritage is always socially constructed and the concept of heritage – what it is and what it should be – has been biased towards the Dutch perspective, particularly when the recognition of a site as part of national cultural heritage occurred predominantly due to Dutch efforts. For example, although officially all projects must be initiated by the partner country, this initiative is often the direct product of preceding appeals by the Dutch partner, who will have created enthusiasm for a project and made the necessary appeals for funding, local partners and necessary political commitment. Old buildings, shipwrecks and cemeteries are thus transformed into cultural heritage by interpreting and 'musealizing' them. This process itself can, however, create dissonance, as it removes sites from their predominantly local context and opens them up to the needs and demands of a much broader circle of stakeholders. The associated extension of the consumer base is likely to be a cause of additional tension as heritage managers struggle to appeal to the various consumers and their often contradictory demands and perspectives.

Common heritage, then, is created at the very start of a project. But labelling it as such does not automatically mean that the site forms part of the identity and history of either or both countries. Our view of the past is always dictated by the present and our independent understanding of the past dictates our interpretations and what we see. For the Dutch government, the common heritage sites are part of national identity and history, even if they are located beyond the national borders. It regards the monuments built by the Dutch or during Dutch periods of administration in any partner country as common heritage. But for the partner country, this need not be the dominant way of seeing, interpreting or presenting these remains. After the Dutch period these sites remained; they received new functions and interpretations, or they received no interpretation at all and were left to slowly collapse.

The passage of time marks both man and monument and the relationship between them. A monument could be a prominent part of the partner country's history and identity, functioning as a symbol of colonial heritage and commemorated or celebrated as such. Alternatively, the colonial nature of a monument may be superimposed by events before or after the colonial period, so that the main narrative of a site can be different or even completely divorced from the Dutch one. Likewise, a site or monument can be part of the identity of a country due to its status or function but not as a historical monument. The Dutch state has to become aware of its role as a creator of heritage and the claims that labelling historical objects, first, as heritage and, second, as common heritage entails. This policy implies not only a change of use but also a change of perspective regarding the involved object.

From this examination of the practice of Dutch policy it is clear that the Netherlands works quite pragmatically within its policy framework, adjusting to the various socio-political agendas and local attitudes. If a partner country's enthusiasm for its Dutch history is apparent, Dutch heritage is highlighted with pride and presented as a primary objective of the heritage and development agenda. But if the Dutch period is associated with colonial guilt or historical shame, its heritage is likely to take a secondary role.

While Portugal appears to employ a similar policy, it was not possible to study the actual execution of its projects and take into account the perspectives of its partner countries. Portuguese and Dutch heritage policies may depart from the same common heritage premise, but the major difference is the binding factor of the Portuguese language and the CPLP union associated with this. It would be very interesting to study how other CPLP countries react to the common heritage policy, whether Portugal is as dominant as the Netherlands in the selection of projects and whether it has found a way of balancing pride in its former empire with feelings of colonial guilt and embarrassment.

The United Kingdom and Spain appear to focus primarily on development in their international heritage policies. This 'culture and development' approach is practiced through institutions with a colonial background, such as the Commonwealth for the United Kingdom and the OEI for Spain. Such organizations can easily incorporate development issues and cultural diversity functions as a starting point.

Most international heritage policies could still be criticized for advocating preservation – sustaining the resource for future generations – as their core activity, with less attention to meeting the demands of contemporary populations. This primacy of preservation results not only from the dominant paradigm, in which a conservation ethic and Eurocentric definitions of heritage are central, but also from the dominant techno-scientific discourse, privileging positivism and processual science that continues to frame the discipline (Williams and Van der Linde 2006; Duineveld 2006). In addition, most international heritage policies and organizations work with a system of selecting and preserving cultural heritage on the basis of 'universal' values and for the global benefit of all humanity (for example the notion of 'outstanding universal value' underlying UNESCO policies; Skeates 2000:12).

This approach implies that, for all of humanity, preservation of the material markers of the past is the underlying vision when dealing with the past. Such ideas of 'universal' value assume that people across the globe prioritize the same aspects of heritage and that a positivist framework for selecting and valuating heritage sites is possible. Some authors even speak of the 'dangers of a fundamentalist ideology apparent in heritage preservationism' (Holtorf 2006), considering the globalizing heritage agencies and the heritage strategies of some Western countries as neocolonial. Although such accusations may be overstated, it is clear that an understanding of the historical and socio-political frameworks and of the concepts underlying Western heritage policies, is crucial for developing more sustainable and ethical forms of interaction.

In a post-colonial world, heritage policies and international collaboration will succeed only as long as they work explicitly from the basis that valorizations and concepts of heritage are subjective, contested and multiple, and that different cultural philosophies and approaches towards heritage management are equally valid. Possible ways to achieve this have been suggested, for instance through dealing with notions of 'dissonant heritage', or with a notion of heritage that encompasses 'care' rather than being based upon 'curation'. It has been argued that this could include care for personal lives, in which development issues and poverty reduction could be more easily incorporated (Rowlands and Butler 2007).

Another possible way forward could be the adoption of heritage approaches and policies based upon a notion of 'human development' as opposed to one of 'preservation' (Van der Linde 2004; Galla 2002). In such models, the function of cultural heritage is seen primarily as a path towards development and progress, endorsed by principles such as empowerment, education, capacity building, knowledge exchange and public involvement.

The fundamental challenge for the heritage management field will be the translation of these postmodern and post-colonial critiques and concepts into workable policy guidelines and financial frameworks. A comparative analysis of how different European countries deal with the legacy of their heritage overseas and with that of their heritage policies, seems crucial.

The overview presented in this chapter is far from complete. More research is needed on the implementation of heritage policies and on the interpretations of related activities in the partner countries. These policies, and the Dutch policy in particular, demonstrate the tension between the desire of the former colonizing countries to engage in what they consider to be heritage of the European expansion and the needs of the former colonies and their priorities in heritage preservation and, indeed, in coming to terms with the past.

It is difficult to overcome this tension, as it is still predominantly the

European countries that fund the training, restoration and so on. But the demands of the partner countries should always be central to these policies, entailing intensive cultural cooperation between the countries where the heritage is located and those with the budget. While European countries may sometimes succeed in stimulating public awareness of heritage, it is important to respect the demands and priorities of the partner countries.

At the moment of writing, the Netherlands is rethinking and rewriting its common cultural heritage policy and the possibilities for cultural cooperation. This process includes a debate on the use of 'common heritage' as a label for the heritage involved. It is evident that friction will remain between generalized notions of commonality and feelings of resentment, pride and embarrassment relating to the colonial past, just as the discussion of the ways to commemorate or celebrate this past will persist. Similarly, the practical implications of a common policy that is mainly financed and controlled by the former colonizing power remain complex. Joint policy frameworks and project proposals have been formulated and projects have been executed in close collaboration.

Evaluating these activities will help to improve the policy field and hopefully also bilateral relations between the Netherlands and its former colonies. Notwithstanding the critical perspective presented in this chapter, the Netherlands does appear to be engaged in an open-minded attempt to deal with its overseas heritage along with its designated partner countries. Common cultural heritage policy thus remains an intriguing, and ongoing, experiment in exploring new avenues for cultural cooperation.

Bibliography

Digital sources

http://culturalpolicies.net/web/index.php
    The Council of Europe/ERI Carts 'Compendium of cultural policies and trends in Europe', ninth edition, 2008.
http://european-heritage.net/
    The European Heritage Network is a permanent system gathering information on governmental services in charge of heritage protection within the Council of Europe.
www.gpeari.pt/english/acordos.asp?zona=relacoes_bilaterais
    Portugal, Ministry of Culture: planning, strategy, evaluation and international relations.
http://www.unesco.org/culture/natlaws/
    UNESCO, Cultural heritage laws database.
http://www1.ci.uc.pt/whpo/home.html
    Website for 'World heritage of Portuguese origin'.

http://whc.unesco.org/en/events/282/
   UNESCO, News item 'World heritage of Portuguese origin'.
http://whc.unesco.org/fr/actualites/239
   UNESCO, News item 'World heritage and Portuguese language'.
http://www.foriente.pt/159/activity-report.htm
   Full list of activities by the Fundação Oriente.
http://www.gulbenkian.org
   Portuguese private institution of public utility whose statutory aims are in the
   fields of arts, charity, education and science.
http://www.thecommonwealth.org
   The Commonwealth is an association of sovereign nations that support each other
   and work together towards international goals.
http://www.britishcouncil.org
   The British Council connects people with learning opportunities and creative ideas
   from the United Kingdom to build lasting relationships around the world.
http://www.culture.gov.uk/
   United Kingdom, Department for Culture, Media and Sport.
http://www.lottery.culture.gov.uk
   National Lottery of the United Kingdom's Department for Culture, Media and
   Sport.
http://www.convenioandresbello.org
   International and intergovernmental organization for education, culture and science. (Members: Bolivia, Chile, Colombia, Cuba, Dominican Republic, Ecuador,
   Mexico, Panama, Paraguay, Peru, Spain and Venezuela.)
http://www.aecid.es
   Spain, Ministry of Foreign Affairs.
http://www.aecid.es/03coop/4program_coop/Patrimonio/index.htm
   Spain, Ministry of Foreign Affairs, Program for Culture and Development.
http://www.mcu.es/index.html
   Spain, Ministry of Culture.
http://cms.ifa.de
   Germany, Institute for Foreign Relations, fostering worldwide art exchange and
   cultural dialogue.
www.windhuk.diplo.de
   German Embassy Windhuk.
http://www.auswaertiges-amt.de/diplo/en/Aussenpolitik/Kulturpolitik/Kulturerhalt.
   html
   The German Federal Foreign Office's Cultural Preservation Programme.
http://www.culture.gouv.fr
   France, Ministry of Culture.
http://www.diplomatie.gouv.fr
   France, Ministry of Foreign Affairs.
http://www.legifrance.gouv.fr/affichCode.do?cidTexte=LEGITEXT000006074236&dat
   eTexte=20080515
   France, Code Patrimoine.
www.isiao.it
   Italian Institute for Africa and the Orient.

www.wbri.be
    International relations of the French community of Wallony and Brussels.
www.kvs.be/index2.php?page=news
    News item concert 'Verscheur de stilte' at the Royal Flemish Theatre website.
www.vliruos.be/index.php?navid=499&direct_to=Congoprogramma
    VLIR-UOS is for the Belgian government the responsible actor for all university
    cooperation regarding development between the universities and university col-
    leges in Flanders, Belgium, and their partner universities in the South.
http://cas1.elis.rug.ac.be/avrug
    Africa Community of Ghent University.
http://www.vvbad.be/node/1293/print
    Bruno Vermeeren, 2007 'Day report Vlaams erfgoed in den vreemde'.
www.africamuseum.be/museum/about/comraf
    African Associations Committee of the Royal Museum for Central Africa.
http://cultuurweb.be/CNETPortal/DetailDossiers.aspx?id_dossiers=2C1A535F-C312-
    FED9-FEBFC34746C17027&language=nl&locale=nl-NL
    Congo section of the Belgium culture portal.

Printed sources

Byrne, Denis
1991   'Western hegemony in archaeological heritage management', *History
              and Archaeology* 5:269-76.
Cleere, Henry
1989a   (ed.) *Archaeological heritage management in the modern world*. London:
              Unwin Hyman.
1989b   'Introduction; The rationale of archaeological heritage management',
              in: Henry Cleere (ed.), *Archaeological heritage management in the modern
              world*, pp. 1-19. London: Unwin Hyman.
Díaz-Andreu, Margarita
2007   *The world history of nineteenth-century archaeology; Nationalism, colonial-
              ism and the past*. Oxford: Oxford University Press.
Dodd, Diana, Melle Lyklema and Kathinka Dittrich-van Weringh
2006   *A cultural component as an integral part of the EU's foreign policy?* Amster-
              dam: Boekmanstudies.
Doortmont, Michael R.
2005   'Cultural heritage, tourism and urban development; The case of Elmi-
              na, Ghana', in: Leo G.W. Verhoef and Ron van Oers, *Proceedings of the
              second international symposium on restoration; Dutch involvement in the
              conservation of heritage overseas*, pp. 33-54. Delft: Delft University Press.
Duineveld, Martijn
2006   *Van oude dingen, de mensen die voorbij gaan...; Over de voorwaarden meer
              recht te kunnen doen aan de door burgers gewaardeerde cultuurhistories*.
              Delft: Eburon.

Eickhoff, Martijn
2007   'Archeologisch erfgoed; Een onbeheersbaar concept', in: Frans Grijzen-
        hout (ed.). *Erfgoed; De geschiedenis van een begrip*, pp. 231-65. Amster-
        dam: Amsterdam University Press.
Fienieg, Anouk
2006   'Gemeenschappelijk erfgoed, gedeeld erfgoed?; Een onderzoek naar
        dissonantie bij gemeenschappelijk cultureel erfgoed in zes landen'. MA
        thesis University of Amsterdam.
Galla, Amareswar
2002   'Culture and heritage in development', *Humanities Research* 9-1:63-79.
Gorp, Bouke van and Hans Renes
2007   'A European cultural identity?; Heritage and shared histories in the
        European Union', *Tijdschrift voor Economische en Sociale Geografie* 98:407-
        15.
Haas, Peter M.
1992   'Introduction; Epistemic communities and international policy coordi-
        nation', *International Organization* 46-1:1-35.
Holtorf, Cornelius J.
2002   'Is the past a non-renewable resource?', in: Robert Layton, Peter G.
        Stone and Julian Thomas (eds), *Destruction and conservation of cultural
        property*, pp. 286-97. New York: Routledge.
2006   'Can less be more?; Heritage in the age of terrorism', *Public Archaeology*
        5:101-9.
Kirshenblatt-Gimblett, Barbara
2006   'World heritage and cultural economics', in: Ivan Karp (ed.), *Museum
        frictions; Public cultures/global transformations*, pp. 1-32. Durham: Duke
        University Press.
Linde, S. van der
2004   'Dealing with conflicts in the management of archaeological sites;
        Balancing immediate activities, sustainable development and ideal
        management planning'. MA thesis University of London.
Lopes Bastos, R. and M. Kanan
2003   Collaborative attitudes in the context of archaeological conservation in
        Brazil; The case study of Campeche Island and Middens Shells in Santa
        Catarina State. Paper submitted at the Fifth World Archaeological Con-
        gress. [http://godot.unisa.edu.au/wac/pdfs/21.pdf, accessed 1-8-2006.]
Maass, Kurt-Jürgen (ed.)
2005   *Kultur und Aussenpolitik; Handbuch für Studium und Praxis.* Baden-
        Baden: Nomos.
Mason, Randall and Erica Avrami
2002   'Heritage values and challenges of conservation planning', in: Jeanne
        Marie Teutonico and Gaetano Palumbo (eds), *Management planning
        for archaeological sites; An international workshop organized by the Getty
        Conservation Institute and Loyola Marymount University, 19-22 May 2000,
        Corinth, Greece*, pp. 13-26. Los Angeles: Getty Conservation Institute.

MCAAH, The Mayor's Commission on African and Asian Heritage
2005   *Delivering shared heritage.* London: Mayor of London.

Overvoorde, J.C. van
1910   'Monumenten van Nederlandschen oorsprong in de vroegere neder-
                zettingen buiten Europa', *Neerlandia* 14:204-5.
1919   'Oudheden (Hollandsche)', in: *Encyclopaedie van Nederlandsch-Indië,*
                Deel 3, pp. 205-15. 's-Gravenhage: Nijhoff, Leiden: Brill.

Pwiti, Gilbert
1996   'Let the ancestors rest in peace?; New challenges for cultural heritage
                management in Zimbabwe', *Conservation and Management of Archaeo-
                logical Sites* 1-3:151-60.

Rowlands, Mike and Beverley Butler
2007   'Conflict and heritage care', *Anthropology Today* 23-1:1-3.

Seif, Assaad
2006   'Lebanon', *Current World Archaeology* 2.7(19):47-8.

Skeates, Robin
2000   *Debating the archaeological heritage.* London: Duckworth.

Smith, Laurajane
2004   *Archaeological theory and the politics of cultural heritage.* London:
                Routledge.

Soejono, R.P.
1984   'On the conditions and scope of the development of archaeology in
                Indonesia', in: Pieter van de Velde (ed.), *Prehistoric Indonesia; A reader,*
                pp. 15-28. Dordrecht: Foris. [KITLV, Verhandelingen 104.]

Tanudirjo, Daud Aris
1995   'Theoretical trends in Indonesian archaeology', in: Peter J. Ucko (ed.),
                Theory in archaeology; A world perspective, pp. 61-76. London/New York:
                Routledge.

Toebosch, Theo
2003   *Grondwerk; 200 jaar archeologie in Nederland.* Amsterdam: SUN.

Trigger, Bruce G.
1989   *A history of archaeological thought.* New York: Cambridge University
                Press.
2006   *A history of archaeological thought.* Second edition. New York: Cam-
                bridge University Press.

Tunbridge, J.E. and G.J. Ashworth
1996   *Dissonant heritage; Management of the past as a resource in conflict.* Chich-
                ester: Wiley.

Ucko, Peter J. (ed.)
1995   *Theory in archaeology; A world perspective.* London/New York:
                Routledge.

Willems, Willem J.H.
2002   'The role of archaeological societies in preserving cultural memorials'
                in: *Encyclopedia of life support systems.* Oxford: UNESCO/EOLSS Pub-
                lishers. [On-line publication.]

Williams, T. and S. van der Linde
2006   'Archaeological site management; Theory, strategies and implementa-
               tion for the archaeological landscapes of Jericho', in: Lorenzo Nigro
               and Hamdan Taha (eds), *Tell es-Sultan/Jericho in the context of the Jordan
               Valley; Site management, conservation and sustainable development; Proceed-
               ings of the International Workshop held in Ariha 7th-11th February 2005 by
               the Department of Antiquities and Cultural Heritage, Ministry of Tourism
               and Antiquities UNESCO office, Ramallah, Rome 'La Sapienza' University*,
               pp. 111-44. Roma: Università di Roma 'La Sapienza'.

Policy documents

Verstrooid verleden. Kamerstukken 1996-1997, no. 25.320, Den Haag, April 1997.

Ruim baan voor culturele diversiteit. Ministerie van Onderwijs, Cultuur en Wetenschappen, Den Haag, 1999.

Raamwerk gemeenschappelijk cultureel erfgoed. Kamerstuk 27.032, no. 2, Den Haag, 26
April 2000.

*Verslag consultatie internationaal cultuurbeleid; De plaats van cultureel erfgoed binnen het
internationaal cultuurbeleid*. Ministerie van Buitenlandse Zaken, Den Haag, 28 May
2004.

*Koers kiezen; Meer samenhang in het internationaal cultuurbeleid; Brief internationaal cul-
tuurbeleid)*. Ministerie van Onderwijs, Cultuur en Wetenschappen en Ministerie van
Buitenlandse Zaken, Den Haag, 10 May 2006.

International strategy. Department for Culture, Media and Sport, London, 2006.

GERT OOSTINDIE

Historical memory and national canons

How is colonial history remembered in the various countries involved, and how in particular have the three themes discussed in the previous chapters – European migration, slave trading and slavery, and indentured labour migrations – found their way into contemporary cultures of remembrance? Not surprisingly, interpretations of this colonial past and the importance attached to it are widely divergent. Historical distance is one crucial factor. The further back in time Dutch colonial presence ended, the more this episode has faded in the respective country's consciousness, eliciting less attention and emotional appeal. As we will see however, there are some interesting exceptions to this rule.

An even more important defining factor seems to relate to the varying degrees of impact of Dutch colonialism. Paradoxically, the greater this impact, the stronger the tendency seems to be to create symbolic distance, either through an emphasis on anti-colonial struggles or by locating historical meaning outside of the (post)-colonial realm. This applies particularly to Suriname and the six islands once known collectively as the Netherlands Antilles.

One factor not addressed in detail in this chapter, but certainly of crucial importance to the development of cultural heritage policies, involves the available financial means. Among the extensive group of countries discussed here, we find large or medium-sized countries with sufficient capital to pursue cultural heritage policies regarding the Dutch episode in their national histories either independently or together with the Netherlands. At the other extreme, we find poor and/or small countries with few resources to invest in such policies and hence a distinct dependence on Dutch or international support and funding. The remaining countries fall somewhere in between. All think of cultural heritage not only as a way of representing their past, but also as a possible asset in the promotion of tourism. These issues of financial means and (a)symmetry in bilateral relations are of evident significance and will have to be addressed in policy debates.

Beyond these generalizations, a focus on the individual countries involved is again appropriate and reveals more remarkable contrasts. This chapter offers a discussion on the canonization – or lack thereof – of Dutch colonialism in Asia, Africa, the Americas and in the Netherlands itself, initially from a wider perspective but zooming in on the three themes addressed in the previous chapters.[1] This is followed by some thoughts on common cultural heritage and contemporary dissonance regarding significance and meaning (Tunbridge and Ashworth 1996) as well as suggestions for future projects, including options for shared colonial *lieux de mémoire*, places of memory.

Asia

Recent historical research has pointed out that Dutch colonialism in the Atlantic was of more significance than has usually been understood. Even so, Dutch exploits in Asia under the banner of the East Indies Company (VOC) no doubt spanned a wider area and had greater repercussions both for global history and for some of the countries involved, including the Netherlands itself. Dutch awareness of this was expressed in the disputed 'celebrations' marking the 400th anniversary, in 2002, of the founding of the VOC, but is also reflected in the inclusion of India, Indonesia and Sri Lanka among the seven former colonies on the list of only eight 'common heritage countries' identified by the Dutch government – the eighth surprisingly being Russia.

The digital *Atlas of mutual heritage*[2] accurately illustrates the enormous expanse once covered by the VOC and the vast number of former settlements, fortifications, trading posts and so on reflecting this history. From the Cape Colony in South Africa, this string of historical places stretches through eastern Africa, the Middle East, South and Southeast Asia to China and Japan. Genuine long-term colonization was only achieved in contemporary Indonesia, South Africa and Sri Lanka. The direct impact of the Dutch in the

---

[1]   The next sections are partly based on a short survey among historians based in the Netherlands. I thank Geert Banck, Leonard Blussé, Jan Breman, Aart Broek, Ronald Donk, Pieter Emmer, Christian Ernsten, Femme Gaastra, Ruben Gowricharn, Oscar Hefting, H.D.S. Hettipathirana, Henk den Heijer, Rosemarijn Hoefte, Han Jordaan, Ineke van Kessel, Gerry van Klinken, Dirk Kolff, Gijs Kruijtzer, Murari Kumar, Susan Legêne, Elsbeth Locher-Scholten, Robert Parthesius, Remco Raben, Robert Ross, Henk Schulte Nordholt, Heather Sutherland, Lodewijk Wagenaar, Abdul Wahid, Marianne Wiesebron, Glenn Willemse and Danielle van Zyl for their responses and comments, and Hanneke Lommerse and Esther Zwinkels for their excellent assistance in conducting the survey. Moreover, I have incorporated findings of the international conference on 'The Atlantic World and the Dutch, 1500-2000' (Amsterdam, 28-30 November 2006), comments made by the participants in the conference on 'Migrations and cultural heritage in the Dutch colonial world' (University of Stellenbosch, South Africa, 25-27 March 2008), as well as critical readings by Peter Boomgaard, Pieter Emmer, Henk den Heijer and Gijs Kruijtzer. I also made good use of Anouk Fienieg'sMA thesis (2006).
[2]   www.atlasofmutualheritage.nl

other territories was of modest significance beyond the realm of commerce. Only a few of the present Asian states that are heirs to the latter category of territories have a distinct interest in the early encounters with the Dutch. The most important common heritage countries are discussed below.

A preliminary note on archival research is requisite. Nearly all of the VOC and other Dutch archives pertaining to the Dutch expansion in Asia and the resulting 'encounters' are in Dutch and therefore present evident obstacles for non-Dutch scholars. In recent years, the Dutch government has sponsored two successive programmes – TANAP and Encompass[3] – developed by Leiden University to teach young Asian historians early-modern Dutch, enabling them to research these archival records. In addition, there have been some translation projects for collections pertaining to Taiwan and Dejima. Important as they are, these endeavours have not yet redressed the dominance of Dutch – and a score of other Western – historians in the field as a whole.

Taiwan

Previously known as Formosa and today a nation of disputed sovereignty, Taiwan was occupied by the VOC between 1624 and 1662. The occupation came to an end when the Dutch were ousted by an army led by the Chinese warrior Zheng Cheng Gong ('Coxinga') for the Ming Dynasty; he was later defeated, in 1683, by the Manchu, supported by the Dutch. The VOC period witnessed European settlement, but to a greater extent Chinese immigration. Mass migration of mainland Chinese and the marginalization of the indigenous population would begin in this period. The short Dutch phase was therefore significant in bringing Taiwan into the Chinese orbit.

A growing interest in the early Dutch period is evident from archival projects, such as the translation of the Dutch governor's *Daghregisters* (Daily Registers) into Chinese for scholarly purposes and the restoration of the governor's Fort Zeelandia in Taiwan. Government support for such initiatives and public education on this formative period are grounded in a volatile political context in which Taiwan claims an individual national character vis-à-vis the People's Republic of China. In the absence of a pre-colonial native voice, the early role of the Dutch seems not to be a sensitive issue.

---

[3]   Towards a New Age of Partnership (TANAP): www.tanap.net/ Encountering a Common Past in Asia (Encompass): www.arts.leidenuniv.nl/history/encompass/

Japan

Dejima

The latter observation certainly applies to contemporary Japanese perceptions of early bilateral links. Dutch officials and traders were allowed to live and work on the small island of Dejima in the harbour of Nagasaki from 1641 until 1859. There was no question of equivalence: the Dutch had no political or military clout whatsoever. Dejima did, however, function as a window to the world for the Japanese court, increasingly so during the eighteenth century. European science and technology were introduced to Japan through Dejima and therefore had a strong Dutch imprint. After the demise of the VOC, exclusive bilateral relations were perpetuated until the mid-nineteenth century, when the Japanese court had to give in to European and American demands to end its self-sought isolation.

A last significant episode in this relationship was the work of the Dutch-employed German scholar Philipp von Siebold, who lived and worked in Japan from 1823 until 1829, and again from 1859 until 1862. His extensive collections – flora, ethnology, art – eventually found their way back to Leiden, where they now form unique museum collections much visited by Japanese tourists.

Arguably, Dutch memory of Japanese-Dutch relations is dominated and often soured by the Japanese occupation of the colonial Dutch East Indies (1942-1945). The early period, in contrast, offers a much less sensitive terrain, which has become enthusiastically researched, discussed and exploited on both sides. Dejima is seen as the historical portal to European Enlightenment and to Dutch expertise, particularly in ecological and environmental matters. There has been a long series of joint projects regarding archival preservation and the translation of Dutch archives into Japanese; historical Dejima (now enclosed in Nagasaki) has been partially restored; Japanese school children learn about the early Dutch presence; Nagasaki has its 'Holland Village'; attraction parks feature typical Dutch architecture and so on. As there was no colonization or Dutch hegemony, the past Dutch presence stirs fascination rather than resentment. Both governments have invested considerably in this uncontested mutual history, and continue to do so.

India

The Dutch presence in India was limited to a handful of short-lived trading posts with little ambition or chance to make a significant impact on the hinterlands. The early Dutch presence forms no part of public memory, where colonialism is entirely associated with the British. Episodes such as the Great Rebellion (1857) and the struggle for independence figure prominently in the national canon – but even these episodes pale in comparison to the Partition that accompanied independence.

Bearing in mind the scant impact of Dutch settlement, the near absence of Indian scholarly interest comes as no surprise. Indian historians are aware that the VOC archives contain important data regarding early Indian history, but also that the same applies to other European archives. Moreover, the language barrier is strong and insufficient funding is available for language training or translation projects. Thus, with the possible exception of Cochin (1663-1795), the Dutch episode is neglected by Indian historians and archeologists.

To a large extent this applies to the awareness of more recent relations as well. Mass emigration of indentured labourers from British India in the nineteenth and early twentieth centuries made a strong impact on a host of Asian, African and Caribbean countries. A marginal proportion of the millions of emigrants ended up in the Dutch colony of Suriname. Yet descendants from British India now make up close to forty per cent of the population of Suriname, as well as of the Surinamese community in the Netherlands. From a Surinamese perspective the Indian connection is thus of paramount importance. For India this diaspora is one of many and numerically insignificant, but even so, oral traditions in the areas of recruitment include references to people going off to Suriname.

Interest in the cultural heritage resulting from these two discrete historical episodes has three possible partners. As one Indian scholar recently remarked, in his country Dutch colonialism, if known at all, is only associated with Indonesia. Arguably, Indian concern for the modest early Dutch role in its history has been lukewarm, although there is some interest in the studies of Dutch historians and a polite tolerance for restoration projects, such as the colonial cemetery in Pulicat. As for archeology and built cultural heritage, in a country full of artifices of a long and rich history, most of these pre-colonial, the scattered remnants of Dutch – or Portuguese for that matter – colonialism inspire no particular interest.

Likewise, from a Dutch perspective, India was only one of the many destinations of the VOC and certainly not the most important. In a way, therefore, it is only through another colonial connection, namely Suriname, that India has recently attracted renewed Dutch interest. This is evinced in the trilateral Dutch-Indian-Surinamese Bidesia project on contemporary immaterial cultural heritage linking the Indian diaspora in Suriname to India and the Netherlands.[4] The third party in this project, Suriname, is arguably the one most interested in this shared cultural heritage. Its interest, of course, has to do with the roots of its own Hindustani population rather than with the scattered remnants of Dutch colonialism in India.

---

[4]   For more information, consult the website of the KIT/Royal Tropical Institute.

Sri Lanka

Whereas the Dutch presence in Taiwan, Japan and India was of a short-lived and limited nature, the VOC did act as a colonial ruler in Sri Lanka from 1655 until the British takeover in 1796, even if the island was never entirely subjugated as a colony. There was long-lasting Dutch control of the coastal lines, there were two 'Dutch' cities (Galle, Colombo) and European immigration resulted in a mestizo *burgher* elite. Otherwise, there were no serious migrations under Dutch rule.

The Dutch period, like the preceding Portuguese and subsequent British ones, is perceived as a colonial occupation. But as in the case of India, a subsequent century and a half of encompassing British colonialism had much more impact and now dominates local memory of colonialism. Some feel that in Sri Lanka the vague awareness of pre-British colonialism is limited to the Portuguese beginnings rather than the subsequent Dutch period. This may be different though in places such as Galle, where colonial architecture serves as an inescapable reminder of the Dutch presence.

Sri Lanka is no exception to the rule that the renovation of historical fortifications and cityscapes is part of a commoditization of history aimed at strengthening the position of the country as a tourist destination. The inclusion of Galle on UNESCO's world heritage list was a major accomplishment in this perspective. Government policies however, whether in local education or tourist marketing, emphasize the Asian history and culture of Sri Lanka rather than European colonialism under whatever flag. After all, the island has a rich cultural history spanning more than 2,500 years, in which the colonial period plays only a very minor part.

The apparent absence of strong feelings regarding the Dutch colonial period has facilitated bilateral cooperation in the fields of urban restoration and maritime archeology. So has consistent Dutch funding of projects in what is genuinely considered shared cultural heritage. For Sri Lanka as in most other countries discussed here, linguistic obstacles stand in the way of extensive use of Dutch archival sources. This is particularly unfortunate as there are few other archival sources for the study of pre-nineteenth century Sri Lanka. In the absence of a tradition of joint historical research projects, the historiography of the Dutch period has largely remained a Dutch affair. Local use of archives relating to the Dutch colonial period is mainly limited to the *tombos*, an indispensable source for genealogical research. Sri Lankan historians strongly argue for more joint research projects in Dutch-language archives.

Indonesia

As indicated in the introductory chapter of this book, the four centuries of 'shared' Indonesian-Dutch history were as significant for the Netherlands as they were for Indonesia – if not more so. Today, the memory of the Dutch colonial period is fading and the younger generations of Indonesians have little knowledge of this distant history. Over sixty years after independence, the Netherlands no longer figures among the foreign countries of major significance to Indonesia, a nation more concerned about present development issues and the relevance of regional diversity to its national identity.

Of course, the colonial period is still relevant to the now vanishing generation of Indonesians with direct recollections of these times, and to younger Indonesians working in the fields of history or cultural heritage. A striking dissonance immediately surfaces. The Dutch rendering of the entire 350 years of 'relations' is usually neatly divided between the first two VOC centuries, the rupture of the English interregnum and next the genuine colonial period. A common Dutch assumption is that the VOC period was not really colonial but one of more or less symmetric commercial relations. The Indonesian perspective, in contrast, qualifies the full period as colonial and defined by Dutch power politics. There is an unbroken line of colonial exploitation and violence from the times of the *kompeni* (Company) to the modern colonial state. Hence the Indonesian discomforts with the Dutch VOC celebrations in 2002 (Oostindie 2003).

Several 'colonial' questions of contemporary relevance are discussed by Indonesian historians. Regionalism is a major issue. Dutch colonialism had a very uneven impact on the various parts of the archipelago, yet in the end defined the present territory. There is a movement away from a Java-centric historiography and a growing interest in the consequences of the later incorporation into the colonial fold for various regions, as well as in the functioning of indirect rule in more remote parts of the archipelago.

On both sides, memories of the violent period of decolonization dominate recollections of the past. While the Dutch in 1949 formally accepted the legitimacy of nationalism and decolonization, symbolic contestations over the exact dating of independence – 1945, according to Indonesia – continued to cast a long shadow over bilateral relations. Only the belated official Dutch recognition of '1945', sixty years after the fact, removed this bone of contention. This bodes well for future cooperation in the field of historical research and cultural heritage.

Indonesia inherited from the Dutch colonial period the definition of its territorial boundaries and a series of governmental and educational institutions, of which today primarily an extended body of legislation based on Dutch-Roman law still stands. Not much of this resounds in everyday life,

View of Malacca

however. Neither is there the extent of colonial material heritage one finds all over Latin America and the Caribbean. Dispersed remnants of colonial architecture and city centres are dwarfed by the post-decolonization urban explosion. Only experts are able to read colonial urban and landscape planning in older urban conglomerations. During the Japanese occupation, Dutch colonial symbols and names were discarded, never to be reinstated.

In the official historical narrative of this large and heterogeneous nation, the Dutch period functions primarily as one of often violent exploitation and denigration, eventually brought to an end by heroic native resistance. In the Republic's gallery of national heroes the majority acquired this status fighting colonialism. Indonesian schools teach the hegemonic narrative highlighting the unity of this geographically and ethnically heterogeneous nation, as well as the national awakening and commitment to development (*pembangunan*) that came with the revolution. Where colonial history figures at all in popular culture, the same tenets usually apply.

Professional historians and university history programmes are interested in more diverse research questions on the colonial period, that is, regional history and ethnicity. A major challenge in this field is of an altogether different nature: the great majority of archival records are in Dutch, the vanished colonial language.

Migration is not a subject privileged even by professional historians. This is not surprising. As we saw, Dutch colonialism sparked migrations of some hundreds of thousands of European colonists and even some millions of Asian slaves and semi-bonded labourers, but the proportional impact of these movements of people was only significant in a few parts of the archipelago. There are two more recent types of migrations in Indonesian history, one to the Netherlands, another the Republic's *transmigrasi* programmes following pre-war colonial models. The first type is relevant here as it belongs to the realm of shared history. The post-1945 'repatriation' of some 300,000 people intimately tied to colonial rule, produced a post-colonial community in the Netherlands estimated at half a million today. This community has contributed to keeping Dutch interest in Indonesia and in a 'shared' history alive. Yet from an Indonesian perspective, the numbers of these emigrants are insignificant, the ethnic composition of the group is unrepresentative, and its political leanings and possible colonial nostalgia are dubious.

Taken together, this is a delicate context for the development of a debate on 'mutual' or 'common' history and cultural heritage. Even so, the recent past has seen constructive cooperation in some fields. This applies first and probably foremost to projects for the restoration of Dutch architecture, both from the VOC and modern colonial periods. Bilateral initiatives in this field have a long tradition, possibly because of their low political sensitivity and their potential for tourism. This does not necessarily imply that these projects have the same relevance to both parties. Some suggest that in Indonesia, Dutch interest in preserving 'shared' material heritage is often politely tolerated rather than applauded. Others, in contrast, point to many local organizations active in conservation programmes, often attached to tourism.

An ambitious attempt to make a new start in the field of joint historical research was the TANAP programme developed at Leiden University, now continued through its sequel, the Encompass programme. The objective of TANAP was the advance of historical research through the preservation and study of the rich VOC archives – now on UNESCO's world heritage list – the training of young historians and the organization of joint research programmes, conferences and the like. Encompass departs from the same principles, but extends the time frame to include the modern colonial period. Both projects are widely seen as a success. One of the explanations for this is that the programme is explicitly not bilateral; it involves a wide range of countries with some historical exposure to the VOC. This is crucial, as it goes some way to diminishing the post-colonial sensitivities that inevitably thwart bilateral Indonesian-Dutch programmes.

Africa

In the seventeenth century, the Dutch divided their modest African 'empire' into zones of influence for the VOC and the WIC. Western Africa was part of the WIC's territory. Most Dutch positions there were established for trading, increasingly in enslaved Africans, rather than as long-term settlement colonies. Dozens of former Dutch fortifications have been identified, from the isle of Arguin off the coast of Mauritania to the north to several forts in Congo and Angola. All of these are now included in the digital *Atlas of mutual heritage*. The bulk of these Dutch trading posts were transitory, left few traces and do not provoke much interest today. The major exception to this rule is Elmina in present-day Ghana, a Dutch fortification from 1637 until 1872.

Surprising from a contemporary perspective, the Cape Colony in South Africa pertained not to the 'Atlantic' WIC, but to the 'Asian' VOC. This resulted from the Cape's designated function as the hub linking Europe and Asia. Owing to its temperate climate, this was to be the only Dutch colony attracting a substantial settler community from the Netherlands, also after the British takeover around 1800. The colony's commercial and demographic relations with Asia remained strong throughout the Dutch and early British colonial periods.

South Africa and Ghana are the two African countries prioritized in the Dutch government's policies for 'common' cultural heritage. Regarding South Africa, this confirms long-standing relations. The inclusion of Ghana in the list of seven former colonies reflects a new Dutch awareness of colonial history wedded to contemporary policy and migration issues.

South Africa

Cape Colony

From its establishment as a VOC colony in 1652 until the British takeover in 1795, the Cape Colony was the only real Dutch settler colony. The Cape had the dual function of transit point between the Dutch Republic and its Asian settlements and, increasingly, as a productive farmers' colony. Much of Cape Town and its environs testifies to these colonial beginnings.

Of course, the territory of the former Cape Colony constitutes only a small part of what is now the Republic of South Africa, the nation's history has many more dramatic episodes than just this early colonial period, and the great majority of its citizens have no direct links to the inhabitants of the erstwhile Dutch colony. And yet the Republic's history is inextricably linked to this early history and to the 'Dutch' Boers who throughout the nineteenth and twentieth centuries would continue to leave strong marks on the country's turbulent history, from the Afrikaner 'free states' in the interior through the Anglo-Boer wars to the apartheid regime.

Colonial migrations, during both the Dutch and the British period, have defined South Africa. These massive movements of people from within Africa, from Europe and from Asia left, inter alia, the legacy of the apartheid regime. Since the demise of this system, the nation's concerted effort to face up to the past has focused on the traumatic post-World War Two period. The Dutch Cape Colony may therefore seem to be a faraway affair. But as we saw, literally all of the migrations that would eventually make South Africa a 'rainbow nation' – European settlers, enslaved and semi-bonded Africans and Asians – are rooted in the Dutch colonial period.

More so than in all the other former Dutch colonies, with the exception of the Antilles and Suriname, the Dutch legacy is immediately visible and audible in South Africa, certainly in the wider Cape Town area, in colonial architecture and particularly in language usage. The delicate nature of this legacy is all too clear. Not only is the very word 'apartheid' derived from Dutch: the descendants of the early Dutch settlers have earned the reputation of having been the staunchest supporters of that regime. In this heavily charged context, there is no longer room for jubilant celebrations of Jan van Riebeeck's 1652 conquest of the Cape; Afrikaans is a contested linguistic heritage and colonial architectural remnants such as the Slave Lodge are only acceptable as historical sites provided they offer a critical perspective of the early colonial period.

Post-apartheid, there seems to be a predictable tendency towards a writing and commemoration of history along ethnic lines. A historical narrative binding the entire nation – regionally as well as ethnically – seems a distant perspective. As one historian remarked, 'Historical writing is very much politicized'. As for preferences for certain historical periods, recent history now takes centre stage, followed by the British colonial period. Once more, it should be borne in mind that the entire South African history and territory far exceed the limits of the historical Dutch Cape Colony. In recent years, several projects were initiated though, for example the transcription of inventories of Dutch archival records and the restoration of Dutch colonial architecture in Cape Town, but these are not particularly a national affair. In this context it should also be remembered that few Afrikaner South Africans define themselves primarily as descendants of Dutch settlers.

In sum, any debate about 'common' cultural heritage linking South Africa to the Netherlands is bound to raise controversy. Recent debates about the possible function of Cape Town's Dutch colonial castle aptly illustrate this conclusion. While some Dutch experts have suggested that the castle could be used to present colonialism including slavery and associated subjects, many South Africans feel the castle should primarily be made a reminder of the horrors of apartheid rather than of early colonialism. Ironically, the latter option could also include references to the Dutch involvement in the anti-apartheid struggle.

The Dutch period does linger in historical memory, but with a twist. The contrast with other early and long-lost colonial possessions is evident, whether we focus on the celebratory mood prevailing in Recife/Brazil and Manhattan or on the virtual absence of memories of the Dutch period in much of Asia. The contemporary relevance of the Dutch colonial era seems even much stronger in South Africa than in Indonesia, in spite of the centuries that have passed since the Dutch state had to cede the 'Cape of Good Hope'.

Ghana

Elmina
Even if at various times the Dutch had many forts along the West African coast, such as at Goeree off contemporary Senegal, the majestic fortress of Elmina has become the undisputed symbol of Dutch colonialism in West Africa. Initially built by the Portuguese, Elmina passed into Dutch hands in 1637 to become a hub in the Dutch transatlantic slave trade. Its heydays in this capacity ended in the 1730s, but the fortress remained in Dutch hands until the British takeover in 1872. It was only under British colonial rule that Elmina became part of the multi-ethnic territorial and administrative entity known as the contemporary republic of Ghana.

In the first centuries of European colonialism and the Atlantic slave trade, all major European slave trading countries had trading settlements along the so-called Gold Coast. At present, a long series of forts in various states of repair testify to the history of European-African commercial and political relations and inter-European rivalries. Elmina is probably the most breathtaking of these forts, and the Dutch history of this slaving post is no secret to the local population. Yet in Ghanaian perceptions of colonial history, the slave trade is only one out of many episodes in the colonial or, for that matter, national history; Elmina is only one out of many hubs for the slave trade; and the Dutch are only one among the European slave trading nations once active on the Ghanaian coast. As in several of the Asian countries discussed here, colonialism is mainly associated with the subsequent, more significant British period. One specific Dutch legacy is the recurrence of Dutch surnames in the Elmina area, a reminder of colonial liaisons.

Contrastingly, for many Antilleans, Surinamese and Dutch Elmina has become the outstanding symbol of Dutch involvement in the Atlantic slave trade. Again, there are historical arguments to nuance this perspective – the majority of enslaved Africans forced into the middle passage across the Atlantic were shipped from other parts of western Africa. But such finesse was understandably lost once the Dutch involvement in the slave trade became a major, perhaps the dominant issue in the contemporary memory of Dutch Atlantic expansion and colonization (Oostindie 2005).

Consequently the Dutch government has engaged in the co-planning and financing of bilateral programmes for the rehabilitation of Elmina and the stimulation of cultural heritage tourism – in the process bringing to the fore delicate questions regarding the commoditization of historical suffering and guilt. Dutch development aid also financed the production of a new guide to the Dutch archival sources for Ghanaian history – the archival records themselves, of course, are in Dutch and therefore virtually inaccessible to historians from Ghana. At the November 2006 AWAD conference in Amsterdam, experts from Ghana strongly recommended continuation of bilateral cooperation in these fields.

The nineteenth-century history of Dutch Elmina witnessed some other migratory links within the Dutch colonial orbit. There was some regulated elite migration to the Netherlands, immortalized in the novel *The two hearts of Kwasi Boachi* by Arthur Japin (2001). Of slightly more numerical significance was the semi-forced recruitment of some three thousand soldiers in Elmina for the Dutch colonial army in Indonesia, between 1831 and 1872. Demographically, this migration was of little significance to either Ghana, Indonesia or the Netherlands, where some descendants now live. Yet this episode has drawn some interest in the Netherlands, due to its strong symbolism. And again, Dutch support contributed to the creation of a small museum on this period in Elmina.

The Americas

Up until the early nineteenth century, the slave trade and African slavery were the defining dimensions of all Atlantic history – the Dutch case is no exception to this rule. Even so, slavery is by no means the only, and in some cases not even the dominant issue in the contemporary canonization of Dutch colonial history in the Americas. This canonization reflects new migratory developments in the nineteenth and twentieth centuries, but also divergent perspectives on early Dutch colonialism in the Americas. Such contrasts became evident again in the recent international conference on 'The Atlantic World and the Dutch, 1500-2000' held in Amsterdam in November 2006. Part of this section derives from presentations and observations made during this conference and the preceding country workshops.[5]

Early Dutch exploits included locations from the far north to the far south of the continent, with Dutch ships sailing to all parts of the Americas. However, the colonial presence was limited to north-eastern Brazil, the Caribbean including the adjacent Guyanas on the northern tip of South America and New Netherland in the contemporary United States. Indeed, apart from these territories, the *Atlas of mutual heritage* only refers to one other location, in Chile.

The Dutch colonial presence in the United States and Brazil was short-lived. Dutch colonial history in the Americas is therefore concentrated in the Caribbean. For brief periods the Dutch settled in many locations all over the Caribbean, but by 1700 the consolidated territory consisted of six tiny islands later known as the Netherlands Antilles as well as several plantation colonies on the 'Wild Coast' of the Guyanas. Of these, Berbice, Demerara and Essequibo passed into British hands around 1800 and eventually became Guyana, while Suriname remained part of the Kingdom of the Netherlands until 1975 and the Antillean islands have chosen to remain within the post-colonial fold.

In comparison to the Spanish, the British and the French, the Dutch were minor players in the Caribbean. Yet Dutch networks were essential in bringing the sugar revolution from Brazil to the Caribbean, and in the next centuries the Antilles would serve as migratory, commercial and at times political nodal points within the circum-Caribbean. In the twentieth century, the oil industry and later tourism would add a new dimension to this tradition. However, perhaps with the exception of Venezuela, the regional impact of the Dutch Antilles has left few traces and little awareness, while archival research on these interconnections is only in its infancy.

Brazil was recently added to the Dutch government's priority list for

---

5   http://awad.kitlv.nl/awad/introduction/conferences/

countries with a 'common' cultural heritage. Suriname already figured on this list. It may appear strange that the six Dutch Caribbean islands are not included. This is due to the fact that they form part of the Kingdom, and as such do not qualify for bilateral cultural heritage programmes. Over the past decades they have, however, been neglected in cultural policy within the Kingdom, as they are responsible for determining and financing domestic affairs themselves.

United States

New Amsterdam, New Netherland
The 1609 'discovery' of Manhattan (New Amsterdam) by the British VOC captain Henry Hudson along with the Dutch roots of contemporary New York and the Albany area, continue to figure in most scholarly accounts of the rise of the United States. Brief as this Dutch colonial prelude may have been, some experts argue that its impact was of major significance, continuing beyond the British takeover (1664) and the formal transition to British rule in 1667. Thus the best-selling book by Russell Shorto, *The island at the center of the world* (2004), celebrates the Dutch colony of New Amsterdam in contemporary Manhattan and the surrounding colony of New Netherland as a decisive formative period in which an American tradition of democracy and tolerance began.

There are objections to this rosy picture of early Dutch American history. Dutch colonization also heralded the successive marginalization of the Native American population and the introduction of African slavery – the first enslaved Africans, incidentally, were disembarked in 1619 from a British ship using Dutch papers, but in Jamestown, Virginia, not Manhattan. And, as Shorto acknowledges, the fact that tolerance for religious and 'racial' diversity was high by contemporary standards does not imply an absence of bigotry. Prejudice was widespread right up to the highest levels (for instance governor Peter Stuyvesant). Yet historians rightly argue that African slavery did not have the crucial impact on New Amsterdam that it did have on the tropical Dutch Americas.

While subsequent Dutch migrations continued to leave distinct marks in American history, the actual colonial Dutch period was brief and seems to have been largely forgotten by non-specialists. Again, it is the British episode that now counts as the colonial one. There are no significant ideological disparities between recent studies of American and Dutch historians on the Dutch period. Linguistic barriers were overcome due to several Dutch scholars simply moving to the United States and pursuing their research there.

While several Dutch-American historical associations exist and while the long-standing New Netherlands project has produced an impressive series of translations into English of Dutch archival sources, there is less funding for joint research or educative projects than one would expect. This was explicitly stated and deplored by the American delegation to the AWAD conference. Perhaps the forthcoming celebrations/commemorations of Hudson's discovery, in 2009, will stimulate the formulation and financing of new projects to this end.

Brazil

New Holland

Although the Dutch colonial period in north-eastern Brazil was both early and short (1630-1654) and left only scattered traces, it continues to evoke much interest among historians and in popular culture – remarkably, far more so in Brazil than in the Netherlands.

One way to look at the Brazilian episode is its initiating function for the Dutch. In Pernambuco they first became involved in the production of slave-grown tropical crops. From Dutch Brazil they first established their own strongholds for the slave trade in West Africa. And after the reconquest of Brazil by the Portuguese, the 'Dutch' played an important role in bringing the sugar revolution and hence African slavery to the Caribbean. Yet slavery somehow seems to be silenced in the historical rendering of Dutch Brazil.

Instead, an altogether different perspective dominates the memory of the 'time of the Dutch' in contemporary Brazil.[6] First and foremost, there is the glorification of the Dutch aristocratic ruler Johan Maurits, who governed the colony from 1636 through 1644. His image is one of an enlightened despot avant la lettre, bringing culture and sciences to the uncultured Americas, eventually bequeathing Brazil with the spectacular ethnographic and landscape paintings of Albert Eckhout and Frans Post, ambitious colonial architecture and city planning, progressive experiments in meteorology and astronomy and so on. Modern scholarship also highlights his policy of toleration of religious difference, allowing Protestants, Catholics and Jews to practice their own creed as long as the non-Protestants did so discretely.

Some outright nostalgia is nurtured, bordering on the absurd – as if 'Mauricio' would have made a New York out of Recife if only he had stayed longer and the Dutch had kept the backward Portuguese out. Conversely, there is the interpretation of the ousting of the Dutch by the local Portuguese colonists as the first historical manifestation of Brazilian proto-nationalism. There is a relaxed juxtaposition of sorts: Recife annually honours both Johan Maurits and the Brazilians avant la lettre who ousted the Dutch.

By all accounts, the Dutch episode is mainly appreciated and possible ill-feelings have long been forgotten. After all, the real colonizers were the

6   See the website of the Brazilian Embassy, www.brazilianembassy.nl/

Portuguese. Although historically not altogether correct, the Atlantic slave trade and slavery are exclusively associated with the Portuguese. In turn there is a wide range of popular stories and sayings in which the Dutch somehow play a part, again mainly in a positive sense.

As early as the nineteenth century, state-sponsored Brazilian historians started studying, transcribing and translating relevant Dutch archival collections. The reappraisal of regional history was stimulated by the gradual eclipse of north-eastern Brazil by the booming regions around Rio de Janeiro and São Paolo. Brazilian scholarship on 'Dutch Brazil' was pioneered by Gonsalves de Mello's classic *Tempo dos Flamengos* (1947). This tradition has been revived in recent years by ambitious projects for the digitization of all relevant archival holdings, new research projects and reprints and translations of older works, the restoration of Dutch fortifications, exhibitions of the paintings commissioned by Johan Maurits and the like.

At the 2006 AWAD conference, experts from Brazil urged for more Dutch commitment and the stepping up of the bilateral cooperation in what they definitely consider to be shared cultural heritage. Their priorities included the facilitation of access to documentation (archives and library collections), translation and digitization of relevant sources, training of young historians in the same vein as in the TANAP and Encompass programmes, continued funding for archaeological and architectural projects, and more systematic bilateral cooperation in historical research and dissemination.

In all of this, Brazil rather than the Netherlands has been the leader both in initiatives and in funding – making it much easier for the Dutch government to belatedly add booming Brazil to its list of priority countries for common cultural heritage, without having to worry about possible avowals of cultural imperialism. Brazilians meanwhile do occasionally express frustration about the little awareness in Dutch society of this, from their perspective, indeed shared history.

Guyana

Berbice, Demerara, Essequibo
Colonized from the first half of the seventeenth century, the three Dutch colonies of Berbice, Demerara and Essequibo were ceded to the British during the Napoleonic wars and subsequently united as British Guyana. The colony attained its independence in 1966 as Guyana. Guyana was developed as a plantation colony by the Dutch and thereafter by the British. Enslaved Africans soon made up the great majority of the population. Large-scale immigration from British India after the abolition of slavery (1834) would again redraw the balance. Today the majority of Guyanese, whether in the country itself or in the second diaspora, are of Asian descent.

Town Hall of Malacca

This has significant consequences for historical memory. For the Afro-Guyanese, the Dutch phase is crucial as it was the long formative period of their culture, including the massive 1763 Berbice slave revolt, a seminal event in Guyanese and Caribbean history. Yet the later part of the history of slavery, including more slave revolts, falls in the British period. For today's Asian majority, there is no direct link to the Dutch period whatsoever. British colonialism therefore is the only pre-independence period of direct relevance to all ethnic groups.

The Dutch language has disappeared from Guyana, and few Guyanese historians are able to read Dutch documents. This implies that almost two centuries of recorded history – archived both in Guyana, the Netherlands and the United Kingdom – are mainly at the mercy of Dutch or Surinamese historians, who have demonstrated little interest in these archives. Consequently, the Dutch period remains virtually a closed book. The National Archives of Guyana are well aware of the richness and vulnerability of their Dutch holdings, but cannot attract funding for preservation or research.

Guyana does not figure on the Netherlands' list of priority countries for shared cultural heritage. Dutch support in this field has been haphazard. With Dutch assistance, some colonial Dutch forts and buildings have been restored. As tourism is little developed in the country, there is not yet a commercial incentive for such projects.

In all, historians and other heritage specialists from Guyana feel that local interest in the Dutch period is scant. At the AWAD conference they emphasized the progressive decay of all cultural heritage resulting from the Dutch colonial period, whether archives or archeological sites. Deploring the lack of Dutch interest and funding, they urged for more Dutch commitment. Their priorities included, again, the facilitation of access to documentation (archives and library collections), translation and digitization of relevant sources and the training of Guyanese historians, as well as the restoration of built heritage from the Dutch colonial period.

Suriname

Formally colonized by the Dutch in 1667, Suriname became an independent republic only in 1975, in a decolonization fully endorsed by the Netherlands. While two to three per cent of the population is of Native American origin, the vast majority descend from enslaved Africans as well as British-Indian and Javanese indentured labourers. Most of the country's history and population are therefore linked to Dutch colonization and its associated migrations. Many ethnic languages are spoken alongside an Afro-Surinamese creole lingua franca, Sranantongo. However, the Dutch language is dominant in institutional life and seems to be replacing Sranantongo even in the private sphere.

Formal decolonization did not sever the links with the former metropolis. Over three decades after the fact, Suriname is still inextricably linked to the Netherlands, economically and politically but most of all demographically. The transfer of sovereignty sparked extensive migration to the Netherlands, to the extent that the Netherlands-based Surinamese community (350,000) today comes close to the total population of Suriname itself (450,000). These figures incidentally also disclose the small scale of these societies and the ensuing asymmetry with the Netherlands, a country with a population of over 16 million. Clearly the combination of scale, power asymmetry and an enduring intense relationship is not an issue for most other common cultural heritage countries discussed in this chapter. In stead, there are clear parallels with the Netherlands Antilles and Aruba.

One of the nation's legacies from colonialism is intense ethnic plurality. There is some discussion regarding the implications of this plurality for social cohesion, the political system and even economics. While feelings range from optimistic to rather pessimistic in this regard, most observers rightly emphasize a long tradition of conviviality and mutual tolerance.

Ethnically and/or regionally divided nations tend to construe neutral and bridging national symbols and narratives of the past which gloss over internal divisions. In authoritarian states, this management of the past belongs to the realm of policy making and is effectuated in top-down policies. Where the state has no such absolute powers and where governance is shared by the major segments of the population, this type of control is not feasible and is often perceived as undesirable. Suriname certainly belongs to the latter category, with an additional defining factor: the greater part of the country's historiography continues to be produced in the former metropolis.

In this context, a public history has emerged in which colonialism and colonial migrations are key elements and where the challenge of ethnic bridging and nation building is stressed. From primary school on, Surinamese children are taught this encompassing narrative, which is also endorsed by the government's support for cultural policies aiming at 'unity in diversity'. In practice, the ethnic segments of the population tend to privilege 'our own things' over an interest in the history and culture of other communities or the national narrative. Amateur and professional historians tend to engage mainly in the history of their own ethnic group. Afro-Surinamese history and in particular narratives of exploitation and resistance have long dominated public history. In the last decades, there is a growing Asian, in particular Hindustani counter current.

While this context in itself poses a challenge for cultural heritage policies, even the periodization of colonial history, and hence the resulting heritage, has a strong ethnic component. The greater part of the colonial period is dominated by two centuries of African slavery. Following this is over a century of Asian immigration and hence the birth of a multi-ethnic nation; modernization, urbanization and democratization; and independence. Much of the material cultural heritage falling within the usual scope of bilateral cooperation – whether fortresses, Paramaribo's historic centre or archives – was produced during the period of slavery; hence any work in this sphere implies the challenge of making history 'work' not only for Afro-Surinamese, but also for the descendants of later arrivals.

No doubt, much of Surinamese history is shared with the Netherlands, and so is virtually all cultural heritage resulting from the long colonial period. It is equally evident that 'shared' in the context of a history of forced and semi-bonded labour migrations implies power asymmetries and possibly contrasting interpretations and valuations of this past and its legacies. Interestingly, the most recent wave of migration in Surinamese history has altered some of the parameters for such contestations. With the emergence of a truly transnational Surinamese community and the gradual rise of Dutch citizens of Surinamese origins in metropolitan institutions, 'Dutch' cultural heritage policies will increasingly be co-defined by Dutch of colonial ancestry. As illustrated during the recent debates on the commemoration of slavery, this has and will continue to have an impact on cultural heritage policies which is absent in Dutch relations with the other priority countries discussed here.

The 2006 AWAD conference in Amsterdam and the preliminary workshops organized in Suriname indeed testified to the progressive overlapping of the 'bilateral' and 'transnational'. Participants emphasized the importance of historical awareness and of investing in cultural heritage – where 'shared' does not preclude 'dissonant'. There was also a widely shared conviction of a Dutch obligation to continued investment in cultural heritage, not only out of respect to Suriname, but equally in recognition of the colonial dimension of Dutch history and as a necessary gesture to the Surinamese community in the Netherlands.

The idea of a Dutch obligation is not formulated in any of the other countries discussed above and there are also divergences in the priorities defined. Certainly some of these are ubiquitous, such as pleas for the restoration and preservation of built cultural heritage, archival management and digitization, the stepping up of cooperation in the fields of museums and historical research and the like. But in addition there were strong recommendations for extensive oral history and oral traditions programmes. Obviously a plea for such projects on the Dutch colonial period would not make much sense in, say, Manhattan, Galle or Recife, and simply reflects the fact that this period ended only recently in Suriname. The emphasis on oral legacies however, also reflects the conviction that too much attention to the 'colonial' in the country's contemporary history provides a distorted picture of everyday life in twentieth-century Suriname.

From a conventional Dutch perspective on international cultural heritage policies, this poses an altogether different question. Over the recent past, there has been relatively generous Dutch funding for shared cultural heritage in Suriname in the traditional spheres, from archives to built heritage. It is fair to say that there has also been a growing Dutch willingness to incorporate highly critical perspectives on colonialism and the concept of 'shared' heritage in its policies. However, the question now surfaces to what extent oral histories on the post-independence period should become a concern of Dutch cultural heritage policies. The debate on that question is still in its infancy.

Netherlands Antilles and Aruba

Colonized from the 1630s onwards, the six islands of the (former) Netherlands Antilles have chosen to remain within the Kingdom of the Netherlands. Recently a dismantlement of the colonial construction of the Antilles-of-six was negotiated, with each of the islands attaining separate and direct relations with the Netherlands.[7]

The three Leeward Islands – Aruba, Bonaire and Curaçao – are located off the Venezuelan coast, the three Windward Antilles – Saba, Sint Eustatius and Sint Maarten (half Dutch, half French) – six hundred miles to the north-east. The vernacular in the Leewards is an Afro-Iberian Creole, Papiamentu. On the Windwards it is English, mainly spoken in a creolized variant. The Dutch language is only dominant in the higher levels of education, bureaucracy and business.

The overwhelming majority of the islands' populations have African roots, while the second largest island, Aruba, has a mestizo Euro-Amerindian population as well. Antillean migration to the Netherlands has been extensive over the past decades. This applies particularly to the main island, Curaçao, with some 130,000 inhabitants as against 100,000 in the Netherlands. As with Suriname, these figures illustrate exceptional small scale and asymmetry with the Netherlands.

Virtually all documented history of the islands pertains to the colonial period and African slavery is the dominant element in this history. However, unlike Suriname, there is also an unbroken European presence on the islands, which makes the slavery issue more delicate. Interestingly, and in contrast to Suriname, external relations have traditionally been strongly oriented towards the Caribbean region and Venezuela rather than to the Netherlands.

---

[7]   Aruba has a separate 'country' status within the Kingdom since 1986. The further dismantlement of the remaining five islands is scheduled to be completed by the end of 2008, but may take longer. The official present designation is 'The Netherlands Antilles and Aruba'. For brevity's sake, 'The Antilles' is used here to refer to the six islands taken together.

These orientations included ongoing migration links to and fro.

Industrialization and more recently the tourist industry caused new labour migrations, this time primarily from the Caribbean and Latin America. All islands harbour substantial recent migrant communities with no previous exposure to Dutch culture or colonialism. And while twentieth-century migrations have resulted in family links between the islands, insular definitions of history and culture are hegemonic. In fact, the absence of a supra-insular identity provoked the dismantlement of the Antilles-of-six, which on the individual islands was perceived as nothing but a colonial construction.

The paradoxes evident for Suriname are no less visible for the Antilles. A 'national', or rather an insular identity is defined in the long shadow of Dutch colonialism and particularly slavery. Yet the Dutch are omnipresent, Dutch funding is required for cultural heritage policies and again, at least for Curaçao, the Antillean population is absolutely transnational. The determined refusal on all islands to accept independence – an outcome long sought for and still not altogether dismissed by the Dutch – considerably complicates the formulation of nationalist narratives. And to complete this picture of post-colonial ambiguity, all islands depend on tourism and consider the built cultural heritage of the colonial period as an invaluable marketing asset.

There has been substantial Dutch investment in the restoration of fortresses, government buildings and the remarkable creolized urban and rural houses of the upper class. This applies particularly to Curaçao, where at the same time angry memories of slavery and critical attitudes towards a celebration or embellishment of the colonial period are most readily voiced. Recently two museums, both housed in a former slave owner's mansion, have taken slavery and slave resistance as the core concern of their exhibitions.

All islands are engaged in the formulation of a 'national' identity, and in all cases the narratives developed tend to take the colonial parameters for granted in order to focus on what is local and unique. This implies defining the national as not-Dutch, as different from each of the other five islands and as dissimilar from what recent immigrants have added to local culture. This strategy for nation building is not made any easier as the islands are becoming increasingly crowded with tourists and Dutch expats.

In addition to urging for more conventional projects such as the digitization of archives, Antillean desiderata expressed during the AWAD conference clearly aimed at the decolonization of cultural heritage policies. Thus there was much emphasis on community-driven research and oral history, and an explicit call to stay away from colonial perspectives. There are obvious parallels with Surinamese priorities. But in addition, language is a crucial element, particularly on the Leeward Islands. Papiamentu is widely seen as the most striking element of the intangible cultural heritage from the colonial period.

This call to favour local over colonial cultural heritage poses dilemmas for Dutch cultural heritage policies. Oral traditions in languages other than Dutch, narratives of local history and research into regional rather than metropolitan connections would generally not be considered as pertinent to the international component of Dutch cultural heritage policy. Yet it so happens that these islands, even if affirming their distinct, non-Dutch character, are constitutionally Dutch so that their local idiosyncrasies somehow belong to the contemporary Dutch cultural landscape, certainly no less so than, say, post-war Mediterranean migrations have altered Dutch metropolitan culture.

While this question will no doubt surface again and again in the coming years, one institutional aberration should be pointed out. The Netherlands Antilles and Aruba do not figure among the priority countries for cultural cooperation defined by the Dutch government, even if the islands share a colonial history with the Netherlands longer than any of the other six nations discussed above. This is of course explained by the fact that the islands are not 'foreign'. It is also true though, with the exception of colonial architecture, that the Antilles seldom qualify for funding from Dutch national institutions in the field of culture – thus, incidentally, fuelling Antillean frustrations regarding the little Dutch interest in Antillean culture and history. As, finally, Antillean local government has modest funds to invest in cultural matters, this means that there may be less spending on local history and cultural heritage in the Antilles than anywhere else in the Kingdom. This certainly is odd and in need of revision.

The Netherlands

This survey would be incomplete without some observations on the way the colonial past is remembered and canonized in the former metropolis itself. This implies a critical take, not only on changing Dutch perceptions of their own colonial past, but also on the context and dynamics of recent debates on Dutch history and identity.

Over the past decade, lively and often acerbic debates have taken place in the Netherlands on Dutch national identity, including its historical roots. As elsewhere on the continent, European integration on the one hand, massive immigration and the ensuing development of a multicultural society on the other, sparked this debate. In the Dutch case, this was a remarkable watershed, as widespread suspicion regarding nationalism and the very concept of 'Dutch identity' had been prevalent during the post-World War Two era.

The question whether the definition and public education of national history enhances the meaning of citizenship and facilitates nation building remains open, as is the question whether it should have these effects in the first place. This debate is not taken up here. It is useful though to reflect on the results of these debates in as much as they have affected the ways colonial history is reinserted into the narrative of the Dutch nation. Two recent authoritative publications provide the material for this analysis. One is the canonical version of Dutch history defined by a government commission chaired by the president of the Royal Netherlands Academy of Arts and Sciences (KNAW) and subsequently accepted as the model for primary and early secondary school history education. The other is the four-volume series *Plaatsen van herinnering* ('Places of memory') written by a set of widely specialized prominent Dutch historians.[8]

Both publications testify to an enhanced awareness of the significance of colonialism in and for Dutch history. Of the fifty 'windows' making up the Dutch history according to the official canon, five focus exclusively on colonial history: the VOC, Atlantic slavery, *Max Havelaar*, the famous nineteenth-century novel criticizing Dutch colonial policy in Java, and two windows on the decolonization of Indonesia and the Dutch Caribbean respectively. Several other windows have a colonial dimension, the founding of the Kingdom (1815; colonial ambitions of King Willem I) and Dutch multicultural society (including post-colonial migrations) being two.

While the first volume of *Plaatsen van herinnering* predates colonialism, the other three volumes do include the colonial dimension. Out of a total of 123 chapters, 19 are devoted to colonial affairs, while again several other chapters have an implicit colonial dimension. Not surprisingly, Indonesia attracts most attention, followed by Suriname and the Antilles. The volume dedicated to the seventeenth and eighteenth centuries however, also contains chapters on Dutch warfare in the Caribbean and Dutch colonization in Brazil, New Netherland and Cape Town.

Nowhere in these respected publications do we come across a glorification of colonialism. The perspectives vary from neutral (for example regarding explorations and the commercial activities of the VOC or post-colonial migrations to the Netherlands) to explicitly critical (towards the Atlantic slave trade or the Dutch foot-dragging in the decolonization of Indonesia).

Once we move to renderings of colonialism outside of academia, the picture becomes more blurred and one encounters more self-congratulatory perspectives on colonialism. This applies particularly to the way the VOC is publicly remembered and was indeed officially celebrated in 2002 – much to the chagrin of South Africa as well as several Asian countries with historical links with the VOC. There is a remarkable contrast between such public celebrations of the VOC and the simultaneous apologetic takes on the WIC. Slavery is one factor explaining this divergence in perspectives, although, as

---

[8]   *entoen.nu* 2006; *entoen.nu en verder* 2007; http://entoen.nu/ The 'canoncommissie' was chaired by the KNAW's president Frits van Oostrom. See Wesseling et al. 2006-07.

indicated above, this does not necessarily reflect a solid understanding of the significance of slave trading and slavery under the aegis of the VOC.

Views on Dutch colonialism in the nineteenth and twentieth centuries are ambivalent. Regarding Indonesia, attention to the ruthless pacification of the archipelago, economic exploitation and so on is complemented by analyses of late-colonial developmental efforts. Criticism on the initial, belligerent Dutch refusal to transfer sovereignty to the Indonesian nationalists has often been muted, out of respect for the large number of involuntary 'repatriates' from the colony. The perspective on Dutch Caribbean history remains dominated by the issue of slavery and its embarrassingly late abolition. Remarkably, the Asian dimension of Surinamese history is much less discussed, even if half of the Surinamese population on both sides of the Atlantic is of Asian descent. The decolonization of the Caribbean again elicits ambivalences: second thoughts about the 'imposition' of sovereignty on Suriname and criticism towards the recent 'recolonization' of the Netherlands Antilles and Aruba.

This lack of balance, particularly in Dutch public history, reflects the contemporary context in which colonial history is reinserted into the national narrative. There is a geopolitical context in which the Netherlands prides itself of having been among the pioneers of globalization, but expresses embarrassment regarding colonialism as such and in particular as to its excesses. This intermingles with a domestic context in which post-colonial migrant communities demand that their voices be heard in the new narrative of Dutch national history.

These factors taken together tend to produce an unbalanced rendering of colonial history. Colonial history tends to be narrowed down to those countries where the Dutch managed to retain their power until the twentieth century and whence substantial numbers of post-colonial migrants 'repatriated': Indonesia, Suriname and the Netherlands Antilles. Moreover, there is a tendency to think of Dutch colonialism in the Atlantic exclusively in terms of the slave trade, slavery and its legacies, hence a past remembered with remorse, while colonialism in Asia more often than not stirs nostalgia and pride. Neither of the two interpretations withstands historical scrutiny.

Within the two Dutch Ministries responsible for cultural heritage policies – Foreign Affairs and Education, Culture and Science – there is an openness to these debates in Dutch society and an awareness of the political sensitivity of these issues in the international arena. It is fair to state that Dutch governmental financing of programmes such as the present one reflects a genuine interest in developing policies for (post)-colonial cultural heritage which offer space for shared as well as dissonant perspectives.

Sharing colonial spaces of memory and policies for cultural heritage

Cultural heritage is not only a contested concept in itself, its very elevation to the status of a privileged concern of national and international policies is disputed. Some argue that from a developmental point of view, heritage discourses are off the mark. In this view, cultural heritage is associated with essentialist constructions of ethnic identities, retrospection and exclusive group thinking, whereas discourses focusing on citizenship are thought to be universalist, future-oriented and inclusive. While there is a point to such concerns, the present project aims to steer away from essentialism in the search to identify common ground in the interpretation of colonial history and its legacies.

In this context, the concept of *lieux de mémoire* ('places of memory'), pioneered by the French historian Pierre Nora, is useful. Inspired by the French initiative, many Western countries have embraced projects aiming to identify such 'places' deemed to be of particular importance to their national history. The ensemble of such historical items – sites, events, texts, traditions and so on – is assumed to encapsulate the core of the nation's historical roots. Thus defining a comprehensive set of places – or to broaden the range of possibilities, 'spaces'– of memory is an exercise in canonization, in the Dutch case by definition including colonialism. This process of selection is an explicitly intersubjective affair. There is nothing self-evident in canonization – debate rules.

While productive debates on these issues continue in the Dutch national arena, we may well broaden the discussion on colonial places of memory to include participants from all places touched by Dutch colonialism. At times, this will elicit heated debates on selection and interpretation. Some dissonance is inevitable and indeed fruitful, and such debates will and need not result in consensus on all accounts. They may, however, inform our understanding of the 'shared', 'common' and 'mutual' – or lack thereof – in the cultural interconnectivity in colonial times and beyond.

Much of the present work in the field of shared cultural heritage centres on the identification and preservation of tangible material remnants of the colonial era, but those involved often have a hard time making this distant history the subject of shared contemporary interest. A focus on the selection and particularly the interpretation of colonial places of memory may help to open up new avenues. The discussion of selection – global, continental, national, local – will force historians from various parts to reflect on the relative importance of the Dutch period in any particular site. The debate on interpretation is an invitation to structured multivocality while at the same time urging us to bring intangible cultural heritage into the equation. After all, historical sites acquire meaning not only through stony structures and dusty paperwork, but just as much through oral traditions and contemporary

Roadstead of Galle

recollections of the past.

What if we would proceed along these lines? Rather than dwelling on the abstract case for this approach, we may reflect on some exemplary places of memory left of this shared colonial history. A focus on episodes related to colonial migrations, and hence on material heritage (sites, buildings) and the interpretations and stories that may come with these, could result in the identification of historical sites such as migration vehicles and hubs (ships, harbours, slave and 'cooli' depots), destinations for labour migrants (plantations, mines), disciplinary institutions (prisons) and metropolitan institutions (museums, scholarly institutions), constructing racial and ethnic categorizations and the like.

A focus on the metropolitan end of colonial and post-colonial migrations would lead us to identify 'places' related to these movements of people in the Netherlands. For one, there are the two companies' headquarters, major harbours and the like, linked to European emigration. But there are also places related to inverse migrations, from the sites frequented by early colonial elites and accompanying servants and slaves through the pensions and societies of colonial students studying at Dutch universities to the late-twentieth century housing projects for successive waves of post-colonial migrants.

As the participants at the Stellenbosch Conference started to ponder the possibilities, all sorts of ideas arose. While much of the present cooperation in this field entails bilateral projects, the focus on migrations presents excellent possibilities to broaden this scope and hence also 'de-centre' the Netherlands. Thus, programmes involving all countries could focus on the comparison of (slave, semi-bonded and free) labour migrations and their legacies; the aftermath and mental legacies of slavery; the emergence of multi-ethnic societies and hence creolization; colonial categorizations and representations; language developments, specifically the (absence of) Dutch language and the emergence of creole languages; religious changes related to the Dutch colonial past; and Muslim migrations under Dutch colonialism.

While some of these ideas are very broad, more specific ones emerged, such as the compilation of a collection of personalized migrant stories linking various parts of the Dutch colonial world and hence demonstrating the multiple migratory trajectories linking Asia, Africa, the Americas and the Netherlands. No great stretch of the imagination is required to see a project of this kind develop from research into a book, a website, exhibitions and more.

In recent years, some exciting projects linking selected countries were initiated, such as the Bidesia project on contemporary memories of Indian indentured labour migration (Suriname, India, the Netherlands); 'Back to the Roots', on the legacies of slavery (Antilles, Africa, the Netherlands, Suriname); and one on Anansie stories and slave narratives (Antilles, Africa, the Netherlands, Suriname). Suggestions for other such multilateral projects include Javanese migration to Suriname and beyond (Indonesia, Suriname, the Netherlands); the origins of Islam in South Africa (Indonesia, South Africa, the Netherlands); and the history of Jews in the Dutch Atlantic.

These and similar ideas all depart from the assumption that such projects are of interest to all countries involved and that there is enough common ground to engage in debates on the contemporary significance and remembrance of colonialism. Migration, a pivotal dimension of colonialism, has been taken as an excellent point of departure here. This of course does not imply that migration should be privileged as the only focal point. Economic and environmental developments left conspicuous legacies in landscapes and cityscapes (water management, polders, transport facilities, urban planning). Belated and mainly half-hearted Dutch efforts to create an imagined community between the metropolis and the colonies were literally cemented in schools, churches, theatres and statues, or alternatively found their way to school books and the media. The Dutch language – widely spoken in a few places, mainly forgotten elsewhere – in itself is a significant *lieu de mémoire* of the divergent trajectories of Dutch colonization. Cultural resistance, anti-colonial struggles and decolonization produced their own tangible remnants and hidden transcripts. So did anthropological and historical museums, colonial scholarly institutions and traditions.

As we reflect on these dimensions of cultural heritage, time and again we come across the same type of questions: how much did colonialism matter then, and how much does its remembrance matter today, for all parties involved? The concerted effort to discuss these delicate issues is in itself an essential contribution to cultural heritage policy and practice, whether this heritage is perceived as shared, mutual and common, or rather as conflicting, contested and dissonant – or, more sensibly, as shared precisely in these very contestations.

Bibliography

entoen.nu
2006   *entoen.nu; De canon van Nederland; Rapport van de Commissie Ontwikke-*
                     ling Nederlandse Canon. Parts A and B. Den Haag; Ministerie van Onder-
                     wijs, Cultuur en Wetenschap.
entoen.nu en verder
2007   *entoen.nu en verder; De canon van Nederland; Rapport van de Commissie*
                     Ontwikkeling Nederlandse Canon. Part C. Amsterdam: Amsterdam Uni-
                     versity Press.

Fienieg, Anouk
2006   'Gemeenschappelijk erfgoed, gedeeld erfgoed?; Een onderzoek naar dissonantie bij gemeenschappelijk cultureel erfgoed in zes landen'. MA thesis University of Amsterdam.
Gonsalves de Mello, J.A.
1987   *Tempo dos Flamengos; Influência da ocupação holandesa na vida e na cultura do norte do Brasil.* Recife: Massangana. [First edition 1947.]
Japin, Arthur
2001   *The two hearts of Kwasi Boachi.* New York: Vintage.
Oostindie, Gert
2003   'Squaring the circle; Commemorating the VOC after 400 years', *Bijdragen tot de Taal-, Land- en Volkenkunde* 159:135-61.
2005   'The slippery paths of commemoration and heritage tourism; The Netherlands, Ghana, and the rediscovery of Atlantic slavery', *New West Indian Guide* 79:55-77.
Shorto, Russell
2004   *The island at the center of the world; The epic story of Dutch Manhattan and the forgotten colony that shaped America.* New York: Doubleday.
Tunbridge, J.E. and G.J. Ashworth
1996   *Dissonant heritage; Management of the past as a resource in conflict.* Chichester: Wiley.
Wesseling, Henk et al (eds)
2006-07   *Plaatsen van herinnering.* Amsterdam: Bert Bakker. Four vols.

PART 2

Migrations under Dutch colonialism

GIJS KRUIJTZER

European migration in the Dutch sphere

Introduction

From the heritage perspective taken in this volume, migration may be described as the flow of genes and memes from one place to another.[1] Genes are the units transmitting physical properties from one generation to the next, while the analogous concept of memes was developed by Richard Dawkins in order to study the transmission of culture in terms of discrete packages of cultural information. Genes and memes are two theoretical tools that help to look at migration as more than simply individuals moving across the globe, for they are what remains after the individual migrant has died – if the migrant has been successful from the genetic or memetic perspective.

The present chapter attempts to trace the European and more specifically the Dutch element through the complex of migrations that took place in the sphere of influence created by the Dutch East Indies Company (VOC) and the West Indies Company (WIC) as well as their precursors and legal successors (hereafter 'the Dutch sphere'). But we wish to avoid the simplification of the past to which the heritage perspective so often gives rise, by conflating genetic and cultural transmission for example. People today cannot be linked to any one set of memes or genes three centuries ago. The European colonial project has ensured that both genes and culture have become thoroughly hybridized in all parts of the world touched by colonialism. Heritage often entails choosing to embrace one part of one's forefathers' and foremothers' culture and to reject other parts, as the ongoing project at the Koninklijk Instituut voor de Tropen (KIT, Royal Tropical Institute) on the roots of Afro-Surinamese people demonstrates (www.mijnroots.nl). This is in no way a new problem, as will

---

[1]   Since this chapter is the outcome of a collaborative project I would like to thank the authors of the other chapters, as well as Hanneke Lommerse, Erik and Niels Sitton and Esther Zwinkels. A collective thanks goes to Peter Boomgaart, Piet Emmer, Victor Enthoven, Femme Gaastra, Henk den Heijer, Gerrit Knaap, Gert Oostindie and Alex van Stipriaan for their critical appraisals of the first draft. I would also like to thank Isabel van der Heiden, David Henley, Kirsten Hulsker, Han Jordaan, Johan van Langen, Wieke Vink and Aukje Zuidema for their input.

be seen later in this chapter: colonial classifiers have always had trouble categorizing people.

While addressing these issues in a quantitative manner, this chapter also devotes quite some space to the qualitative information necessary to put the figures into perspective. The section on 'European migrants' discusses the various segments of these migrants moving within the Dutch sphere. They are divided into two groups: 'real' migrants and employees of the WIC, the VOC or the state. Next the various estimates of the total flows of European migrants within the Dutch sphere are discussed, followed by a closer look at the provenance of both the employees and 'real' migrants. That section also looks at Dutch colonial policies of inclusion and exclusion of non-Dutch migrants and at the effectiveness of those policies.

In the following section, 'Demography of the colonial populations', the emphasis shifts from population flows to the demographics of individual places in the Dutch sphere and the share of the colonial groups in the total population of places under Dutch sway. The next section, 'Ways of counting', looks at the categorizations employed by the colonial authorities with respect to the colonial populations and the usefulness (or uselessness) of the colonial categories for tracing European genes from our present-day vantage point. The final section describes the most quantifiable flows of memes, namely those of language and religion, from a comparative perspective. To conclude, a short Epilogue draws attention to some of the paradoxes of migration in the Dutch sphere from the heritage perspective, and brings this colonial history home.

European migrants

Grades of volition

Who is a migrant? It seems difficult to leave volition out of a definition of migration, but it is equally difficult to establish volition. In a brief overview of colonial migration of the 1980s, E. van den Boogaart and P.C. Emmer (1986:3) write: 'in comparison with the emigration to the New World, it is somewhat warped to speak of European emigration to Asia and Africa. In fact, the majority of Europeans set off for African and Asian trading posts, firmly resolved to return again after a few years'. Even if that were the case, many might have changed their minds while in the East or dithered long enough to never make it back to the Netherlands. Studies like those by Marion Peters and Ferry André de la Porte (2002) and Lodewijk Wagenaar (1994) show that many continued to renew their contracts while in Asia. In other words, the VOC was not just an employer, it was a way of life. Moreover, the dream of returning, however unrealistic, is what gets most migrants of all epochs through the day.[2] Even in Suriname, in the West, an eighteenth-century governor complained about the *animus revertendi* that motivated the Dutch planters in the colony (Oostindie 2005:7). Rather than draw a clear-cut distinction between people with a desire to migrate and people with a desire to return we may look at the will to migrate as a gradual scale between those two extremes. The question as to whether those Company employees who did not return from the Indies are to be considered emigrants becomes crucial if one is to make a comparison between East and West.

Company and state employees

The first group we would like to consider here are the personnel of the Dutch East and West Indies Companies. These men[3] in particular are generally assumed to have planned a return to Europe at some point, as was exemplified in the quotation in the previous paragraph. If, however, we are to take the place of death as the final destination of this group, as has been done for other groups of people moving around the globe, we end up with a significant stream of migrants.

How long must these Company servants have lived to qualify as migrants? Those dying on the outward voyage, before reaching their initial destination, we may perhaps discount. Their number was quite significant. On an average VOC voyage to Asia somewhere in the order of ten per cent of the passengers and crew lost their life, as a detailed calculation in the standard work of Bruijn, Gaastra and Schöffer, *Dutch Asiatic shipping* reveals. Figures for the Dutch Atlantic voyages are much less precise (an issue that will be dealt with in more detail below), partly due to the fact that it was not only the WIC that was operating on these routes. According to a study concerning voyages to Berbice, the death rate was only one per cent, whereas on the slave carrying voyages by the Middelburgsche Commercie Compagnie between West Africa and the Americas the death toll among Europeans seems to have been as high as eighteen per cent. On the basis of these figures, along with some figures for French ships, Victor Enthoven assumes that on average a seaman had a

[2]   Lucassen and Penninx (1994:69) compare the return rates of would-be permanent emigrants from the Netherlands in the 1970s to the return rates of supposedly temporary labour migrants to the Netherlands. The return rates do not match the expectations of the migrants or society and the opposition between 'temporary' and 'permanent' collapses in the face of the figures. Compare also the considerations of the East Indies 1930 census office regarding the distinction between *blijvers* (stayers) and *trekkers* (drifters) (*Volkstelling 1930*, VI:6-7).
[3]   After 1632 the VOC employed only one woman, as a midwife (Blussé 1986:161). There were, however, a few women who posed as men. See Bruijn, Gaastra and Schöffer (1987:148) and, in the database discussed below, the category 'vrouw' under the search option 'einde dienstverband manier'.

'Old Dutch street within the Fort of Colombo'

five per cent chance of not surviving a voyage across the Atlantic,[4] which was generally much shorter than a voyage to the East Indies.

Death rates were also high after arrival in both the West and the East Indies. Peters and André de la Porte (2002) provide a qualitative insight into the dying of VOC personnel and their families in Coromandel, while Harvey M. Feinberg (1974) gives a quantification of the death rates among Europeans in WIC service on the African west coast in the eighteenth century: around twenty per cent per annum, mostly due to disease. But the African west coast was among the more deadly places for Europeans, as was the Dutch fortress of Concordia on Timor, where the VOC was forced to send mainly Germans, because Dutchmen preferred to go elsewhere.[5]

It was the newcomers who were especially hard hit in most places. Even on breezy Curaçao 23 per cent of the soldiers arriving from Europe between 1702-1744 died during their first year.[6] Batavia became very unhealthy after 1733 when a malaria epidemic broke out, as P.H. van der Brug demonstrates in an important study on mortality in Batavia and Ceylon and on VOC ships. Before 1733, about five to ten per cent of the newly arrived soldiers in Batavia died during their first year, a figure that climbed to forty-fifty per cent after 1733 and to a grisly sixty-seventy per cent in 1775. A small comparative sample from Ceylon shows that in the latter year 'only' about thirteen per cent of the newcomers died during their first year there. It was, incidentally, not only the European newcomers to Batavia that were hit, but also the Chinese migrants to the city, Javanese fishermen, canal diggers from the region and the slaves who were brought in from elsewhere in Asia, although precise figures for these groups are absent (Van der Brug 1994:56-9, 237-8). In Malacca the death rate among Europeans was also higher than the local average, as a small sample study by A.P.M. Ketelaars (1985:73-4) indicates. It was, and is, however, thought that those who survived their first year in the tropics built up some sort of immunity.

Yet these death rates only reveal part of the story regarding the flows of people from the Netherlands to the Indies. A useful distinction may be made between soldiers and sailors. It seems that there was a higher return rate

---

[4]   Bruijn, Gaastra and Schöffer 1987:163; Enthoven 2005:161. Note that the mortality figure of four per cent that Enthoven gives for Asiatic voyages on p. 170 is a misreading of Bruijn, Gaastra and Schöffer p. 162, who have in turn misread Schoute (1929:46), who thought that death rates of two to four per cent on ships were the norm if there was no outbreak or epidemic of any kind. Schoute's figure must, however, be considered outdated because he did not have access to the comprehensive numerical data that Bruijn, Gaastra and Schöffer had.

[5]   The remark on Timor is derived from Hans Hägerdal, who is preparing a monograph on the region during the VOC period.

[6]   Enthoven 2007:25. This figure is derived from a study in progress by Han Jordaan, who is planning to augment his data for the later part of the eighteenth century.

among sailors than among soldiers, 59.3 per cent and 30.2 per cent respectively for those recruited in the eighteenth century for the Delft Chamber. Jan Lucassen concludes from this that soldiers were apparently much more vulnerable than sailors, and Van der Brug similarly assumes that non-return equalled death as a premise for his calculation of the average mortality of VOC personnel in Asia, which consequently turns out to be much higher for military personnel than for sailors (Lucassen 1991:11; Van der Brug 1994:186-8). It was, however, the soldiers who were the most keen to settle down and marry local or mestizo women. By 1616, only three years after the foundation of a fortress at Pulicat, eleven of the garrison's Dutch soldiers were living there as married men; two married to Dutch women and nine to local women (Kruijtzer 2008: Chapter 1). Non-return therefore did not equal prompt death for soldiers.

The Company men who married local women tied themselves to Asia – as some contemporary authors graphically put it. In 1649 the High Government at Batavia passed a by-law forbidding Asian and mestizo women along with their European husbands to leave for the Netherlands on any ship, whether VOC or non-VOC. This measure was intended more as a means of tying the personnel to Asia or, in the High Government's words, 'to the advancement and establishment of a good, stable and well-regulated colony in these lands', than to deter people from marrying. Apparently many were willing to forego their right of passage to Europe (Peters and André de la Porte 2002:45-7).

Apart from remaining in Company service, the VOC personnel had two options in the *Octrooigebied*. First, upon the expiry of their contract,[7] they could become a *freeburgher* or free settler under VOC protection. Second, they could desert the Company and find a new employer. Once completed, the vocopvarenden.nationaalarchief.nl database should make it easy to calculate the percentages of people choosing either option in the eighteenth century; so far the data indicate that desertion was somewhat more popular than becoming a *freeburgher*.[8] The *freeburgher* community will be discussed in more detail later. As far as desertion is concerned, we have no aggregate figures, although deserters were a constant source of complaints for the VOC management.

Desertion was especially prevalent in South Asia, because there the VOC settlements and trading posts were often close to English, French, Danish and Portuguese establishments and there was a large demand for European military labour and expertise from the Indian courts. During the VOC war

---

[7]   Initially, three years for seafarers and five years for other personnel, but after 1658 the lower ranking seafarers also saw their contracts extended to five years (Bruijn, Gaastra and Schöffer 1987:147).

[8]   The database should be completed around 2010; the search option 'einde dienstverband manier' provides a great number of possible career endings.

at Cochin with the Travancore kingdom in the 1740s, a great number of Europeans deserted the VOC and joined the ranks of the enemy; as many as 87 in the years 1647-1648 (Singh 2007:124-5). Frank Lequin has calculated that Bengal saw on average sixty desertions from VOC service per year, though it is unclear if they were all Europeans. Still, in 1756 as many as 56 Europeans deserted the VOC for the Mughal governor of the province (Lequin 2005:150-2). With an average force of 145 European and 47 Indian military personnel in Bengal over the period 1700-1789, this represented a substantial loss (Lequin 1982, II:357). Many Europeans entering the service of Indian kings and nobles became Muslim and established families, but were no longer part of the European colony (although cities like Hyderbad had special streets for their European military personnel as early as the seventeenth century) and dropped out of the VOC records. They may, however, well have been among the more successful migrants with respect to progeny. They were joined by a trickle of Dutch fortune seekers making their way over land to South Asia (Kruijtzer 2008: Chapter 1).

Desertion also took place on some scale in the WIC sphere. In 1719 nine new recruits for Curaçao took off within a few days after their arrival on the island. At the time of the Fourth Anglo-Dutch War (1780-1784) 23 soldiers of a 40 men-garrison disappeared in Berbice and in 1792 eight soldiers destined for that colony took off before even arriving there (Enthoven 2005:162-4). These figures are, however, only indicative. It would be desirable to have a proper quantification of desertion both in the VOC Octrooigebied and in the Dutch Atlantic.

In the period following the VOC and WIC, the Netherlands continued to send out people to administer and pacify the colonies. Between 1815 and 1909 156,482 military men were recruited in the Netherlands for the East Indies (Bossenbroek 1986:193). The number of civil servants recruited in the Netherlands for the colonies was smaller. Cees Fasseur's calculation of the number of home recruits for administrative service in the Dutch East Indies suggests an annual average of just over 40 between 1907 and 1939 (Fasseur 1994:434-5). An overall computation for the entire post-VOC/WIC period is desirable, however.

Settlers arriving as settlers

Finally there was a category of people leaving the Netherlands who were not in the service of the VOC, WIC or the state. Perhaps many of them had the intention of staying for good, but even among these groups many kindled the hope of returning, as was already noted with regards to the Suriname planters; five of the indentured servants for New Netherland discussed below contracted a free return trip before even disembarking (Van den Boogaart

1986:64). Also with regard to this group the contrast between the East and
the West should not be overstated. The East had its colonization schemes as
well as the West.

In its early days the VOC also sent a number of single women. In 1610 the
first governor general brought 36 along. During the 1620s Jan Pieterszoon
Coen in particular insisted that families and orphans be sent from Holland
to populate the colonies. As a result, a number of single women were sent
and an orphanage was established in Batavia to raise Dutch orphan girls to
become proper East India brides. Exact figures are not available, but we do
know of thirty girls reaching Batavia on the ship *Leiden* (Blussé 1986:158-60;
Bruijn, Gaastra and Schöffer 1987:148). In 1625 six single women sent out
under this colonization programme, known as 'Company daughters', married Dutchmen at Pulicat and were provided with a dowry of fifty rixdollars
by the Company (Peters and André de la Porte 2002:45-7).

Although the programme of sending 'Company daughters' was abandoned in 1632, women continued to arrive in Asia as wives of personnel, as
stowaways or as paying passengers. The latter were bound by the VOC to
stay at least fifteen years in the Octrooigebied, although in 1669 that period
was reduced to five years for those marrying in the Octrooigebied. Women
needed to have good connections with the VOC management in order to have
a chance of embarking, because, as retired ship surgeon Nicolaus de Graaff
remarked in the 1680s, 'if the gentlemen directors would allow all those who
wanted to sail, I believe there would be more women folk on the ships than
men folk' (Peters and André de la Porte 2002:45-7).

In the years after 1669, European colonization reappeared on the agenda
of the VOC directors in the Netherlands and the High Government in
Batavia. In 1672 the directors gave those wishing to settle at the Cape, Ceylon
or Batavia permission to take 6,000 guilders to their destination. The ships
of the 1671-1672 season carried 33 male *freeburghers* from the Netherlands to
Batavia as well as 84 women and 91 children, who for the most part would
have been associated with these *freeburghers* (Bruijn, Gaastra and Schöffer
1987:147-8). According to Ad Biewenga, a large part of the immigrants to the
Cape between 1680-1700 came directly from Europe, but almost a decade
after the foundation of the colony in 1652, the number of wives and children
of VOC personnel was still greater than the number of wives and children
of burghers (113 versus 37). Part of these immigrants came as *knechten* (farm
hands) in VOC service to assist the burghers in establishing agriculture (Shell
1994:12-5). In 1706, and more definitely in 1717, the Cape was, however,
closed to direct migration from Europe (Biewenga 1999:23; Giliomee 2003:2;
Moritz 1938:76-8).

At various times during the seventeenth century the Dutch developed
policies to settle the island of Mauritius, which was uninhabited when they

first arrived. As early as 1606 VOC ships brought plants, including grain and fruit trees, goats and pigs in order to develop the island as a supply station. In the 1640s, a substantial number of slaves were brought to the island and its governor Adriaen van der Stel requested Batavia to send Chinese labourers to advance the agricultural frontier on the island, but none were sent. In the late 1670s governor Isaac Lamotius decided to develop the island into a colony for *freeburghers*, who were bound to remain on the island for fifteen years and engage in agriculture. But the Company also decided twice to evacuate the island because of the rising costs, lastly in 1706 (Moree 1998).

For the area under the *Octrooi* of the WIC, there were a number of colonization schemes. Though much more known, these schemes relied on stopgap measures akin to the schemes of the VOC. In 1654-1655, for instance, 47 orphans were sent to New Amsterdam. Dispatching Europeans as indentured agricultural servants, which the VOC only did for the Cape, was done on a larger scale for the West, however. Moreover, one mechanism of colonization was developed for the WIC area that did not exist in the VOC sphere of influence: the *patroonship*. The *patroons* or patrons were assigned a certain area to populate and establish agriculture. The best-known *patroonship* was that under the Van Renselaer dynasty in New Netherland, but there were also a number of *patroonships* on the Wild Coast. Of the estimated total of 5,700 people migrating to New Netherland during the span of its existence (1624-1664) it seems that around 35 per cent were indentured to the WIC and the city of Amsterdam and another six per cent to the Van Renselaers. Of the remaining 59 per cent coming directly from the Netherlands it is unclear what percentage were free colonists as opposed to Company servants – although the latter group probably constituted the majority. A large part of the colonists went in family units; only 39 per cent of the WIC-supported colonists were adult males, although the corresponding percentage among the Van Renselaer colonists was 81. Nevertheless, this contrasts with the pattern of migration to the VOC Octrooigebied. Another contrast of sorts is the frequency of desertion among the indentured servants in New Netherland, which seems to have been low, although no precise figures are available (Van den Boogaart 1986:60-6).

The colonization projects along the 'Wild Coast' or the Guyanas, and on Tobago, then known as Nieuw Walcheren, were mostly directed from Zeeland. Particularly active senders of colonists were Abraham van Pere, recognized as the proprietor of an area along the Berbice River, to which he sent the first sixty male Zeelander colonists in 1627 (he found no women prepared to travel), and Pieter de Moor, who had established a colony on the Wiapoco River in 1615 and seems to have sent around 200 people from the Netherlands to New Walcheren between 1628 and 1632. Many of the colonization attempts on the Wild Coast ended in sickness and disaster. A particularly disastrous attempt was the colony on the Oyapoc River, to which 350 men, children and women (including Elisabeth van der Woude who survived to tell the tale) were sent in 1676, but tropical downpours, sickness, internal strife and conquest by the French, who took the captive survivors to Martinique, ended the operation. Henk den Heijer puts forward the question as to why colonists kept coming to the Wild Coast. He suggests that the propaganda for settlement in the region by people like Willem Usselinx was as unrealistic as it was effective.[9]

One of the reasons why both the WIC and the VOC at times encouraged European settlement was simply to find strength in numbers. The Portuguese example played a large role in this, as some early-seventeenth century Dutchmen believed that the flourishing Portuguese overseas communities had contributed to the Portuguese success in dominating trade and trade routes (Kruijtzer 2008: Chapter 1). For Dutch Brazil for instance, the WIC actively sought northern European colonists, because the circa 12,000 Dutch and Europeans allied with them (excluding Jews) in the colony were far outnumbered by the 30,000 odd 'Portuguese' that remained around 1640 (Schalkwijk 1998:47-9).

Similarly, in the late 1630s, the great influx of Chinese into Taiwan or rather the imbalance between the number of Europeans and Chinese, became a source of concern for the High Government, just as in Suriname the ratio of Europeans to African slaves became a concern during the eighteenth century. Governor Hans Putmans of Taiwan therefore proposed that immigration of men from Europe be stimulated and that these men be allowed to marry local women and engage in trade. But the High Government deemed it more realistic to institute a poll tax in order to discourage Chinese settlement to some extent and to generate the funds for the maintenance of a larger regiment to keep the Chinese in check (Van Veen 2003:149-50). Nevertheless, the Chinese population of the island continued to grow at a fast pace.

In the case of Suriname, the first regulations to address the imbalance between whites and blacks in the colony were promulgated in 1684 by governor Cornelis van Aerssen van Sommelsdijk. According to Van Sommelsdijk's by-law, the plantation owners were to hire one white person for every ten black persons they employed (as slaves), on pain of a fine of 10,000 pounds of sugar. Similar by-laws were promulgated in 1692, 1724, 1768, 1773 and 1785, but only the first of these seem to have had any effect – the percentage of whites in the colony continued to drop after a very slight rise (Goslinga 1985:536-7).

In the post-Company period only the 1840s saw the development of some agricultural colonization programmes for Europeans within the Dutch

---

9   Goslinga 1971:410-32; Den Heijer 2005; Barend-van Haeften 2005.

sphere. This time frame was marked by a 'craving for migration' as a com-
mittee of private citizens for the propagation of European colonization on
Borneo put it. Their observation was of course based on the small stream of
Dutchmen migrating to the United States at the time, but their aim was to
channel this 'craving' towards the Dutch colonies. The governor general of
the Dutch East Indies, however, thought the plan undesirable because he did
not deem physical labour by Europeans in the tropics feasible and because it
might offend the indigenous rulers. But the Minister of Colonies was of the
opinion that people could live in all climates and that a bit of physical exercise was healthy; it was his Ministry that in 1844 finally agreed to absorb the
expenses of a long-pushed white colonization plan for Suriname (later known
as 'Groningen plan'). In 1845, 208 people arrived, comprising 29 families and
over 30 single men. They settled at Voorzorg on the Saramacca River, but
many of that and the two subsequently dispatched groups died not long after
they had arrived. The survivors were moved to the Groningen Estate on the
opposite bank of the river. By 1852 the state subsidy for the plan was termi-
nated and the remaining settlers were moved closer to Paramaribo.[10]

Later agricultural colonization plans were directed not so much at people
coming from Europe, but at European people already in the overseas possessions or at non-Europeans. The slave emancipation bill of 1863 stated
that free colonization of Suriname was to be encouraged. For the most part
this role was taken up by the Asians who had come as indentured labourers
and served their term, especially the Javanese and Hindustanis (Goslinga
1990:224-5, 475, 503). The major twentieth-century colonization scheme in
the Dutch East Indies involved Javanese, who were sent to other islands of
the archipelago to redress the presumed overpopulation of Java (see section
'Local people' and Chapter VI). Around 1930 there was much pressure from
the Indo-Dutch community to give its members land to engage in small-scale
agriculture, but the ensuing colonization schemes failed dismally, including
the Indo-Dutch colony in New Guinea, involving some 600 colonists in total.
The scheme was briefly revived around 1950 to provide a home for the dis-
placed Indo-Dutch, but would fail once again (Meijer 2004:128-37, 310-2).

Total flows from and to the Netherlands

The previous subsection attempted to shed some light on the gradations of
intentionality in 'Dutch' migration and colonization. Such subtleties are lost,
however, in the mass of figures we face in this subsection, as the two main
authors discussed here, the historians Jan Lucassen and Victor Enthoven,

---

[10]   NA, Kabinet des Konings, 4199, *verbaal* 30-1-1848 X3; Ministerie van Koloniën, 1856, *verbaal*
20-5-1848 no. 1. For the Groningen plan see Goslinga 1990.

seem quite agreed that anyone who does not return is a migrant. This is a rather fortunate circumstance because taking volition into account would only further complicate the already complex task of working around the few data in our possession.

The often cited figure of 973,000 people leaving the Netherlands on VOC ships over the entire span of its existence, is the only one of its kind based on an addition of numbers found in records. But even this figure is not as firm as it appears. Apart from the fact that for some voyages passenger lists are una-vailable – for which averages have been extrapolated – the figure is certainly somewhat high, because it does not take into account the number of people sailing for a second or multiple time from the Netherlands, which a study by K.L. van Schouwenburg (1988) of the Delft Chamber recruits reveals to have been significant. Calculating the total number of returnees, and hence the net migration, is even more hazardous. Estimates range from 366,900 (based on the assumption that the category 'crew at the Cape' represented those return-ing to Europe) to 483,835 returnees (based on an extrapolation of percentages found for the Delft Chamber in the eighteenth century). This means that somewhere in the order of half a million, give or take a hundred thousand, Europeans sent out by the VOC ended their lives in the Octrooigebied or on VOC ships. One may want to subtract a further ten per cent from that number for the people who never made it to their initial destination in the Octrooigebied, as was noted above.[11]

For the WIC area, no such aggregate figures are available. Taking issue with an off-the-cuff calculation of the number of crew consumed by the Dutch Atlantic – on the basis of the mortality rates aboard VOC ships – by Emmer and Klooster (1999:57-8), Enthoven (2005) has made a daring effort to mirror the calculations around the figure of 973,000 outbound VOC passen-gers for the West. But his calculation too suffers from a lack of data so that his equations are anchored to (sometimes very rough) estimates only. Enthoven starts from an estimate of an average of 180 outbound and 160 homebound voyages per annum for the period 1600-1800 and then proceeds to calculate the average number of sailors, military men and other passengers on board. The most well-founded of these estimates seems to be that of the sailors, for which he cites a good number of studies. He arrives at an average of 52 passengers, times the 180 voyages times 200 years, yields a total of 1,872,000 outbound individuals according to Enthoven's table. He then proceeds to calculate the percentages of sailors, military men and passengers who did not return at 5, 90 and 50 per cent respectively, from which he calculates the average number of returnees, and arrives at a total of 1,209,510. This means

11   Bruijn, Gaastra and Schöffer 1987:144, 163; Van Gelder 1997:40-1; Lucassen 1991:12, 18, 40-2 (Van Schouwenburg cited there).

that more Europeans would have remained in the West through Dutch transportation – Enthoven makes it a round 700,000 – than in the East.

This figure seems inflated, however. First, the manner in which Enthoven arrives at an average of seven non-crew and non-military passengers per outbound voyage is unclear, although he gives a few figures for the Jews in the Dutch Atlantic and the Pennsylvania Dutch. We shall return to these groups below. Second, nine out of fifteen of Enthoven's net migrants are military men, constituting 397,494 people. But the biggest deployment of military men in the West consisted of 6,000 odd troops sent by the States General to Dutch Brazil in the 1640s; between 1740 and 1794 only some 13,343 soldiers were recorded as having been sent to Suriname. Will a comprehensive count of recorded numbers eventually add up to the total figure mentioned above?

Third, Enthoven deflates the figure of returnees by not only reducing each category of voyagers by a percentage for those remaining, but also by reducing the multiplier from 180 to 160 (that is, the estimated number of return voyages). This double reduction means that 35 per cent of the voyagers would have remained in the Octrooigebied as opposed to the 27.4 that would have been the weighted average of Enthoven's category percentages. The difference of 7.6 per cent translates into 142,272 people that Enthoven includes in the net migration figure.

Another problem is the difficulty in distinguishing between voyagers and individuals. This problem also arises with the figure of VOC departures, but to a lesser extent than for the West. If 95 per cent of the Atlantic sailors returned to the Netherlands, as Enthoven has it, as opposed to the 59.3 per cent of VOC sailors who returned (see above), is it not likely that a greater percentage signed up for a second or multiple voyage for the West than for the East, also considering the shorter duration of the westward voyages? Supposing that sailors made an average of two voyages to the West would already reduce the number of outbound individuals by some 650,000. In this scenario one would of course also have to reduce the number of returnees, while the net 'migration' of sailors would remain the same because the five per cent reduction estimate concerns the number of voyages and not individuals, but the triangular Atlantic system suddenly appears as a gigantic treadmill. It would be very useful to have for the West a (sample) survey comparable to that by Van Schouwenburg on the percentage of sailors who signed up for multiple voyages.

By thus trimming Enthoven's figures one must arrive at a figure lower than 700,000, even if with his method it is hard to arrive at a figure as low as that which David Eltis ventures of a total net migration of 20,000 people from the Netherlands to the Americas before 1760. His figure is based on the very rough estimates by Jan Lucassen of 15,000 migrants from the Netherlands to South America, the Caribbean and West Africa for the seventeenth, eight-

Village on Manipa near Fort Wantrouw

eenth and nineteenth centuries and a maximum of 10,000 for emigrants to North America for the seventeenth and eighteenth centuries.[12] But Lucassen himself is sceptical of his estimates and Eltis seems interested in making the figure of European migration to the Americas pale in comparison to the figure of Africans transported to the New World (see Chapter V). Therefore the figure probably lies somewhere between his and Enthoven's. A more solid footing for calculations of 'Dutch' migration to the West is duly required.

As for the nineteenth and twentieth centuries, many more precise figures should be available, but only Lucassen (1991:43-5) has attempted to calculate net migration flows between the Netherlands and its colonies. His calculation of the net migration flows is, however, very preliminary, as the author himself notes. He arrives at a net migration from the East Indies to the Netherlands for the nineteenth century and at a net migration in the other direction for the early twentieth century, but there are far too many extrapolations and uncertainties in the calculation to consider these figures here. For one thing, the tables of Ferenczi and Willcox (1929:743-4) he uses, concern migration from and to all the Dutch colonies, and do not specify whether or to what extent civil servants and military personnel are counted.[13]

Provenance of the migrants and transmigrants

Civil and military personnel recruited in the Netherlands

As Malthus already noted in the early nineteenth century, the Netherlands and its empire of trade were once widely seen as the 'grave of Germany', because so many Germans moved to and through it (quoted in Lucassen 1991:9). Lucassen introduces the term 'transmigrants' for the foreign VOC employees (and by extension all non-Dutchmen signing up in the Netherlands for service in its empire), because they were neither immigrants to the Netherlands, nor emigrants from the Netherlands.

The percentages of foreigners in VOC service are quite well established through an evaluation of a large number of random samples by Bruijn and Lucassen (1980) and some studies conducted for individual VOC Chambers. On the whole it may be said that over the entire period of the VOC's existence, sixty per cent of the soldiers and forty per cent of the maritime personnel came from outside the Dutch Republic. These percentages fluctuated to some extent, however. Before 1660 the percentages of foreigners were about 65 and

---

[12]   Eltis deducts from these figures twenty per cent for returns (Lucassen 1991:22-3; Eltis 1999:28-9).
[13]   Lucassen does not seem to have noticed the tables in *Volkstelling 1930*, VI:18-9 with a bearing on this topic.

35 for soldiers and mariners respectively, to drop somewhat in the later part of the seventeenth century, after which they steadily increased again, to reach roughly eighty and fifty per cent around 1770. Bruijn and Lucassen also give some data regarding the geographical origins of recruits from within the Dutch Republic, of which it can very generally be said that the majority hailed from the seaside provinces, while the percentage of soldiers from the inland provinces rose steadily in the eighteenth century along with the number of foreigners (Van Gelder 1997:53-4; Bruijn and Lucassen 1980:21-4, 139-40).

For the West, again, the percentages are less well established. Lucassen assumes an inverse relation between the length of the sea voyages and size of the ships on the one hand and the remuneration and number of Dutchmen among the crew on the other hand, to conclude: 'our assumption concerning the relationship between the duration of voyages and the percentage of non-Dutch crew leads us to suggest that, in the case of the WIC [...] and related companies sailing to Africa and America, we may expect between thirty and forty per cent of crews to have been foreign'. A study of the Middelburgsche Commercie Company's personnel operating on the slave routes in the eight-eenth century indicates that 35 per cent of the crew were foreign, mostly of German and Scandinavian origin (Lucassen 1991:12).

Many, but not all, of the foreigners in VOC service were similarly confined to the lower ranks. The Germans cited in Roelof van Gelder's *Het Oost-Indisch avontuur* complained that it was very difficult for non-Dutchmen to be hired as anything but a soldier, and some quantitative studies confirm this picture. Samples of the personnel for the VOC Chambers of Hoorn and Enkhuizen in the eighteenth century reveal that 92 per cent of the ships' officers were Dutch, against 76 per cent of the subaltern officers. Studies for the Zeeland Chamber have yielded a similar 86 per cent Dutchmen among the higher officers, although in the 1770s that figure dropped to 75 per cent. As Van Gelder notes: the lower the rank, the higher the percentage of foreigners (Van Gelder 1997:31-3, 56).

Some foreigners still managed to rise through the ranks, however, as is illustrated in the following overview of the origins of the higher VOC per-sonnel in Bengal. This table, compiled by Lequin, also reveals the wide geo-graphical spread of those origins.

During the nineteenth century military recruits for the East Indies con-tinued to include a large number of foreigners, about one third on average. There were also years when the number of foreigners exceeded the number of Dutchmen in the legions. It must be noted that the meaning of 'foreign' shifted somewhat during this period, because between 1815 and 1830 the Kingdom of the Netherlands included the southern Netherlands, which after the latter date became Belgium. So while in the early century Southern Netherlanders were not counted as foreigners, they were mostly barred from

Table 4.1 Birthplaces of members of the Bengal directorate in the eighteenth century

Region	Number	%
Netherlands	94	81.7
Germany	9	7.8
Austrian Netherlands	1	0.9
France	2	1.7
Denmark	1	0.9
Russia	1	0.9
VOC Octrooigebied	7	6.1
Total	115	100

Source: Lequin 2005:249-50.

service between 1833 and 1846, and hired as Belgians in the later part of the century. On the whole, foreigners included mostly Germans, Frenchmen, Belgians and Swiss. French veterans of the Napoleonic Wars were a prominent presence in the years after 1815. A great wave of Swiss soldiers came from British legions that had fought in the Crimean War, but they mutinied in 1860 and were subsequently barred for some time (Bossenbroek 1986:31-4).

Settlers departing from the Netherlands

There were also foreigners amongst those boarding ships in the Netherlands in order to settle in the Dutch sphere. Their numbers are to be reconstructed from censuses of the colonies rather than from passenger lists or the like. Most thoroughly researched is perhaps the European population of New Amsterdam. According to Joyce Goodfriend (1992:16) the influx arriving from the Netherlands was already quite heterogeneous. Some Europeans

Table 4.2 Ethnic origins of 222 identifiable male settlers in New Amsterdam at English takeover

Ethnicity	Number	%
Dutch	168	76
German	24	11
French	15	7
English	10	4.5
Scandinavian	3	
Irish	1	
Jewish	1	
Total	222	100

Source: Goodfriend 1992:15-6.

also arrived from elsewhere in the Americas, especially Jews, who will be discussed below. As a result, about a quarter of the free population of New Amsterdam was not ethnically Dutch. The table below is based on Goodfriend's research into the nature of New Amsterdam at the time of the English takeover in 1664.

After the revocation of the Edict of Nantes in 1685, quite a number of Huguenots were carried to the Cape by the VOC. After three years of deliberation over the request of Huguenot leader Marquis du Quesne, the VOC directors decided to grant this group permission to settle at the Cape. The Huguenots were, however, barred from engaging in so-called private trade (that is, non-Company trade). Those who could not bring the capital or equipment to set themselves up in a trade or in agriculture, were to take service with their compatriots. Eventually, many established vineyards. We do not have exact numbers for the immigration of Huguenots to the Cape, but it seems that in the first year, 1688, at least 140 disembarked (Verstegen 2001:91-2).

Suriname also attracted a number of non-Dutch immigrants over the years. Among them a number of Huguenots after 1685, and followers of the egalitarian sect of Jean-Pierre Labadie, which included some Frenchmen. In the 1680s and in 1747 there was an effort to establish a colony of Swiss and Germans from the Pfalz (Van Lier 1977:24-7). In the eighteenth and nineteenth centuries some Herrnhutter missionaries from Moravia came to Suriname and the Cape to proselytize among the slaves. A mission station in the Netherlands directed their efforts.

In the late seventeenth century there were calls from among the higher echelons of the VOC to encourage the immigration of German settlers to the Cape, as long as they were Protestant.[14] In 1698 a pamphlet appeared in Hamburg in which poor Germans were enjoined to migrate to the Cape. There are no total numbers of such German migrants, but Eduard Moritz (1938:76-8) speaks of at least fifty male German settlers who either alone or with families arrived between 1670 and 1700.

In his study of Germans at the Cape, which appeared in 1938 in a series entitled 'Die deutsche Leistung in der Welt' (The German achievement in the world), Moritz gives a table of *Stammväter* and *Stammütter*, that is to say, of the founders of South Africa's 'Old Families'. The ethnic breakdown of these founders, both settlers arriving as settlers and as (former) VOC personnel, is as follows:

---

[14]   It may also be noted in this context that of the 47 Germans in VOC service whose memoirs Van Gelder (1997:68) studied, 43 were Lutherans, 2 were otherwise Reformed and only 2 were Roman Catholics.

Table 4.3 Ethnic origins of founders of Afrikaner old families arrived between 1657-1806

Ethnicity	Number of men	Number of women
German	913	63
Dutch	520	312
French	90	77
Scandinavian	67	2

Source: adapted from Moritz 1938:92.

The Dutch, French, Scandinavian and especially German ethnicities he saw as the ingredients of what became, under British rule, the Afrikaner community of South Africa. The first application of the term 'Afrikaner' to a member of the European community with roots in the Dutch period dates from one year after the British takeover in 1806 (Giliomee 2003:23). The other major European Creole group in the Dutch sphere, which in the twentieth century came to be known as Indische Nederlanders, must also have had many Germans among its ancestors. By 1930 still 2.2 per cent of the 'European' population of the Dutch East Indies were born in Germany, putting those born in Germany in fourth place, after those born locally (70.7 per cent), those born in the Netherlands (21.2 per cent) and those born in Japan (2.3 per cent).[15]

Dutch shipping also facilitated the arrival of the so-called Dutch (or Deutsch = Germans) of Pennsylvania. In the eighteenth century as many as 100,000 may have migrated to North America via the Netherlands (Enthoven 2005:167). But for the most part this migration flow took place outside the Dutch sphere. Moreover, it does not seem to have left many traces in Dutch archives (Fertig 1994:198).

Dutch policies of inclusion and exclusion of free settlers

It was noted above that a high percentage of the military and naval personnel operating in the Dutch sphere were not Dutch. Also, in both the East and the West the Dutch authorities encouraged certain non-Dutch groups to settle, Jews and Chinese in particular. Furthermore, in Brazil and in Suriname, the original European settlers, Portuguese and English respectively, were encouraged to stay when the rule over their colonies was transferred to the WIC (although the WIC sought to balance the Brazilians with northern Europeans). Similarly, in New Netherland, the Swedes of New Sweden were absorbed and Europeans of all hues were allowed to settle in the colony.

---

[15] *Volkstelling 1930*, VI:25. For an elaboration on the 'European' population of the Dutch East Indies in 1930 see below.

Goodfriend (1992:17) therefore states that 'the Company's willingness to tol-
erate all nationalities in its colony was paralleled by the acceptance of ethnic
intermarriage in New Amsterdam as a necessary way of life'. The image
of toleration – not to be confused with equality, as Goodfriend (1992:218-9)
rightly notes – of all kinds of settlers in the Dutch colonies requires some
adjustment, however, especially for the East, which we may contrast to the
West in this respect.

With respect to other Europeans, the most tolerant of the Dutch colonies
were the three settlements on the Wild Coast run from Zeeland that survived
into the eighteenth century: Berbice, Demerara and Essequibo. Especially
after 1738 British citizens were encouraged to settle there and establish plantations. Johan van Langen (Van Langen 2003:122 and elsewhere) suggests that
one of the reasons the Zeeland authorities were so tolerant towards the British
settlers was that they were trying to keep the Hollanders of the Amsterdam
Chamber of the WIC out of the affairs of these colonies. By 1800 the ratio of
Dutchmen to British was 1:7 and this preponderance of British settlers played
a role in the decision of the British government not to return the colonies to
the Dutch after the Napoleonic era. Yet also in Amsterdam-run Suriname an
English element persisted throughout the existence of the colony, which was
perhaps reinforced during the brief British interregnum in the early nineteenth century, so that the English and Scottish presence was marked, particularly in the Nickerie District, although in 1823 only fifty to sixty English
people were reported to be residing in Suriname (Van Lier 1977:24-7).

In the VOC Octrooigebied the overwhelming trend was one of exclusion
of European competitors, in view of the trade monopolies and monopsonies
the VOC sought to enforce. VOC commissioner Hendrik Adriaan van Rheede
tot Drakestein noted in 1677 that the most important privilege 'the honourable Company enjoys by right of alliance and conquest' on the Malabar coast
was the exclusion of all Europeans from the area (s'Jacob 1976:177). Van den
Boogaart (1986:70) also supposes that the burgher right of New Amsterdam
was instituted in part to keep out unwanted competitors. In the same vein
Eric Jones (2003:31, 40-50) suggests that the dual system of justice at Batavia
– administered to Company personnel by the Council of Justice and to others by the much less professional *Schepenrechtbank* – originated in the desire
of the Company to set competitors and especially Englishmen at a disadvantage. And in 1707 all Englishmen and Scots were banned from Batavia
altogether. In a recent article on Scots in the VOC Octrooigebied during the
seventeenth century Steve Murdoch (2002) therefore speaks of 'a particularly
hostile environment'.

Furthermore, lessons were learned from the West. While the VOC conquest of Malacca in 1641 ushered in a brief period of toleration of the Catholic
faith with the explicit aim of retaining the 'Portuguese' and black Christian

populations in the city, after the successful revolt of the Portuguese of Brazil against Dutch rule, the directors of the WIC convinced those of the VOC that the success of the Portuguese in Brazil might encourage their brethren in the East to revolt against the Dutch. In 1646 the Batavia High Government gave orders to the Malacca authorities to rid the city of all Catholics refusing to practice their religion in a covert manner (as was mandatory in the Netherlands as well). As a result, most of the more properly Portuguese left, although many of the less properly 'Portuguese' mestizos and black Catholics remained (Ketelaars 1985:63-5). And in stark contrast to the initial treatment of the Portuguese in Brazil, the Portuguese of Ceylon were in 1656, after the VOC conquest of the island, shipped to the South Asian mainland in some eight shiploads, with the exception of several 'widows and daughters' who chose to stay and were destined to become the wives of VOC personnel (Raben 1996:102). Similarly, at the conquest of Cochin in 1663, the Portuguese of the town were moved to Goa (s'Jacob 1976:lii).

On the other hand the VOC authorities did welcome deserters from other European companies and the like, just as the latter welcomed defectors from the Dutch side. It would be desirable to have a calculation of the net result. From qualitative data it appears that the advantage was on the English side. Wrote the English directors during the Fourth Anglo-Dutch War: 'we conceive it will be easy to prevail upon soldiers in the Dutch service in India, to bear arms in our service' (Lequin 2005:150-2).

Certain non-European groups were discouraged from settling in the Dutch enclaves or encouraged to leave them. In 1678 the Batavia High Government ordered the governor of Malacca to bar 'Moors' (in this case Indian and West Asian Muslims) from trading in the town. As a result, a large number of Indian merchants were forced to leave the town in 1680, so that the share of 'Moors' and Hindus in the population dropped from 11.2 to 3.6 per cent (Ketelaars 1985:66-8). Finally, the Chinese massacre of 1740 was less than an expression of Dutch tolerance, though not official policy. A number of historians have tried and are still trying to 'place' this event in the Dutch colonial past and compare it to similar outbreaks of violence against Chinese populations elsewhere in Asia, especially in the Spanish Philippines (Blussé 1986:89-95).

To sum up, the Dutch authorities did not just want anyone to settle in their colonies, they wanted specific groups, or people who could perform certain functions. As the governor of Malacca wrote in 1677 the colony needed more manpower 'especially of the hard-working Chinese, to promulgate the necessary agriculture and engage in other handwork and trades, to and for which the black Christians are mostly disinclined, too lazy or too slow' (Ketelaars 1985:68). The Chinese, who played an important role in the VOC area, are not discussed here but the Jews, who played an equivalent role in the Dutch West are the topic of the next subsection.

Jewish settlers

Jews played a very significant role in Dutch colonization in the Americas. It is unclear how many reached the colonies directly from the Netherlands, but most seem to have come from elsewhere. The paths of migration of groups of Jews in this early modern period were full of twists and turns, wherefore they merit a separate discussion here.

The mother of all Jewish communities in the Dutch West was the community of Jewish descent that 'migrated' into the Dutch sphere with the conquest of Portuguese Brazil. Often its members were nominally Catholic as Portuguese law required but many reconverted to the Sephardic rite of Judaism in the Dutch period. When a return of Brazil to Portuguese rule was imminent this group was presented with a problem and some opted to betake themselves to other places in the Dutch sphere. One of the refugees from fading Dutch Brazil, David Nassy, seems to have first obtained a patent to settle with 'a large number' of Jews on Curaçao, but never seems to have gone there, perhaps because the terms were less favourable than the Jews had enjoyed in Dutch Brazil and the Curaçao governor Peter Stuyvesant was less than inclined to accept them on the island. In 1659, however, Nassy obtained a patent, also from the Amsterdam Chamber of the WIC, to be the *patroon* of a Jewish colony to be created on Cayenne island in the Cayenne River, where they met some opposition from the Dutch governor but were finally allowed to settle at one end of the island. The original group seems to have been composed of Jews from Brazil and a few from Amsterdam, but they were joined by two or more shiploads of Jews recruited from Livorno, bringing the colony to some 300 to 400 individuals. Most of these people were, however, expelled or set to flight by the French who occupied Cayenne in 1664. It seems that the greater part of these refugees made their way to the so-called Jewish Savanna in the then still English Suriname colony, where a small group of Jews was already established, including those who had come from England in 1652. This group was joined in the eighteenth century by 'German' or Ashkenazic Jews recruited in Amsterdam.[16]

As the case of Nassy illustrates, Jews from Brazil were much in demand in the European colonies in the Caribbean, so much so that the English lieutenant general William Willoughby in 1667 found it expedient to carry the Jews remaining in Nassy's settlement at Cayenne with him to Barbados. Jews from Brazil brought along the expertise in sugar cane planting and refining that was highly sought after in the European colonies in the Caribbean and the Guyanas (Arbell 2001:300; Oostindie 2007). In New Amsterdam, however,

---

[16]   Arbell 2001:296-301; Israel 2001:345; compare and contrast the account of Nassy's career given in Goslinga 1971:424-5.

the 23 Jewish refugees from Brazil arriving in 1654 were not well received and were even asked to leave by Stuyvesant. He was soon corrected by the WIC directors (after a petition from the Amsterdam Portuguese Jewish community), as a result of which a small Jewish community developed in New Amsterdam (Williams 2001:377-81).

Table 4.4 Jewish population centres in the Dutch sphere

Area	Census date	Population (est.)
Recife (Brazil)	1645	1,450
New Amsterdam	1654	100
Sint Eustatius	1722	21
Curaçao	1702	>600
	1789	>1,095
	1870	878
	1905	686
Aruba	1833	31
Suriname	1684	163
	1787	1,311
	1830	1,324
	1890	1,208
	1919	1,185*
	1921	671*
Cochin	1676/1685	2,000
	1767	>2,000

Source: adapted from Drescher 2001:460 (estimates Recife and New Amsterdam); additional sources: Israel 2001:337 (Sint Eustatius 1722); Israel 2001:336-7 (Curaçao 1702) and Klooster 1994:289 (Curaçao 1789, figure does not include the Jewish servants; Israel 2001:336-7 gives 1,495); *Koloniaal Verslag* 1871 and 1906 (Curaçao 1870 and 1905); Teenstra 1836-37, II: opposite 196 (Aruba); Enthoven 2005 (Suriname 1684); Klooster 2001:350-1 (figures given by Nassy for late seventeenth-century Suriname overstated); Van Lier 1977:24 (Suriname 1787-1830; note that the figures for 1810 and 1787 are mixed up by Drescher 2001); *Koloniaal Verslag* 1891 (Suriname 1890); Segal 1993:45-6 (Cochin 1676 25 'white' families, and 1685 465 'black' families, multiplied by 4; 1767 40 'white' and 470 'black' families).

* The figures for the years 1919 and 1921 in Suriname were provided by Wieke Vink on the basis of sources in the National Archives. The figure for 1919 is based on a count by the synagogues, the 1921 figure is based on the official census count.

In the VOC Octrooigebied the only significant Jewish population was the ancient community at Cochin. This community too 'migrated' into the Dutch sphere by an act of conquest from the Portuguese. Although the Jews of Cochin lived outside the limits of Dutch jurisdiction (which extended only to the fort area and to the Christians of the region), they had welcomed the

Ruins of the old VOC fort in Sawaai Bay

VOC takeover of the fort from the Portuguese and some of them maintained close economic ties with the Dutch (Segal 1993:40-6; Singh 2007:31, 48-9, 121). For these reasons they have been included in the chart below.

Otherwise Jews were exceptional in the VOC towns (and Jews in VOC service even rarer). The foundations of today's relatively large Jewish community in South Africa were laid only after the British takeover. The first group of Jews, consisting of British and Germans, arrived in 1806 (Weisbord 1967:233). From the late nineteenth century Jews made up a small part of the European population of the Dutch East Indies, but they were subsumed under the heading of the 3.68 per cent 'other religions' (or perhaps under the 7.10 per cent 'no religious membership' or the 7.58 per cent 'religion unknown') (*Volkstelling 1930*, VI:123).

Demography of the colonial populations

A promising avenue of comparison between East and West regarding 'Dutch' migration lies in the statements we have of the relative size of population groups in various places under the Dutch flag. Although most of those statements hardly merit the name 'census', there are some for every settlement. For some places – such as Batavia and Colombo – far more such figures are to be found than for others. Moreover, the categories used in one place do not match with those used in another place or at another time. Despite these obstacles, we propose to look at the population of the 'Dutch' colonies as if they were composed of six categories, three categories of Christians and three categories of (mostly) non-Christians. First, European Christians both straight from Europe and born overseas. Second, the groups of part European descent, that is 'Eurasians', 'Eurafricans' and 'Euramericans'. Third, the groups that were otherwise produced by colonialism, namely Christian client communities and freed slaves and their descendants. Fourth, non-Christian groups that were attracted by the relatively favourable conditions the Dutch settlements offered them, most importantly the Jews and Chinese, of whom only the Jews were discussed in this chapter. Fifth, enslaved people, to be discussed in a later chapter. And sixth, local people under Dutch jurisdiction, whom we shall commence with in this section.

The reality of colonial populations was of course more complex. The graveyard at Galle yields an interesting insight into how the important colonial boundaries between Christian and non-Christian and between free and unfree intersected in Ceylon society. The graveyard was divided into four parts: the inner churchyard for European Christians and probably also mestizos considered European enough, and the outer graveyard for the rest subdivided into three sections, one for black (*swarte*; here meaning Asian, not

African) Christians both free and unfree, one for free non-Christians and one
for bonded non-Christians (Wagenaar 1994:58). In short, the markers of race
and religion were not absolute in the European colonial context, as an increasing body of literature attempts to demonstrate (for example Cannadine 2001;
Bosma and Raben 2003:12-36), nor should local deviations be ignored. With
these caveats in mind, we will attempt below to lay down some figures in
comparative tables, while trying to stay away from the patently unreliable
data.[17]

Local people

It would be somewhat pointless to attempt making a table relating to the
numbers of local people under Dutch sway, since such a table could not
indicate the various degrees to which those people were subject to Dutch
writ. Still, it is useful to put the migration flows created by the Dutch into
the perspective of the numbers already present and to give an impression
of the extent to which the Dutch presence affected the demography of those
populations.

In South Asia, on the Malay peninsula and in the archipelago, the number
of Europeans and other migrants in Dutch settlements was dwarfed by the
numbers already present. The Dutch records of the Company period furnish
some useful estimates of the population of the regions in which the VOC men
found themselves. An early and very detailed example of such an estimate is
the district-wise count of the armed population of Malabar by Van Rheede,
which is undoubtedly based on a local source, perhaps even a translation of
a locally acquired document, seeing that the Indian states of the period were
highly bureaucratic. Van Rheede calculated a number of 1,511,000 armed
Nayars (the military caste) in all of Malabar (s'Jacob 1976:92-6). He did not
try to estimate from that number the total population, but obviously the
Europeans in Cochin and the other smaller Company establishments on the
coast made up only the tiniest fraction of that number. Around 1726 François
Valentijn estimated that the population of Java was 31,161,250, an incredible
figure. More serious estimates of the last quarter of the eighteenth century,
mostly based, again, on the number of arms-bearing men or a theoretical family unit called a *cacah*,[18] arrived at somewhere in the region of two to three
and a half million.

[17]   David Henley has warned us about all the censuses conducted in the Dutch East Indies
except the 1930 census. Han Jordaan has warned us about the inflated figures laid down by Claus
van Laar for 1749 Curaçao. Wieke Vink, finally, has warned us about the figures provided by the
Jewish communities of Suriname of their own numbers (see table 4.4).
[18]   For a discussion of this term see Boomgaard 1989:207-13.

The Caribbean and South America, by contrast, were sparsely populated, especially due to the impact of diseases brought by the Spanish and the Portuguese a century before the arrival of the Dutch (McNeill 1976). The Dutch presence in the New Netherland region was only one more stage in this process. The Amerindians of the area suffered more from the diseases brought by the Dutch than they did from warring with the Dutch. The Huron and Iroqois confederations were perhaps reduced by as much as ninety per cent during several smallpox epidemics in the New Netherland period. Emmer and Klooster (1999:54-5) note that this figure was comparable to the English and French colonies in North America, while the small number of European victims of these epidemics in the Dutch colony was unique. By way of explanation, they suggest that the exposure of the Europeans who came to New Netherland to the smallpox epidemics raging around the theatres of the Thirty Years' War (1618-1648) had been greater because the catchment area of 'Dutch' migrants was closer to those theatres than the French and English catchment areas.

The only area under Dutch control in the West where Native Americans remained the majority into the nineteenth century was Aruba, with 1,401 Free Coloured people 'mostly of Indian origin' (although all Christian) in 1825, compared to only 169 whites and 399 slaves (Coomans-Eustatia, Coomans and Van der Lee 1998:219). In 1950, in Suriname, Native Americans made up only around one per cent of the population of Paramaribo and the plantation zone/coastal line, that is 1,846 people, with another 1,700 living in the less accessible areas (Van Lier 1977:297).

But this effect of Dutch colonization was not confined to the New World. In some ways Taiwan was comparable to the New World, witnessing both the displacement of the indigenous people whose existence depended in part on hunting and fishing by colonists engaged in plantation agriculture and the wiping out of part of the indigenous population by diseases carried by colonists from Europe. In 1636 it was reported that

> the Almighty, Who is our unfailing Guardian, had inflicted over the past year such pestilential diseases upon the villages of the murderers [the indigenous Taiwanese] that about half of the inhabitants had died, so that hopefully it will be less difficult to reach the objective of our intentions (Van Veen 2003:149).

The decimation of the indigenous population of Taiwan paved the way for Chinese migration to Taiwan in the Dutch period,[19] which laid the foundation for the present-day identity of the island. But we can not devote any more space to that here in view of the European heritage perspective we are taking in this chapter.

---

[19]   Van Veen 2003:147-50; Yao 2003:137; Oosterhoff 1985:54-5.

The Dutch also brought disease to the Cape, smallpox in particular. In 1713 great numbers of Khoikhoi died and 'lay everywhere on the roads [...] cursing at the Dutchmen, who they said had bewitched them' (Crosby 1993:35). This epidemic was followed by a further two in 1755 and 1767; the latter leaving the Swellendam area virtually empty of Khoikhoi, because those who had fled the epidemic found their lands taken over by *trekboers* upon their return (Viljoen 2006:17).

In Elmina the population was also greatly reduced by a smallpox epidemic at the end of the seventeenth century (Feinberg 1989:77-92), although in the literature this has not been attributed to contact with the Dutch. Still, Elmina was isolated by the Sahara from the densely populated belt stretching from Europe and North Africa to China, through which viruses could spread and mutate easily, according to the theory of Alfred Crosby as elaborated by Jared Diamond.

In the Indonesian archipelago, on the other hand, the local population seems to have increased under Dutch rule, especially in the later period. Gerrit Knaap has painstakingly gathered evidence from the mass of VOC data on the population of the Spice Islands to demonstrate that it did grow somewhat in the third quarter of the seventeenth century, although the population never recovered from the huge casualties sustained during the VOC wars to enforce a monopoly in the early century (Knaap 2004:127-58).

On Java the indigenous population was long supposed to have grown at a very fast rate during the nineteenth century (supposedly due largely to smallpox vaccination introduced around 1820!), but Widjojo Nitisastro has cast aspersions on the official nineteenth-century figures and on the late eighteenth-century estimates of J.C.M. Radermacher, W. van Hogendorp and S.C. Nederburgh, cited above, which he considers too low (Nitisastro 1970:40-7; Gooszen 1999:3-7). More recently, however, Anthony Reid, Peter Boomgaard, R.E. Elson and David Henley have upheld modified versions of the high growth rates, attributing these to different causes related to a greater or lesser extent to the Dutch presence. According to Elson, even the most far-reaching of the Dutch colonial policies, the implementation of the Cultivation System (see Chapter VI), which Nitisastro thought detrimental, stimulated population growth.[20] According to the only reliable census conducted in the Dutch East Indies, that of 1930, the population of Java and Madura stood at 41,719,364 and the total population of the Dutch East Indies at 60,727,233 (*Volkstelling 1930*, VI:18).

[20]   Henley 2005; Elson 1994; Boomgaard 1989.

Europeans in the colonies

Emmer and Klooster (1999:57-8) suggest that the average mortality rate was higher in the Dutch Atlantic sphere than in comparable European Atlantic empires. Of course, as will be clear from our discussion in section two, we have no such figure as the average mortality rate in the Dutch Atlantic, but Emmer and Klooster's observation that after the fall of New Netherland the Dutch Atlantic sphere 'did not include any settlement colonies with a benign disease environment' is noteworthy. At that time the only remaining Dutch possession in the temperate zone was the Cape Colony, which, although situated on the Atlantic, was part of the VOC Octrooigebied.

Yet the birth rates of Europeans in the tropics should not be underestimated; a substantial number of the 'European' VOC personnel were born in Asia, as can for instance be seen in table 4.1 listing the birthplaces of the Bengal directorate. Furthermore, after the advent of modern medicine, living in the tropics became less of a problem for Europeans. The officers in charge of the 1930 census in the Dutch East Indies suggest that the greater part of the accretion of the European population between 1860 and 1930 was due to natural increase rather than immigration. It must be noted, however, that the category 'European' had been considerably enlarged in the meantime and by 1930 seems to have included the greater part of the Eurasians (Meijer 2004:26, 31-3), as well as *gelijkgestelden* or people granted equivalent standing, including Japanese, Egyptians, Armenians and Turks, although the Chinese with such a status were counted with the Chinese.

Included in the next table are some of the more reliable figures we have for the (Christian) European populations of the Dutch sphere. The numbers given there are as inclusive as possible. In general they include both European settlers and Company/state officers, as well as the families of those European men. With respect to the latter, these figures create a somewhat inflated image of the European gene pool in the colonies, because in the pre-1800 period in particular, most European men married mestizo or local women. Furthermore, mestizos were sometimes counted along with the Europeans anyway (see below).

The right-hand column of the table gives the percentage of Europeans among the total population of each locality. These figures do, however, not always give a meaningful insight into the proportion of the Christian Europeans relative to the population of the host societies, especially in the Asian sphere. As was noted in the previous section on local people, it is often quite impossible to put a precise figure to the local population just outside Dutch jurisdiction. Rather, the right-hand column figure should be seen as an index of the concentration of Europeans in the limited area defined by the place name given in the first column. As such, these figures reflect the different settlement patterns in the Dutch sphere. While in the East Europeans initially lived concentrated in harbour towns, in Suriname they lived both in Paramaribo and on the plantations among great numbers of slaves and later indentured labourers. These figures also reflect the dramatic change that took place in the East in the post-Company period when the Dutch acquired jurisdiction over large numbers of local people and the Europeans fanned out over the Indonesian Archipelago to administer districts and establish plantations.

Euramericans, Eurafricans and Eurasians

In 1633 and 1663 the kings of Siam issued edicts stipulating that Siamese women and women of the Mon minority were not to marry *farang*, European men. By 1689, however, there were seventeen children with Dutch fathers and Siamese or Mon mothers in the Dutch compound beside Ayutthaya, the capital of Siam (Pombejra 2000; Ruangsilp 2007:39-45). Apparently it was difficult to implement population policies in the early modern period, unless there was great determination on the part of the authorities and drastic measures were taken – such as the banishment from Japan of all Europeans, along with their wives, concubines and mixed offspring in the late 1630s, as well as the consequent isolation of the remaining Dutchmen from local people (Blussé 1986:184-5).

As was already noted, in the early years of the VOC's existence the establishment of colonies (in the sense of procreating groups of people) was encouraged by a number of prominent VOC figures in the East, although the directors at home remained sceptical. In several places VOC men were encouraged to marry local women. Coen sought to make his colony at Batavia a decent one and made cohabitation out of wedlock punishable in 1620, but the Plakkaat (by-law) of 1649, which tied European men married to local women to the Octrooigebied, might have indirectly encouraged concubinage (Blussé 1986; Bosma and Raben 2003:26, 38-45, 68-9). It would be of some use to have a percentage-wise overview of European VOC personnel married to

---

of the European VOC servants and the circa 50 family members of the freeburghers); Ketelaars 1985:66 (Malacca 1681 figure includes 'Dutch' *freeburghers* and families, and householding VOC personnel and families); Knaap 2004:132 (Kota Ambon, figure does not include VOC personnel); Raben 1996:87-100, 305-32 and Lequin 2005 (Batavia figures for city and Ommelanden added up, 1673 figure only partly includes VOC personnel, 1729 figure 1,755 burghers and 4,778 Company personnel of whom 118 indigenous and 172 born in Asia); Boomgaard and Gooszen 1991 (Batavia 1844, Surabaya, Semarang); *Volkstelling 1930*, VIII:2, 18 (Dutch East Indies).

local women in relation to those cohabiting with local women. The prime obstacle to marriage was religion: women had to be or become Christians in order to be allowed to marry European VOC personnel. Racial difference in marriage was perhaps frowned upon by some Company managers, but such objections never materialized into official policy, although after the 1630s marriage in general was somewhat discouraged, especially with regard to the lower ranks of the VOC (Kolff and Van Santen 1979:18-31; Bosma and Raben 2003:26-45, 68-9; Jones 2003:33-5).

In any case, the result of both concubinage and marriage was that most Dutch establishments in the East had a number of people drawing on both European and non-European gene pools. As early as the seventeenth century, while abolishing the policy of bringing Company daughters to the Indies, the directors believed that 'when our men marry native women, strong robust children are produced, who stay alive' (Blussé 1986:161). The directors may have had something of a point when they highlighted the health of mestizo offspring. Van der Brug (1994:61-2) has calculated that the mortality rate in Batavia was lower among mestizos and Mardijkers (see below) than among European women (it is not possible to calculate a general figure for European men), although the mestizos and Mardijkers too suffered from the malaria epidemic of the 1730s. Still, Batavia was a somewhat unhealthy place even for those born in the city, such as the mestizos and Mardijkers, among whom the mortality rate was about twice the average rate for city dwellers in contemporary Europe.

In general, the mixed relationships were between European men and non-European or mestizo women, not the other way around. In the late eighteenth century it even became good practice among the higher European echelons to maintain a number of non-European women. In the period that was perhaps the most decadent – the short period around 1800 between the end of the Company and the British interregnum – Dutch officials flaunted their '*serails*' openly and sometimes publicly celebrated the birth of children by their concubines, as three examples cited by Boomgaard (1989:159) show. Concubinage of European men with Asian women continued into the twentieth century, while the opposite remained quite unthinkable. When one of the Javanese princes who had attended the coronation of Wilhelmina in 1898 in the Netherlands, planned to bring back the Dutch prostitute he had been living with during his stay, the Minister of Colonies suggested to the Indies government that the prostitute should be refused entry into the country and sent a photograph to help customs identify her.[21] It may be noted in this context that Meijer (2004:31) suggests that the greater part of the present-day Indo-Dutch community is not descended from the old mestizo community,

[21]   NA, Ministerie van Koloniën 6256, secret *verbaal*, 27-9-1898 no. Y18.

but from the nineteenth- and early twentieth-century European soldiers and their indigenous concubines. Between 1888 and 1911 almost half of the subaltern officers and one in five of the common soldiers had a local woman living with them in the barracks.

Concerning the Cape colony, there is an ongoing debate as to what percentage of its society might be considered the result of mixed relations and how any such percentages can be explained. As can be seen in table 4.3 the European male genetic input into the Afrikaner community far outweighed the female European input. The number of *freeburgher* men per 100 *freeburgher* women dropped only slowly, from 260 in 1690 to 140 in 1770. The surplus men would supposedly have satisfied their sexual needs with local or slave women, mostly out of wedlock, because mixed marriages made up only around two per cent of the marriages recorded at the Cape church over the entire VOC period (Elphick and Shell 1979:128-32; see also Shell 1994:173).

A traveller of the 1780s suggested that a sixth of the Khoikhoi population was in fact of mixed descent. The offspring of Khoikhoi women and European or slave men were referred to as *bastaards*. Perhaps *bastaards* of part European descent had a bigger chance of surviving smallpox, as the case of Jan Paerl suggests (see Viljoen 2006:17). But since these *bastaards* were not generally recognized by their fathers, they were considered part of Khoikhoi society. In the late eighteenth century sometimes a distinction was made between the terms Bastaard-Hottentots for the children of slave fathers and Khoikhoi mothers, who were indentured as a group, and *bastaards* for the Khoikhoi of part European descent (Viljoen 2006:3, 16-7, 175; Elphick and Shell 1979:133-4).

While the Bastaard-Hottentots inherited a modified degree of their father's status (not slave but still indentured), the offspring of European men and female slaves most often retained the slave identity of their mothers in the Cape as well as in the West. Although there are cases in which the father tried to obtain *freeburgher* status for his (male) children, there is a significant contrast between the treatment of mestizos as a group in the Asian establishments of the VOC and in its Cape establishment. In the Cape the rights of mestizos were not clearly defined but varied greatly, along with the category under which they were subsumed: that of slave, Khoikhoi, 'Free Black' and occasionally European. The slave status of the mestizo children of Company slave women and Europeans – nearly half of the children under twelve at the Company slave lodge in 1685 – shocked the influential commissioner Van Rheede, who ruled that these children should be manumitted and absorbed into European society, while also laying down regulations to stop further miscegenation. Neither of these measures seem to have had much effect (Elphick and Shell 1979:127, 133-5).

The situation in Suriname was comparable to the Cape in that people of mixed descent were divided between the slave and free categories. In 1830 about 43 per cent of the people of part European descent (Eurafricans) found themselves in slavery, the remainder formed part of the Free Black population (Van Lier 1977:71). But the situation in Suriname also differed from the Cape in that the great majority of 'mixed' people were not the offspring of Europeans and indigenous people like the *bastaards*, but of Europeans and African slaves, who will be discussed in Chapter V.

In the early seventeenth century, the more successful of the Dutch ventures on the Essequibo seems to have been sustained by marital alliances with the Native Americans of the region. A 1637 Spanish letter reported that 'the Dutch being so mixed with the Indians that they marry with the Carib women, as well as with those of other tribes'. This close alliance seems to have been the work of governor Adriaan Groenewegen, who was reported to understand the 'humours' of the Indians well, and upon whose death, in 1664, the colony was wiped out by the English (Goslinga 1971:413-25). In Dutch Brazil there were also marriages between Europeans and Native American women, with official approval, although in the Ceará region such unions led to some acrimony and were consequently forbidden (Schalkwijk 1998:49-50).

Like all Europeans engaged in the European expansion, the Dutch used a bewildering array of terms for the offspring of Europeans and non-Europeans. It seems that in the West the term 'mulatto' was the most common and in the East 'mestizo'. In Africa the term 'tapoeier' also occurs for those of mixed European and African descent. Most confusing are the terms used for the different grades of 'European-ness'. The term 'castizo', which the Portuguese used for people of 'pure' European descent born in Asia, was adopted by some Dutchmen for people of mixed descent. Nieuhoff averred that it was used in Pulicat for the offspring of two mestizos, but noted in the context of Nagapatnam that it was used for the offspring of black (*swarte*) fathers and Portuguese mothers (Nieuhoff 1682:107, 113). For the 1790 census of Cochin the term 'white castizo' was invented and applied to 469 people, distinguished from a group of 180 mestizos (Singh 2007:172 and Appendix 1). Lodewijk Wagenaar gives a tabular exegesis of the use of the terms 'castizo', 'mestizo' and 'pustizo' in Ceylon, on the basis of a list of names of Galle inhabitants in 1755, which we insert here:

In the West a similar array of terms existed – perhaps even more complicated because the people making up colonial society originated from three continents rather than two – which were employed in as confusing a manner to the present-day observer. It appears, for instance, that the term 'mestizos' (*mustiezen*) was in late eighteenth-century Curaçao used for the children of mulattos and whites (Klooster 1994:294), while mulattos were really the equivalent of the mestizos of the East. Other terms were 'sambos' for the children of mulattos and blacks and 'pardos' for the offspring of Africans and

The 'New Dutch Church' in Ambon

Amerindians (Klooster 1994:294; Enthoven 2007:18).

The numbers of people of part European descent were generally under-estimated in official counts. For reasons discussed in the following section 'Ways of counting', they were often counted with the Europeans in the East and counted with the 'Free Blacks' or slaves in the West. Moreover, it is difficult to find two censuses using the same criteria. For late seventeenth-century Malacca we know that in the censuses of 1680, 1687 and 1688 non-Dutch wives of Dutchmen were not included in the number of Dutchmen, but for the years 1675, 1678 and 1681 they were (Ketelaars 1985:67). One is advised to keep these caveats in mind when reading the following table.

Topasses/Mardijkers/'Free Blacks'

While the groups discussed in the sections 'Europeans in the colonies' and 'Euramericans, Eurafricans and Eurasians' represented the genetic drift of Europe into a new environment, this section looks at what may be called 'memetic drift', to wit the proliferation of European ideas and ways. The groups dealt with in this section were all to some extent Europeanized but not generally descended from Europeans.

The Topasses of southern India, Ceylon and Timor were one such group. They were often of purely 'Asian' descent but baptized and Lusified to a certain extent. They were closely associated with the Portuguese by the Dutch and in fact often included in the term 'Portuguese'.[22] On Ceylon, however, they were considered a nuisance and in the early 1660s there were several plans to ship them off the island, as had been done with the other 'Portuguese' right

Table 4.6 Terms for people of mixed descent in Ceylon in 1755

Father	Mother	Child
European	Native	Mixties
European	Mixties	Casties
European	Casties	Casties
Casties	Casties	Poesties
Casties	Mixties	Not found
Casties	Native	Mixties
Mixties	Mixties	Not found
Mixties	Native	Mixties

Source: Wagenaar 1994:48.

---

[22]   Also in other places the term 'Portuguese' as used by the Dutch was somewhat open-ended and did not necessarily include only persons of (part) European descent, for example in Malacca (Ketelaars 1985:65-6).

after the conquest. In 1663 Rijklof van Goens wrote that 'Colombo and Galle are swarming with evil-disposed Portuguese of the lowest kind who refuse to work and, increasing fast like weeds, are a great danger to the community'. As this quotation also indicates, not much seems to have been effected in the way of removing the Topasses from the island, although a considerable drop in their number may be noted for Colombo between 1684 and 1694 (Raben 1996:102-3).

In Cochin the Topasses were also considered a danger in the first period after the conquest in 1663, although the treaty with the raja of Cochin stipulated that all Roman Catholic Christians would come under the jurisdiction of the Dutch as inheritors of the Portuguese position, while the Syrian orthodox or St. Thomas Christians were to remain under the jurisdiction of the raja. This was something of an irony because conqueror Van Goens hoped to find the most loyal allies of the Dutch among the latter Christians and toyed with the idea of letting them renounce the Pope explicitly, but the High Government dissuaded him. After the Dutch takeover, only some 22 Topass households remained within the walls of the fortress, which the Dutch greatly reduced in size; the remaining 4,000 odd Topasses were left to live on the surrounding islands, making up about half the population of the agglomeration of Cochin, which was spread over a few islands. Apart from

Table 4.7 Free people of part European descent in the Dutch sphere, 1673-1854

Area	Census date	Population (est.)
Sint Eustatius	1829	196
Curaçao	1825	2,358
Bonaire	1833	860
Suriname	1830	3,947
Elmina	End of 18th century	1,500
Cochin	1760	415
	1790	649
Colombo	1684	640
Galle	1760	208
Malacca	1681	322
Batavia	1673	726
	1729	1,050
	1769	1,224
Java	1854	9,360

Sources: Teenstra 1836-37, II:330 and opposite 190 (Sint Eustatius and Bonaire); Coomans-Eustatia, Coomans and Van der Lee 1998:199 (Curaçao); Doortmont and Smit 2007:312 (Elmina); Singh 2007:172 and Appendix I (Cochin); Raben 1996:104 (Colombo) and 305-32 (Batavia: figures for city and Ommelanden added up); Wagenaar 1994:46 (Galle: 123 Eurasian VOC servants and their circa 85 family members); Ketelaars 1985:66 (Malacca); Prins 1933:670 (Java).

the Lusified Topasses (whose Lusification was especially manifest in dress and speach), there were Malayalam-speaking Roman Catholics, from whose ranks were drawn the so-called Lascarins, indigenous Christian troops. The Lascarins were allowed to settle on the land owned by the Company around the city.[23] One might say that the Topasses and Lascarins represent different degrees of memetic drift.

In Southeast Asia the most important Europeanized group were the so-called Mardijkers. This word originated in the application of the term *orang merdeka* or free man to the free Moluccans educated and baptized by the Portuguese. In Batavia, Mardijker came to be applied to Christian Portuguese-speaking people of Asian origin, many of them freed people who had arrived as slaves from South Asia, others former inhabitants of Portuguese colonies who had moved to or remained in Dutch establishments (Blussé 1986:165). In late seventeenth-century Kota Ambon the Mardijkers were not listed separately, but were initially counted mostly under the native category and later largely transferred to the European category along with some Makassarian burghers. This largely explains the rise in Europeans that one may note in table 4.5 (Knaap 2004:132).

A group somewhat comparable to the Mardijkers of Southeast Asia was the 'Free Black' category at the Cape. This group consisted of manumitted slaves and their descendants as well as the Asian exiles and convicts whose term had expired. As elsewhere in the VOC Octrooigebied, the term black (*swart*) did not apply only to Equatorial Africans (who were mostly referred to by the term Caffers, which the Dutch derived from the Arabic word for unbelievers), but to anyone not of European descent. In fact, the 'Free Black' community consisted for the greater part of Asians. A difference with the Mardijker community, however, was that part of the Free Blacks were Muslim, and managed to make some converts to Islam among the slave population. In 1722 the community was given its own militia company and the two artillery companies that developed from this played an important role in the defence of the colony against the English in 1806. This group was thus sufficiently associated with the Dutch colonial establishment to be included here in the Europeanized groups, its boundaries being at times clearly demarcated from the burgher community, but at other times not (Elphick and Shell 1979:116, 145-55).

The following table lists the Topasses, Mardijkers and Cape Free Blacks as well as 'Free Blacks' of the West in so far as we found them listed separately from people of part European descent:

---

[23]   Roelofsz 1943:366; Singh 2007:43, 99, 103; s'Jacob 1976:lii-liii, 164-8 (Memoir of Hendrik van Rheede 1677).

Table 4.8 Europeanized groups in the Dutch sphere

Area	Census date	Population (est.)
Sint Eustatius	1829	89
Curaçao	1825	2,969
Bonaire	1833	1,069
Aruba	1833	1,888
Cape	1670	13
	1711	63
	1770	352
Cochin	1663	4,000
Colombo	1684	172
	1694	25
Malacca	1681	1,409
Batavia	1673	5,362
	1729	8,026
	1769	5,204

Sources: Teenstra 1836-37:330 and opposite 190 (Sint Eustatius, Bonaire and Aruba, Free Blacks, not including Free People of Colour); Coomans-Eustatia, Coomans and Van der Lee 1998:199 (Curaçao: Free Blacks, not including Free Coloureds); Raben 1996:104-6 (Colombo: Topasses); Singh 2007:43 (Cochin: Topasses estimate after conquest); Ketelaars 1985:66 (Malacca: 'Free Black Christians' and 'Portuguese'); Elphick and Shell 1979:148 (Cape: Free Blacks); Raben 1996:305-32 (Batavia, figures for city and Ommelanden added up).

Ways of counting

Because the censuses conducted in the West did often not enumerate separately the groups discussed above under the headings 'Euramericans, Eurafricans and Eurasians' and 'Topasses/Mardijkers/"Free Blacks"', it is difficult to compare the figures from that hemisphere to the ones we have for the East. Furthermore, the modes of enumeration used by the Dutch authorities changed over time and developed in different directions in East and West, with regional variations again within the two hemispheres. Perhaps there was an inverse relation between the inclusion of non-Dutch Europeans in the colonial elite (see the subsection 'Dutch policies of inclusion and exclusion of free settlers') and the inclusion of mixed offspring of Europeans in the same elite during the WIC/VOC period. But although the policies in East and West with regard to the inclusion/exclusion of other Europeans converged after that time, the official views of people of part European descent continued to diverge.

In Suriname mulattos (were) moved away from the white category over time. An important date in this respect is 1754. Before that year the Jewish mulattos of Suriname were considered full members of the Jewish community, but after that they became mere 'congregants' (Frankel 2001:409). After circa 1900 the term 'Creoles' came in vogue to describe the collective of the mulattos and blacks (except the Maroons) in Suriname. The 1950 census distinguished the following six categories within the 'Creole' or 'Black-Coloured' category: Surinamer, Neger, Bosch-neger, mixed for one generation, mixed for two generations and mixed for three generations or more (*Volkstelling* 1950, X:42) As it turned out, 58 per cent of the Creoles considered themselves 'mixed' for two or more generations. At that time the Creoles were the largest group in Suriname, making up 40.8 per cent of the population (Van Lier 1977:297-300; *Voorlopig resultaat* 1971:4).

On Curaçao more 'in between' categories were officially recognized and the European category there was somewhat more permeable than in Suriname. The militia of Curaçao, for instance, was divided into three units: one of whites, one of Free Blacks and one of mulattos. A parade in 1740 saw an interesting debate over precedence, at which the Free Blacks argued: 'That they should be more esteemed than the mulattos [and] that they had kings of their race and that the mulattos did not have any, also if there were no negroes there would have been no mulattos, they negroes had also been on the island before the mulattos' (Enthoven 2007:36).

The Free Blacks and mulattos, however, were also collectively set apart from the white population of Curaçao in that by 1816 they were all (except for twenty people) Roman Catholics, in common with the slave population, while nearly all Europeans were either Protestant or Jewish. Only the *musties* offspring of mulattos and whites were counted among the *freeburghers* in the second half of the eighteenth century and were enrolled in the white militia of the island, made up of about one fifth *mustiezen* in 1789 (214 out of 1,063 men) (Klooster 1994:293-4; Coomans-Eustatia, Coomans and Van der Lee 1998:106, 159).

In the East the European category was still more permeable than on Curaçao and the developments there sharply contrast with those in Suriname. While the number of mestizos was already systematically underestimated during the VOC period, in the course of the nineteenth century the census category 'Europeans' became more and more inclusive. The patrilinear character of this category was also continued in the post-Company period.

Bosma and Raben suggest that the registered number of mestizos in Batavia was depressed by two factors. First, the mestizos working and living at the Batavia castle were not counted. Second, the term 'mestizo' was as much a social as a racial term – people who had acquired a high status may simply not have been counted as mestizos (Bosma and Raben 2003:67-8). What may also have contributed to the low figure of mestizo registrations in the VOC period was that being a mestizo became a disadvantage with respect to employment by the VOC. In 1727 the High Government instituted a by-law which stated that 'Indian children' were only to be hired in emergencies

(Bosma and Raben 2003:63-70). The Ceylon government laid down that of the total number of clerks on the island two thirds were to be European and one third castizos and pustizos, 'but no mestizos' (Wagenaar 1994:48).

In 1818 a Civil Register was established for Europeans and their descendants and further regulations laid down in 1828 ensured that only the European father could enter a child with a non-European concubine in the register. After 1867 such 'natural' children could also become 'legal' children if recognized by the father (Boomgaard and Gooszen 1991:67; Meijer 2004:389, note 70). Although many Europeans did not recognize their offspring – Meijer (2004:32-3) estimates that 'thousands' were thus left out of the European category – many others did, even if sometimes imparting the child out of wedlock with their family name spelled in reverse. When Governor General A.J. Duymaer van Twist had a survey prepared of the exact number of mestizos in Java in 1854, it turned out that half of the registered Europeans were mestizos (9,360 out of circa 18,000). And even that may have been an underestimation, since the local officials who were asked to provide the figures were not supposed to investigate people's family background but only to look for the 'distinguishing skin colour' among the registered Europeans in their locality (Prins 1933:670).

A further contribution to the growth of the European category was the regulation of 1896 laying down that women were to follow their husbands into any one of the three status categories of the Dutch East Indies: Native, Foreign Oriental or European. Since around 1900 only two per cent of the (formerly) European women were married to non-Europeans and thirteen per cent of the European men were married to non-Europeans, this meant a net increase of the European category, even more strongly when the percentage of non-European wives increased to 27.5 per cent in 1925 and only gradually decreased to twenty per cent in 1940. European women entering into mixed marriages remained few, but nevertheless became the subject of great controversy in the late 1930s, drawing much attention to the double standards for women and men and for Europeans and Natives maintained by Europeans in the Dutch East Indies and in the Netherlands (Locher-Scholten 2000:147, 187-209).

The result of all this was that by 1930 the majority of the people in the European category in the Dutch East Indies were wholly or partly of Asian descent, while in Suriname the 'mixed' people fell outside the European category. We may juxtapose Figures 4.9 and 4,10.

The variation in the modes of enumeration over space and time in the Dutch sphere needs to be further researched. Why did the Curaçaoan authorities stop counting people along colour lines in 1841 (compare Renkema 1981:338)? Why did, by contrast, descent or *landaard* and racial mixture become such all important concerns in Suriname censuses up until the mid-

Table 4.9 Suriname: 'free people', including people of part European descent

Area	Census date	Population (est.)
Suriname	1738	598
	1787	650
	1791	1,760
	1812	3,075
	1830	5,041
	1910	52,369 (Creoles)
	1950	74,918 (Creoles)

Source: Van Lier 1977:71, 190, 297.

Table 4.10 The Dutch East Indies: 'Europeans', including free people of part European descent

Area	Census date	Number
Java	1853	18,000
Dutch East Indies	1860	43,876
	1900	91,142
	1930	240,417
	1946	283,000

Sources: Prins 1930:670 (Java); *Volkstelling 1930*, VIII:18 (Indies 1860-1930); Beets et al 2002:37 (Indies 1946).

twentieth century? Why did the category 'Europeans' become so narrow in early twentieth-century Suriname that it probably did not even include Jews? Why did the same category become so widely encompassing in the Dutch East Indies? A thorough investigation of the modes of counting will give a valuable insight into which group boundaries mattered in different contexts.

The spread of culture

Is it possible in any way to relate the figures of migration flows and populations (genes) given in the tables above to the spread of culture (memes)? As a measure of the cultural impact, or memetic drift, of Dutch colonization we propose to briefly look at the spread of Dutch and other languages and religions in the different parts of the Dutch sphere.

Very generally it may be said that the Dutch language had little impact. For that reason Hein Eersel (1998:208) states that it should be investigated why the formidable colonial power that the Netherlands was, left so little of its language in the former colonies. In many places where the Dutch arrived, there was already a language in place that could carry, as it were, a colonial society. This was the case in most of the Asian establishments, where (Creole) Portuguese continued as the lingua franca and turned out to be inexterminable, to the grief of some VOC officials (Blussé 1986:165; Groeneboer 1998:55). This was also the case on Curaçao, where the lingua franca Papiamentu owed its roots to the Spanish and Sephardic presence on the island as well as to the Portuguese presence on the African slave coasts. On the Dutch Windward Antilles Creole English persisted and continues to be spoken till the present day. A nineteenth-century visitor remarked that 'not one of the citizens understands a word of Dutch' (Teenstra 1836-37, II:370). In Suriname the Creole language Sranantongo ('Negro-English') was already so well established when the Dutch arrived that it continues to be the first language of the Creole community.

There were, however, times and places where the Dutch language did gain a foothold. In Suriname Dutch is used beside Sranantongo in everyday business as well as in official matters and some argue that a Surinamese Dutch exists (Van Donselaar 2005). Pidgin languages based on Dutch arose in the Berbice region and on three of the Virgin Islands. The latter language, called 'Negro Dutch', continued to be spoken after the islands were taken over by the Danes and became extinct only in the twentieth century (De Vries, Willemyns and Burger 1993:275-9). In New Amsterdam too, Dutch appears to have been commonly used, also by non-Dutch Europeans. When the Lutherans, many of whom were German, requested a pastor, they asked for a 'Hollander', because 'the Dutch language is most commonly used here'. The Dutch language and culture would remain important for a long time after the English takeover. Some thirty years later, Charles Lodwick observed that New York was 'too great a mixture of nations and English the least part' (quoted in Goodfriend 1992:3, 16). Finally, at the Cape, Dutch slowly replaced Portuguese; Afrikaans is still a major language in South Africa.

It is well known among historians of the European expansion that the Dutch Indies did not have a Thomas Macaulay who made it government policy to turn the Indians of British India into Englishmen in all but skin colour in 1835. It seems that the Dutch colonial authorities even took the British policy as an example of how not to proceed (Groeneboer 1998). Consequently, the proliferation of the Dutch language in the Dutch East Indies lagged far behind the spread of the English language in British India. Even among the Indo-Dutch community only about a quarter seems to have had an active command of the Dutch language around 1900, although after the First World War a certain Hollandization occurred among this group and Dutch became their language for the public space (Meijer 2004:33, 68-79). The report of 1930 census applauded the great increase in the number of people able to write Dutch, but the percentage of people able to write Dutch was still only 6.1 per cent among literate Javans and 11.1 per cent among the literate Foreign Orientals (*Volkstelling 1930*, VIII:31).

The lack of zeal of Dutchmen in spreading their language should, however, not be overstated. In 1659 the Dutch governor of Ceylon issued a Plakkaat in order 'to propagate and establish the Dutch language, while rooting out and abolishing the Portuguese language, so that [...] the name and memory of our enemy may be forgotten and ours engraved'. Despite the severe punishments for speaking Portuguese laid down in the Plakkaat, the measure remained ineffectual; Dutch did not become more than an official language of government and the language of the Dutch Reformed Church on the island (Groeneboer 1995:2). There were also voices in nineteenth-century Dutch colonial politics demanding more schooling in Dutch for the people of the Dutch East Indies, although the policies which they initiated were as a rule quickly withdrawn (Groeneboer 1998). In Suriname, moreover, language policies took a remarkable U-turn in the late nineteenth century. While slaves had been strongly discouraged from learning Dutch, and the Herrnhutter missionaries proselytized in Sranantongo, in 1876 it was suddenly ordained that all school instruction should be in Dutch. This policy was more or less pursued until some years after the Second World War and is responsible for the continued importance of Dutch in Suriname, up until the present (Eersel 1998).

Most interesting, if one wants to pursue the analogy between memes and genes, is the mixing of languages that occurred within the Dutch sphere. Most thoroughly researched are the complex roots of Afrikaans, to which Malay, Portuguese, German and French contributed and which developed parallel strains among the Khoikhoi and white population (Ponelis 1993). The first known written sentence of Afrikaans reflects the colonial competition for territory amid which this Creole language came into being: "'t Za lustigh duytsman; een woordt calm, ons u kelum'/'Be quiet Dutchman, speak one word and we will slit your throat' (De Vries, Willemyns and Burger 1993:279-84). In the Dutch East Indies a Creole Dutch also developed, called Petjok, but this was only used by the Indo-Dutch population and opposed by the school authorities. It is now practically extinct. Yet despite the meagre investment in Dutch education in the Dutch East Indies and the fact that Dutch is now treated in Indonesia as a dead language (only used to gain access to old texts), there are some 7,000 Dutch loan words in the form of Malay called Bahasa Indonesia (De Vries 2005; Eersel 1998:207). In Suriname, Sranantongo and Surinamese Dutch borrow from each other's vocabulary, although there also seems to be such a thing as 'deep' Sranantongo, using few Dutch words (De Haan 1994:10).

The most enduring effect of the Dutch colonial enterprise with regards to language was the spread of languages other than Dutch (and also in this respect the meme-gene analogy presents itself). Many European languages were disseminated through Dutch efforts: Portuguese to Batavia and German to the furthest corners of the Dutch sphere, such as the Cape, where it seems

The Ambon market

to have survived until the end of the Dutch period (Moritz 1938:98-102). But also Chinese languages to Taiwan and Suriname, and Malay through the Indonesian archipelago (Groeneboer 1998).

As the examples of South Africa and Taiwan demonstrate, the spread of language was often related in some way to the spread of genes. But this was not the case for lingua francas such as Malay in Indonesia and Dutch in Suriname, nor was it the case for Negro Dutch and Sranantongo, which started out as pidgin languages for basic communication between uprooted people. In the case of lingua francas and pidgin languages there seems to be an inverse relation between the concentration index of Europeans (see table 4.5) and the promulgation of such languages, perhaps precisely because the greater mingling of people in the more intensively colonial contexts where the Dutch were able to spread out over large areas required such common languages.

Although language and religion were seen to be closely linked by contemporaries, the spread of religions is an even more complex subject than the spread of languages. In seventeenth-century Ceylon, for instance, the propagation of Dutch was thought necessary to aid the propagation of the Dutch Reformed religion (Groeneboer 1995:8), and the German missionary G. Simon, active in the Dutch East Indies, thought that with their support for Malay, the Dutch authorities were also aiding the spread of Islam (Steenbrink 1993:107-8). But while language and religion are often tied up in group identities, there are several more factors involved in the dissemination of religion than in the spread of language.

On the whole, the Dutch colonial authorities failed to spread their religion (that is, the Dutch Reformed religion and after 1848 also other Christian denominations, including the Catholic), except in South Africa, the Moluccas and some other areas in the Dutch East Indies where Islam had not gained a foothold by the time Dutch missionaries arrived. While the relatively small number of Dutchmen in the Dutch sphere may have played a role in the failure to spread 'Dutch' religion (in the nineteenth century, for instance, not enough people could be found to fill the posts created for Dutch missionaries), there were also three other factors that impeded the spread.

First was the somewhat greater reticence on the part of the Dutch colonial authorities to offend local people than was found among other European imperial authorities. This reticence can be traced from the works of Grotius in the early days of the VOC (Van Ittersum 2006) down to the early twentieth century, when the admission of missionaries to districts of the Dutch East Indies was strictly monitored by the governor general. In Suriname this reticence received a further impetus from the fear of the slave-owners that they could no longer keep their slaves as slaves once they would have become Christian.

But there were always voices among the Dutch favouring missionary programmes, and it is certainly an overstatement to say the Dutch empire was there only for the purpose of commerce and utterly lacked any imperial ideology in stark contrast to the other European empires of the early modern period (Kruijtzer 2008: Chapter 1; contrast Pagden 1995:4, 114). And while it is clear that missionary activity did not really get off the ground in the Netherlands until the foundation of Protestant missionary societies in the 1790s and Catholic missionizing did not really start until the mid-nineteenth century, in the early twentieth century Dutch missionaries made up for the past centuries, to such an extent that Pope Pius XI remarked in 1925: 'Hollandia docet' – Holland leads the way (De Graaf and De Valk 2007:6-11).

After a brief stay in Suriname in the 1730s G. Kals published the tract entitled *The principal and basic inequities of the Netherlands; The neglect of the conversion of the heathen.* His plea was ignored, however, and missionizing in Suriname was left mostly to the Moravian brotherhood of the Herrnhutters who arrived in the second quarter of the eighteenth century. Because making contact with the slaves proved difficult, due to the reluctance of the slave owners, their initial successes were among the Free Blacks in Paramaribo. After the slave emancipation, however, most descendants of slaves became Christians of the Herrnhutter denomination (Goslinga 1985:370, 1990:291; Oostindie 2005:29-31). The fact that the handful of Moravians in Suriname managed to have such a great cultural impact, confirms our idea that in circumstances like those obtaining in colonial Suriname there could be an inverse relation between the concentration of an ethnic group and its cultural influence.

A second factor was the relative difficulty in becoming a Calvinist Protestant. While the Catholic Portuguese were often content with a nominal conversion – as Protestant Dutchmen and Englishmen observed in the early seventeenth century when they entered the Portuguese sphere – Dutch Protestantism required a confession of faith that was more far-reaching. In early seventeenth-century Batavia the authorities toyed with the idea of separating the sacraments of baptism and communion and reserving the latter only for the purer souls, but in the end it was decided to keep them combined – meaning that only the purer souls could become Protestant at all (Blussé 1986:169-70). This reluctance to admit none but those on whom God's grace had fallen (*sola gratia*) tied in with the very strict belief in predestination to which the Dutch state church had confirmed its allegiance in 1618. Considerations of this nature may also have played a role in the abandonment of the black and coloured population of Curaçao to the care of Catholic missionaries from the mainland. In the 1820s reverend G.B. Bosch noted that although he thought that the colour segregation between the Protestant and Catholic churches was due to a desire of the white elite to distance itself in order to remain in control, the white elite itself generally thought the reason was 'the appropriateness of the Roman church for ignorant people' (compare Oostindie 2005:39-43). The nineteenth-century African recruits for the Dutch East Indies army (see Chapter VI) were for much the same reasons left to Roman Catholicism, although this was frowned upon at the Ministry of Colonies.[24]

A third factor in the limited spread of the Dutch religion were the types of non-Christian religion that Christianity had to compete with in the Dutch sphere. Some anthropologists as well as the historian Anthony Reid have argued that in Africa and the Indonesian archipelago both Christianity and Islam were more fit for the conditions prevailing in the early modern and modern age than the polytheist and animist beliefs present at an earlier stage because as monotheist religions they offered a more comprehensive world-view. Karel Steenbrink rightly notes, however, that another important aspect shared by Islam and Christianity is the exclusivity they claim on the basis of their scriptures (Steenbrink 2000). This exclusivity was also recognised by the Ministry of Colonies. It became official policy in 1841 to disallow Christian missionising among the Muslims of Java and Sumatra, in view of their '*Fanatismus*'.[25]

It was precisely in the area of the East that was longest part of the Dutch sphere that Christianity and Islam competed. The idea that Islam and Christianity were engaged in a centuries long 'race' for the souls of the people in the archipelago was most clearly put forward by the scholar B.J.O. Schrieke in the 1950s (Azra 2000), but it was already perceived as such long before that. As early as 1612 two Dutch ministers active in the Moluccas thought that the local people were 'weeping in heathendom' and were so desperate for education that as soon as Muslim preachers set foot amongst them they converted.[26] In the late seventeenth century Wouter Schouten, who was also very much in favour of spreading the gospel among pagans and other non-Christians, observed in a poem:

> And how the Moor steadily attempts, pants and tries/
> to imprint the Qur'an into the souls of those who fell into the cunning net/
> of Muhammad's deceptive teachings/
> which teachings spread more and more/
> through Asia, the finest kingdoms/
> that are unsurpassed by any parts of the world/
> including the east, yes, even upto Moluccas' beach/
> his teachings are well received and implanted.[27]

[24] NA, Ministerie van Koloniën, 1403, *verbaal* 2-11-1841 no. 2.
[25] NA, Ministerie van Koloniën, 1403, *verbaal* 2-11-1841 no. 2 and *verbaal* 19-6-1848 no. 2.
[26] 'Soo wanneer bij hen maer Moorse paepen en comen, datse haer datelijck laeten besnijden, door gebreck van ander onderichtinge.' NA, Letter Casparus Wiltensis and Matthias Paludanus 29-7-1612, VOC 1056:171.
[27] Autographic poem by Wouter Schouten in Schouten 1676, Part 3: opposite p. 35.

Some even thought that the Dutch colonial efforts themselves aided the spread of Islam. That idea was most clearly put forward by the previously mentioned early twentieth-century German missionary Simon in his phrase: 'Islam accompanies the colonial government' (Steenbrink 1993:107).

Once more this confirms our hunch that the Dutch spread many kinds of genes and memes through the Dutch sphere but only few of their own. And while it seems that memes and genes did not move completely independently of each other in the Dutch sphere, working out the nature of the link between the flows of people and the flows of cultural expressions remains the real challenge.

Epilogue

Decolonization brought colonialism back to Europe with the immigrant communities from the former colonies. In the case of the Netherlands these communities included some of the ones we have discussed here, most importantly the Creoles of Suriname and the Indo-Dutch, both of which included a majority of people with a heritage of both European and non-European genes. Both groups were also Christian and had Dutch as their first or second language. And in both cases the post-colonial migration was a continuation of the temporary migration to the Netherlands of the younger age groups for study purposes,[28] especially during the last decades before independence (1947-1949 for the Dutch East Indies and 1975 for Suriname).

But the diverging trends towards exclusion and inclusion from/in the European community respectively, meant that the overwhelming majority of the Indo-Dutch came to the Netherlands in the period between 1945 and 1968 but the majority of Creoles remained in Suriname at the time of Independence.[29] The inclusion of the Indo-Dutch was of course only partial (Meijer 2004 sketches their ambiguous position in great detail), but the sense of exclusion of the Surinamese Creoles has been such that in recent years there has been a growing demand for an apology by the Dutch government for slavery.

---

[28]   For some figures regarding Suriname see Oostindie 2000:202 and for the Dutch East Indies see the section on the *katjangs*, or study migrants, in Beets et al. 2002.

[29]   It is estimated that only 31,000 of the 294,000 Indo-Dutch (the part of the 'European' category that was to qualify for Dutch citizenship) opted for Indonesian citizenship in the two years following Indonesian independence, the remainder moved to the Netherlands or was already there for study purposes etcetera (Beets et al 2002:38). On the eve of Suriname's independence roughly a third of the Surinamese population was in the Netherlands and with that opted for Dutch citizenship (Oostindie 2000:212). In both cases the community in the Netherlands was later joined by '*spijtoptanten*', again relatively more in the Indonesian case. The oft-cited figure of 6,000 Indo-Dutch finally remaining in Indonesia, however, is an underestimation that has everything to do with the colonial ways of counting (Zuidema forthcoming).

While the latter group is, as Gert Oostindie remarks in Chapter I, visibly of African ancestry and in that way easily identified with the victims of the history of slavery, its members are also paradoxically more likely to be descended from slave owners or at least Europeans who lived in Suriname than the average Dutch person, as the 'Back to the Roots' programme is revealing through genetic research. The programme emphasises the difference between female and male lines or 'roots', and rightly so because genetic research with a historical angle tends to underscore the genderedness of the human past, including the probability that our common female ancestor preceded our common male ancestor by some 84,000 years (basically meaning that the common male ancestor had children with more than one woman). We may draw a comparison here with genetic research revealing other past patterns of male migration and domination, like the 'Aryan' expansion into South Asia sometime before Christ. Controversial research in recent years has demonstrated that some male members of the upper or 'Aryan' castes carry a Y chromosome resembling the Y chromosome deemed typically European, while their mitochondrial DNA, which reveals the female ancestry, matches that of lower caste Indians (Bamshad et al. 2001; Bezbaruah and Choudhury 2001). From a genetic world historical perspective the Dutch overseas expansion is not all that exceptional.

Such genetic research takes its meaning, however, from historical studies like this one, which present us with the quantitative data to construe a statistical likelihood of ancestry as well as the qualitative aspects of past migrations – which one may or may not want to fit into a heritage narrative. The differing attitudes towards the European genetic element in the heritage of Surinamese Creoles and Indo-Dutch reflects the different colonial experiences of Suriname and the Dutch East Indies as well as the different attitudes towards the mutual colonial heritage outlined in Chapter III.

Bibliography

Archives

NA (Nationaal Archief, The Hague)
- VOC (Verenigde Oostindische Compagnie)
- Kabinet des Konings
- Ministerie van Koloniën

Digital sources

www.mijnroots.nl
   A joint project between the Tropenmuseum and Erasmus University which

involves young people and artists from the Netherlands with an Antillian, Aruban and Surinamese background.
www.vocopvarenden.nationaalarchief.nl
'The European labour market and the Dutch East India Company (VOC)' – a database of the personnel of the Dutch East India Company in the eighteenth century (NWO Project).

Published works

Arbell, Mordechai
2001   'Jewish settlements in the French colonies in the Caribbean (Martinique, Guadeloupe, Haiti, Cayenne) and the "Black Code"', in: Paolo Bernardini and Norman Fiering (eds), *The Jews and the expansion of Europe to the West, 1450 to 1800*, pp. 287-313. New York: Berghahn Books.

Azra, Azyumardi
2000   'The race between Islam and Christianity theory revisited; Islamization and Christianization in the Malay-Indonesian archipelago 1530-1670', *Documentatieblad voor de Geschiedenis van de Nederlandse Zending en Overzeese Kerken* 7-2:26-37.

Bamshad, Michael, Toomas Kivisild, W. Scott Watkins, Mary E. Dixon, Chris E. Ricker, Baskara B. Rao, J. Mastan Naidu, B.V. Ravi Prasad, P. Govinda Reddy, Arani Rasanayagam, Surinder S. Papiha, Richard Villems, Alan J. Redd, Michael F. Hammer, Son V. Nguyen, Marion L. Carroll, Mark A. Batzer and Lynn B. Jorde
2001   'Genetic evidence on the origins of Indian caste populations', *Genome Research* 11:994-1004. [http://www.genome.org/cgi/content/full/11/6/994]

Barend-van Haeften, Marijke
2005   'Een mislukte kolonisatie aan de Oyapoc door vrouwenogen bezien; Het verslag van een reis naar de Wilde Kust door Elisabeth van der Woude (1676-1677)', *De Zeventiende Eeuw* 21-1:79-90.

Beets, Gijs, Corina Huisman, Evert van Imhoff, Santo Koesoebjono and Evelien Walhout
2002   *De demografische geschiedenis van de Indische Nederlanders*. Den Haag: Nederlands Interdisciplinair Instituut. [NIDI Rapport 64.] [http://www.nidi.knaw.nl/en/output/reports/nidi-report-64.pdf/nidi-report-64.pdf]

Bezbaruah, Supriya and Samrat Choudhury
2001   'White India', *India Today* 30:34-6.

Biewenga, Ad W.
1999   *De Kaap de Goede Hoop; Een Nederlandse vestigingskolonie, 1680-1730*. Amsterdam: Prometheus/Bert Bakker.

Blakely, Allison
1993   *Blacks in the Dutch world; The evolution of racial imagery in a modern society*. Bloomington: Indiana University Press.

Blussé, Leonard J.
1986   *Strange company; Chinese settlers, Mestizo women, and the Dutch in VOC Batavia*. Dordrecht: Foris. [KITLV, Verhandelingen 122.]

Boogaart, E. van den
1986   'The servant migration to New Netherland, 1624-1664', in: P.C. Emmer (ed.), *Colonialism and migration; Indentured labour before and after slavery*, pp. 55-81. Dordrecht/Boston/Lancaster: Nijhoff.

Boogaart, E. van den and P.C. Emmer
1986   'Colonialism and migration; An overview', in: P.C. Emmer (ed.), *Colonialism and migration; Indentured labour before and after slavery*, pp. 3-15. Dordrecht/Boston/Lancaster: Nijhoff.

Boomgaard, Peter
1989   *Children of the colonial state; Population growth and economic development in Java, 1795-1880*. Amsterdam: Free University Press.

Boomgaard, Peter and A.J. Gooszen
1991   *Changing economy in Indonesia; A selection of statistical source material from the early 19th century up to 1940; Vol. 11: Population trends 1795-1942*. Amsterdam: KIT.

Bosma, Ulbe and Remco Raben
2003   *De oude Indische wereld 1500-1920*. Amsterdam: Bert Bakker.

Bossenbroek, M.P.
1986   *Van Holland naar Indië; Het transport van koloniale troepen voor het Oost-Indische leger 1815-1909*. Amsterdam: De Bataafsche Leeuw.

Brug, Peter H. van der
1994   *Malaria en malaise; De VOC in Batavia in de achttiende eeuw*. Amsterdam: De Bataafsche Leeuw.

Bruijn, J.R., F.S. Gaastra and I. Schöffer
1987   *Dutch-Asiatic shipping in the 17th and 18th centuries; Vol. I: Introductory volume*. The Hague: Nijhoff.

Bruijn, J.R. and J. Lucassen (eds)
1980   *Op de schepen der Oost-Indische Compagnie; Vijf artikelen van J. de Hullu, ingeleid, bewerkt en voorzien van een studie over de werkgelegenheid bij de VOC*. Groningen: Wolters-Noordhoff/Bouma's Boekhuis.

Cannadine, David
2001   *Ornamentalism; How the British saw their empire*. New York: Oxford University Press.

Coomans-Eustatia, Maritza, Henny E. Coomans and To van der Lee (eds)
1998   *Breekbare banden; Feiten en visies over Aruba, Bonaire en Curaçao na de Vrede van Munster, 1648-1998*. Bloemendaal: Stichting Libri Antilliani.

Crosby, Alfred W.
1993   *Ecological imperialism; The biological expansion of Europe, 900-1900*. Cambridge: Cambridge University Press.

Donselaar, J. van
2005   'Surinaams-Nederlands', in: Nicoline van der Sijs (ed.), *Wereldnederlands; Oude en jonge variëteiten van het Nederlands*, pp. 111-30. Den Haag: Sdu Uitgevers.

Doortmont, Michel R. and Jinna Smit (eds)
2007   *Sources for the mutual heritage of Ghana and the Netherlands; An annotated guide to the archives relating to Ghana and West Africa in the Nationaal Archief, 1593-1960s*. Leiden: Brill.

Drescher, Seymour
2001   'Jews and new Christians in the Atlantic slave trade', in: Paolo Bernar-
               dini and Norman Fiering (eds), *The Jews and the expansion of Europe to
               the West, 1450 to 1800*, pp. 439-70. New York: Berghahn Books.

Eersel, Hein
1998   'De Surinaamse taalpolitiek; Een historisch overzicht', in: Kees Groene-
               boer (ed.), *Koloniale taalpolitiek in Oost en West; Nederlands-Indië, Surina-
               me, Nederlandse Antillen en Aruba*, pp. 207-23. Amsterdam: Amsterdam
               University Press.

Elphick, Richard and Robert Shell
1979   'Intergroup relations; Khoikhoi, settlers, slaves and free blacks, 1652-
               1795', in: Richard Elphick and Hermann Giliomee (eds), *The shaping of
               South African society, 1652-1820*, pp. 116-69. Cape Town: Longman.

Elson, R.E.
1994   *Village Java under the Cultivation System, 1830-1870*. Sydney: Allen and
               Unwin.

Eltis, David
1999   'Slavery and freedom in the early modern world', in: Stanley Lewis
               Engerman (ed.), *Terms of labor; Slavery, serfdom, and free labor*, pp. 25-49.
               Stanford: Stanford University Press.

Emmer, Pieter C. and Willem W. Klooster
1999   'The Dutch Atlantic, 1650-1800; Expansion without empire', *Itinerario,
               European Journal of Overseas History* 23-2:48-69.

Enthoven, Victor
2005   'Dutch crossings; Migration between the Netherlands and the New
               World, 1600-1800', *Atlantic Studies* 2:153-76.
2007   'Onder de wapenen; Burgersoldaten in de Atlantische wereld', *Leid-
               schrift* 22:13-41.

Fasseur, C.
1994   *De Indologen; Ambtenaren voor de Oost 1825-1950*. Amsterdam: Bert Bak-
               ker.

Feinberg, Harvey M.
1974   'New data on European mortality in West Africa: The Dutch on the
               Gold Coast 1719-1760', *Journal of African History* 15:357-71.
1989   *Africans and Europeans in West Africa; Elminans and Dutchmen on the
               Gold Coast during the eighteenth century*. Philadelphia, PA: American
               Philosophical Society.

Ferenczi, Imre and Walter F. Willcox
1929   *International migrations; Vol. 1, Statistics*. New York: Arno Press. [Publi-
               cations of the National Bureau of Economic Research 14.]

Fertig, Georg
1994   'Transatlantic migration from the German-speaking parts of Cen-
               tral Europe, 1600-1800; Proportions, structures, and explanations', in:
               Nicholas Canny (ed.), *Europeans on the move; Studies on European migra-
               tion*, pp. 192-235. Oxford: Oxford University Press.

Frankel, Rachel
2001   'Antecedents and remnants of Jodensavanne; The synagogues and cemeteries of the first permanent plantation settlement of New World Jews', in: Paolo Bernardini and Norman Fiering (eds), *The Jews and the expansion of Europe to the West, 1450 to 1800*, pp. 395-436. New York: Berghahn Books.

Gelder, Roelof van
1997   *Het Oost-Indisch avontuur; Duitsers in dienst van de VOC (1600-1800)*. Nijmegen: SUN.

Giliomee, Hermann
2003   *The Afrikaners; Biography of a people*. Cape Town: Tafelberg.

Goodfriend, Joyce D.
1992   *Before the melting pot; Society and culture in colonial New York City 1664-1730*. Princeton: Princeton University Press.

Gooszen, Hans
1999   *A demographic history of the Indonesian archipelago, 1880-1942*. Leiden: KITLV Press. [Verhandelingen 183.]

Goslinga, C.Ch.
1971   *The Dutch in the Caribbean and on the Wild Coast, 1580-1680*. Gainesville: University of Florida Press.
1985   *The Dutch in the Caribbean and in the Guianas, 1680-1791*. Assen: Van Gorcum.
1990   *The Dutch in the Caribbean and in Surinam, 1791/5-1942*. Assen: Van Gorcum.

Graaf, Gerrit de and Hans de Valk
2007   'Een "Repertorium van Nederlandse zendings- en missiearchieven" (ca. 1800-1960)', *Documentatieblad voor de Nederlandse Kerkgeschiedenis na 1800* 66:3-16.

Groeneboer, Kees
1995   'De Nederlandse taalpolitiek op Ceylon ten tijde van de VOC (1656-1796)', *Gramma/TTT; Tijdschrift voor Taalwetenschap* 3-2:1-12.
1998   'Nederlands-Indië en het Nederlands', in: Kees Groeneboer (ed.), *Koloniale taalpolitiek in Oost en West; Nederlands-Indië, Suriname, Nederlandse Antillen en Aruba*, pp. 55-83. Amsterdam: Amsterdam University Press.

Haan, Dorothee Marian Petra de
1994   *Deep Dutch; Towards an operationalization of school language skills*. Amsterdam: IFOTT. [Studies in Language and Language Use 9.]

Harris, Karen L.
2006   'Not a Chinaman's chance; Chinese labour in South Africa and the United States of America', *Historia* 52-2:177-97.

Henley, David E.F.
2005   'Population and the means of subsistence; Explaining the historical demography of island Southeast Asia, with particular reference to Sulawesi', *Journal of Southeast Asian studies* 36:337-72.

Heijer, Henk den
2005   '"Over warme en koude landen"; Mislukte Nederlandse volksplantin-
               gen op de Wilde Kust in de zeventiende eeuw', *De Zeventiende Eeuw*
               21-1:79-90.
Israel, Jonathan I.
2001   'The Jews of Dutch America', in: Paolo Bernardini and Norman Fiering
               (eds), *The Jews and the expansion of Europe to the West, 1450 to 1800*, pp.
               335-49. New York: Berghahn Books.
Ittersum, Martine Julia van
2006   *Profit and principle; Hugo Grotius, natural rights theories and the rise of
               Dutch power in the East Indies, 1595-1615.* Leiden: Brill.
s'Jacob, H.K. (ed.)
1976   *De Nederlanders in Kerala, 1663-1701; De memories en instructies betref-
               fende het commandement Malabar van de Verenigde Oost-Indische Compag-
               nie.* 's-Gravenhage: Nijhoff. [Rijks Geschiedkundige Publicatiën, Kleine
               Serie 43.]
Jones, Eric Alan
2003   *Wives, slaves, and concubines; A history of the female underclass in Dutch
               Asia.* PhD thesis University of California, Berkeley.
Ketelaars, A.P.M.
1985   'Van inheemse stapelmarkt tot tweederangs koloniale stad; Een geschie-
               denis van Malakka van 1403 tot omstreeks 1690'. MA thesis University
               of Utrecht.
Klooster, Wim
1994   'Subordinate but proud; Curaçao's free blacks and mulattoes in the
               eighteenth century', *Nieuwe West-Indische Gids* 68:283-300.
2001   'The Jews in Suriname and Curaçao', in: Paolo Bernardini and Norman
               Fiering (eds), *The Jews and the expansion of Europe to the West, 1450 to
               1800*, pp. 350-68. New York: Berghahn Books.
Knaap, Gerrit
2004   *Kruidnagelen en christenen; De Verenigde Oost-Indische Compagnie en de
               bevolking van Ambon, 1656-1697.* Second revised edition. Leiden: KITLV
               Uitgeverij. [Verhandelingen 212; First edition 1987.]
2006   'Kasteel, stad en land; Het begin van het Nederlandse imperium in de
               Oost', *Leidschrift* 21-2:17-30. [Special issue 'Van verovering tot onaf-
               hankelijkheid; De koloniale relatie tussen Nederland en Nederlands-
               Indië'.]
Kolff, D.H.A. and H.W. van Santen (eds)
1979   *De geschriften van Francisco Pelsaert over Mughal Indië, 1627; Kroniek en
               remonstrantie.* 's-Gravenhage: Nijhoff. [Werken Linschoten-Vereeniging
               81.]
Koloniaal Verslag
1868-1924 *Koloniaal verslag; Bijlage C van de Handelingen der Staten-Generaal.* 's-Graven-
               hage: Algemeene Landsdrukkerij.
Kruijtzer, Gijs
2008   *Xenophobia and consciousness in seventeenth-century India; Six cases from
               the Deccan.* PhD thesis University of Leiden.

Langen, Johan van
2003   'De Britse overname van de Nederlandse koloniën Demerary, Esse-
          quebo en Berbice (Guyana); Van economische overvleugeling naar
          politieke overheersing (1740-1814)'. MA thesis University of Amster-
          dam.
Lequin, F.
1982   *Het personeel van de Verenigde Oost Indische Compagnie in Azië in de acht-*
          tiende eeuw, meer in het bijzonder in de vestiging Bengalen. PhD thesis
          University of Leiden. Two vols.
2005   *Het personeel van de Verenigde Oost Indische Compagnie in Azië in de acht-*
          tiende eeuw, meer in het bijzonder in de vestiging Bengalen. Alphen aan den
          Rijn: Canaletto/Repro-Holland. [Revised, abridged edition of Lequin
          1982.]
Lier, Rudolf van
1977   *Samenleving in een grensgebied; Een sociaal-historische studie van Suriname.*
          Third revised edition. Amsterdam: Emmering. [First edition 1949.]
Locher-Scholten, Elsbeth
2000   *Women and the colonial state; Essays on gender and modernity in the Nether-*
          lands Indies 1900-1942. Amsterdam: Amsterdam University Press.
Lucassen, Jan
1991   *Dutch long distance migration; A concise history 1600-1900.* Amsterdam:
          International Institute of Social History. [IISG Research Paper 3.] [A
          shorter version of this paper was published as 'The Netherlands,
          the Dutch, and long-distance migration in the late sixteenth to early
          nineteenth centuries', in: Nicholas Canny (ed.), *Europeans on the move;*
          Studies on European migration, 1500-1800, pp. 153-91. Oxford: Clarendon
          Press, 1994.]
Lucassen, Jan and Rinus Penninx
1994   *Nieuwkomers, nakomelingen, Nederlanders; Immigranten in Nederland*
          1550-1993. Amsterdam: Spinhuis.
McNeill, William
1976   *Plagues and peoples.* New York: Doubleday.
Meijer, Hans
2004   *In Indië geworteld; De twintigste eeuw.* Amsterdam: Bert Bakker.
Moree, P.J.
1998   *A concise history of Dutch Mauritius, 1598-1710; A fruitful and healthy*
          land. London: Kegan Paul, Leiden: IIAS.
Moritz, Eduard
1938   *Die Deutschen am Kap unter der holländischen Herrschaft 1652-1806.* Wei-
          mar: Böhlau.
Murdoch, Steve
2002   'The good, the bad and the anonymous; A preliminary survey of Scots
          in the Dutch East Indies 1612-1707', *Northern Scotland* 22:63-76.
Nieuhoff, Johan
1682   *Zee en lant-reize, door verscheide gewesten van Oostindiën [...].* Amsterdam:
          De weduwe van Jacob van Meurs.

Nitisastro, Widjojo
1970   *Population trends in Indonesia.* Ithaca: Cornell University Press.
Oosterhoff, J.L.
1985   'Zeelandia; A Dutch colonial city on Formosa', in: Robert J. Ross and
                Gerard J. Telkamp (eds), *Colonial cities; Essays on urbanism in a colonial
                context*, pp. 51-63. Dordrecht/Boston/Lancaster: Nijhoff.
Oostindie, Gert
2000   *Het paradijs overzee; De 'Nederlandse' Caraïben en Nederland.* Third edi-
                tion. Leiden: KITLV Uitgeverij. [Caribbean Series 20; First edition
                1997.]
2005   *Paradise overseas; The Dutch Caribbean, colonialism and its transatlantic
                legacies.* Oxford: Macmillan.
2007   'Een paradox van vrijheid en slavernij; Joden en slavenhandel in de
                Nieuwe Wereld', *Academische Boekengids* 61:13-5.
Pagden, Anthony
1995   *Lords of all the world; Ideologies of empire in Spain, Britain and France.* New
                Haven: Yale University Press.
Peters, Marion and Ferry André de la Porte
2002   *In steen geschreven; Leven en sterven van VOC-dienaren op de Kust van
                Coromandel in India.* Amsterdam: Bas Lubberhuizen.
Pombejra, Dhiravat na
2000   'VOC employees and their relationships with Mon and Siamese
                women; A case study of Osoet Pegua', in: Barbara Watson Andaya
                (ed.), *Other pasts; Women, gender and history in early modern Southeast
                Asia*, pp. 195-214. Honolulu: Center for Southeast Asian Studies, Uni-
                versity of Hawaii.
Ponelis, F.A.
1993   *The development of Afrikaans.* Frankfurt am Main: Peter Lang.
Prins, W.F.
1933   'De bevolkingsgroepen in het Nederlandsch-Indisch recht', *Koloniale
                Studiën* 17:652-88.
Raben, R.
1996   *Batavia and Colombo; The ethnic and spatial order of two colonial cities 1600-
                1800.* PhD thesis University of Leiden.
Renkema, W.E.
1981   *Het Curaçaose plantagebedrijf in de negentiende eeuw.* Zutphen: Walburg
                Pers.
Roelofsz, M. Antoinette P.
1943   *De vestiging der Nederlanders ter kuste Malabar.* 's-Gravenhage: Nijhoff.
                [KITLV, Verhandelingen 4.]
Ruangsilp, Bhawan
2007   *Dutch East India Company merchants at the court of Ayutthaya; Dutch per-
                ceptions of the Thai kingdom c. 1604-1765.* Leiden: Brill.
Schalkwijk, Frans Leonard
1998   *The Reformed Church in Dutch Brazil (1630-1654).* Zoetermeer: Boeken-
                centrum. [Mission 24.]

Schoute, D.
1929   *De geneeskunde in den dienst der Oost-Indische Compagnie in Nederlandsch-Indië.* Amsterdam: De Bussy.

Schouten, Wouter
1676   *Aanmercklijke voyagie gedaan door Wouter Schouten naar Oost-Indiën.* Amsterdam: Jacob van Meurs and Johannes van Someren.

Schouwenburg, K.L. van
1988   'Het personeel op de schepen van de Kamer Delft der VOC in de eerste helft der 18e eeuw', *Tijdschrift voor Zeegeschiedenis* 7:76-93.

Schutte, Gerrit
1979   'Company and colonists at the Cape', in: Richard Elphick and Hermann Giliomee (eds), *The shaping of South African society, 1652-1820*, pp. 173-210. Cape Town: Longman.

Segal, J.B.
1993   *A history of the Jews of Cochin.* London: Vallentine Mitchell.

Shell, Robert C.-H.
1994   *Children of bondage; A social history of the slave society at the Cape of Good Hope, 1652-1838.* Hanover/Johannesburg: University Press of New England.

Singh, Anjana
2007   *Fort Cochin in Kerala 1750-1830; The social world of a Dutch community in an Indian milieu.* PhD thesis University of Leiden.

Steenbrink, Karel
1993   *Dutch colonialism and Indonesian Islam; Contacts and conflicts 1596-1950.* Amsterdam: Rodopi.
2000   'A history of Christianity in Indonesia as an exercise in comparative religion', *Documentatieblad voor de Geschiedenis van de Nederlandse Zending en Overzeese Kerken* 7-1:67-78.

Teenstra, M.D.
1836-37   *De Nederlandse West-Indische Eilanden in derzelver tegenwoordigen toestand.* Amsterdam: Sulpke. Two vols.

Veen, Ernst van
2003   'How the Dutch ran a seventeenth-century colony; The occupation and loss of Formosa 1624-1662', in Leonard Blussé (ed.), *Around and about Formosa; Essays in honor of Professor Ts'ao Yung-ho*, pp. 141-60. Taipei: Ts'ao Yung-ho Foundation for Culture and Education.

Verstegen, Math
2001   *De Indische Zeeherberg; De stichting van Zuid-Afrika door de VOC.* Zaltbommel: Europese Bibliotheek.

Viljoen, Russel
2006   *Jan Paerl; A Khoikhoi in Cape colonial society, 1761-1851.* Leiden: Brill.

Volkstelling 1930
1933-36   *Volkstelling 1930 = Census of 1930 in Netherlands India.* Batavia: Landsdrukkerij. Eight vols.

Volkstelling 1950
1956   *Tweede algemeene volkstelling Suriname 1950; Vol. 10. De eigenlijke volkstel-*
            ling. Paramaribo: Welvaartsfonds Suriname.
Voorlopig resultaat 1971
1971   *Voorlopig resultaat vierde algemene volkstelling; A preliminary report.* Para-
            maribo: ABS.
Vries, Jan W. de
2005   'Indisch Nederlands', in: Nicoline van der Sijs (ed.), *Wereldnederlands;*
            Oude en jonge variëteiten van het Nederlands, pp. 59-78. Den Haag: Sdu
            Uitgevers.
Vries, Jan W. de, Roland Willemyns and Peter Burger
1993   *Het verhaal van een taal; Negen eeuwen Nederlands.* Amsterdam: Prome-
            theus.
Wagenaar, Lodewijk
1994   *Galle, VOC-vestiging in Ceylon; Beschrijving van een koloniale samenleving*
            aan de vooravond van de Singalese opstand tegen het Nederlandse gezag,
            1760. Amsterdam: De Bataafsche Leeuw.
Weisbord, Robert G.
1967   'The dilemma of South African Jewry', *The Journal of Modern African*
            Studies 5:233-41.
Williams, James Homer
2001   'An Atlantic perspective on the Jewish struggle for rights and opportu-
            nities in Brazil, New Netherland, and New York', in: Paolo Bernardini
            and Norman Fiering (eds), *The Jews and the expansion of Europe to the*
            West, 1450 to 1800, pp. 369-93. New York: Berghahn Books.
Yao, Keisuke
2003   'Two rivals on an island of sugar; The sugar trade of the VOC and
            Overseas Chinese in Formosa in the seventeenth century', in: Leo-
            nard Blussé, *Around and about Formosa; Essays in honor of Professor Ts'ao*
            Yung-ho, pp. 129-40. Taipei: Ts'ao Yung-ho Foundation for Culture and
            Education.
Zuidema, Aukje
forthcoming *'Warga Negara bukan asli'; Dutch and Indies-Dutch children of colonialism*
            in Indonesia: Citizenship, integration trajectories and identity. PhD thesis
            University of Amsterdam.

RIK VAN WELIE

Patterns of slave trading and slavery in the Dutch colonial world
1596-1863

Introduction

From the early seventeenth to the mid-nineteenth century, slavery played a fundamental role in the Dutch colonial world.[1] All overseas possessions of the Dutch depended to varying degrees on the labour of slaves who were imported from diverse and often remote areas. The slaves were almost exclusively of African and Asian descent, as it was no longer deemed morally acceptable to enslave fellow Europeans and early experiments with Native American slaves had quickly been abandoned due to a lack of success. Meanwhile, in the Dutch Republic and selected other parts of early modern Europe, slavery and serfdom had almost entirely disappeared, even though an official moment of abolition eludes us.[2] Historians have often been struck

[1] I would like to thank Peter Boomgaard, David Eltis, Pieter Emmer, Henk den Heijer, Han Jordaan, Gerrit Knaap, Gert Oostindie, Alex van Stipriaan and Jelmer Vos for their many insightful comments on earlier drafts of this chapter.
[2] There is sparse evidence suggesting the presence of African and Asian slaves in the Low Countries from the sixteenth until the eighteenth centuries, but this is almost entirely drawn from the commercial juggernauts of Antwerp and Amsterdam, global ports with strong connections to overseas colonies. Our understanding of this 'metropolitan slavery' is still scanty, partly due to the scarcity of the source material – the numbers cannot have been very high – and partly due to the line dividing slave from servant appearing rather blurred here, if not de jure then certainly de facto. Slaves brought back on return voyages from the colonies – generally considered an illegal practice – were often manumitted on arrival in the Netherlands and became personal servants, with their daily tasks arguably differing very little from those serving as domestic slaves in the colonies. For a general overview of this reverse migration, see Poeze 1986 and Oostindie and Maduro 1986. As a cultural theme, African 'slaves' – especially young children – figured prominently in contemporary paintings of wealthy burghers. See Blakely (1993) for the African presence in the Dutch Republic. The unique but numerically insignificant presence of slaves in metropolitan society falls outside the scope of this chapter.

by this curious paradox: that the seventeenth-century Dutch took great pride in their hard-fought freedom and climate of tolerance at home, while simultaneously exploiting hundreds of thousands of slaves in their overseas dominions (Drescher 1994; Eltis 1993, 1999).

But perhaps this paradox holds the explanation as to why public awareness of slavery in Dutch history has until recently been so limited. In sharp contrast with most other lucrative commodities bought and sold by the merchants of the East Indies Company (VOC) and the West Indies Company (WIC), slaves seldom passed through the Dutch Republic. The trade in slaves, even then considered a rather 'uncommon market' (Gemery and Hogendorn 1979), was always held at a relatively comfortable distance. And whenever this physical distance was occasionally bridged, as in the frequently-cited Middelburg case of 1596, the Dutch commitment to freedom was instantly tested.[3] Colonists returning to their homeland were generally prohibited from taking their slaves along and, when doing so anyway, risked the loss of their property by implicit manumission. The eminent historian of Western slavery, David Brion Davis (2000:458), spoke of these moral and legal boundaries as 'primitive "Mason-Dixon" lines, now drawn somewhere in the Atlantic, separating free soil master-states from tainted slave soil dependencies'.[4] Because of this physical and psychological separation, there was hardly any need to come to terms with colonial slavery in the metropolis.

How much more direct is the awareness of slavery in the United States – or most other former colonies in the Americas – where the institution had been planted in its very midst and functioned as a foundational theme in the national history? With the descendants of slaves visibly and ever more vocally present, citizens could not afford the luxury of ignoring an ignoble past. It may perhaps not come as a surprise that until this very day many Europeans, when confronted with the topic, still conjure up a Hollywood-type image of black slaves picking cotton in the antebellum South, as if slavery was an exclusively American invention.[5]

---

[3]   In 1596 a ship carrying 130 Angolan slaves, most likely captured at sea from the Portuguese enemy, entered the province of Zeeland with the intention of selling this human cargo for profit on the local market. However, these plans were, as far as we can tell now from the available documentation, prevented by the protests from several concerned citizens.

[4]   Sue Peabody (1997) has given a masterful historical analysis of this paradox in early modern France and its colonies. Recently, Susan Amussen (2007) explored how English metropolitan society came to terms with colonial slavery during the seventeenth century. The 'Mason-Dixon line' separated the free northern territories of the United States from the slave states of the South.

[5]   This traditional overemphasis on slavery in the antebellum US South is, undoubtedly, a result of the powerful influence of the African American civil rights movement of the 1950s and 1960s and the popular portrayal of history by Hollywood. But in a sense, the European fascination with US slavery dates back to the success of Harriet Beecher Stowe's classic *Uncle Tom's cabin* (1852).

The post-colonial migration of descendants of Caribbean slaves to the Netherlands in the twentieth century confronted the Dutch more directly with their slavery past. Simultaneously with this migration, and often stimulated by it, numerous academic publications have shed light on the history of the Dutch Atlantic slave trade and of slavery in the Dutch Americas.[6] These scholarly contributions, in combination with the social and political activism of the Afro-Caribbean Dutch, have helped to bring the subject of colonial slavery into the national public debate. The ongoing discussions about an official apology for the Dutch role in slavery, the erection of monuments to commemorate that history, and the inclusion of some of these topics in the first national history canon are all testimony to this increased attention to a troubled past.[7] To some this recent focus on the negative aspects of Dutch colonial history has already gone too far, as they summon the country's glorious past to instil a new sense of pride and patriotism – instead of political correctness – in the Dutch.[8] And while the Dutch Prime Minister Jan Peter Balkenende should perhaps be given the benefit of the doubt for his call for a return to the 'VOC mentality' – after all, there were plenty of inspiring aspects to the history of the Dutch East Indies Company – it nevertheless demonstrated a lack of tact and historical understanding.[9]

This continued admiration for the VOC signals that the Dutch historical imagination still connects most negative aspects of colonialism with the history of the West Indies Company and its Caribbean possessions. That slavery also played a prominent role in the VOC domain has seemingly been forgotten. This public ignorance merely reflects the state of academic scholarship on the subject. Slavery has never been a fashionable topic among historians of the VOC and its absence in the literature is not an exclusively Dutch phenomenon either.[10] In fact, the historiography of Indian Ocean World slavery

---

[6]   This historiography is far too extensive to be fully mentioned here. A few recent works representing the major scholars in the field that are used for this chapter are Emmer 1998, 2000; Den Heijer 1997; Jordaan 2003; Klooster 1997; Oostindie 1995; Postma 1990 and Van Stipriaan 1993.

[7]   See Oostindie 1999 and 2008 for some insightful readings on this current struggle with the Dutch slavery past.

[8]   Dutch politician Rita Verdonk's inaugural speech (3-4-2008) for her political movement 'Trots op Nederland' (ToN, 'Proud of the Netherlands') lamented the presence of an anti-Dutch culture in the Netherlands which 'seeks to erect slave monuments all over the place in order to depict us as evil'. The fact that she, as a cabinet minister (of Immigration), was verbally harassed at the inauguration of the national slavery monument in Amsterdam a few years earlier may have influenced these remarks.

[9]   Balkenende made these ill-advised comments during the *Algemene Beschouwingen* in Dutch parliament (28-9- 2006). He does not of course stand alone in this celebratory attitude regarding the history of the VOC; see Van Stipriaan and Bal (2002) and Oostindie (2003) for a critical commentary on the uncritical public commemoration of the 400-year anniversary of the VOC in 2002.

[10]   This implies that the strong political mobilization by the African-American descendants of slaves was an essential factor in stimulating the historiography of slavery in the Americas.

in general is still in an embryonic stage. Fortunately, propelled by the recent efforts of a small number of historians, we are learning more about the nature of European colonial slavery in the East and can begin, in the words of one of these scholars, 'to "unsilence" this part of our history and "re-Orient" the historiographical imbalance' in slavery studies.[11]

In this chapter I will present a global comparative overview of Dutch colonial slavery, with a heavy emphasis on the history of the slave trade in the VOC and WIC domains. In the previous chapter the free European migrations within the Dutch colonial orbit have been mapped in detail. In order to assess their relative demographic and cultural importance, it is necessary to look at the concurrent forced migrations as well.[12] First, some of the fundamental differences between the origins of slavery in 'the East' and in 'the West' will be addressed. Then, in two longer sections, the nature, volume and directions of the long-distance slave trades to the Dutch colonies are sketched over time. Finally, some admittedly rough observations are made regarding the nature of slavery and abolition in the Dutch colonial world. Only by establishing the geographical and ethnic origins of the slaves and their demographic, economic and cultural contributions to the varying destinations, can we begin to estimate their overall impact in what should essentially be seen as a shared history. Future in-depth comparative research will hopefully lead to a greater understanding and public awareness of the significance of slavery in the Dutch colonial sphere.

The different origins of slavery in the Dutch colonial sphere

While slavery was of great importance in both the VOC and the WIC domain, the origins and general nature of the institution differed fundamentally due to some grand historical contrasts. From the dominant perspective of American plantation slavery, the demand for slaves in Asia does at first not seem very urgent. Traditionally, the VOC has been portrayed as seeking an empire of

---

[11]   Vink 2003b:135. The major historians working on slavery in the Indian Ocean World are well represented in the general overviews of Reid (1983c) and Campbell (2004a, 2004b), while Knaap (1981, 1991, 1995), Vink (2003b), Boomgaard (2004) and, most recently, Raben (2008) have focused more specifically on the Dutch role in it. Vink's comment about 'historiographical imbalance' is particularly interesting in light of the general view among historians of Dutch colonialism, namely that the Dutch Americas have often been neglected in favour of the more celebrated history of the VOC. This further proves that when it comes to the study of colonial slavery, attention has almost completely been centred on the New World.

[12]   The discussion on forced migrations will be limited here to the long-distance (oceanic) slave trades, although other migration flows within the Dutch colonial sphere were certainly not always free either. See for example the dissertation of Kerry Ward (2001) on the transports of convicts and exiles in the Dutch Indian Ocean World.

trade, without real colonizing ambitions. The primary objectives of that trade – the highly coveted spices of the Moluccas and various other lucrative commodities – were usually produced by indigenous Asian societies themselves; Dutch merchants mainly desired the direct, cheap and unhindered access to these products, preferably by shutting out their European commercial rivals. However, long-distance shipping to the production zones and dealing with both indigenous traders and European competitors proved incredibly risky and unpredictable. Therefore it was imperative to establish some kind of military presence at the source of the trade. Even the tiniest factory or fort could in fact be seen as a form of 'indirect' or 'mini-colonization', since an all too rigid division between traders and colonists simply does not fit with the complex historic realities.[13]

As the commercial and territorial interests of the VOC expanded at a dramatic speed, the need for manpower to perform a whole range of tasks intensified accordingly. In the previous chapter we have seen that the Dutch encountered, to a greater extent than the other European colonial powers, difficulties in meeting these labour demands with fellow countrymen. It was therefore a motley and multicultural crowd that enlisted with the VOC to undertake the dangerous voyage to the East, yet few were willing to perform arduous work under unfamiliar and unhealthy conditions for meagre pay. With sizeable Asian populations nearby, tapping into local labour resources seemed the most logical solution.

By utilizing Asian and African slaves, the VOC essentially adapted to age-old practices in the Indian Ocean World. This is neither the time nor place to decipher the long and complex history of slavery in that region. Local traditions of slavery and serfdom had continuously been blended with and transformed by the activities of Indian, Arab and Chinese traders, making the European newcomers only the latest contributors to a history of overlapping frontiers in the Indian Ocean World (Vink 2007). When the Dutch entered this already highly commercialized region in the mid-1590s, the many shapes and forms of coerced labour they came upon often thoroughly confused them.

Some of that initial bewilderment can be distilled from the famous *Itinerario* in 1596, which signalled the dawn of Dutch overseas expansion (Terpstra 1955). Van Linschoten's lengthy descriptions of the servile aspects of the Portuguese Asian colonial society of Goa in the 1580s, and particularly the many images accompanying the text, must have fascinated the interested

---

[13] Knaap 2006. A similar critique of the traditional division in the historiography between indirect commercial rule in British Asia and direct colonization in the British Atlantic is provided by Stern (2006) who, in his reassessment of colonization in the East, speaks of 'the English East India Company-State' (701, note 11).

'The Old Hospital or Town Hall' in Ambon

reader from the egalitarian confines of the Dutch Republic.[14] By addressing the morally corrupting effects of colonialism and slavery Van Linschoten's message served, according to a recent analysis (Van den Boogaart 2000), a dual purpose: as a condemnation of the lifestyle of the Portuguese enemy and as a cautionary vademecum to the nascent Dutch explorers.[15] That those Portuguese predecessors, due to their extensive experience with slavery at home and abroad, would function as important examples to the Dutch 'apprentice' has been sufficiently demonstrated (Emmer 2006).

Scholars usually emphasize the uniquely pre-modern characteristics of African and Asian types of slavery, primarily in order to distinguish them from the dominant image of European colonial slavery. Thus in a classic statement on 'slavery' [their quotation marks] in Africa, Kopytoff and Miers (1977) perceived the system as an important societal process in which dependency on and protection by an influential person was generally preferred to individual freedom, as the latter effectively meant isolation from the larger community. Slaves were customarily the product of tribal warfare and were traded regularly on local markets, but the institution – so the story goes – was only dramatically transformed with the sudden growth of external (European and Arabian) demands for slaves (Lovejoy 1983; Manning 1990).

Anthony Reid's pioneering volume on slavery in Southeast Asia (1983c) felt the need to address 'slavery, bondage and dependency' together, thus acknowledging that chattel slavery was but one of many conditions of unfreedom common to the region. Certain Asian paths to slavery, particularly those relating to debt (pawn slavery) or the inability to take care of oneself or one's family, were considered to be more or less temporary and offered much-needed protection.[16] Furthermore, slave status could, particularly in the case of young females, often result in a remarkable upward social mobility. There

---

[14]   In his condemnation of Portuguese slavery, Van Linschoten fell squarely within the anti-Spanish ideology of the time. A recent study by Schmidt (2001) brilliantly demonstrates how during the Eighty Years' War the Dutch compared their own struggle with Spanish tyranny and 'slavery' to the victimization of the 'innocent' Native Americans at the hand of ruthless Spanish conquistadores. 'Slavery' in the Dutch-Spanish ideological conflict had of course little to do with forced labour in the colonies. See Van Gelderen (1992) for an erudite analysis of the meaning of slavery in the ideology of the Dutch Revolt.

[15]   Considering the aforementioned historiographical imbalance in slavery studies, it is quite telling that Van den Boogaart, who has primarily written on Dutch colonial expansion and slavery in the Atlantic World, focuses so closely on this particular aspect of Van Linschoten's work.

[16]   Campbell (2004a:xxiii) talks in this context about 'slavery as a form of social security'. It can of course be argued whether strictly temporary conditions should still be labelled as chattel slavery. Boomgaard (2004:87) distinguishes between three broad categories of servile labour on Java: 'slaves, who can be bought and sold, serfs, who can neither be traded nor leave their masters, and debt bondmen and bondwomen who in principle can regain freedom by paying off their debts'. In reviewing Reid's 1983 volume, James Scott (1985:142) suggested that 'it might perhaps be more accurate to speak of 100 percent slaves, 80 percent slaves, 20 percent slaves, and so on'.

even exists evidence suggesting that some slaves, given the opportunity for manumission, declined out of fear that freed status would automatically be followed by intensive compulsory labour demands from the local state apparatus (Campbell 2004a:xxiii-xxv). Such ambiguous and somewhat redeeming qualities, these scholars argue, are often lost from view because the historiography of slavery is so thoroughly dominated by the exploitative European colonial type, in which the contrast between slavery and freedom was nearly absolute.

While such alternative perspectives on slavery have significant merits, they sometimes employ a rather one-dimensional view of European colonial slavery, as if based solely on evidence from eighteenth-century Caribbean plantations. There is, however, good reason to believe that Europeans in the Indian Ocean World remained much closer to local customs and that 'no clear demarcation existed between a "native" and "white man's" slave trade, or even between the functions of slaves in local and European communities' (Sutherland 1983:264). With the production of agricultural commodities for the European market firmly in indigenous hands, the influx of slaves into colonial trading posts did not signify any real dramatic break with the past. Demographically, it must be said, slaves were more important in the European trading posts than in pre-colonial towns or indigenous communities (Raben 2008), but this only goes to show that Natives procured labour services in different ways. Europeans may have come to dominate the maritime routes of the Indian Ocean, subsequently enhancing the transoceanic movements of slaves, but their power on the Asian and African continent was extremely limited and largely dependent on friendly relations with local rulers.[17] Reid's plea to research the interaction between indigenous and colonial forms of slavery is still as valid today as it was a quarter century ago:

> Southeast Asia provides the most important evidence of European colonists taking over and interacting with an existing Asian system of slavery, rather than imposing their own system in a vacuum as in the New World or South Africa. We should therefore examine carefully how far the new patterns which emerged were determined by the masters or the slaves; by Europe or by Asia; by legal theory or by the political and social environment (Reid 1983a:14).

The demographic, economic and political-military dimensions of European colonization in the Americas were radically different, and so was the demand for and usage of slaves. Though Iberian colonists relied heavily on Native

---

[17]   Only in the second half of the nineteenth century did European powers have the wherewithal to make inroads on land and establish colonial domination over indigenous societies in Asia and Africa. Ironically, this colonial expansion was often justified by European theorists as a way of putting an end to the remaining indigenous institutions of slavery.

Americans working in various forms of unfree labour, the catastrophic mortality rates caused by the 'Columbian Exchange' (Crosby 1972) had decimated many tribal societies and economies. The rapid depletion of indigenous American populations almost seemed to post-mortem validate Eurocentric terminology pertaining to the 'discovery' of a 'New World' and the abundance of 'virgin land' just begging to be settled. The moral indignation of a few enlightened witnesses from Europe (most notably Las Casas) and the strong resistance of surviving Amerindians, gradually led to a decline in the exploitation of 'red' slaves.[18]

European colonial domination in the Americas was extensive, but consisted by and large of the control over unexplored natural resources; the commercial prospects of indigenous labour and trade were, barring a few important exceptions, trivial at best. And while the prospect of free and uninhabited land appealed to economic and political-religious refugees alike, the profitability of such 'bottom-up' colonization was minute in the short term. Experiments with transporting contract and convict labour from Europe were quite substantial – although much less so in the Dutch case – but remained circumscribed by how far one could legally push his fellow countrymen.[19]

The decision to transport slaves from sub-Saharan Africa to the Americas, a forced migration that began in earnest around the 1530s, generated a genuinely 'new world'. Not only did African slaves ensure the survival and commercial success of many European colonies in the greater Caribbean, in the process they also transformed themselves into a people with an entirely unique identity and culture (Mintz and Price 1992). Since almost all slaves in the Americas were black and of African background, and nearly all slave owners of white European descent, the history of slavery in the Americas has become closely intertwined with that of racism. The origin, nature and impact of colonial slavery in the New World were therefore quite exceptional. And its compelling history has dramatically shaped our modern-day image of the institution.

Despite these fundamental differences in origination, holding up the evidence on European colonial slavery in the Indian Ocean World against

---

[18]   Native American societies were familiar with slavery, but not as an economically productive system. The Tupinamba of Brazil, for example, used slaves for ceremonial sacrifices. In this 'uneconomic' use of slaves, Native Americans probably shared characteristics with indigenous slavery in Africa and Asia.

[19]   Europeans utilized the forced banishment of convicts and war captives, the system of indentured servitude and the sending of widows and orphans and other dependent people. But the acclaimed free and relatively egalitarian nature of the Dutch Republic conflicted with many of these practices. Moreover, the overall productivity of these coerced Europeans in the colonies was often not that high. In a counterfactual argument David Eltis (1993) states that, if European nations had not been restricted by certain cultural limits, they would have used cheaper white European slaves.

our more extensive knowledge of the institution in the American context may lead to fresh insights into both subjects. Slavery has often functioned as an exciting field for comparative exercises, yet few historians have dared to take it to a truly global level.[20] Even David Brion Davis' inspirational call (2000:454) to start 'looking at slavery from broader perspectives' somehow manages to exclude the entire Indian Ocean World from the 'big picture', as if that region existed in some historical vacuum.[21] The historiographical dominance of American slavery is in fact so glaring that its historians rarely ever feel the urge to look beyond the Atlantic World. On the other hand, the few historians looking at slavery in the Indian Ocean World can hardly escape drawing contrasts and similarities between the two systems.

The Dutch case promises to be particularly rewarding in a comparative exercise, as the VOC and WIC did, mutatis mutandis, resemble each other fairly well and their slavery operations were, from a quantitative perspective at least, quite similar. It also handily avoids the debate about cultural differences that usually forms such a grand obstacle in cross-national comparative history. And, finally, it will hopefully render us a more complete picture of Dutch slavery abroad.[22] This somewhat provocative comparison is, needless to say, primarily intended as an inventory of the quantitative data available, as a survey of the relevant historiography and as a challenging sketch of the major contrasts at hand. As the Dutch colonial orbit virtually encompassed the entire globe, one simply has to favour general patterns above specific detail.

---

[20]   Most comparative histories of slavery remain confined to the Americas. Some outstanding exceptions are Frederickson (1981), who compared slavery and racism in the settlement colonies of North America and South Africa and Kolchin (1987), although his comparison moved beyond slavery to include Russian serfdom. Pétré-Grenouilleau (2004) discusses the European and Arabian slave trades together, while Christopher, Pybus and Rediker (2007) takes an even broader look at forced migrations. Daalder, Kieskamp and Tang (2001) focuses on Dutch colonial slavery and slave trading around the globe.

[21]   Davis arguably can be forgiven, as he faults a mainly U.S. American audience on their provincialism regarding slavery. The fact that he does mention Mauritius and Réunion in the Indian Ocean in a footnote on page 454 perhaps suggests that he draws the line at modern plantation slavery. Even so, his statement that 'the multinational Atlantic Slave System can be seen as the first stepping stone toward the multinational corporations that today employ millions of virtual slaves in various construction and production projects in Asia, Africa, and Latin America' (p. 466) is rather odd when seen from the colonial Indian Ocean World perspective. Despite its title Moitt's collection (2004) is also predominantly focused on sugar and slavery in the Caribbean.

[22]   Of the major European colonial powers (Spain, Portugal, United Kingdom, France and the Dutch Republic), the Dutch had the smallest presence in the Americas, but were arguably the most dominant colonial power in Asia until the second half of the eighteenth century, when the British empire – on the heels of the American Revolution – began reorienting its focus to the Indian subcontinent. Recent findings (Postma and Enthoven 2003) suggest that the West may have been equally or even more important to the Dutch than the East with regard to trade and migrations of people. From a European comparative perspective, however, the Dutch were much more dominant in the East.

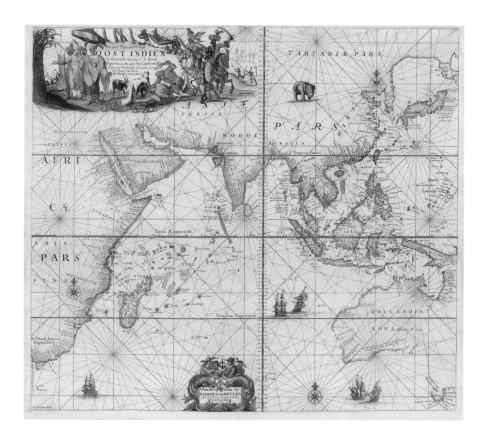

Map of the East Indies

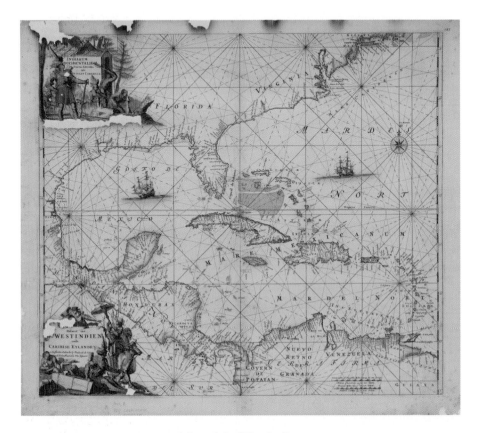

Map of the West Indies

The house of the medical officer in Dejima

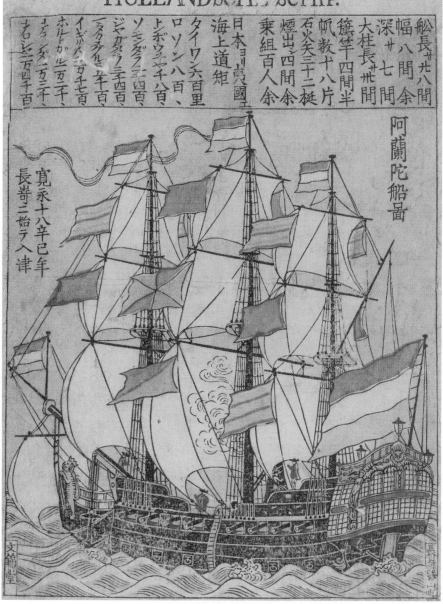

Japanese print of a 'Dutch ship'

View of Dejima

Dutch Reformed Church, Galle

Map of Batavia

Castle and church of Batavia

Town hall of Batavia

Fort Belgica on Banda

Joden Savanne, Suriname

Saba

Willemstad

African KNIL soldier

Slave houses on a plantation, Suriname

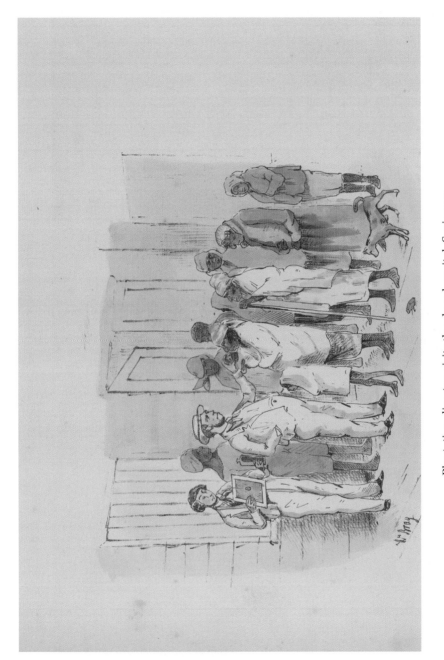

Plantation director visits the slave hospital, Suriname

The Dutch and the transatlantic slave trade

The slave trade has often been labelled a forced migration.[23] This migratory aspect is, naturally, most apparent in the transoceanic slave trades, with people being shipped over long distances, often to different continents. During the seventeenth and eighteenth centuries, hundreds of thousands of slaves were moved between the Dutch colonial possessions. In the following pages the larger migratory patterns of the slave trade in the Dutch colonial sphere will be addressed: how many slaves were transported over time, where did they come from and what were their primary destinations? To answer these questions, we gratefully draw on the extensive empirical work undertaken by some of the leading historians in the field. Since scholars generally adhere to the historic and historiographical divisions between the VOC and WIC, it makes sense here to discuss both slave trades independently, before drawing some general comparisons.

Quantifying the transatlantic slave trade

The transatlantic slave trade was a remarkably straightforward and one-directional migration, the key component of an ingenious triangular commercial system that has been well documented. Ships loaded with a carefully-selected assortment of products sailed from diverse ports in Western Europe to the West African coast, where European merchants exchanged these commodities for African slaves sold by local traders. The human cargo was then transported to strategic locations in the Americas, before returning home carrying slave-produced commodities such as sugar, coffee and tobacco to the European market. It was a good example of the emergence of global trade in the early modern period. If the voyage went as planned – this included keeping slave mortality on board to a minimum – investors stood to profit from several transactions,

For the African victims the so-called middle passage was merely one part of their tragic journey to the Americas. First, they experienced enslavement, coerced transportation and confinement in Africa itself, before being sold to what must have seemed strange white men who subsequently moved them

---

[23]   To define the slave trade as a forced migration fits nicely within the larger project. In essence, each transaction that moved a slave from one owner to the next was a highly dramatic passage, underlining the sheer powerlessness of the slave regarding his or her future. One of the greatest fears confronting slaves in the antebellum United States was, if we go by their own scattered testimonies at least, the prospect of being sold 'down South' or 'down the river', a change of venue which not only implied harsher working conditions and treatment, but also a dissolution of the established family, community and cultural bonds, no matter how feeble and meaningless these may have seemed in the eyes of the people closing the deal.

under excruciating circumstances across the Atlantic Ocean. Finally, after disembarking in the New World, they often faced further regional trading and transport. For the majority of them, backbreaking labour on large commercial plantations under the tropical sun loomed as the final destination. The forced alienation of those surviving the entire ordeal – the aggregated mortality rate must have been considerably higher than the estimated 14.5 per cent for the transatlantic crossing alone[24] – undeniably impacted their identity: from local or tribal affiliations within Africa to a more diffused African identity vis-à-vis the Europeans on board and, with the passage of time, to the birth of uniquely African American slave cultures.[25]

Depicting this forced migration in broad dramatic strokes is far easier than charting its precise directions in time and space. To pinpoint the exact origination of the slaves in Africa on the one hand – the so-called provenance zones or 'catchment' areas – one needs to be well-versed in regional African history, where primary evidence is often deficient. Establishing the specific end destinations in the Americas on the other hand, requires a deep understanding of multiple colonial histories. Furthermore, the records left of the slave ship voyages themselves and their actual embarkation and disembarkation ports are vast, yet still far from complete. It may not come as a surprise that African Americans with the desire and means to discover their genealogy are currently putting more faith in the scientific path of modern DNA research.[26]

Due to its highly organized and businesslike character, with slave embarkation, mortality and disembarkation being meticulously registered, historians have been left with large amounts of administrative evidence from which the business, volume and direction of the transatlantic slave trade can be reconstructed. They have been mainly occupied with three research objectives: first, the 'numbers game', or closely estimating the volume of slaves traded, transported and having perished along the way; second, determining which European nations were involved in slave trading and to what degree; and, finally, establishing which specific African groups fell victim to this

---

[24]   The estimated mortality rate is based on the current version of the Trans-Atlantic Slave Trade Database (TSTD2). It should be added here that very high mortality rates applied to the European crew of the slave ships as well, primarily due to the unhealthy tropical conditions on the African coast, where ships could experience long waiting periods before setting sail for the Americas.

[25]   The scholarly debate on 'Creolization' is an important one; a good place to start is the classic statement by Mintz and Price 1992. To emphasize the important role of the transatlantic slave trade in fostering Creolization, the cover of their book shows the famous abolitionist sketch of slaves crammed into a British ship during the middle passage. For a more recent assessment of the concept, see Price 2006.

[26]   This kind of research has become especially popular in the United States, where celebrities like Oprah Winfrey have given it ample attention. See, for example, www.AfricanAncestry.com In the Netherlands, Alex van Stipriaan is currently doing research on this topic.

forced migration and where and how their lives and cultures in the Americas continued. The first modern quantitative overview of the Atlantic slave trade by Philip Curtin (1969) inspired many historians to conduct empirical research in archival depositories. Eventually, the various cliometric data sets emerging from this were combined in the Trans-Atlantic Slave Trade Database (TSTD), an ongoing and truly collaborative project of a global community of scholars.[27] The current version of the database (TSTD2) contains a total of 34,850 registered slave voyages between 1501 and 1866, and based on these records estimates that around 12,521,300 slaves departed Africa with about 10,702,700 making it to the Americas. These modern estimates are only slightly above the total numbers Curtin proposed almost four decades ago, but are now corroborated by a wealth of supporting evidence.[28] Table 5.1

Table 5.1 Estimated African slave exports by national carrier, 1501-1866*

	1501-1600	1601-1700	1701-1800	1801-1866	Total
Spain/Uruguay	120,000	146,300	10,700	784,600	1.061,600
Portugal/Brazil	154,200	1.011,200	2.213,000	2.468,900	5.848,300
United Kingdom	1,900	428,300	2.545,300	284,000	3.259,400
Netherlands	1,400	219,900	330,000	3,000	554,300
United States**		4,200	189,300	111,900	305,300
France	100	38,400	1.139,000	203,900	1.381,400
Denmark/Baltic		27,400	67,300	16,300	111,000
Totals	277,500	1.875,600	6.494,600	3.873,600	12.521,300

Source: Trans-Atlantic Slave Trade Database (TSTD2), www.slavevoyages.com, www. slavevoyages.org, (http://wilson.library.emory.edu:9090/tast/assessment/estimates. faces?permlink=1788875).

*   For purposes of calculation, estimates of embarked and disembarked slaves in TSTD2 have not been rounded off. To avoid reading these numbers as precise totals, I have rounded the estimates up to the nearest hundred. Since I have done so with the aggregated 'totals' as well, they may not always be the exact sum of the individual estimates in these tables.
**   The database assigns slave voyages that were organized and departed from colonial North America in the seventeenth and eighteenth centuries (mainly Rhode Island) to what would later become the United States.

[27]   Work on the TSTD dates back to the 1980s, when computer and database technologies were still rather simplistic. For the first officially published version, including a database on CD-ROM, see Eltis et al 1999. The new and improved dataset, TSTD2, is an online version that has become interactive and accessible to the general public in 2008 (www.slavevoyages.com, www.slavevoyages.org). It is a truly revolutionary project aimed at bringing professional research and public education closer together.
[28]   Curtin (1969:87) downgraded Noel Deerr's estimate of 11,970,000 slaves imported into the Americas to 9,566,000, stating that 'it is extremely unlikely that the ultimate total will turn out to be less than 8,000,000 or more than 10,500,000'. TSTD2 thus appears to fall right between Curtin's and Deerr's estimates.

gives a general overview of the volume of the transatlantic slave trade, broken down by century and national carrier.

At present the database contains 1237 officially documented Dutch slave voyages with a total of 408,658 slaves departing from Africa. Through elaborate, but by no means flawless, methods these data are extrapolated to an estimated total of 554,300 slaves exported by the Dutch or roughly 4.4 per cent of the total volume of the transatlantic slave trade. Of these slaves around 475,200 reached the Americas alive (suffering a mortality rate of 14.3 per cent). These figures are fairly close to what the classic account of the Dutch Atlantic slave trade proposes (Postma 1990:295), which makes perfect sense, as the database relies heavily on the primary research by Johannes Postma.[29] Recently, Postma (2003a:137) downgraded his own assessments quite substantially to 501,409 slaves exported or 4.6 per cent of the total trade, with an annual average of 2,458 slaves embarking on the African coast.[30] Based on new empirical research by several historians, Postma now believes that a large number (207) of eighteenth-century voyages to Africa, ones he previously assumed to be slave voyages, were actually bilateral commodity traders returning directly to Europe. He thus changed from a 'maximalist' approach, 'wanting to make certain the volume of the slave trade was not understated', to a 'minimalist' one, 'including only those ships for which there is clear evidence that they carried slaves' (Postma 2003a:129).

The compilers of TSTD2, after incorporating the data collected by Postma, Den Heijer and several others, make 'slightly more aggressive assumptions' and argue, for example, that very few Dutch vessels sailing to the Angola region went there to trade in produce only (Vos, Eltis and Richardson 2008:232). And when Postma (2003a:121) decides to leave out approximately 3000 slaves captured from Dutch ships 'because they were presumably disembarked in the Americas by ships of other nations', TSTD2 still assigns those to the Dutch slave trade based on their original African departure. Such quibbles are exemplary of the many judgement calls historians are forced to make in order to cope with gaps in the historical records and with

---

[29]   Although the parameters are slightly different, estimating 542,972 slaves exported from Africa in the period 1600-1803 (Postma 1990:295). Johannes Postma has been working on the Dutch Atlantic slave trade since the 1960s, when he wrote his dissertation at Michigan State University, and acknowledges being influenced by Curtin's landmark study at the time (Postma 2003a:118-9).

[30]   Postma's revisions lower his previous estimates by seven per cent and the Dutch share of the entire transatlantic slave traffic from 4.7 to 4.6 per cent. He is, in my opinion, rather harsh on himself, calling the reassessment 'a humbling experience', showing 'that assumptions and speculation, however reasonable they may seem, are always inferior to verifiable evidence' (Postma 2003a:137). Note furthermore that Postma's estimate for the Dutch trade is lower in absolute numbers, but higher in its relative share of the total trade compared with TSTD2, suggesting that he still uses a significantly lower estimate for the total volume of the transatlantic slave trade.

evidence that defies easy categorization. For example, a recent dissertation (Paesie 2008) argues for a substantial increase in the volume of the Dutch slave trade based on hundreds of illicit slave voyages originating from the Dutch Republic, primarily from the maritime province of Zeeland. However, quite a few of these interlopers sailed – partly to escape the harsh WIC reprisals – under foreign flags. Based on this, TSTD 2 would qualify these voyages under other European states, even though it is fairly clear that these were predominantly Dutch-led operations. Working with a modern database fortunately allows the researcher some flexibility to adjust such ambiguous cases according to his or her personal preferences. But the decisive factor in establishing the nationality of a slave voyage – the investors, the owner of the vessel, the captain and crew, the flag – will likely remain elusive. Breaking down the transatlantic slave trade by national background therefore remains a complex and subjective exercise.

Despite the inherent subjectivity of all assumptions, extrapolations and estimations involved, historians generally agree that slightly more than half a million Africans were transported on Dutch ships with somewhere between 50,000 to 100,000 perishing before reaching the New World.[31] While research on specific periods and aspects of the trade will likely continue, any dramatic alterations to this general picture may no longer be expected. With regard to sheer volume the Dutch are regarded as a second-rate player in the transatlantic slave trade, certainly important, yet not comparable to the massive numbers transported by Portuguese and British vessels.

Such grand total figures can sometimes be misleading, however, or at least conceal interesting historical patterns. For example, as table 5.1 indicates, the Dutch were only truly active slavers during the seventeenth and eighteenth centuries, so if we limit our calculations to that period, their share of the total volume moves upward to 6.6 per cent. The Dutch commanded an even stronger position during the seventeenth-century 'Golden Age' (11.7 per cent), and in the period 1650 to 1675, more or less the age of the Caribbean sugar revolution, Dutch vessels were responsible for over twenty per cent of the entire transatlantic slave trade. Thus, to properly understand the relative impact of the Dutch, one needs to place the aggregated totals in their specific historical context. The volume and direction of the Dutch transatlantic slave trade will therefore be situated in time and space, in a modest attempt to historicize and interpret some of the general data presented in table 5.2 and 5.3.

---

[31]   Once again, Curtin's (1969:85) guesstimates were remarkably close to the mark: 'While a reliable estimate is not possible from the present literature, 500,000 is accepted here for the whole of Dutch America during the whole of the slave trade, including present-day Guyana'. This was especially accurate considering the prior estimates by Deerr (1950:284), who arrived at a total of 900,000 slaves imported into the Dutch Guyanas and the Dutch West Indies combined.

Fort Nassau, Berbice

Table 5.2 Estimated Dutch slave exports per African region, 1596-1829

	1596-1650	1651-1700	1701-1750	1751-1800	1801-1829	Total
Senegambia		8,400	400	400		9,200
Sierra Leone		800		800	700	2,300
Windward Coast			13,500	64,600	1,100	79,100
Gold Coast	800	18,200	41,700	42,500	300	103,400
Bight of Benin	5,400	71,300	47,500	2,700		126,900
Bight of Biafra	6,900	20,300	500	1,000	100	28,700
West Central Africa	21,900	67,400	53,400	61,100	900	204,800
Total	34,900	186,400	156,900	173,100	3,000	554,300

Source: Trans-Atlantic Slave Trade Database (TSTD2), www.slavevoyages.com, www.slavevoyages.org; (http://wilson.library.emory.edu:9090/tast/assessment/estimates.faces?permlink=1788878).

Table 5.3 Estimated Dutch slave imports per region, 1596-1829

	1596-1650	1651-1700	1701-1750	1751-1800	1801-1829	Total
Europe	100	1,900				2,000
North America		1,200				1,200
British Caribbean	900	4,700	400	700	300	7,000
French Caribbean		11,600	600	600		12,700
Danish Caribbean			5,200			5,200
Dutch Caribbean*		81,500	40,000	20,200		141,700
Dutch Guyanas		34,000	84,300	130,200	1,800	250,300
Dutch Brazil	26,600	1,100				27,700
Spanish Americas	1,300	17,800	3,300	1,400	400	24,200
Africa		3,000			300	3,200
Total	28,800	156,800	133,700	153,100	2,800	475,200

Source: Trans-Atlantic Slave Trade Database (TSTD2), www.slavevoyages.com, www.slavevoyages.org; (http://wilson.library.emory.edu:9090/tast/assessment/estimates.faces?permlink=1788879).

* The term 'Dutch Caribbean' is used here in its narrow definition, only consisting of the Dutch Caribbean islands, while Suriname and the other Wild Coast settlements fall under the 'Dutch Guyanas'.

When dealing with a sensitive subject such as slavery, quantitative studies are often criticized for being cold-hearted accounts, with the slaves amounting to little more than lifeless numbers on paper.[32] This chapter easily serves

---

[32] This should hardly come as a surprise, since we are left with a wealth of data from the European trade records, several descriptive accounts from European witnesses to the slave trade, but with almost no authentic sources from the African or slave perspective. In the preface to his classic Philip Curtin (1969:xix) wrote: 'Some readers may miss the sense of moral outrage tradi-

as a typical example of this. But while statistical tables and graphs cannot adequately describe the individual and collective human tragedies of the middle passage, they are nevertheless an unmistakable reflection of the bulk of source material historians are left with.[33] Furthermore, recent publications have shown how a mastery of hard data can ultimately lead to excitingly fresh and culturally sensitive interpretations, or towards the debunking of them (Eltis 2000). The greatest challenge for future research will remain the exploration of the directional patterns of this forced migration, connecting specific provenance zones in Africa with their particular destinations in the Americas. Only then, for example, can historians and anthropologists make accurate observations about the cultural impact of the slaves on their respective New World settlements.[34]

Historicizing the Dutch transatlantic slave trade

The incidental slave trade, 1596-1635

Given that their commercial activities on the African coast dated back to the mid-1590s, the Dutch waited several decades before actively participating in the slave trade. Initially, Dutch African trade was primarily focused on gold and, to a much lesser extent, ivory.[35] Their first official settlement on the African coast, Fort Nassau (1612) at Mouri on the Gold Coast, did not spark any serious slaving activities either. Perhaps this hesitation was caused by initial moral reservations regarding the traffic in humans or, more plausibly, can be attributed to the fact that the Dutch still lacked a suitable American

---

tional in histories of the trade. This book will have very little to say about the evils of the slave trade, still less in trying to assign retrospective blame to the individuals or groups who were responsible. This omission in no way implies that the slave trade was morally neutral; it clearly was not. The evils of the trade, however, can be taken for granted as a point long since proven beyond dispute.'

[33]   Recent studies focus on the treatment of slaves during the middle passage and particularly the relationship between the largely European crew and the African 'cargo'; see Christopher 2006 and Rediker 2007.

[34]   Of course, research on African retention in the Americas is by no means new. As early as the 1920s and 1930s, the famous anthropologist Melville Herskovits studied the culture of the descendants of slaves and Maroons in Suriname, looking for specific African elements. The point is that with the aid of the TSTD such observations and assumptions can be cross-checked with our own empirical findings.

[35]   For the relative importance of the gold and ivory trade in relation to the slave trade for the seventeenth-century Dutch on the African coast, see Van den Boogaart 1992 and the response by Eltis 1994. As early as around 1615 the Portuguese were complaining to the Spanish king that the Dutch dominated all African trades, except for the one in slaves (Ratelband 2000:34, 45).

colony with a strong demand for slave labour.[36]

As the rise of Dutch colonial expansion was closely tied to the enduring conflict with Spain (as well as with Portugal from 1580), Iberian shipping became fair game for Dutch privateers. The capture of Portuguese slave ships in and around the Atlantic Ocean resulted in what has been labelled an 'incidental slave trade' (Emmer 1972b:728-9). Slaves carried by the enemy were defined as 'contraband' and, when possible, sold to the nearest friendly buyer.[37] This incidental slave trade reached a peak during the first full decade of the WIC, but the 2,356 slaves – if we accept WIC official Johannes de Laet's count – taken between 1623 and 1636 (Van den Boogaart and Emmer 1979:355) were, despite their value as propaganda, rather insignificant from a quantitative perspective.[38]

From a qualitative viewpoint, however, some of these slaves caused a historic impact far greater than their numbers may suggest. Which slaves, for example, received more attention than the twenty Africans delivered in 1619 by 'a Dutch man of warre' to the English settlers at Jamestown, Virginia?[39] In various other Protestant settlements in the New World (New Netherland, Bermuda, Barbados, Tobago, Guyanas) warfare and privateering were often responsible for the arrival of the first Africans.[40] Almost all originated from

---

[36]   One of the first board meetings of the WIC, in 1623, revealed some reservations regarding the moral legitimacy of the Angolan slave trade. Even so, there is evidence that the Dutch already made use of slaves on the African coast itself, as suggested by early Dutch activities on Cabo Verde and on the island of Príncipe. See De Jonge 1862, I:235 and Enthoven 2003.

[37]   The term 'incidental' occurs several times throughout the historiography of the Dutch slave trade, but Emmer developed it most clearly. The famous case of 1596 (see note 3) illustrates that this initial trade did not go entirely unquestioned: an attempt to sell 130 captured Angolan slaves in Middelburg resulted in protest rather than profit. There is some scattered evidence that several Portuguese slave ships captured by the Dutch in the 1620s were released with their slaves, either for practical reasons (no market to sell them, other sailing priorities) or perhaps because the captains personally abhorred the practice. Later on, slaves based on Curaçao who served on intra-Caribbean vessels often received fake freedom papers so that, in case of a hostile attack in open waters, they could not be confiscated as 'contraband'. I thank Han Jordaan for pointing this interesting fact out to me.

[38]   Because the TSTD assigns nationality of slave voyages based on ship registration at the African coast, these incidental slaves are all listed under the Portuguese flag, even if they disembarked in the New World from Dutch ships.

[39]   Most histories of slavery in the United States begin with this shipment arriving at Jamestown. Slavery in seventeenth-century colonial Virginia in general has received much more attention than its historical proportions justify. For recent information on these particular slaves, see Sluiter 1997 and Thornton 1998b. One question that continues to preoccupy historians of colonial North America is whether these Africans were treated as slaves or not; that they departed Africa as slaves is clear, however.

[40]   Wim Klooster (1998:105) mentions Angolan slaves at the Dutch forts on the Xingú River in 1623 and hundreds of slaves among the Dutch at Cayenne in 1644; the patroonship of Jan de Moor on the island of Tobago, established in 1628, was arguably the first Dutch plantation colony in the Americas. The English slave trade also began with privateering activities, namely by the Elizabethan 'sea dog' John Hawkins in the 1560s.

West Central Africa (Congo-Loango, Luanda, Benguela), which between the 1580s and 1640s possessed a virtual monopoly on slave exports. Some of the names assigned to the first African residents of New Amsterdam – Paulo d'Angola, Anthony Portuguese, Simon Congo, Assento Angola – confirm this Portuguese-Angolan connection.[41] As the first and rather isolated Africans among small communities of struggling settlers from north-west Europe, this 'charter generation' of 'Atlantic creoles' (Berlin 1996, 1998; Heywood and Thornton 2007) witnessed the slow crystallization of slavery before its own eyes. At times, they may have experienced a level of freedom and social mobility that was generally absent among future generations of African American slaves.

Dutch Brazil and the emergence of the WIC slave trade, 1630-1654

The conquest of Pernambuco and several other Portuguese captaincies in north-east Brazil during the early 1630s handed the WIC the richest sugar-producing area in the world, and a full-blown slave society at that. The Company officials soon came to realize that without slave labour sugar cultivation was in danger. After the surrounding rural areas were sufficiently 'pacified', the WIC began expanding its commercial interests on the African coast by simply conquering long-established Portuguese trading posts. Earlier attempts to do so had failed miserably (Ratelband 2000; Den Heijer 2006), but victories at Arguin (1633), Elmina (1637), São Paulo de Luanda and São Tomé (1641) guaranteed an unprecedented Dutch dominance on the African coast. Never would the Dutch have easier access to slaves than during the 1640s (Ratelband 1953, 2000).

The history of Dutch Brazil can be divided into three acts: first, the conquest and consolidation of a sizeable territory for sugar cultivation, followed by a decade of relative peace and prosperity under the enlightened governorship of Johan Maurits van Nassau and, finally, renewed warfare with the local Portuguese colonists leading to the ultimate surrender of the colony in 1654. During Maurits' years, thousands of slaves were imported by the WIC, heralding the official involvement by the Dutch in the transatlantic slave trade. At first, these slaves were mainly procured from the Calabar region (Slave Coast, Bight of Benin and Bight of Biafra) and the region north of the Congo River (Van den Boogaart and Emmer 1979:360). But, partly fuelled by the traditional preferences of the Portuguese-Brazilian sugar planters (*moradores*) for Angolan slaves, the main port of Luanda was taken in 1641.

The increasing volume of slave imports and sugar exports in the 1640s

---

[41]   Berlin (1996:265).This historic connection between New York and West Central Africa (Congo and Angola) has recently been reawakened through cultural exchanges.

Table 5.4 Estimated slave imports and sugar exports in Dutch Brazil, 1630-1654

Period	Slave imports	Sugar exports**	Political developments
1630-1635	280*	154,169	Conquest and pacification
1636-1645	23,500	2,433,742	Relative peace and prosperity
1646-1654	1,700	240,848	Renewed guerrilla warfare

Sources: *Slave imports*: TSTD2 comes close to the classic work by Wättjen (1921), who gave a total of 23,163 slaves imported by the Dutch during the peak decade, especially considering that TSTD2 includes 210 slaves imported by the Dutch to Bahia and 140 slaves to an unspecified destination in Brazil. Wättjen's figures for 1642-1643 are lower than those given by Johan Maurits van Nassau in a report to the States General of the Dutch Republic in 1644: according to that report the slave trade registers revealed that between 7 February 1642 and 23 July 1643, roughly one and a half years, 6468 slaves had embarked, of whom 1524, or almost a quarter, would perish during the middle passage (Gonsalves de Mello 2001:199-200). *Sugar exports*: Wättjen (1921:316-23) as cited in Den Heijer 2003:88; these export figures start in 1631 and end in 1651, but except for the sugar looted at the conquest of Pernambuco, I do not foresee substantial additions here.

*   The 280 slaves imported in 1630 were incidental Angolan slaves, taken from a captured Portuguese vessel (and as such should not fall under Dutch slave imports in TSTD2, see Van den Boogaart and Emmer (1979:358).
**   Sugar was measured in *arrobas* – one *arroba* being approx. 14.75 kilograms (Den Heijer 2003:88) – which would imply that during the peak decade the Dutch exported almost 36 million kilograms of sugar from Pernambuco to Europe.

came to a sudden halt when renewed hostilities broke out shortly after Maurits had returned to Europe. Everywhere sugar plantations and mills were burned to the ground or halted their production. The effects of war and peace on sugar and slavery in Dutch Brazil are clearly visible in table 5.4; the first official decade of Dutch participation in the transatlantic slave trade was quite impressive.[42]

While the 'Brazilian adventure' was, for the shareholders of the WIC at least, a financial disaster, it also taught the Company important lessons about the operation of the transatlantic slave trade and the organization of slave-based sugar production; and that trusting a policy of religious tolera-tion to secure the loyalty of resident Portuguese planters had been naive. For Brazilians today, this era of religious toleration spurred by the charisma of the 'humanist prince' of Nassau and the many cultural and architectural

---

[42]   While most periodizations are inherently subjective, this one may have its merits. My main concern here is to make visible the sudden rise and fall of the Dutch Brazilian plantation com-plex which, for example, would be missed when one sticks to the annual average of 721 slaves exported by the Dutch in the period 1600-45 (Postma 2003a:137).

achievements stimulated by him are exactly what makes this Dutch episode so unique and admirable.[43]

Even so, the import of thousands of African slaves during Maurits's reign hardly deviated from the slave trading patterns before and after the Dutch period. In the first quarter of the seventeenth century alone, the Portuguese shipped approximately 150,000 bonded Africans to Brazil.[44] In this respect, the Dutch slave trade to Brazil may have generated less of a historic impact than the few incidental slaves delivered to other locations in the New World in the previous decades. The Dutch did introduce more slaves from West Africa to Brazil, primarily from the Slave Coast, thereby perhaps introducing the first Igbo from the Bight of Biafra in Pernambuco as well (Vos, Eltis and Richardson 2008). As a result, the diversity of the local African population was somewhat augmented, although this was arguably but a marginal number compared to the great majority of Angolan slaves imported from West Central Africa during the entire seventeenth century.

The rise of the Dutch slave trade in other European colonies, 1646-1674

War undoubtedly had a dramatic but also liberating effect on the lives of slaves in Brazil. New slaves arriving from Angola could no longer be sold or fed by the Company. The Hoge Raad in Recife begged its WIC colleagues in Luanda to stop sending slaves across the Atlantic, and those who had already arrived were now redirected north. In January 1646 the *Tamandare* sailed with a cargo of slaves from Fernando da Noronha via Barbados to New Amsterdam. The relative ease with which this merchandise was sold appeared as a harbinger of things to come (Ratelband 2000:225, 259). With Dutch Brazil sliding into the chaos of civil war in the mid-1640s, the WIC faced a dilemma: what should be done about the slave trade, especially after its short-lived supremacy on the African coast was eroded with the Portuguese recapturing Luanda and São Tomé (1648) and the expansion of English slaving activities? (see table 5.2)

Past historians have argued that the Dutch opened new markets for slaves in the English and French Caribbean by introducing slave-based sugar cultivation closely resembling the Brazilian model.[45] This interpretation seems to fit the historic timeline quite nicely, just as the fact that during

---

[43] For a recent assessment of the Dutch policy of religious toleration in Brazil, see Israel and Schwartz 2007.
[44] Klein (2004:230). That a significant proportion of the Brazilian sugar produced in the first two decades of the seventeenth century was traded on the Amsterdam exchange, only indicates that the Dutch were already profiting from plantation slavery before they began directly participating in it themselves; see Ebert 2003.
[45] For example, Curtin (1969:125-6); elsewhere (p. 55) he states that '[u]p to 1663, the slave trade to Barbados was practically a Dutch monopoly'.

the 1650s and 1660s, before the acquisition of Suriname and the rise of the Curaçaoan *asiento* trade, the Dutch mostly transported slaves to colonies of other Europeans (see table 5.3). However, recent empirical research by John McCusker and Russell Menard (2004) strongly diminishes the Dutch role in the so-called 'Barbadian sugar revolution' by pointing at a much greater English involvement than previously thought.[46] The First Navigation Act (1651) established under Cromwell was mainly intended to suppress Dutch trade to the English colonies and fuelled the growing animosity between the two maritime superpowers, eventually leading to three naval wars between 1652 and 1674. Increasingly stifled by the mercantilist policies of England and France, the Dutch looked – ironically perhaps – to the colonies of their former enemy Spain to provide new markets for the slave trade.[47] Between 1646 and 1657, Dutch traders sold about 3,800 slaves to Santo Domingo, Puerto Rico and Tierra Firme (Klooster 1998:106), while between 1657 and 1663 fourteen Dutch slave ships arrived at Buenos Aires in the Rio de la Plata region alone.[48]

It is in this volatile arena that the emergence of Curaçao as a slave trade entrepôt for the Spanish Americas should be situated. No longer useful as a military base for the Company, now the war with Spain was over, and not suitable for commercial plantation agriculture, the island needed a different niche. For the next half century, Curaçao would take advantage of the *asiento* trade, receiving 'saltwater' slaves from Africa and distributing them to the Spanish Americas according to contracts made in Europe. The *asiento* contracts were renewed and reconfigured several times during the second half of the seventeenth century, thereby consolidating the Dutch position as a major player in the transatlantic slave trade.[49]

Altogether almost a 100,000 slaves, or roughly twenty per cent of the entire Dutch slave trade, accordingly found their way to the Spanish Americas

---

[46]   The authors are diminishing the Dutch role, while at the same time suggesting its continued importance. It remains hard to establish and measure the more immaterial contributions. After the first Navigation Act, the English colonists were most likely inclined to hide any illicit Dutch trade from the records. At the same time, the Company records at Elmina (Ratelband 1953) show an increase in English shipping for slaves in the mid-1640s.

[47]   The end of the Eighty Years' War (1648) created new possibilities for Dutch traders in slaves and other colonial goods. Because Spain was still in conflict with Portugal – until 1640 the primary slave carrier for the Spanish Americas – its colonists were searching for other ways to procure slaves.

[48]   Moutoukias 1988:143-7. Rio de la Plata had a notorious reputation as a smuggling port at the periphery of the Spanish Americas. Klooster (1998:53) notes, based on Moutoukias, that it was the most frequently visited place in Spanish America by the Dutch between 1655 and 1665, with 63 voyages in total, and that there even existed a small resident population of Dutch and Flemings in Buenos Aires.

[49]   Klooster 1997, 2003. In 1667 and 1668 contracts were drawn to move 4000 slaves on an annual basis, and in the period 1679-1681 it peaked to 9,800 slaves to be delivered at Curaçao.

between 1658 and 1729, with a sizeable number from the Slave Coast, thus further diversifying the ethnic make-up of the Spanish colonies (Klooster 1998:107). Except for their short 'layover' at Curaçao and their impact on the island economy, most of these Africans quickly disappeared from the Dutch colonial realm. And while this transit trade enhanced the historic reputation of the Dutch as slave traders, the slaves themselves ended up in Spanish, not Dutch colonies.[50]

With Curaçao evolving into 'Amsterdam's Caribbean counterpart' (Klooster 1998:59), other Dutch colonies in the Americas received slaves only sparingly during the 1650s and 1660s. Governor Peter Stuyvesant of New Netherland repeatedly requested slaves from Curaçao, but only a few actually arrived (84 between 1659 and 1661) (Emmer 1972a:115). Sound business acumen, not national solidarity, ensured that most surplus or 'refuse' slaves were sold closer to home, and usually at much better prices. New Netherland simply could not compete with the Caribbean plantation colonies in their demand for slave labour. Of the two large slave cargoes arriving in New Amsterdam, most of the slaves of *Het Witte Paert* (1654) were quickly resold to tobacco planters in the Chesapeake, and the 290 slaves disembarking from the *Gideon* were just in time to witness the non-violent surrender of New Amsterdam to the English.[51] New Netherland was by all accounts never more than a peripheral destination in the slave trade, even if the small stream of slaves arriving would lay the foundation of a vibrant African American community.[52]

The slave trades of the second WIC and the interlopers, 1674-1730

The Peace of Breda (1667), settling the Second Anglo-Dutch War and swapping New Netherland (New York) for Suriname, would greatly impact the future of the Dutch transatlantic slave trade. For the next century and a half, the Dutch colonial possessions in the Americas would remain largely

---

[50]   The English were also important in the slave trade to the Spanish Americas, with Jamaica functioning as a competing slave entrepôt to Curaçao. However, Jamaica differed from Curaçao, as the island was also home to a substantial plantation sector, thereby giving it a more diversified economic character than the Dutch colony.

[51]   In 1655 the governor and council of New Netherland supported a ten per cent duty on the sale of each slave exported from the colony, because almost all slaves brought by *Het Witte Paert* had left the colony again. This was the moment when the Chesapeake tobacco plantations began replacing British indentured servants with African slaves. For the connections between Chesapeake planters, some of whom had Dutch backgrounds, and New Amsterdam-based merchants, see Hatfield 2003.

[52]   That around 1664 New Amsterdam possessed 'the largest urban slave population on mainland North America' (Berlin 1996:269) says more about the slow emergence of racial slavery in the Chesapeake and the stunted growth of its cities than any acute demand for slaves in the Dutch trading post.

unchanged. One could even say that the failed colonization of New Holland (Dutch Brazil) and New Netherland (Dutch New York) made the WIC domain leaner and meaner, heavily concentrated on the lower Caribbean. This suited the financial and structural reorganization of the Company in the early 1670s very well. With Curaçao now in its golden age as a slave trade entrepôt to the Spanish Americas and with Suriname emerging as the quin-tessential Dutch plantation colony, the future opportunities for the slave trade looked promising.

The original documentation of the Second WIC (1674-1792) has fortu-nately been much better preserved than that of its predecessor. From the viewpoint of the transatlantic slave trade, this entire period is best divided into two parts: the era of the WIC monopoly and, from the early 1730s on, the era of the private slave trade. Henk den Heijer's (1997) research on the slave trade of the Second WIC gives a good impression of the origin, volume and destination of these voyages (see tables 5.5 and 5.6).

Table 5.5 Slave exports Africa under the second WIC, 1674-1740

Period	Elmina	Slave Coast	Angola	Various	Total
1674-1689	10,553	16,543	22,207	14,861	64,164
1690-1704	3,745	22.035	17,017		42,797
1705-1719	4,712	18,433	7,640	1,248	32,033
1720-1740*	24,028	18,099	9,356		51,483
1674-1740	43,038	75,110	56,220	16,109	190,477
Percentage	22.6%	39.4%	29.5%	8.5%	100%

Source: adapted from Den Heijer 1997:151.

* This period is six years longer than the others.

Table 5.6 Slave imports Americas under the second WIC, 1674-1740

Period	Curaçao	Suriname	St. Eustatius	Essequibo Berbice	Various	Total
1674-1689	31,642	12,490	668	754	7,758	53,312
1690-1704	17,849	10,180		1,659	5,985	35,673
1705-1719	10,726	12,549	446	1,536	480	25,737
1720-1740*	2,270	25,565	9,747	2,503	1,916	42,001
1674-1740	62,487	60,784	10,861	6,452	16,139	156,723
Percentage	39.9%	38.8%	6.9%	4,1%	10.3%	100%

Source: adapted from Den Heijer 1997:152.

*   This period is six years longer than the others.

Five Surinamese girls with different ethnic backgrounds

According to table 5.5 the forced migration of Angolan slaves gradually declined during this period, while the Slave Coast remained a relatively stable supplier throughout (primarily from the Bight of Benin, as the Bight of Biafra was increasingly dominated by English slavers, see table 5.2) and Dutch Elmina underwent a dramatic transformation from gold to slave exporter. As this transformation took place after Curaçao had lost its function as a slave entrepôt, it is plausible that most slaves from the Gold Coast found their way to Suriname through Elmina, confirming the oft-celebrated historic connections between these two colonial possessions of the Dutch.

Curaçao and Suriname were the primary beneficiaries of the Company slave trade in this period, receiving almost equal numbers, with the crucial difference being that most slaves to Curaçao were transferred to Spanish colonies, while Suriname functioned as an end destination (see table 5.6). Between 1676 and 1716 over 42,000 African slaves arriving at Curaçao were distributed among Spanish traders (Klooster 2003:205-6; Postma 1990:45, 48). When, after the Spanish Succession War (1701-1714), the *asiento* contracts fell squarely into English hands, the slave trade to Curaçao rapidly declined.[53] Not only did this have immediate effects on the island's economy and the activities of the local Company slaves (Jordaan 1997, 1999, 2003), but it would also result in a rapid creolization of its African American population and the sustained growth of a Free Black community.[54] It appears that Sint Eustatius took up some of the slack of the transit trade in the 1720s, but the island's trade was more focused on the French Caribbean and, later in the century, on North America as well.[55]

Although the WIC attempted to monopolize the Dutch slave trade, since the second half of the seventeenth century interlopers had been operating in the same business. Postma and others have generally argued that the triangular trade was too complicated and risky for smugglers to be very successful, and have accordingly assessed low figures when compared with the Company trade. Recent archival research by Paesie (2008) however, has provided us with numbers that are impressive, with the interlopers reaching up to a third of the WIC slave trade in the first three decades of the eighteenth century. This would mean a substantial increase of the volume and impact of

---

[53]   According to Jordaan (2003:220) 'independent shippers landed nearly 10,000 slaves at Curaçao between 1730 and 1795, illustrating the island's diminished role in the traffic'.

[54]   Klooster 1994, 1999. For the remainder of the eighteenth century Curaçao nevertheless continued its other – mostly illegal – trade relations with the Spanish Americas, particularly with the eastern parts of Venezuela; see Klooster 1998.

[55]   During the 1770s, at the time of the American War of Independence, Sint Eustatius earned the nickname 'the Golden Rock' owing to its free trade and smuggling activities. In the period 1775-79 the island received around 4,000 slaves from Africa – most were undoubtedly intended for further trading.

Table 5.7 Estimated volume of illicit slave trade by Dutch-based interlopers, 1674-1730

Period	Embarked on African coast	After leaving African coast*	Arriving in the Americas	Distributive trade**
1674-1699	19,000-21,000	15,500-17,500	13,000-14,000	5,000-6,000
1700-1730	50,000-53,000	40,000-43,000	33,000-35,000	5,000-10,000
Totals	69,000-74,000	55,500-60,500	46,000-49,000	10,000-16,000

Source: Paesie 2008:51-2, 242-58.

*   Paesie assesses a substantial reduction between the first embarkation of slaves and the actual transatlantic voyage. Because interlopers were operating illicitly, they were more vulnerable to attack by both Company ships and foreign (enemy) vessels. The shipboard mortality of the slaves is only assessed in the third column.
**   These slaves should be counted separately from the other three columns as they were distributed along the African coast, on the nearby islands or in the Iberian peninsula to other slave traders. Most of these slaves still embarked on the middle passage, but not as part of the cargo of Dutch-based interlopers.

the Dutch slave trade, even though many of the slaves transported ended up in non-Dutch colonies.

The private slave trade: Zeeland's return to the Wild Coast, 1730s-1803

During the 1730s the WIC relinquished its monopoly on the transatlantic slave trade, leading to the emergence of a large private slave trade and the end of its illegal forerunners, the interlopers. Companies such as the Middelburgsche Commercie Compagnie (MCC)[56] and the Rotterdam-based firm of Rochussen were now mainly responsible for delivering slaves to Suriname and the smaller Dutch plantation colonies on the Wild Coast (Berbice, Essequibo and Demerara).[57] As a consequence, the historic connections between Zeeland and the Wild Coast were rekindled, with almost eighty per cent of the Dutch private slave trade organized by companies from that maritime province.

The extent to which this trade expanded dramatically in the mid-eight-

[56]   Several historians have researched the extensive archives of the MCC and written on the private slave trade in the eighteenth century, particularly Unger (1961), Priester (1987) and most recently Reinders Folmer-van Prooijen (2000).
[57]   The Dutch presence on the Wild Coast dated all the way back to the end of the sixteenth century, but had frequently suffered from hostilities with Native Americans, as well as Spanish, English and French colonizers. Interestingly, Berbice and Essequibo, with an older Dutch history than Suriname, were ultimately incorporated into British Guyana, while Suriname, which began as an English colony, remained Dutch. Demerara was only opened for colonization in the mid-eighteenth century and attracted mainly British planters from Barbados.

Table 5.8 Estimated slave imports into Dutch colonies in the 18th and 19th century*

Period	Dutch Caribbean**		Dutch Guyanas		British Guyanas***
	Dutch voyages	Other voyages	Dutch voyages	Other voyages	
1701-1725	29,200	0	24,200	0	
1726-1750	10,800	2,100	60,000	0	
1751-1775	16,100	100	100,700	1,200	
1776-1795	4,100	3,600	29,500	5,500	
1795-1800	0	0	0	7,900	30,600
18th century	68,300	5,900	214,500	14,700	
1801-1808	0	0	1,200	19,800	41,700
Prohibition of the international slave trade					
1820-1825	0	0	600	3,700	0

Source: Trans-Atlantic Slave Trade Database (TSTD2), www.slavevoyages.com, www.slavevoyages.org; (http://wilson.library.emory.edu:9090/tast/assessment/estimates.faces?permlink=1788951; http://wilson.library.emory.edu:9090/tast/assessment/estimates.faces?permlink=1788952).

*   These estimates only pertain to the data in TSTD2. After the transatlantic slave trade became illegal, slave imports into the Guyanas came primarily from elsewhere in the Caribbean; this topic will be discussed in the section under abolition.
**   The term 'Dutch Caribbean' is used here in its narrow definition, only consisting of the Dutch Caribbean islands, while Suriname and the other Wild Coast settlements fall under the 'Dutch Guyanas'.
***   The British Guyanas are, in this table, the Dutch Guyanas during the English occupation.

eenth century, before decreasing just as rapidly during the latter decades, becomes clear from table 5.8. This decline can be attributed to two factors: first, the state of the Surinamese plantation society itself, which suffered from a financial crisis and limited profitability,[58] partly related to the continuous resistance of the Maroon communities; second, the general decline of the Dutch Republic, no longer a major player in Europe, with English supremacy in the Fourth Anglo-Dutch War (1780-1784) confirming the loss of their maritime prowess.

A further breakdown of the Dutch slave trade to the Guyanas gives an estimated 160,200 slaves disembarking in Suriname during the eighteenth century according to Postma (2003b:306), whereas a much smaller figure of 20,300 slaves went to Essequibo and Demerara on Dutch ships (Van der Oest 2003:335). This would leave – barring dramatic differences between these various estimates – about 34,000 slaves brought to Berbice on Dutch vessels during the eighteenth century. Essequibo and particularly Demerara, which

[58]   For a critique of this colonial crisis thesis, see Van Stipriaan 1995.

opened for settlement in the 1740s, were promising and quickly developing plantation colonies, with most of their slaves arriving in the latter decades of the eighteenth century.

The inability of the Dutch to keep pace with these economic developments was quickly answered by increased British and US slave trading activities: Postma (2003b:306) mentions a total of 7,011 slaves arriving in Suriname on US ships during the 1780s and 1790s, with the British focusing predominantly on Essequibo and Demerara, especially after occupying these colonies in 1795.[59] The colonies were briefly returned to the Dutch during the era of the Batavian Republic (1795-1805), much to the chagrin of even the Dutch planters. A total of six Dutch slave voyages in 1802-1803 delivered an estimated 1,287 slaves to Suriname (Postma 2003b:306). The TSTD2 projects that during this Dutch interregnum British slavers still brought 18,200 of the foreign slave imports to the 'Dutch' Guyanas, mostly to Essequibo and Demerara, and another 71,500 slaves in the English period before the prohibition of the international slave trade.

Based on the provenance zones of the Dutch private slave trade in the eighteenth century (see table 5.2) it becomes clear that besides a continuous stream of slaves from West Central Africa, the Wild Coast settlements were mainly supplied with slaves from the Gold Coast and, in an entirely new development, from the Windward Coast. This may have been a reaction to the Dutch being driven away from the Slave Coast by the British, but other factors relating to the operation of the private slave trade could also have influenced this change.[60] Approximately 100,000 Africans were imported into the Dutch Guyanas in the third quarter of the eighteenth century; of this total, West Central Africa and the Windward Coast supplied around 40,000 slaves each, with the Gold Coast adding the remaining 20,000. These migration streams influenced the diversity of the slave population of Suriname substantially and gave the colony a continued African impulse largely absent from the rapidly creolizing African population of Curaçao.

The slave trade in the Dutch Indian Ocean World

Compared with our remarkably detailed knowledge about the transatlantic slave trade, our understanding of the slave trade in the Indian Ocean World

[59] Logically, as English colonists already owned a third of the 130 young plantations in Demerara during the 1760s and worked by slave labour '[b]etween 1789 and 1802, export ts of sugar rose by 433 percent, coffee by 233 percent, and cotton by 862 percent[; f]abulous fortunes were made in a short period' (Viotti da Costa 1994:43).
[60] See Vos 2008 for an in-depth look at Dutch slave trading on the Windward Coast in the eighteenth century.

is astonishingly poor. If not for the ubiquity of slaves in the historical documents, it would be easy to forget that slave trading had taken place there at
all. Until recently, it certainly had not preoccupied historians to any great
extent. One reason for this is that slave trading constituted only a minor
part of the commercial activities of the Company. Historian Els Jacobs has
estimated its net worth at only 0.5 per cent of the entire VOC trade in the
eighteenth century (Vink 2003b:235). It was thus insignificant in comparison
with the bright profits from the pepper, coffee and tea trades. The Company
was apparently 'content to leave this trade to "private enterprise", albeit
under certain restrictions' and *freeburghers* in Batavia – European, mestizos
and in the eighteenth century the Chinese – became 'the biggest slave traders
in Asia'.[61] But the documentation regarding this private slave trade, including
that of already established indigenous merchants, is more scattered, incomplete and anecdotal than we would like.[62] This makes it extremely difficult
to make even guesstimates about the nature, volume and directions of these
forced migrations. The following pages are, therefore, of a more tentative
nature and will often gaze through the prism of the better-known transatlantic slave trade.

First of all, the national involvement in the Indian Ocean slave trade is infinitely more complicated and diverse, which makes the temporal boundaries
much harder to define. The transatlantic slave trade has, as we have seen, a
clearly demarcated history from beginning to end, spanning almost four centuries. Because it was an entirely European affair – if we accept that the participation of independent American nations such as the United States and Brazil
can be attributed to the descendants of European settlers – it is relatively easy
to oversee. The vast majority of Atlantic Ocean slave voyages were organized
in, departed from, and returned to European ports, even if quite a few were
illicit. This metropolitan origination was entirely absent from slave voyages
in the Indian Ocean World, and as a consequence they remained more hidden
from public view and administrative record-keeping in Europe.

Furthermore, since an extensive regional slave trade already existed
before the arrival of the Europeans in Asia, and sometimes persisted after

---

[61]   Van der Kraan 1983:330. Van der Kraan (1983:339, note 10) points out that since the 1720s
the VOC levied an extraordinarily high duty of ten *rijksdaalders* per slave sold on the Batavian
market. Sutherland (1983:270) tentatively suggests that the private trade could have been at least
six times the size of the Company trade in the mid-eighteenth century.
[62]   For the sake of historical documentation, it of course did not help that, according to
Sutherland (1983:283, note 2), 'at various times limits were placed on private trade' and 'what
was prohibited was the trade in people who were not legitimately enslaved [...]. In theory, since
1699, all slaves had to be properly documented and sales had to be registered, but given the high
profits, this stipulation was evaded by many traders, and a high proportion of slave transactions
involving Europeans were in fact illegal, while the indigenous trade was beyond the Company's
reach'.

Europeans had relinquished the practice, a clear beginning and end to this slave trade are missing. Europeans never monopolized this economic activity in Asia, although Raben (2008) suggests that their presence caused a decided intensification of the slave trade. A reliable estimate of the total volume of the slave trade in the Indian Ocean World therefore seems well-nigh impossible. After all, we cannot simply rely on the European and colonial archives alone, but need some understanding of the absolute and relative shares of Chinese, Indian, Arabic, African and local traders, and to what extent they operated independently from, or in cooperation with the Europeans.

With local African and Asian forms of slavery rooted in pre-modern traditions, Europeans may have influenced or even transformed these systems through increased demand, but they could never fully command its perimeters. Slavery in the New World consisted entirely, after the gradual exclusion of Native American slaves, of sub-Saharan Africans. Such a clear racial identification of, and connotation with slavery never materialized in the Indian Ocean World, even though in the ethnocentric mindset of Europeans, both Africans and Asians alike could be defined as 'black'.[63] True, lightness of skin had its positive merits in the Indian Ocean World as well, but theoretically a wide pool of racial, ethnic, national and religious groups were eligible for enslavement, at times even including Europeans themselves. Comparable to the often irrational preferences that European colonists in the New World showed for specific Africans, an abundance of theories existed regarding the attributes of particular slaves in the Indian Ocean World. Here, as in the West, African slaves were often considered ideal for hard, backbreaking labour conditions.[64] Additionally, Hindu slaves from Malabar were praised for their technical skills, female slaves from Bali for their domestic labour and as potential future marriage partners, while Buginese Muslims from South Sulawesi were frequently shunned for their supposed rebelliousness, to give but a few of the existing stereotypes.

Yet, despite such ethnic typecasting, slave identity in the Indian Ocean World was never encapsulated in one clear racial classification. This situation was further complicated by the presence of much larger free popula-

---

[63]   Had it been profitable to transport Asian labour to the Caribbean sugar plantations – which was not the case before the mid-nineteenth century – then slavery in the Americas may have lost some of its racial exclusivity. But the absence of a large free population sharing an ethnic background with the slaves would still have kept the unique power dynamics of colonial slavery in the Americas intact.

[64]   In his *Itinerario*, Van Linschoten already commented that the slaves from Mozambique (East Africa) were in high demand all across the East, 'because they are the strongest of the entire Orient, and do the dirtiest and harshest work, and only for that they are used' (Terpstra 1955:25). This perception may have been intensified by the use of African slaves by Portuguese colonists during the sixteenth century.

tions sharing ethnic and religious backgrounds with the slaves. A simple demographic breakdown of a colonial settlement can, therefore, tell us little about who had in fact arrived as a forced migrant and who came out of free will. Since dependency – not outsider status – was almost equally distributed among a great mixture of peoples, it was then, and still is now, extremely difficult to establish one single, unambiguous slave identity.

This multi-ethnic character of Indian Ocean slavery creates even more confusion if we attempt to chart the geographic directions of the regional slave trade. There may have been 'many middle passages', as a recent comparative treatment of forced migrations in the modern world puts it (Christopher, Pybus and Rediker 2007), but none was as clearly a physical and cultural transition as the one-way journey of African slaves to the Americas. If we reasonably exclude the more than half million Southeast African and Malagasy slaves shipped to the Americas, then most forced migration patterns in the Indian Ocean World appear to crisscross one another, demonstrating a multi-directionality unseen in the Atlantic system.[65] Slaves could embark virtually anywhere within the region and be shipped to a variety of destinations and destinies. Monsoon winds further dictated seasonal shipping patterns and prevented the transoceanic slave trade from any year-long regularity, making estimates even more complicated.

The widespread use of slaves as domestic servants by their European owners made it more likely that a single slave was subjected to several long-distance migrations in his life, often in opposite directions. Obviously, this significantly increases the risk of a slave being counted two or even three times, a key obstacle to assessing the total volume of the slave trade. In the previous chapter we encountered similar problems regarding the free European migration streams to and from the colonies. Once again we are struck by what a uniquely one-directional voyage the transatlantic slave trade really was. For that matter, the Indian Ocean slave trade bears more resemblance to the intra-American slave trade, as colonists and their slave property moved from one colony to the next, for example, from Barbados to South Carolina or from Saint Domingue to Louisiana. Yet such slave migrations have wisely been left outside the definition of the *trans*-atlantic slave trade.

Because the informal VOC empire spanned across and beyond the Indian Ocean World (ranging all the way from Cape Town, South Africa, to Dejima, Japan), the multi-directionality of the slave trade was only further stimulated.

---

[65]   TSTD2 estimates that a total of 542,700 slaves were exported from Southeast Africa and the Indian Ocean islands, a number similar to the entire Dutch transatlantic slave trade. Of those slaves, an estimated 436,500 arrived in the New World, suggesting a mortality rate of almost twenty per cent (19.6). The greater length of the middle passage should largely account for this stunningly high mortality rate, although most of these slaves were transported during the nineteenth century, when shipping technology had clearly improved.

Rik van Welie

Batavia was the uncontested central cog in this supra-regional trade system, but key VOC possessions such as the Banda Islands, Ceylon and the Cape Colony all demonstrated a relatively independent pull for slaves, and adequate oversight on this traffic was usually absent. VOC officials and private burghers travelling between these Dutch trading posts often brought their personal and trade slaves along, thereby adding to the administrative confusion and cultural diffusion. Non-Dutch traders, Europeans as well as non-Europeans, transporting slaves on water and over land, further complicate the issue.

Faced with some of the challenges and difficulties addressed above, Markus Vink (2003b) has attempted to assess the volume of the Dutch Indian Ocean slave trade by using a method not uncommon to scholars of the transatlantic slave trade. As the records of slave departures and arrivals are simply too patchy, and to circumvent the problem of double-counting, he decided to approach the problem from the demand rather than the supply side: how many slaves had to be imported each year into the VOC possessions to keep their slave populations at a relatively steady level? Vink's provisional results are displayed in table 5.9.

Table 5.9 Number of Company slaves and total of Dutch slaves with estimated size of accompanying annual slave trades, ca. 1688

VOC domain	Company slaves	Total Dutch slaves	Size of annual Company slave trade	Size of annual total Dutch slave trade
Ambon	74	10,569	6-7	800-900
Banda	166	3,716	10	150-200
Batavia	1,430	26,071	70-140	1,300-2,600
Cape	382	931	20-40	45-60
Ceylon	1,502	ca. 4,000	75-150	200-400
Makassar	112	ca. 1,500	6-11	75-150
Malabar	32	ca. 1,000	2-4	50-100
Malacca	161	1,853	8-16	90-180
Moluccas	0	ca. 400	0	20-40
Others*	268	16,308	15-30	1,000-1,800
Total	4,127	ca. 66,348	ca. 200-400	ca. 3,730-6,430

Source: Vink 2003b:166-7. I have decided to remove the dates given for these census figures because all Company slaves were assessed on the last day of 1687, except those at the Cape. As that figure stems from 1688, all total Dutch slaves estimates are taken from 1688, except Batavia (1689), Makassar (1687-88), Malabar (1687), Malacca (1682) and the Moluccas (1686). Barring any dramatic natural disasters in these years, I see no problem with these slight variations in dates.

* The category 'Others' includes the settlements at Amoy, Bantam, Bengal, Coromandel, Jambi, Japan, Japara, Palembang, Persia, Siam, Sumatra, Surat, Timor and Tonkin.

While slave population figures are taken from original VOC documentation, the estimates for slave imports are deduced from a variety of primary and secondary sources listed in the footnotes. Vink subsequently calculates that around the year 1688 between 4,476 and 7,716 slaves had to be exported annually to allow – after assessing a twenty per cent morality rate – for the necessary slave imports. Based on these estimates, he draws the conclusion that 'the volume of the total Dutch Indian Ocean slave trade was therefore 15-30% of the Atlantic slave trade [...] and one-and-a-half to three times the size of [...] the Dutch West India Company slave trade' (Vink 2003b:168).

Anyone familiar with the Dutch Atlantic slave trade will likely be stunned by this bold assertion, even after realizing that the statement is merely valid for the late 1680s. Upon checking with the most recent estimates for the transatlantic slave trade, it appears that Vink's comparison holds up for the entire volume of this trade, yet he substantially underestimated the Dutch role: 1687 and 1688 were actually peak years for the Dutch slave trade, as they were then in command of the *asiento* trade, with an estimated 6,900 and 5,900 slaves exported respectively (TSTD2). But if we consider, in line with renowned scholars (Postma 2003a; Klooster 2003), that the Dutch transatlantic slave trade was actually at its zenith during this period, Vink's estimates for the eastern trade continue to impress us. Putting both slave trades together would suddenly make the Dutch a major, if not the dominant, player in the colonial slave trade of the late seventeenth century.[66] This was surely the 'Golden Age' of the Dutch slave trade.

A twenty per cent mortality rate may strike the reader as rather high, especially considering that the maritime routes were generally shorter than in the Atlantic Ocean and that many slaves could be procured from the nearby hinterlands. But, as will be discussed later in this chapter, some of the slave voyages organized by the VOC suffered from catastrophic mortality rates and it appears that the overall disease climate in the Indian Ocean World was far more debilitating than in the West.[67] Admittedly, Vink uses a very wide definition for 'Dutch slaves', as he incorporates all slaves within the VOC jurisdiction, regardless of the nationality and ethnic background of their owners. Perhaps 'slaves within the VOC domain' or 'slaves under Dutch control' would have been a more suitable description, but even then one can debate whether the several thousand slaves belonging to the indigenous Ambonese

---

[66] Without even taking into account that, judging from Paesie 2008, the volume of the illicit Dutch slave trade to the Americas in this period might have to be upgraded as well.

[67] Drawing from the work of Blussé, Reid (1983a:29) states that during the 1760s and 1770s an average of 1325 persons were buried each year in Batavia's two slave cemeteries. This would imply that Vink's estimates would only grow larger in the second half of the eighteenth century.

Hindustani gather to celebrate in Suriname

truly fit this classification.[68] Assuming for the moment that Vink's calculations are reasonably accurate though – and there is no apparent reason to
believe otherwise – the pressing question that remains is how these estimates
for the year 1688 relate to the entire span of the Dutch Indian Ocean slave
trade. What can one year tell us about two centuries?

Vink (2003b:167) humbly underlines that he is only providing a 'tentative
census' and that much more archival research is needed to begin sketching
a historical development over time. Using his techniques this would be an
extremely taxing exercise, as one would need access to yearly slave population counts for each individual settlement, their respective birth, death and
manumission rates, mortality rates for the various slave trading routes and
many other important contingencies. It is not difficult to imagine how such a
method could lead to dramatic misrepresentations. If, for example, we took
a snapshot of Dutch Brazil in the early 1640s and extrapolated this over the
entire 25-year lifespan of that colony, its slave imports would easily be exaggerated up to five times their actual size. Supply of, and demand for, slaves
are always highly volatile forces in history.

It is, nevertheless, quite reasonable to think that the slave trade in the
Indian Ocean World operated more independently of market fluctuations
than its Atlantic variant. Slaves in the VOC domain were seldom directly
used in the production of commodities for the European market. Even in
the exceptional case of nutmeg cultivation on the Banda Islands, where
slave labour was utilized in ways resembling the Caribbean-style plantations, the VOC monopoly prevented a market-driven expansion of the slave
population.[69] In general, most slaves in the Indian Ocean World functioned as
domestic servants to free European and Asian burghers in the trading towns.
Evidently, the demographic ebb and flow of these residents and their respective slave holdings was closely related to the health of the colonial economy.
Yet an estimation based on the perspective of supply may have its merits
here. The general size of the free populations of various VOC possessions
certainly appears to reveal a more direct correlation to its slave holdings than
was the case in the Western hemisphere. Lacking sufficient data to assess the

---

[68]   Knaap (1987:129, 133, 137) estimates the native Ambonese population in the VOC govern-
ment at 49,168 in 1671 and 57,605 in 1692 (the latter demographic count containing 7,232 slaves).
The remaining slaves at the colonial town of Kota Ambon of course much more fit the description
'Dutch slaves'.

[69]   Through its worldwide monopoly on both the clove and nutmeg production, the VOC
essentially controlled the market forces and could therefore afford to slow down production (and
keep prices artificially high). Els Jacobs (2006:18) lists many ways through which the Company
attempted to slow down the production of cloves in the Ambonese archipelago, even its con-
templation of 'importing opium, in the expectation that it would make the Ambonese lose their
work motivation'. Nutmeg cultivation on Banda did not suffer from an overproduction of cloves,
partly because it took a good ten years for a nutmeg tree to bear fruit (Els Jacobs 2006:20, 23).

regional trade and transoceanic movement of slaves, the approach by Vink
may very well be the most valid option to quantify the volume of the Dutch
slave trade in the Indian Ocean World.

Major provenance zones of the Dutch slave trade in the Indian Ocean World

From the perspective of the supply of slaves a closer look is necessary to
establish the major directional patterns of these forced migrations in the
Indian Ocean World. In an attempt to give order to this rather chaotic picture
and to make the topic more manageable, historians have subdivided the VOC
domain into three distinct regional systems: Southeast Asia with Batavia
as the undisputed centre of the VOC empire, South Asia with Colombo as
the most important colonial town, and southern Africa with Cape Town as
primary settlement and halfway station between Europe and Asia. Here we
follow this schematic division to establish the most important provenance
zones of Indian Ocean slaves, the destinations of these slaves and the period
in which these forced migrations took place. Many slaves acquired in one
of these three regions first remained within that area, but depending on the
labour demands of the time and the decisions of the VOC officials in Batavia,
they could be shipped to another region. One could even speak of a 'triangular' trade in this respect, in which slaves usually shared cargo space with
other, often more profitable commodities.

South Asia: different paths to enslavement

Although the Dutch acquired slaves from South Asia throughout the seventeenth and eighteenth centuries, the region's significance as a slave supplier
was most pronounced in the first half century after the foundation of Batavia
(Vink 2003b:140). In 1623 and 1624, for example, the Dutch at Batavia witnessed
the arrival of three large slave ships carrying a total of 1,700 slaves from the
Coromandel Coast.[70] According to the local Company officials in Nagapatnam,
thousands more could have been purchased for very little money, a pleasing
notion as the construction of the Company's headquarters was in full swing
and slavery had recently been codified in colonial legislation (Fox 1983).

---

[70]   Niemeijer 2005:53-4. The VOC had established several trading factories on the Coromandel
Coast, many of them dating back to the first decade of the seventeenth century: Masulipatnam,
Petapoelie, Tegenapatam or Tierepopelier and Nagapatnam. Ultimately the town of Pulicat with
Fort Geldria would function as the headquarters of the Company in this area. In these early years
(1621-24) the VOC also exported an undisclosed (but likely small) number of slaves from Surat,
a practice soon discontinued for unknown reasons; see Van Santen (1982: table 1). Raben 2008
arrives at a total of 3,051 registered slaves imported into Batavia between 1622 and 1624.

The Coromandel Coast would serve as an important but dramatically volatile provenance zone for slaves, due to specific local circumstances and traditions. Each time a combination of religious strife, civil war, bad harvests and large-scale famine plagued this densely populated region of India, it created desperate refugee streams with no place to go or food to still their hunger. Under such conditions it was customary for parents to sell their children, for men to sell their wives, and eventually even allow themselves to succumb to slavery. Each time the events of the early 1620s repeated themselves in some shape or form, they represented an opportunity for the VOC and other slave traders to acquire a substantial number of inexpensive slaves.

Vink (2003b:141) has listed several of these 'boom' periods in the seventeenth century, with 2,118 slaves acquired by the VOC in 1645-1646, 8,000-10,000[71] between 1659 and 1661, 1,839 in the mid-1670s and another 3,859 in the mid-1690s. There is no apparent reason to suspect that these human dramas did not reoccur during the eighteenth century. When bad harvests and skyrocketing rice prices caused another famine-slave cycle around Nagapatnam in 1729, at least 2,000 desperate victims jumped to their death in the local river, while the VOC only managed to purchase 189 slaves, and 62 of them soon perished from a combination of disease and weakened resistance. The following year the Company issued an official statement condemning the prevalence of suicide around town (Peters and André de la Porte 2002:63, note 40).

Because the supply of Coromandel slaves was highly unpredictable and fluctuated rather independently of Dutch demand, it is not easy to estimate their total share in the Dutch Indian Ocean slave trade. If the pattern of 'boom' periods from the seventeenth century persisted into the eighteenth, the Dutch could possibly have taken an average of 4,000 to 5,000 slaves from this region every fifteen or twenty years; and such an estimate excludes the slave trade during 'normal' or 'slow' periods.[72]

Dutch officials overseeing the purchase of these desperate 'coastal souls' (*Custsielen*) from Coromandel often justified the practice as 'a work of compassion', but it is all too obvious that in most cases self-interest was king (Vink 2003a). Great was the disappointment when, due to peaceful conditions and abundant harvests, no slaves could be purchased or when, in a time of severe crisis, such as at Masulipatnam in 1687, even the local VOC officials

---

[71]   According to Philippus Baldaeus, who witnessed the dramatic events in Nagapatnam around 1660, the VOC transported at least 4,000-5,000 slaves to Jaffnapatnam, an equal number to Colombo and several thousand more to Batavia and elsewhere. His estimate of the total volume appears thus somewhat higher than that given by Vink (Peters and André de la Porte 2002:62).

[72]   We still need to know the number of slave exports in 'normal' times from the Coromandel Coast. It seems that the VOC trading post in Burma, for example, requested Coromandel slaves on a regular basis although numbers were few. See Dijk 2006:140-2.

were too sick and incapacitated to broker a good deal (Peters and André de
la Porte 2002:63). Perhaps this emphasis on compassion must be read in light
of the rather unique form of slave acquisition on the Coromandel Coast:
usually, the Dutch bought slaves through indigenous and Asian merchants
and middlemen, but in this case they were more directly involved in the
actual enslavement of fellow human beings, even if most of them 'voluntarily'
agreed to it. It would be interesting in this regard to ascertain whether these
unfortunate Indians viewed such enslavement as a temporary measure that
could be reversed in the future, thus as a traditional custom that was likely to
be at odds with contemporary Dutch concepts of slavery (Guha 2005:182).

Although slave exports from the Bengal-Arakan region were much smaller
in size, they also seemed more reliable and systematic throughout the seventeenth century (Van Galen 2008). Between the 1620s and 1660s the VOC transported hundreds of Bengali slaves on a yearly basis to Batavia, most of them
bought from the *feringhi* (Portuguese and mestizo) traders in the Arakan port
of Dianga.[73] The predominance of Bengal and other South Asian slaves in mid-
seventeenth-century Batavia can be assessed from recorded manumissions
between 1646-1649:[74] of the 211 slaves receiving their freedom, 86 originated
from Bengal, fourteen came from Coromandel, sixteen from Malabar, five from
India through Ceylon and five from Arakan – a total of 126 slaves from South
Asia or 65 per cent if we eliminate the seventeen slaves listed with an unknown
origin. While some of these slaves were perhaps purchased as concubines and
marriage partners and therefore quickly manumitted,[75] we may assume that
many others had 'earned' their freedom through years of loyal service.[76]

Compared to most Coromandel slaves, those from Bengal were more
traditionally 'produced' during 'just wars' between the Arakan kingdom of
Mrauk U and the Indian Mogul empire and then sold by slave traders to the
Dutch. Due to changes to the power balance in the region that fell completely

---

[73]   Sutherland 1983:266. The peaks were 1,046 slaves in 1647 and 1,803 slaves in 1655 (Raben
2008). A short contemporary account of a slave voyage with more than 200 Bengali slaves from
Arakan to Batavia can be found in Schouten 1676:159-60.

[74]   Raben 1996:121. Raben (1996:121, table 5.1) mentions the primary source ANRI Schepenen
827 A, Register of manumitted slaves 5-9-1646 – 20-8-1649 (damaged: lacuna between 10-10-1646
and 12-2-1647).

[75]   Over two thirds of the manumitted slaves were female, although the Balinese slaves tend
to skew the data slightly, thus confirming the specific nature of the Balinese slave trade in which
females were often sold to function as 'slave brides', associated especially with the Chinese
population of Batavia. It is not unlikely that female slaves from Bengal were also used as slave
brides, so these manumissions could be related to the substantial slave imports between 1644 and
1647 (Vink 2003b:141).

[76]   The nature of domestic slavery, so widespread in the Indian Ocean World, had a much
greater propensity for manumission than plantation slavery as the social intimacy between the
masters and their slaves was much higher.

outside the control of the VOC, this source suddenly dried up during the mid-1660s. There is no evidence that this area recaptured some of its earlier importance as a provenance zone for the Dutch slave trade in the eighteenth century, although the activities of private slave traders never leave many traces in the archives.[77] It probably had little effect anyway, as the decline of Bengali slave exports 'was compensated for by developing new suppliers' such as Madagascar and sources within the Indonesian archipelago itself like Makassar (Sutherland 1983:266).

Another area in South Asia taking over some of this trade was the Malabar Coast (Kerala) of India, where between 1657 and 1663 the Dutch successfully ousted the Portuguese enemy from their colonial trading posts. Like it had been the case in the Dutch conquests in Ceylon and elsewhere in Asia, the real victims of such European colonial wars were generally the local allies unfortunate enough to support the losing party.[78] So, in yet another type of enslavement, several thousand prisoners of war on the Malabar Coast were transported to Ceylon and Batavia. After the hostilities had ended, the Dutch continued to export a small but continuous stream of slaves, mostly taken from the hinterland of Cochin and estimated to consist of 50-100 slaves to Batavia and 80-120 to Ceylon on an annual basis (Vink 2003b:141). This Malabar slave trade was maintained well into the eighteenth century.[79]

Based on these scanty historical records and given the high population density of this region it would not be far-fetched to suggest that approximately 100,000 slaves were taken from South Asia by the Dutch, and possibly more, if we include the slaves that served the Dutch locally in their many trading posts on the Indian coast and at Ceylon. Hopefully, future archival research will shed more light on this rather obscure part of the Dutch slave trade in the Indian Ocean World.

Southeast Asia: Bali and Makassar and the role of Asian slave traders

The principal VOC possessions in Southeast Asia – Batavia, Ambon and the Banda Islands – were all 'consumers' of slaves for several centuries. Besides imports from South Asia, local resources were eagerly and often ruthlessly

---

[77]   Lequin 2005:196. For example, the well-known physician Nicolaas de Graaff lost a total of 57 female slaves as the vessel *Buinskerk* sank on a river in Bengal in 1672. It had been his plan to send these slaves as 'a gift' to Batavia (Peters and André de la Porte 2002:63).

[78]   Naturally, the slaves of the surrendering Portuguese residents were also acquired, as specifically stipulated in the second term of the capitulation of Cochin on 7-1-1663.

[79]   Singh 2007:106-7. Shortly before taking over Cochin from the Dutch in 1795, an English official commented – in the abolitionist spirit of the time – that such a move 'would totally put a stop to the barbarous traffic in slaves, which is at present most shamefully carried on to a considerable extent by the Dutch' (cited in Lequin 2005:196, note 181). See also Allen forthcoming.

Table 5.10 Slave imports into Batavia on Asian ships (and annual averages), 1663-1682

	Bali		Makassar		Buton		Total imports	
1663-1668	564	(94)	8	(1)	154	(26)	1053	(178)
1669-1672	461	(115)	2828	(707)	705	(176)	4691	(1173)
1673-1682	1327	(133)	1250	(125)	325	(33)	4065	(407)

Source: *Daghregister Casteel Batavia*, rendered in Raben 1996:123, table 5.2.

exploited. When the conquest of the Banda island of Ai, in 1616, left the original population either dead or in refuge on the neighbouring island of Run, the Dutch expeditionary fleet imported a workforce of around 800 people to attend to the abandoned nutmeg trees: among them was the entire population (446) of the island of Siau, to the north-west of Halmahera, where the Dutch had defeated the Spanish, some 100 people taken in a similar fashion from Portuguese Solor and another 350 prisoners, convicts, slaves and freed slaves, among them sixty Spanish and Indian soldiers (Hanna 1978:40). The fate of the indigenous population of Banda was sealed at the hands of the infamous Jan Pieterszoon Coen only five years later, during the Bandanese massacre of 1621. Several thousand were killed or died from diseases and starvation; most of the survivors were deported as slaves. One consignment shipped off to Batavia consisted of 883 people (287 men, 356 women and 240 children); of these 176 would perish during the voyage (Hanna 1978:54). Many other islands, large and small, provided slaves with some regularity. One could even say that, with the exception of Java, the entire Indonesian archipelago functioned as a potential market for slaves.[80] However, during the seventeenth century two specific areas emerged as the main slave suppliers to Batavia and other VOC possessions in the Indian Ocean World: the island of Bali and the port of Makassar on Sulawesi.

Makassar had risen as an important commercial town and a slave trading post during the sixteenth century and continued to operate relatively independently of the VOC until its conquest by the Dutch in 1667 (Treaty of Bungaya).[81] After such a military victory, it was fairly common to enslave any enemies captured and export them from their homeland, as had been the case on the Malabar Coast, at Ceylon and on the Banda Islands. As is seen in table

---

[80]   Sutherland 1983:266-7. Java had been an important source of slaves during the sixteenth century. In the seventeenth century two factors reversed this trend: the rise of a strong Mataram monarchy and a VOC policy deliberately aimed at preventing the purchase of Javanese slaves for Batavia. The VOC feared that the presence of Javanese slaves in Batavia would encourage marronage and slave revolts by the dominant ethnic group (Reid 1983b:174).

[81]   It has been suggested that the early presence of the Portuguese here may have transformed local forms of slavery and slave trading; see Sutherland 1983:266.

5.10, there is a sudden peak in the slave trade to Batavia from Sulawesi, with Makassar and Buton as the main provenance zones.

Considering these events it is not surprising that during the 1680s 'the largest single ethnic category (over thirty per cent) among the Company's slaves were the Buginese and Makassarese' (Sutherland 1983:268). In the historical documents of the VOC one finds many references to the troublesome and rebellious nature of these slaves from South Sulawesi. This stereotype was partly based on their strong Muslim identity, partly on the fact that these ethnic groups continued to resist their social, political and especially commercial displacement by the Dutch and partly on the continued loyalty of their allies to Sulawesi.[82] Buginese, Wajorese and other Sulawesian enemies of the Dutch who managed to avoid captivity and enslavement would form a 'substantial diaspora' that 'became the backbone of a trading network which remained outside Dutch control' (Knaap and Sutherland 2004:4).

Sulawesian allies of the Dutch carried on the previous role of Makassar as one of the primary slave trading stations in the archipelago, which became increasingly focused on the trade to Batavia. A good share of these slaves were procured from the large island of Sulawesi itself, by preying on the territories of their traditional rivals or by kidnapping local people. Others were taken through large-scale maritime raids in the relatively defenceless eastern parts of the archipelago. While the Company officially attempted to curtail this trade in 'stolen people' and only condoned the sale of 'legitimate' slaves, it was ultimately too dependent on the commerce of Makassar to adopt such a principled stance.

The surviving records of the harbour masters at Fort Rotterdam allow for a better understanding of the volume and operations of the Makassar slave trade in the eighteenth century (Knaap and Sutherland 2004:116-20). While the data still remain patchy, we now possess annual averages for private sector slave imports and exports during the 1720s (266 to 99) and the 1780s (807 to 1,168), while the daily register (*Daghregister*) of Batavia records annual imports from Makassar of about 400 slaves during the years 1766-1769 and circa 550 slaves between 1774-1777, figures that may have to be augmented by some fifty per cent to reflect the real volume of this trade more accurately (Knaap and Sutherland 2004:117). Of these imports into Batavia during the second half of the eighteenth century, about 200 to 300 slaves were destined for the Company workforce, while the great majority was sold to private merchants and residents.[83] Even so, Sutherland's (1983:270) estimate of 3,000

---

[82]   During the eighteenth century the VOC sometimes prohibited the forced migrations of these ethnic groups within the Indian Ocean World, possibly to avoid social unrest and slave resistance.

[83]   Governor Clootwijk (1752-56) actively pursued this trade for the VOC, exporting around

slaves being shipped annually from Makassar to Batavia throughout the
entire eighteenth century now appears highly exaggerated.

Slaves entering Makassar during the 1720s were primarily drawn from
Sumba (32 per cent), Sumbawa (18 per cent) and Ende (17 per cent), while
in the 1780s once again Ende (42 per cent), Bugis (20 per cent) and Buton (16
per cent) became major provenance zones. In the 1720s, Sulawesian skippers
had still dominated this transport, but their role was gradually taken over by
mainly Makassar-based Malay traders (50 per cent), together with Chinese
(18 per cent) and Company subjects (17 per cent) in the 1780s. The Company
servants and *freeburghers* residing in Makassar's Vlaardingen district were
understandably of much greater importance in redirecting these newly
arrived slaves toward Batavia (63 per cent), while the Chinese also plied this
trade (seventeen per cent).[84] By the 1780s these Dutch-organized slave voyages carried an average cargo of 30 slaves for the Company and 72 for the free
market, plus a crew of 28. While these small vessels were certainly 'terribly
crowded', it remains a matter for debate whether conditions on board were,
especially considering the short duration of the voyage, 'comparable to those
on the Atlantic slave route', as Knaap and Sutherland (2004:119-20) suggest.

The slave trade from Bali was of a rather exceptional nature, reflecting the
unique history of this island society, the last remaining vestige of Hinduism
in the archipelago. Historians generally agree that Bali began exporting a sizeable stream of slaves to Batavia from the mid-seventeenth until the early nineteenth century, with a total volume roughly estimated at 100,000 to 150,000
slaves (Schulte Nordholt 1996:41). They disagree substantially, however, on
the grounds for this trade. For some it appears entirely rooted in internal
developments and Bali's otherness, suggesting that 'while Balinese society
steadily "produced" new slaves, the opportunities for utilizing slave labour in
Bali itself were rather restricted [...] a tendency which made it possible for the
island to support a regular slave exporting trade' (Van der Kraan 1983:326-7).

While not ignoring the internal dynamics of Balinese society, Schulte
Nordholt (1996:41-4) clearly perceives the impact of an external demand for
slaves. By exchanging local slaves for Spanish dollars, weaponry and opium,
Balinese rulers were able to increase their wealth and power in society. This
process seems eerily similar to the so-called war-slave cycles that have often
been demonstrated in pre-colonial African societies: 'wars generated slaves,

---

1,500 slaves from Makassar during his short reign. This led Sutherland (1983:270) to believe that
the private slave trade was six times higher than the Company slave trade, but her estimate for
the overall trade may have been misleading in this regard.
[84]   Knaap and Sutherland 2004:119. When compared to the other trades around town 'the
slave trade had [...] become the last commercial niche for the Burghers of Makassar' (Knaap and
Sutherland 2004:119).

but it seems likely that the demand for slaves also generated wars'.[85]

During the seventeenth and eighteenth centuries the great majority of slaves went, via Chinese middlemen in the ports of Kuta and Buleleng, to the Batavia market. The seventeenth-century *Daghregisters* list slave arrivals at a rate of up to one hundred for a single month and this volume appears to have remained fairly steady over the entire period of the slave trade. In the early decades of the nineteenth century, slaves from Bali were also (illegally) transported by French ships to the sugar plantations of Mauritius and Bourbon (500-600 annually) and between 1827 and 1831 the Dutch shipped over a thousand 'slaves' from Bali to serve as soldiers in the wars on Java. As late as 1837 the Dutch government at Batavia entertained plans to send 400 females from Bali to the nutmeg plantations at Banda; their local expert on Bali suggested that it would take approximately a year to acquire such a number of female slaves (Van der Kraan 1983:328).

While traditional customs may have ensured that 'the position of women in Balinese society was one of potential slavery' (Van der Kraan 1983:323), the outside demand for female marriage partners, particularly by Chinese male residents in Batavia, must have further intensified this export trade in women, so much so that the female slave of Bali became something of an exotic fixture in the Southeast Asian imagination.[86] The Chinese controlled the purchase of slaves for export on Bali (the Dutch did not have an established residence there until the late 1820s), transporting them to Batavia, and selling them to mainly Chinese and Dutch *freeburghers*. The Chinese domination of this Balinese slave trade, and their role along with other Asian traders in the import and export of slaves from Makassar, begs the question of how 'Dutch' this slave trade really was. Admittedly, these forced migrations were strongly stimulated by, and directed towards the growing empire of the VOC in Asia. If the slave traders resided and operated under VOC jurisdiction, there is little reason to exclude them from the 'Dutch' slave trade; but if these voyages were explicitly carried out under different flags and outside Dutch control, we should apply the same rigorous standards of the transatlantic slave trade and place these outside the perimeters of the Dutch slave trade.[87]

---

[85]   Schulte Nordholt 1996:41. As an example Schulte Nordholt (1996:41) cites the *patih* of Karangasem in 1808: 'We wage upon the others when we, lords, lack money; at such times we swoop down on the weakest of our neighbours, and all prisoners and their entire families are sold as slaves so that we [...] have money to buy opium.'

[86]   This image seems to have lingered on even after the abolition of slavery, considering the 'modern' photographs of scantily-clad Balinese slaves in Reid (1983c:324, 333). It has further been suggested that their willingness to prepare meals using pork made them attractive as household servants and cooks to the Chinese and other non-Muslim groups.

[87]   British vessels transporting slaves to Suriname form part of the British slave trade, regardless of the fact that Suriname was a Dutch colony at the time. This is currently the accepted basis for subdividing the transatlantic slave trade among the various European nations. It allows

Suikeronderneming Mariënburg, Suriname

Designating the slave trade from Bali as non-Dutch evidently does not change the fact that these slaves ultimately ended up within the Dutch colonial sphere and as such became part of a shared colonial history. It is tempting to pose the counterfactual question if, without the presence of the VOC in Southeast Asia, this trade would ever have reached such dimensions. Seen from the perspective of demand, this appears unlikely, even though Van der Kraan (1983) suggests that Balinese slaves were 'produced' relatively independently of outside market forces. Considering Makassar's history before the Dutch conquest and its (semi-legal) continuation of the slave trade after the Dutch prohibition, one gets the impression that there had always been buyers for slaves in the archipelago.[88]

Even so, when Batavia was closed as a central market for slaves in the early nineteenth century, due to abolitionist pressures from Europe, Bali and Makassar suffered a period of economic readjustment (Reid 1983a:33; Schulte Nordholt 1996:167). The arrival of the Dutch in Southeast Asia did not start the regional slave trade, but without a doubt intensified the activities of its local networks (Sutherland 1983:267; Raben 2008). As a consequence, several hundred thousand slaves were transported to different locations and, unlike most of the provenance zones in the South Asian region, the island societies where these victims were taken from often paid a hefty demographic, cultural and socio-economic price.[89]

Greater Southern Africa at the junction of two oceanic slave-trading networks

With the VOC possessions depending primarily on Asian slaves, it is relatively unknown to the general public that sub-Saharan Africa, the single source of slaves to the Americas, also contributed a substantial number of people to the Indian Ocean slave trade. The African continent was as such tragically situated between two supra-regional slave-trading networks, with forced migrations moving in opposite directions.[90] The main African provenance zones

---

historians to differentiate between the involvement of a nation in the slave trade and in colonial slavery itself. In a serious comparison between two different slave-trading systems, such basic assumptions should at least be equal.

[88] Schulte Nordholt (1996:167) states that around the time of the Peace of Kuta (1849) in Bali, 'the Dutch [...] closed their eyes to the export of slaves, which was still going on, though in lesser numbers than before'.

[89] Schulte Nordholt 1996:41, note 55. But according to Boomgaard (2004:92) the demographic loss on Bali due to the slave trade cannot have been too disruptive. He even suggests that slave exports may have functioned as an alternative form of birth control.

[90] Besides these two oceanic slave-trading systems there was a substantial export of slaves via land-routes, mostly to Islamic Africa and the Middle East; see for example Pétré-Grenouilleau 2004. Further research on the 'catchment areas' of these various Atlantic and Indian Ocean export

located in the Indian Ocean World were Southeast Africa (Mozambique) and Madagascar, areas that provided slaves for the Americas as well, with Brazil and Cuba as major recipients. Reports from early Dutch voyages to the East Indies already mention the potential of Madagascar as a source of cheap slaves and by 1616 VOC officials at Batavia were seriously contemplating the import of Malagasy slaves.[91] The first recorded VOC voyage to procure slaves there, in 1626, proved a failure, however, with high mortality rates and slave prices unable to compete with those of the more densely populated South Asian provenance zones (Barendse 1995:140).

Though strategically located on the shipping routes to the core Dutch possessions in Asia, its hostile environment and unhealthy climate prevented any serious consideration of Madagascar as the refreshment station the VOC was so desperately looking for.[92] The uninhabited island of Mauritius, several hundred miles to the east of Madagascar, was deemed more suitable for this purpose and Dutch colonization there proceeded in 1638.[93] Fairly soon after that time slave voyages were organized between Mauritius and Antongil Bay on the north-east coast of Madagascar, obtaining the much-needed labour to develop the small Dutch settlement.[94] Between 1641 and 1647 a small slave trade moved approximately 500 Malagasy slaves to Mauritius (Moree 1998:31-7). Some of the 'excess slaves' were transported further east toward Batavia, where complaints were lodged concerning the health and character of these Malagasy slaves (Barendse 1995:141-3). Those remaining on Mauritius caused the Dutch colonists all kinds of problems as well, judging from the high levels of resistance, rebellion and *marronage* (Moree 1998). After the foundation of

slave trades (especially Angola and Mozambique) may establish if they were at times supplied by the same hinterland.

[91]   Stapel 1929:653. See, for example, the December 1595 comments in the travel journal of Frank van der Does, cited in De Jonge 1864, II:309-10. For the VOC interest in Malagasy slaves, see Böeseken 1977:62. VOC historian Pieter van Dam specifically mentions the resolution of 17-8-1616 (Stapel 1929:653), which came after the suggestions of Governor-General Gerard Reynst in 1614 and 1615 (Coolhaas 1960:44-6).

[92]   The establishment of such a supply station was considered imperative from the early days of the trade with the East Indies. Balthasar de Moucheron's attempt in the late 1590s to create such a station on the West African island of Principe (Prinseneiland), with the aid of several slaves from Cabo Verde, had turned out disastrous. His interest in Madagascar in this regard is duly noted; see De Jonge 1862, I:225-6.

[93]   The Dutch first came to the island in September 1598, when Admiral Van Warwijck christened it in honour of Prince Maurits. After that time it became a popular refreshment station, as well as a source of ebony bark, while ships sometimes stayed there for several weeks to undergo repairs.

[94]   On 12-6-1641 the Portuguese-Dutch peace negotiations established that the eastern coast of Madagascar would fall within the Dutch sphere of influence, while the western coast was visited by Portuguese traders; see Armstrong 1983-84:216. The following year the Dutch were the first European power to sign a treaty with the local ruler at Antongil Bay to secure a monopoly on the local slave trade.

the Cape Colony in 1652, voyages to procure slaves followed the same pattern, by sailing (often via Mauritius) to Antongil Bay, although early attempts met with little success (Armstrong 1979:77). Given the superior strategic location of the Cape, the Company decided to cut costs and abandon Mauritius as a refreshment station, albeit only temporarily.[95]

As a European settlement colony on the tip of the African continent and straddling the borders of two supra-regional slave-trading networks, the Cape occupied a unique place in history. Given the proximity of the West African coast and the extensive Dutch experience with slave trading there[96] – the VOC was initially interested in tapping into this labour reservoir. In 1658 the *Hasselt* returned from Allada on the Slave Coast with 228 slaves, while in the same year the *Amersfoort* delivered 174 Angolan child slaves taken from a Brazil-bound Portuguese slaver.[97] Given the small settler population in Cape Town at the time, these slave imports had a great impact, even if a substantial number were transported onto Batavia. VOC commissioner Rijklof van Goens considered Angola's proximity to the Cape actually problematic, as it might entice slaves to escape to their homeland. But his alternative proposal – to exchange African slaves in Batavia for Bengali slaves – never materialized.[98] The initial (and secretive) influx of West African slaves into the VOC domain was almost immediately halted when the WIC protested this intrusion of their chartered monopoly.[99] After that time, slaves were incidentally

---

[95]   Mauritius was given a second chance between 1664 and 1710, mainly in order to prevent other European powers from settling on the island; see Moree 1998. Indeed, French colonists quickly colonized Mauritius (Ile de France, 1715) – following nearby Réunion – and imported an estimated 44,394 slaves into the Mascarenes until 1769, with over 30,000 coming from Madagascar. After 1769 the islands were opened up to French private traders and slave imports expanded so that by the end of the eighteenth century approximately 100,000 slaves were toiling there; Allen 2004:34, 41. So, if the Dutch have the dubious distinction of introducing African slavery to the island, the French can be said to have 'perfected' the system.

[96]   Given the history of the Dutch slave trade in the Atlantic Ocean, the timing of this voyage is quite interesting. Dutch Brazil had already been lost, Suriname was still an English colony and Curaçao was only a few years away from acquiring its position in the *asiento* slave trade. VOC officials could easily have entertained the idea that the West African slave trade was theirs for the taking.

[97]   Armstrong 1979:77. The *Hasselt* sent out on secret instructions from the Heeren XVII, had embarked 271 slaves, so 43 of them perished en route. The Portuguese slaver carried approximately 500 slaves, but this proved too voluminous a load for the Dutch to carry. They took 250 children on board the *Amersfoort*, of whom only 174 survived the trip to the Cape (Shell 1994a:78). The latter is an interesting but quite exceptional case of slaves entering the transatlantic slave trade, yet ending up in the Indian Ocean World system.

[98]   Barendse 1995:141; Böeseken 1977:63-4. In a similar vein the first governor of the Cape Colony, Jan van Riebeeck, had proposed sending rebellious Khoikhoi as slaves to Batavia.

[99]   The WIC also staked a claim to Cape Town itself, perhaps not entirely unjustified as the town is situated on the Atlantic Ocean littoral. The VOC remained interested in the West African slave trade as late as 1704 (Shell 1994b:13), but only in the 1790s – after the WIC had been disbanded – were Cape slavers allowed to venture westward.

procured at Cabo Verde and other places along the VOC shipping lanes, but West Africa would never form a major provenance zone for Dutch colonies in the Indian Ocean World.

Thus, with the western coast of Africa off-limits and its eastern coast still predominantly under the control of Portuguese and Arab traders, Madagascar remained the most viable and consistent source of African slaves. During the second half of the seventeenth century, the VOC organized regular slave voyages to the island from Batavia and Cape Town, but often with dramatic results. Dutch vessels began looking beyond Antongil Bay to the more commercialized western coast of Madagascar, often sailing between trading posts (Maningaar, Magelage and Boina Bay, Tulear and St. Augustine's Bay) to acquire a sufficient cargo. The time-consuming character of this slave trade, combined with the delays caused by the changing monsoon winds and the general inexperience of these VOC slave traders, often caused astonishing mortality rates (Stapel 1939:653-70).

This was especially true for the forced migration of Malagasy slaves to the Sillida gold mines at West Sumatra during the 1670s and 1680s, which was 'every bit as horrific as the "middle passage" across the Atlantic', with several hundred slaves packed into extremely crammed conditions (Barendse 1995:141-5). In their organization, distance travelled, duration and shipboard mortality, these voyages easily rivalled the triangular transatlantic slave trade. Ships sailed for several months from Batavia to the Cape, then proceeded to trade slaves at various points along the Madagascar coast, before riding the monsoon winds to Cochin or Ceylon and further on to Padang on West Sumatra. Specifically built for the occasion – likely with the help of slaves – the *Sillida* left Batavia late December 1680, purchased 236 slaves at Magelage and Maringado in August 1681 and arrived at Padang in early February 1682 with only 97 slaves (41.1 per cent) alive, of whom more than half died within four months of their arrival (Stapel 1939:655-8). The *Hogergeest* took almost a year to sail from the Cape to Padang, embarking 274 slaves at Augustin Bay, but delivering only 108 slaves (39.4 per cent) upon arrival at their final destination.[100] If Madagascar was widely considered 'the most dangerous trade of the Arabian seas' (Barendse 1995:155), no one felt this more than the slaves exported from the island.

Borrowing ideas from the more experienced slave trading WIC (Stapel 1939:665-70), the VOC began transporting Malagasy slaves to Cape Town first, where they could recuperate before moving on to Batavia or Padang

---

[100]   Stapel 1939:660. The Heeren XVII commented in a letter (8-10-1685) on the long trip of the *Hogergeest* 'that it can even be considered a miracle, that of the 274 purchased slaves, after such a long and hazardous voyage, there were still 108 left' according to VOC historian Van Dam (Stapel 1939:665).

on the larger Company ships coming from Europe (Barendse 1995:144, 154; Böeseken 1977:68). Of the documented slave voyages organized by the VOC from Cape Town, more than eighty per cent (33) went to Madagascar, returning with an estimated 2,820 slaves (Armstrong 1979:78). This slave trade was remarkably consistent over time, with twelve voyages between 1652 and 1699 (1,064 slaves), nine between 1700 and 1749 (779 slaves) and twelve in the period 1750-1799 (977 slaves).[101] The remaining slave voyages in the eighteenth century all went to the eastern coast of Africa. During the 1720s the VOC exported a small trickle of slaves (288) from its short-lived trading post at Delagoa Bay (Maputo) (Eldredge 1994:133) and in the 1770s Mozambique and Zanzibar rose to prominence (974 slaves).[102] Combining all these VOC slaving voyages, Armstrong (1979:78-9) arrives at a total of 4,300 African slaves imported into Cape Town and estimates an additional ten per cent (430) for the illicit private slaves brought on these trips.[103] However, the number of slaves exported by the Company – including those to West Sumatra – must have been significantly higher considering the abnormal mortality rates in the African slave trade of the Indian Ocean.

The Cape Colony did not rely solely on Company-organized voyages for its slave supply, although private slaving voyages from the Cape were officially prohibited until 1793 (Ross 1988:214). Sometimes the Company simply embarked a sizeable load of slaves onto one of its vessels returning from Ceylon.[104] Of a much more substantial impact, however, was the practice of *freeburghers* and Company officials 'taking advantage of (and stretching) a Company rule which allowed them to be accompanied by personal slaves as far as the Cape' (Armstrong 1979:79). Because it was illegal to return with slaves to the Dutch Republic, Cape Town offered the last viable opportunity for these repatriating individuals to sell their human property, and often at better prices than elsewhere in the Indian Ocean World.[105] As a result a

---

[101] The first slave voyages from Cape Town to Madagascar were undertaken in 1654 on the *Roode Vos* and the *Tulp* (Armstrong 1979:77), while the final one, the *Jagtrust*, returned with 59 slaves in 1779 (Ross 1988:315). For a detailed description of the operations of this regional slave trade, see the recent publication of the journals of the *Leijdsman* (1715) (Westra and Armstrong 2006).

[102] Armstrong 1979:78. Ross (1986:324) argues that the slaves imported from Zanzibar and the East African coast in general suffered even higher mortality rates than those from Madagascar, especially after their arrival at Cape Town.

[103] Armstrong (1979:79) states that this private slave trade 'was defended as a customary usage, without any specific known authorization, which compensated the ships' officers and supercargoes for the dangers and discomforts they underwent in the trade, and as an encouragement for them to go on future voyages'.

[104] Armstrong (1979:79) gives examples of 93 Tutucorin (Coromandel) slaves in 1677, and 36 and 80 slaves sent from Jaffnapatnam (Ceylon) in 1712 and 1719 respectively.

[105] Ross 1988:211. This prohibition was established on 15-9-1636 in a Batavian law code; Armstrong (1979:79-80, 110, note 22) mentions the idea that slaves would be 'legally free on

private 'peddling trade' (Van der Kraan 1983:331) emerged between ship passengers and residents at the Cape. This partly explains why Cape Town in the course of the seventeenth century witnessed the arrival of 657 slaves from South Asia (227 from the Coromandel Coast, 214 from the Malabar Coast, 198 from Bengal and 18 from Ceylon), 166 from Southeast Asia (76 from Makassar, 32 from Batavia, 12 from Ternate, 11 from Bali, etcetera) and several more from Mozambique (34) and other places along the African coast (Böeseken 1977:74-5).

As most of these private trade slaves had either been previously acquired or born into Dutch colonial slavery elsewhere in the VOC domain, perhaps they should not be included in the total volume of the Dutch slave trade (Shell 1994a:81). Even so, they unmistakably changed the face and history of colonial society at the Cape. The total number of slaves imported into the Cape (1652-1808) has been estimated at approximately 63,000, originating from four almost equally important provenance zones: Southeast Asia (22.7 per cent), South Asia (25.9 per cent), Madagascar (25.1 per cent) and Southeast Africa (26.4 per cent).[106] 'The complexity of early Cape culture', Shell (1994b:11) therefore concludes, 'was in part the result of a constantly changing slave trade to the Cape. Slaves were drawn from a multitude of starkly different geographic and cultural origins, constituting easily the most diverse population of any recorded slave society.'

Shell (1994b:12) has nicely displayed the historic patterns of this multicultural slave trade to the Cape. The individual peaks of the early slave voyages to Madagascar stand out clearly among the more continuous streams of slaves from South and Southeast Asia. Moreover, a decided intensification and 'Africanization' of the slave trade can be detected in the second half of the eighteenth century, but this was due to Dutch weakness rather than strength. In 1767 the VOC prohibited the import of (private) Asian slaves on Dutch ships into the Cape, at a time when their maritime power was already declining in both relative and absolute numbers.[107] Foreign slavers – English, French, Portuguese and Danish – handsomely exploited this niche, especially during and after the Fourth Anglo-Dutch War that crippled Dutch shipping

---

arrival' in the Netherlands, but that the execution of these ordinances was haphazard at best. According to the laws of Batavia, there was a limit of four slaves per VOC official or private burgher.

[106]   Shell 1994a:40-1, 1994b:14. Slaves from West Africa are included in the East African (continent) category. Of the total volume, 7.4 per cent came from Makassar, 3.7 per cent from Batavia, 2.2 per cent from Bali, 1.6 per cent from Bugis and 1.2 per cent from Buton.

[107]   Whether this prohibition was introduced out of fear of the 'violent' nature of Sulawesian Muslim slaves (Armstrong 1979:80; Van Duin and Ross 1987:83; Ross 1988:212), or because of stinginess by the Company (Shell 1994a:43, 1994b:35, note 7; Ross 1988:212), it ultimately did not prevent the illicit continuation of this practice.

even further.[108] The 'Africanization' of the slave trade to the Cape therefore occurred in tandem with the 'Europeanization' of the slavers. The French were particularly active during the 1780s, shipping thousands of Southeast African slaves to their sugar plantation colonies in the Mascarenes (Mauritius, Réunion) but also to the Caribbean (Saint Domingue); the Portuguese plied a similar route to Brazil. As these transatlantic slavers took on provisions at the Cape, they were exposed to the temptation of quick profits.[109]

Slave imports into the Cape tapered off during the 1790s, with a suggested 2,000 slaves entering the colony during the First British Occupation (1795-1802) (Ross 1988:216), another 1,039 slaves, of whom at least 790 from Mozambique, during the period of the Batavian Republic (1803-1806) (Shell 1994a:45) and a few hundred (300) more before the prohibition of the international slave trade (Ross 1988:216). If we subtract the numbers during the British occupation from the total volume rendered by Shell, we arrive at 60,000 slaves imported during the VOC era. A sizeable amount of these had previously been slaves in other parts of the Dutch Indian Ocean World, whereas the intensification of slave imports in the second half of the eighteenth century must be attributed to foreign slavers. It would only be a matter of time before the slaves at the Cape fell under British instead of Dutch jurisdiction.

Towards a global picture of the Dutch colonial slave trade

To suggest an estimate for the entire volume of the Dutch slave trade in the Indian Ocean World would be irresponsible, based on the scattered data I have given. Needless to say, more rigorous archival research is required to get closer to an accurate figure for this slave trade, and fortunately there are signs that area specialists are picking up on this theme. It will be a momentous and nearly impossible task to integrate their future findings into something resembling the TSTD2, considering the many pitfalls involved in the multi-directional Indian Ocean slave trade. Even if we accept that around 60,000 slaves were disembarked at Cape Town during the VOC period, how many of them had been previously

---

[108]   Shell (1994a:45) cites this war as 'the true watershed date for the origin of Cape slaves' – understandably, with the dramatic change in the nationality of the slave traders came a change in provenance zones as well. Van Duin and Ross (1987:127) show that during the eighteenth century, with the exception of the aforementioned war, Dutch shipping continued at a relatively consistent rate (between forty to seventy ships yearly), with in the 1770s foreign shipping suddenly expanding; 1772 was the first year with more foreign than Dutch ships stopping at the Cape Town harbour and this trend would only grow stronger during the last decades of the century. This development is of course closely related to the growth of the East African slave trade to both the Mascarenes and the Americas.

[109]   It was not allowed to purchase slaves for the Company from foreign traders, but Company officials and *freeburghers* could always buy slaves for private use (Böeseken 1977:70).

traded in the South Asian or Southeast Asian region, either by Dutch or other merchants? Perhaps we should stop trying to measure this unique slave trade in transatlantic terms and assess it solely on its own patterns. Broadly speaking though, the number of slaves entering the Dutch colonies in the Indian Ocean World during the seventeenth and eighteenth centuries must have amounted to at least several hundred thousand. Raben (2008) guesstimates that to Batavia alone – by far the greatest consumer of slaves in the VOC domain – between two and three hundred thousand slaves were shipped. It is, in fact, possible that the slave trade to Dutch colonial towns in the East approached the half million mark of the Dutch transatlantic slave trade. But regardless of the exact numbers, the available evidence certainly warrants a reappraisal of the overall role of the Dutch in the colonial slave trade.

The Dutch transatlantic slave trade can be relatively easily divided between the period of the WIC monopoly and the era of the private slave trade that followed it. The most significant gaps in our knowledge relate to the illicit private slave trade (interlopers) during the era of the Company trade and the recent study by Ruud Paesie (2008) has shed valuable light on this topic. In the Indian Ocean World, the Company's involvement in slave trading was arguably more heavily centred on the seventeenth century as well. Since its trading empire was still expanding, each territorial conquest was followed by the building or strengthening of fortifications and warehouses, backbreaking work that was preferably done with slaves and convicts rather than by Company personnel. The VOC organized several long-distance slave voyages (Coromandel, Bengal-Arakan, Madagascar) but most slaves were transported in smaller shipments, often as additional freight stowed away with the primary commodities. Future research may perhaps reveal whether slaves shipped in this way had a better chance of surviving the voyage or not. The private slave trade in the Dutch Indian Ocean World was more hidden and, apart from the personal trade slaves of Company officials and *freeburghers* travelling on VOC ships, more limited to regional networks. A sizeable share of this trade remained in the hands of Asian merchants (Southeast Asia) or was carried on by ships sailing under different European flags (southern Africa). If we apply the same strict national compartmentalization that has been customary in the transatlantic slave trade, a substantial downsizing of the Dutch Indian Ocean slave trade is likely in order.

In recent quantitative assessments of the transatlantic slave trade, the Dutch are often relegated to the status of a minor or second-rate carrier (Eltis 2001). It is difficult to argue with the mass of compiled data spanning more than three centuries. But if we narrow the time frame to the period of the Golden Age (*Gouden Eeuw*), Dutch participation in the transatlantic slave trade grows significantly in importance. Furthermore, if we compare this with the Dutch stake in American slavery, the oft-repeated idea that the Dutch were more successful at trading than at colonizing is confirmed once again. In the Atlantic World the Dutch shipped more slaves to colonies of other nations than vice versa and were thus, in sheer numerical and historical impact, of greater importance on the supply side (Africa) than on the demand side (Americas) of the slave trade. This contrast is even further enhanced when we consider that substantial parts of the European population in the Dutch colonies, particularly the planters, were of a non-Dutch background, while Dutch investors and skippers often attempted to evade the WIC monopoly by trading slaves under different Protestant flags or illicitly.[110] Even the Company itself was not opposed to allowing its former Portuguese-Brazilian enemies to take slaves along the Gold Coast, as long as they paid a generous duty of ten per cent per slave (Schwartz and Postma 2003).

Looking back at Dutch colonial migration in its entirety, it is safe to say that no European power demonstrated a greater discrepancy between sending their own citizens overseas and transporting others, either through force or on a more voluntary basis (Eltis 1999:28). How great the destructive impact of these forced migrations was on the various provenance zones in Africa has been the subject of an extensive and often heated debate. For the Indian Ocean World, it seems that the densely populated South Asian societies – especially when considering their massive indentured labour migrations that came after the abolition of slavery – were relatively unaffected by the small drainage of manpower. For the major slave-exporting regions in Southeast Asia (Sulawesi, Bali) however, as well as for the island of Madagascar, the effects of the export slave trade must have been more dramatic, both in terms of demographic loss and in stimulating internal warfare, enslavement and general disorganization. It is moreover quite conceivable that some of the smaller island societies in the eastern parts of the Indonesian archipelago were in fact destroyed beyond repair by slave raiding expeditions instigated directly or indirectly by the Dutch.

The nature of slavery in the Dutch colonial sphere

As slaves from widely diverging backgrounds continued to arrive in Cape Town during the eighteenth century, colonial farmers (Boers) trekked fur-

---

[110] Ratelband 1953; Paesie 2008. Although I realize that, on the other hand, the mercantile connections of Sephardic Jews played an important role in the early development of the Dutch slave trade and that there are sporadic cases of Dutch planters settling in foreign colonies. For example, Klooster (1998:41-2) and Paesie (2008:248-9) mention a significant population of Dutch planters on Danish St. Thomas, with many coming from Curaçao and Sint Eustatius. By 1765 they were still the single largest group on the island, outnumbering the Danes two to one; there was also a Dutch presence on St. John after that island became a Danish colony in 1717.

De directrice van het Gouvernementshospitaal te Paramaribo (midden) met haar staf

ther into the interior, in search of new land and opportunities. Far removed from the bustling port, and generally unable to afford the slaves offered for sale there anyway, these frontiersmen turned to native African labour. The incorporation of Khoikhoi children and other local captives through systems such as the *inboekstelsel* has traditionally been described as a form of forced apprenticeship, a type of 'enserfment' to be clearly distinguished from the slavery that existed around the Cape. Eldredge and Morton (1994:1) blur this distinction however, by arguing 'that thousands in the interior were indeed captured, traded, or held as chattel[; o]n the expanding "Dutch frontier", slave raiding was part of a process of dispossessing indigenes of their cattle and land for commercial gain'.[111] Established historians of colonial South Africa generally criticized the authors' flexible use of the term 'slavery'.[112] And there were unmistakably important legal differences between the two. Nevertheless, who could argue that the de facto condition of an African captive forced to work for a white European farmer on the rural frontier was inherently better than that of, say, a domestic slave in Cape Town?[113]

The history of the Indian Ocean World is littered with such ambiguities questioning the Western conception of chattel slavery vis-à-vis more 'lenient' forms of servitude. Considering the widespread 'uneconomic' use of slaves as status symbols to the wealthy, it is perhaps understandable that such slaves occasionally experienced higher material living standards than other dependents in society. It is, however, slightly more difficult to comprehend that free people sold their children and themselves willingly into slavery, even if it were to escape starvation and receive protection, or that enslaved people refused an offer of freedom because they thought themselves better off in their current situation (Campbell 2004a:xi-xxvi). Apologists of slavery do not

[111] If defined as slavery, this practice should perhaps have been included in the previous section, since it clearly added new slaves to the Dutch colonial sphere. However, the topic of this chapter has been restricted to the larger maritime slave trades, where people were forced to migrate to completely new environments. It will be infinitely more difficult to establish the volume and directions of the short-distance slave trades over land. In this specific situation at the South African frontier, it was the European colonists who were primarily doing the migrating, while the future slaves or serfs essentially remained in their traditional environment.

[112] Pamela Scully (1997:607) states that some chapters of the book 'do not add much to our knowledge of slavery except to rename coercive labour relations as slavery. However, the book does demonstrate that scholars have tended to overlook relations of servitude because they did not fall under the category of de jure slavery.' Robert Ross (1995:512) argues that '[t]he problem derives from the resolutely ethic criteria employed in this book for the identification of slavery. As is not seldom the case, the subtitle of this book [*Captive labor on the Dutch frontier*] is a far better description of its contents than the main title [*Slavery in South Africa*]'.

[113] Although James Scott was referring to Southeast Asia, his comment (1985:143) that 'the function of the slave is a better indication of his or her condition than legal status per se' seems appropriate for this context as well.

have to look very hard to come across such historic evidence.[114]

We thus have to accept that many victims of debt bondage, serfdom, forced labour and various other forms of 'virtual slavery' that characterize the Indian Ocean World 'have often been more exploited and worse off than slaves'.[115] Even in the comparatively transparent slave-free dichotomy of the American colonies, sporadic cases can be found of expensive slaves being spared hard and dangerous labour that instead was performed by expendable hired hands and convicts of European backgrounds; or of emancipated slaves complaining that their new-found freed status was somehow 'worse than slavery'. This is not to say that most slaves in history did not wholeheartedly desire freedom – after all, Patterson (1982) has argued that the idea of freedom itself originated from the slave. It merely goes to show that the reality of freedom, after it was granted, was not very 'free'.[116]

The decision to focus only on de jure slaves in this chapter may therefore appear somewhat arbitrary to some, but it is not. The primary objective was to outline the forced migrations in the Dutch colonial sphere and these were, with the exception of convicts and exiles (Ward 2001), by and large consisting of 'true' slaves. If the Dutch had transported the aforementioned Khoikhoi to Cape Town and from there to other colonial settlements, the pretence of apprenticeship and serfdom certainly would have been lifted. Jan van Riebeeck, the first governor at the Cape, already proposed this as a remedy for unruly Natives, but for various reasons the Company never considered it wise to enslave the local population. While unfree labour conditions showed a perplexing variety around the Indian Ocean World, it appears that the finer details were generally lost on the Dutch. However, when slave trading and slavery were abolished during the nineteenth century, alternatives had to be considered. Only then did the Dutch begin exploiting native populations more directly, even transporting them over great distances, but under different terms of labour (see Chapter VI).

Yet even when we confine ourselves to de jure slaves, a theoretical definition can only be of limited use. The actual lived experience of slaves simply varies too dramatically over time and space to make it truly workable. And even when a particular system of slavery is labelled as either extremely harsh

---

[114]   One of the classic examples is George Fitzhugh's defence of slavery in *Cannibals all! Or slaves without masters* (1854), arguing that the European and North American working class had to toil harder, yet were not taken care off by their modern employers.

[115]   Miers 2004:9. The article of Miers offers an excellent introduction into the many problems associated with defining slavery. Her take (2004:4) on 'virtual slavery' is that it is 'a term used as loosely as slavery itself, when no more precise definition can be found, for a situation in which the victim has most but not all the attributes of a slave'.

[116]   See Cooper, Holt and Scott (2000) for an excellent methodological survey of the various problems facing former slaves in the post-emancipation era.

or rather mild by its historians, the nature of the human relationship between a master and his or her slave can play out in a myriad of ways. One finds the most despicable punishments alongside surprisingly intimate bonds of friendship. Being the subject – or should I say object? – of enslavement and slave trading always had something of a cruel lottery to it.

Of course, it is a primary task of historians to look beyond such idiosyncratic experiences and establish more general patterns in time and space. Ever since the classic study by Frank Tannenbaum (1947), historians have been comparing the various manifestations of New World slavery in an attempt to explain the roots of their differences. To some, the key factor was the cultural background of the European colonizer: Iberian slavery was supposedly rather mild, while English and Dutch slavery was harsh and more brutally exploitative.[117] Others have objected to these arguments by attributing more weight to the environmental and demographic conditions in the colonies themselves. Since we are here primarily concerned with a comparison of Dutch colonial slavery, we can – in the footsteps of Harry Hoetink's study of race relations (1967) – safely eliminate the metropolitan cultural factor. At the same time, our wide global perspective enables us to focus even more closely on the importance of various local conditions in the historic development of colonial slavery. By looking at the demographic size of the slave populations in the Dutch colonial sphere and the specific labour conditions the slaves faced, we can offer some tentative suggestions on how these factors impacted the sociocultural position of the slaves and their historic legacy.

The size of slave populations in the Dutch colonies

The absolute and relative size of slave populations can be helpful indicators to determine to what extent a particular society was dominated by slavery. Table 5.11 and 5.12 are admittedly modest attempts to gather some relevant demographic data for slavery in the Dutch colonies. Given the limitations of the historical records it is, certainly in the Indian Ocean World, difficult to show a clear development over time. Nonetheless, these figures irrefutably prove the heavy dependency of the Dutch colonial settlements on slaves.

---

[117] See Foner and Genovese (1969) for an overview of the classic positions on this debate. The cultural arguments by Tannenbaum and Elkins have recently been given new life by scholars like Blackburn (1997) and Eltis (2000) who both argue that certain 'progressive' developments in the metropolis (growth of capitalism, freedom, possessive individualism) can be indirectly related to the rather harsh treatment of slaves by the British and Dutch. Eltis (1999) sees it as a most tragic irony that the rights to liberty and personal freedom these early modern Europeans enjoyed at home, also allowed them to act relatively unfettered and unchecked towards outsiders beyond the European continent.

Rik van Welie

Table 5.11 Assorted slave and free populations in the Dutch colonial world (VOC domain)

Colony	Year	Slaves (Company and private slaves)		Europeans and mestizos		Free Non-Europeans	
Zeelandia (Taiwan)	1650	ca. 500	(10.0%)	ca. 1,800	(36.0%)	ca. 2,700	(54.0%)
Kota Ambon	1694	2,870	(52.3%)	1,008	(18.4%)	1,609	(29.3%)
Banda Islands	1638	2,190	(57.0%)	539	(14.0%)	1,115	(29.0%)
	1687	3,731	(58.5%)	1,111	(17.4%)	1,533	(24.0%)
	1854	1,890	(29.8%)	487	(7.7%)	3,962	(62.5%)
Makassar (Sulawesi)	1730	2,915	(58.5%)	622	(12.5%)	1,448	(29.0%)
Batavia	1632*	2,724	(33.8%)	2,368	(29.4%)	2,968	(36.8%)
(inner city)	1673	9,938	(56.0%)	2,336	(13.2%)	5,466	(30.8%)
	1699	12,505	(57.1%)	2,453	(11.2%)	6,953	(31.7%)
	1729	14,760	(62.3%)	2,135	(9.0 %)	6,806	(28.7%)
	1759	10,046	(59.4%)	2,170	(12.8%)	4,698	(27.8%)
	1797	4,339	(51.1%)	785	(9.2%)	3,373	(39.7%)
Batavia	1673**	3,343	(35.9%)	414	(4.4%)	5,554	(59.6%)
(Ommelanden)	1699	13,216	(26.6%)	982	(2.0%)	35,490	(71.4%)
(surrounding areas)	1729	15,729	(19.9%)	670	(0.9%)	62,558	(79.2%)
	1759	17,111	(15.4%)	802	(0.7%)	93,259	(83.9%)
	1789	32,906	(23.0%)	748	(0.5%)	109,685	(76.5%)
Batavia (total)	1850	7,556	(2.2%)	3,774	(1.1%)	336,995	(96.7%)
Java and Madura	1850	9,646	(0.1%)	16,172	(0.2%)	9,544,205	(99.7%)
Malacca	1678	1,780	(35.2%)	814	(16.1%)	2,463	(48.7%)
- Fort	1678	511	(43.9%)	652	(56.1%)	n.a.***	
Silida(West Sumatra)	1681	131	(76.6%)	40	(23.4%)	n.a.	
Colombo	1694	1,787	(53.3%)	ca. 881	(26.3%)	ca. 684	(20.4%)
- Fort	1694	787	(55.9%)	ca. 473	(33.6%)	ca. 148	(10.5%)
- Town	1694	1,000	(51.4%)	ca. 408	(21.0%)	ca. 536	(27.6%)
- Surrounding area	1683	591	(22.3%)	n.a.		2,059	(77.7%)
Galle	1760	393	(21.3%)	559	(30.4%)	889	(48.3%)
Jaffnapatnam	1694	558	(52.5%)	504	(47.5%)	n.a.	
Cochin	1760	1,275	(62.5%)	508	(24.9%)	257	(12.6%)
	1790	1,299	(56.1%)	804	(34.7%)	214	(9.2%)

*   In 1632 there was no strict division between the inner city and the surrounding suburbs (Ommelanden).

**   In 1673 and 1679 only a small part of the Ommelanden are included in the census, explaining the jump of the total population from 13,593 in 1679 to 45,550 in 1689 (Raben 1996:89); the southern suburb of Batavia (Zuidervoorstad) is, together with the inner city, included in these 1670s counts.

*** N.a., or numbers not available – usually this means that the remaining census data do not give clear distinctions between the European/mestizo free population and the rest of the free population. They are therefore included in the other free category. It can be assumed that the free non-European, non-mestizo populations of Fort Malacca and Jaffnapatnam were really small, whereas at the Cape Colony the absolute and relative size of the Free Black population (Asians and Africans alike) decreased as one moved further away from Cape Town.

Colony	Year	Slaves (Company and private slaves)		Europeans and mestizos		Free Non-Europeans	
Mauritius	1706	71	(29.1%)	173	(70.9%)	n.a.	
Cape Colony	1750	5,327	(51.9%)	4,932	(48.1%)	n.a.	
- Cape Town (fort)	1731	1,333	(42.2%)	1,624	(51.4%)	200	(6.3%)
- Cape district	1750	3,188	(58.5%)	1,939	(35.6%)	320	(5.9%)
- Stellenbosch district	1750	765	(57.0%)	576	(43.0%)	n.a.	
- Drakenstein district	1750	1,115	(43.0%)	1,476	(57.0%)	n.a.	
- Swellendam district	1750	259	(29.4%)	621	(70.6%)	n.a.	
- Graaf-Reinet district	1790	597	(17.5%)	2,805	(82.5%)	n.a.	

Table 5.12 Assorted slave and free populations in the Dutch colonial world (WIC domain)

Colony	Year	Slaves		Europeans		Free Non-Europeans	
Gold Coast	1645	409	(64.9%)	221	(35.1%)		
(all Dutch forts)	1736[*]	ca. 700	(72.0%)	262	(27.0%)	ca.10	(1.0%)
	1773	ca. 700	(68.2%)	180	(17.0%)	146	(13.7%)
- Fort(s) Elmina	1645	192	(60.4%)	126	(39.6%)		
	1700	ca. 300	(69.8%)	130	(30.2%)		
	1736	ca. 300	(74.4%)	103	(25.6%)		
- Fort Nassau	1645	156	(80.4%)	38	(19.6%)		
Dutch Brazil	1645/6	2,671	(20.0%)	7,114	(53.2%)	3,583	(26.8%)
Suriname	1683	4,281	(84.1%)	811	(15.9%)	?	
	1738	ca.24,047	(89.8%)	2,133	(8.0%)	598	(2.2%)
	1791	48,155	(91.2%)	2,900	(5.5%)	1,760	(3.3%)
	1830	48,784	(86.8%)	2,373	(4.2%)	5,041	(9.0%)
- Paramaribo	1791	ca. 8,000(	68.0%)	2,000	(17.0%)	1,760	(15.0%)
	1850	6,139	(37.6%)	ca. 2,500	(15.3%)	ca.7,699	(47.1%)
- Plantations	1774	56,834	(98.4%)	914	(1.6%)		
	1791	45,000	(98.0%)	900	(2.0%)		
	1850	33,408	(96.7%)	1,141	(3.3%)		
Berbice	1720	895	(89.0%)	111	(11.0%)		
	1762	4,077	(92.2%)	346	(7.8%)		
	1796	8,232	(88.6%)	860	(9.3%)	200	(2.2%)

[*] Doortmont and Smit (2007:325) give the following Dutch castles and forts (and African towns) on the Gold Coast during the era of the slave trade: Fort Crèvecoeur (Accra) 1649-1868; Fort Good Hope (De Goede Hoop, Senya Beraku) 1705-1868; Fort Patience (Lijdzaamheid, Apam) 1697-1868; Fort Amsterdam (Abandze, Kormantin) 1665-1868; Fort Nassau (Mouri) 1612-1868; Cabo Cors (Cape Coast) 1660s; Castle St. George d'Elmina (Elmina) 1637-1872; Fort Coenraadsburg on St. Jago Hill (Elmina) (1637) 1660s-1872; Fort Vredenburg (Dutch Komenda) 1689-1872; Fort St. Sebastian (St. Sebastiaan, Shama) 1638-1872; Fort Orange (Oranje, Dutch Sekondi) 1670s-1872; Fort Witzen (Takoradi) 1680s-1872; Fort Batenstein (Butre) 1656-1872; Fort Dorothea (Akwida) 1717-1872; Fort Gross Friedrichsburg (Hollandia, Pokesu) (1717) 1725-1872; Fort St. Anthony (Axim) 1642-1872; Fort Ruyghaver (Ankobra River) 1654-1659.

Colony	Year	Slaves		Europeans		Free Non-Europeans	
Essequibo	1700	426	(87.7%)	60	(12.3%)		
and	1735	2,600	(95.9%)	110	(4.1%)		
Demerara (1746)	1796	28,000	(89.3%)	2,700	(8.6%)	650	(2.1%)
Tobago	1665	c. 7,000	(84.8%)	1,250	(15.2%)		
Curaçao	1720	2,238	(55.9%)	c.1,720	(42.9%)	48	(1.2%)
	1789	12,864	(61.3%)	4,410	(21.0%)	3,714	(17.7%)
	1833	5,894	(39.2%)	2,602	(17.3%)	6,531	(43.5%)
- Willemstad	1789	5,419	(46.9%)	3,507	(30.4%)	2,617	(22.7%)
	1825	1,731	(25.6%)	2,443	(36.1%)	2,590	(38.3%)
- Countryside	1789	7,445	(78.8%)	903	(9.6%)	1,097	(11.6%)
	1825	4,383	(61.7%)	523	(7.4%)	2,197	(30.9%)
Bonaire	1806	364	(38.5%)	72	(7.6%)	509	(53.9%)
	1833	567	(32.4%)	112	(6.4%)	1,069	(61.2%)
Aruba	1816	370	(21.4%)	210	(12.1%)	1,150	(66.5%)
	1833	393	(14.3%)	465	(16.9%)	1,888	(68.8%)
St. Eustatius	1715	750	(58.9%)	524	(31.1%)		
	1747	1,513	(60.2%)	1,002	(39.8%)		
	1790	4,944	(63.1%)	2,375	(30.3%)	511	(6.5%)
	1816	1,784	(67.5%)	507	(19.6%)	336	(13.0%)
St. Maarten	1715	244	(30.1%)	361	(59.7%)		
	1750	1,795	(73.5%)	648	(26.5%)		
	1790	4,226	(75.9%)	1,151	(20.7%)	194	(3.5%)
	1816	2,551	(71.7%)	715	(20.1%)	293	(8.2%)
Saba	1715	179	(35.0%)	336	(65.0%)		
	1790	564	(43.4%)	730	(56.1%)	7	(0.6%)
	1816	462	(40.3%)	656	(57.3%)	27	(2.4%)
New Netherland	1664	ca. 400	(5.3%)	ca. 7,000	(93.3%)	ca. 100	(1.3%)
New Amsterdam	1664	ca. 300	(12.6%)	ca. 2,000	(84.2%)	ca. 75	(3.2%)

We must keep in mind that most of these population figures pertain to the Dutch-controlled areas only and give little indication of the indigenous populations surrounding these colonies. The size and strength of these native societies were undoubtedly the main difference between European colonization in the Americas and elsewhere around the globe, and of fundamental importance to the development of slavery.

In the New World, most of these native populations were not only relatively sparse, especially after coming into contact with European colonists, but their societies were relatively 'underdeveloped' and defenceless against European might. Direct territorial colonization was therefore not merely a possibility, but almost obligatory if Europeans were hoping to make longterm profits. To provide for the much-needed labour, first indentured servants from Europe, then African slaves were imported in droves.[118] Generally speaking,

---

[118] Only early Spanish colonization of mainland America, which focused on the more densely populated – though ultimately powerless – Aztec and Inca empires, did rely substantially on

the population structure of most American colonies became characterized by 'Black majorities' and, despite occasional hostilities with surrounding Native American tribes, control of these slaves was of primary concern to the colonial order. From the lower US South all the way to central Brazil, African slaves always made up more than half of the total population and their labour was indispensable to the raison d'être of these societies: the plantations. The Dutch era in Brazil and their later settlements on the Wild Coast (Suriname, Berbice, Essequibo and Demerara) certainly fit this mould. The major insular Caribbean colonies of the Dutch (Curaçao, St. Eustatius, St. Maarten) possessed slightly lower percentages of slaves, primarily because these islands did not fully adhere to the classic American plantation model. They were either too small or the climate was too arid for plantation agriculture to be truly viable. The islands were still characterized by 'Black majorities', partly due to their specific historic roles in the transatlantic slave trade and partly because European immigrants generally avoided such unhealthy tropical climates. New Netherland easily came closest to resembling the natural environment of Western Europe and accordingly witnessed a sizeable (family) migration of European colonists and had no strong demand for African slaves, except in trading them onward to more plantation-oriented colonies.

While slave populations in most Dutch VOC possessions were substantial as well, the comparison with the American colonies completely falls apart if we take the surrounding indigenous populations into account.[119] In the Indian Ocean World the 'Natives' formed the true 'Black' or non-European majorities and as such were both respected and feared by the European colonizer. Their indigenous production and extensive Asian trade networks allowed European colonists to limit direct control to fortified trading posts and their immediate hinterlands. Of course, they had but little choice in this matter. In this maritime network of colonial towns, slaves formed a unique element occupied with serving the Dutch inner circle: they worked on the docks, erected fortifications, tended to Company garden plots, functioned as artisans and complemented the European households as domestic servants, concubines or even as future wives. But they were almost never involved in commercial agriculture for the European market. In the Indian Ocean World, commercial production remained squarely in the hands of indigenous societies.

Slaves were thus numerically important only if we concentrate on the various VOC ports, from Batavia to Colombo, Cochin to Makassar. Their demographic impact gradually loses significance if we extend the concentric

---

coerced native labour. But the rather unique development of African slavery in these colonies only confirms the essential role played by indigenous populations in this process.

[119] Raben 2008 points out that the VOC towns had remarkably high slave populations when compared to pre-colonial towns and nearby indigenous communities.

circle around those colonial towns (Raben 2008). The Dutch fort and town of Zeelandia (Taiwan), for example, had in 1650 around 5,000 residents, of whom more than 1,000 were VOC soldiers and 500 were slaves; but they were easily outweighed by a Chinese population of approximately 20,000 on the island and another 70,000 native inhabitants of Formosa in the surrounding villages 'controlled' by the VOC (Van Veen 1996:77; Oosterhoff 1985:55). On the Gold Coast (current-day Ghana), the demographic and military strength of the local African states made the forts-factories of the WIC resemble those of the VOC much more closely than its other possessions across the Atlantic. The six to eight hundred African slaves that manned these trading posts during the eighteenth century easily outnumbered the free Company servants, who between 1700 and 1760 were on average 253 men strong, with a gradually increasing share of Free Black and mulatto personnel.[120] The few hundred WIC servants and their Company slaves who resided in and around the two forts at Elmina were insignificant when placed against the demographic and military strength of the town on the African mainland, with a population (including slaves) fluctuating somewhere between 12,000 and 16,000 during the eighteenth century (Feinberg 1989:65, 85; Van Kessel 2002:25, 101). Friendly relations with the local rulers were, understandably, an absolute priority to the Dutch.

Slavery in the European trading posts across the Indian Ocean World had a decidedly urban and domestic character. Slaves performed a much wider variety of service-oriented tasks than their 'colleagues' in the Americas, who were primarily occupied with plantation production of an industrial nature. In their attempts to estimate the relative harshness of the slave's condition, historians have often judged urban slavery to be rather mild. Such a judgement is primarily based on the harsh and monotonous working conditions that field slaves encountered, but also on the limits of social control in the city and the general mobility that characterizes most seaports throughout history.

This distinction between urban and rural slavery is captured quite well by slavery in the Dutch Cape Colony. Historians who stressed the outright inhumanity of 'the Cape of torments' (Ross 1983; Worden 1985), have generally focused their archival research on slavery in the rural areas of the Western Cape, while a Cape Town-oriented perspective can lead to seeing a more familial relationship between the paternalistic master and his 'children of

---

[120]   Feinberg 1989:35-6; Den Heijer 1997:81-2. Den Heijer (1997:81-2) suggests an average WIC personnel on the Gold Coast – including the coastal vessels – fluctuating between 180 and 380 around this period (1674-1740), with the percentage of Europeans from outside the Dutch Republic rising from 32.5 per cent in 1700 to 56.6 per cent in 1740. The Dutch forts on the African coast were rather unique in that they, according to Feinberg (1989:36), only contained Company employees, but no European *freeburgher* class; a similar situation, though for different reasons, developed in the VOC post of Dejima in Japan.

bondage'.[121] Moreover, if one takes American, and thus basically rural slavery as a measuring rod, which Shell does throughout his work, then the working and living conditions of slaves at the Cape may appear relatively humane in comparison. But looking at other VOC possessions – all mostly cosmopolitan trading posts – leaves one with the distinct impression that Cape slavery was very exploitative, and much more racially defined, in nature. A study of Dutch colonial society around the provincial town of Stellenbosch confirms this image once more, by providing some horrific examples of the ways in which slaves were punished on the rural frontier (Biewenga 1999:108-15). The colonial environment and its economy were understandably of fundamental importance in defining the lives of the slaves.

The various roles of slaves in the colonial economy

In an attempt to assess the relative importance of slavery, M.I. Finley (1968) made a now classic distinction between 'societies with slaves', encompassing most civilizations throughout human history, and a few historic 'slave societies', in which the entire socio-economic structure was based on slavery as a mode of production. His definition of 'slave society' was a very narrow one and, besides his fascination with classical slavery, fitted only the European plantation colonies in the Americas. Historically, the rise of the 'plantation complex' was firmly based on the production of sugar for the European market. All the major importers of slaves in the Americas, from Brazil in the sixteenth to Cuba in the nineteenth century, were essentially addicted to this combination of 'sweetness and power'.[122] The plantation colonies of the Dutch, New Holland (Dutch Brazil) in the first half of the seventeenth century and Suriname and the other Wild Coast settlements thereafter, did not significantly differ from this pattern (see table 5.4 on Dutch Brazil). Suriname had 171 sugar plantations by 1713 (Van Stipriaan 1993:33), but underwent a dramatic intensification of plantation agriculture during the eighteenth cen-

---

[121] Shell 1994a. Such different interpretations are undoubtedly also influenced by the historiographical trends of the time, in which the 'victimization' of slaves gradually became replaced by a search for more 'agency' and 'resistance' in the face of oppression.

[122] Mintz 1985. The powerful role of sugar is sometimes overlooked when focusing on slavery in the North American mainland, where tobacco and, in the nineteenth century, cotton were king. Only in the Mississippi River Delta of Louisiana did sugar plantations operate, which goes to show that the cultivation of sugar cane is limited to unhealthy subtropical climates. Not surprisingly, slavery in the rest of the southern United States was rather exceptional considering that its slave population showed a positive natural growth and, as a result, high levels of creolization. Even within the South, slave life and culture manifested themselves in different ways according to the agricultural organization (tobacco, rice, indigo) of the colonies; see both Morgan 1998 and Berlin 1998.

Indiaans kamp (Kalebaskreek), tekening A. Borret

tury, as the production of coffee began surpassing that of sugar. This explains in large part the increased volume of the Dutch transatlantic slave trade during the middle decades of the century. Table 5.13 based on the most thorough quantitative study of Suriname during its last hundred years of slavery, shows the development of this commercial plantation sector.

Table 5.13 Suriname plantation slaves producing for the export market, 1750-1863

Plantation sector	Year	Number of plantations	Total slaves (average per plantation)		Field slaves (number per plantation) and % of total	
Sugar	1750	141	19,008	(135)	9,835	(70) 52%
	1770	111	16,584	(149)	8,411	(76) 51%
	1790	102	12,232	(120)	5,243	(51) 43%
	1810	100	10,108	(101)	4,196	(42) 42%
	1825	95	12,352	(130)	5,925	(62) 48%
	1862	86	19,789	(230)	7,876	(92) 40%
Coffee	1750	225	16,029	(71)	9,332	(41) 58%
	1770	295	37,179	(126)	20,087	(68) 54%
	1790	248	26,710	(108)	12,390	(50) 46%
	1810	235	21,968	(93)	10,668	(45) 48%
	1825	178	17,363	(98)	8,132	(46) 47%
	1862	37	3,892	(105)	-	
Cotton	1825	73	8,290	(114)	4,145	(57) 50%
	1862	15	2,551	(170)	-	
Cacao	1862	23	1,225	(53)	-	

Source: Van Stipriaan 1993:128-44, 438-9.

The other Dutch plantation colonies on the Wild Coast grew even more dramatically during the second half of the eighteenth century (see tables 5.8 and 5.12), though this expansion was mainly instigated by British and North American planters and merchants. When the English occupied these colonies during the Napoleonic era, the slave population of Essequibo and Demerara quickly increased from 28,000 in 1796 to circa 60,000 slaves in 1806, working a total of 700 plantations (Van der Oest 2003:329). They produced the same commodities for the European market as nearby Suriname and in fairly identical patterns, with sugar and coffee closely rivalling each other, followed at some distance by cotton and then cacao.

Sugar cane never wavers too far from the equator but, as its history shows, experienced a clear westward migration across the globe. Sugar production was an essential feature of several economies around the Indian Ocean World, but it never became so closely connected to the tragedy of slavery as in the greater Caribbean. Sugar plantations around Batavia and on Taiwan during the VOC period, for example, may occasionally have turned to slave labour as well, but they were predominantly run by Chinese merchants (Niemeijer 2005: table 9) who usually imported cheap 'coolies' from China to do the drudgery.[123] Later, during the Cultivation System on Java, the Dutch began forcing native labour into sugar production, often through more indirect, feudal means (see Chapter VI).Only the tiny island of Mauritius showed a glimpse of slave-based sugar production during its Dutch occupation, but its true maturation as a plantation colony took place later, during the eighteenth and nineteenth centuries. The main reason why the Mascarenes eventually developed according to a Caribbean pattern was because they were largely uninhabited and more or less 'open' to European colonization.

The closest the Dutch came to slave-based plantation agriculture in the Indian Ocean World was in the Moluccas (Maluku), the famous 'spice islands' located a thousand miles to the east of the VOC capital of Batavia. But even here, specific local conditions and historic events were of prime importance in the development of slavery. On Ambon, where the Dutch had expelled the Portuguese at an early stage (1605), the production of cloves remained in the hands of the large indigenous population, sometimes aided by local or imported slaves.[124] The VOC merely arranged the fixed purchase and shipment of these cloves and frantically oversaw its coveted monopoly, for example by deploying island raids to extirpate clove trees outside Ambon (the so-called *hongi* expeditions). Its headquarters in the Ambonese archipelago, the city of Kota Ambon, certainly depended on the services of an extensive – and almost entirely imported – slave population, but few of them were directly occupied with the production of cloves (Knaap 1991).

The Banda Islands to the south, the sole place in the world to grow nutmeg trees at the time, could perhaps have developed in a similar direction as Ambon. The indigenous population made a comfortable living by a 'not especially arduous mode of horticulture' (Hanna 1978:6, 9). Nutmeg and its by-product mace were accordingly sold to various competing Asian and European merchants. But the VOC demanded exclusive rights to these spices and, through a series of ruthless expeditions, took hold of the island group in the early seventeenth century. Both fierce resistance by the Bandanese against

---

[123]   The VOC on Formosa mainly profited indirectly, by taxing the Chinese on almost all their economic activities, even on the right to collect these taxes. In 1651, at a time when Dutch Taiwan finally became profitable for the Company, the Chinese produced 4,400,000 pounds of sugar, while the average sugar yields for that period are estimated between one and two million kilos annually (Van Veen 1996:71, 77). Van Veen states that '[t]he process of colonization of Formosa was very similar to what had happened in South America [as in, the Spanish Americas?] and what would take place more than two hundred years later in Africa [during its colonial era]'.
[124]   Knaap (1987:129, 133, 137) estimates the native Ambonese population during the VOC government at 49,168 in 1671 and 57,605 in 1692, with the latter population containing 7,232 slaves, or 12.6 per cent.

such a monopoly and Dutch acknowledgement that these islands were in fact small and isolated enough to be controlled directly, contributed to one of the most tragic chapters in Dutch colonial history.[125] After the Bandanese population had almost been annihilated, the Company resumed the production of nutmeg and mace through a system of Dutch planters (*perkeniers*) and imported slaves working the small-scale plantations (*perken*). The Banda Islands under the Dutch became, in the words of one historian, 'nothing less than a Caribbean cuckoo in an Asian nest'.[126]

Yet what the VOC created on Banda in the 1620s was rather unique due to its rigid monopolistic character. The productive area of the three main islands were divided into 68 *perken* of almost equal size (33 on Lonthor, 31 on Ai and three on Neira, where the Company headquarters were located), and each *perk* was provided with 25 slaves whom the VOC delivered at a fixed price of forty *rijksdaalders* (96 guilders) each (Hanna 1978:59-60). Most of these starting conditions remained unchanged for over two centuries. For example, the loss of 1,529 slaves in several epidemics in 1693, 1702 and 1715 was still calculated at forty *reaal* a piece (Hanna 1978:55). Lonthor, by far the largest island, continued as the most important producer of nutmegs, while Neira Town – similar to Kota Ambon – arranged the export of spices and the import of necessary goods and foodstuffs. In 1854 one can still detect the clear relationship between the urban nature of Neira, with its European population served by domestic slaves, and the more production-oriented Lonthor and Ai (table 5.14):

Table 5.14 Selected population groups of the three main Banda Islands, 1854

(Number of perken)	Perk slaves	House slaves	Europeans and mestizos	Total *perk* labour force (% total pop.)	Total Population
Neira (3)	174	513	340	236 (7.4%)	3,201
Lonthor (25)	864	158	96	1,836 (73.3%)	2,504
Ai (6)	144	16	10	384 (72.6%)	529

Source: Bleeker Report 1856, as cited in Hanna 1978:111-2.

[125] Hanna (1978:3) estimates the size of the island group at 1/25,000 of the entire Indonesian archipelago. J.P. Coen headed the final conquest of the islands in 1621 and it is often suggested that this was revenge for the massacre of a group of VOC officials by locals in 1609, events a young Coen probably witnessed first-hand. A report by VOC official Jacques l'Hermité in the early 1610s (De Jonge 1865, III:380-94) already suggested a 'final solution' of similar proportions.

[126] Loth 1995:35. I generally agree with Loth's treatment of Banda under the Dutch as a Caribbean plantation model. It would be interesting to see if the architects of the *perkenier* system referred to concrete examples from the European colonization of the New World. At the beginning of the VOC experiments with *perken* on Ai in 1616, the Caribbean plantation system was arguably still in a developmental stage, but perhaps Spanish colonization in the West Indies or, more likely, Portuguese sugar captaincies in Brazil provided the Dutch with a model.

The stationary character of the Banda economy stands in stark contrast with the market fluctuations affecting the American plantation sector. The monopoly on nutmeg and mace enabled the VOC to keep both prices and production stable. In the 1630s, the Company had extirpated all nutmeg trees on the island of Run, for fear of possible resettlement by the English. They could easily have expanded cultivation to Run in the late 1660s, when the United Kingdom officially relinquished all its prior claims on the island.[127] But they felt no need to do so until 1862, when new *perken* were laid out on Run.[128] The monopoly thus ensured that the slave population on the *perken* 'stagnated' between 2,000 and 3,000 throughout the seventeenth and eighteenth centuries. During the nineteenth century, as table 5.14 demonstrates, slaves were gradually replaced by other, possibly cheaper forms of labour. The prohibition of the slave trade and pending abolition were certainly important factors in this development.

Even though the slaves on Banda produced for the European export market, there was no pressure to overwork the slaves as was often the case in the highly competitive Caribbean plantation sector.[129] Their lot was certainly preferable to that of Malagasy slaves put to work in the Silida gold mines on West Sumatra (1671-1739). As mentioned before, the Madagascar slave trade had stunning mortality rates and the situation only moderately improved upon arrival. While the VOC made ample use of Asian slaves throughout their possessions, it generally regarded African slaves more suitable for the harshest labour (Barendse 1995:142). Malagasy slaves were only used as 'chattel slaves instead of house slaves' (Barendse 1995:143), which also implies that the Dutch organized their slave workforce along ethnic distinctions.

This pattern of Asian slaves concentrated in the urban economy and African slaves relegated to more physically strenuous field labour seems to have persisted in South Africa as well (Shell 1994a:160-5). At the Cape the demographic and military weakness of the indigenous pastoral societies also allowed the Dutch to colonize more according to an American settlement pattern. Fortunately for the slaves, a moderate climate prevented any large-scale commercial plantation agriculture. That slavery nevertheless became such an important feature of the Cape economy has everything to do with its geographic location in the middle of two large slave-trading networks. In the

---

[127]   As part of the Peace of Breda (1667) which settled the Second Anglo-Dutch Naval War (1665-67). In this peace settlement the English took over New Netherland (New York), while the Dutch in turn claimed Suriname, a swap that has often been ridiculed with the benefit of hindsight, but at the time cannot have seemed too disadvantageous.

[128]   Hanna 1978:66. The termination of the monopoly was officially decreed on 31[!]-4-1864, but only became effective in 1873 (Hanna 1978:105).

[129]   To state that working conditions of slaves were either good or bad should not automatically lead to conclusions regarding their general treatment, but it certainly can be a useful indicator.

early stages of its development, there were still signs that the colony would follow a pattern similar to New Netherland, relying predominantly on immigrant labour – either indentured or not – from Europe.[130]

If slave labouring conditions on Banda and in the rural Cape districts were exceptional compared to most other VOC possessions, the lower Dutch Caribbean islands were a bit of an aberration to the general West Indian pattern. Though the WIC made several efforts to establish sugar and tobacco plantations on Curaçao, the arid climate generally confirmed earlier Spanish observations that these were, at least from the perspective of commercial agriculture, 'islas inútiles'.[131] Curaçao and its port Willemstad functioned as a naval base, a slave-trading emporium and a free haven for illicit trading with the Spanish Main, but never as a slave-based plantation economy producing for the European market. Looking at their roles in the colonial economy, slaves on Curaçao often performed tasks quite similar to those of slaves in the VOC trading posts.[132]

From New Amsterdam to Cape Town, from Elmina to Zeelandia, slaves in Dutch colonial ports were occupied with a great variety of work activities: building fortifications, loading and unloading ships, growing food for local consumption in Company gardens, being hired out as urban artisans or apprentices, serving European families as domestic servants, or pleasing transient sailors and soldiers as prostitutes. There was always something to do in the bustling trading posts of the Dutch colonial empire and slave labour was used accordingly. One gets a vivid sense of this diversification of work from a list of runaway slaves who left Curaçao between 1729 and 1775:[133] among the 500 male runaways, there were 129 field slaves (25.8 per cent), 82 seamen (16.4 per cent), 47 carpenters (9.4 per cent), 32 fishermen (6.4 per cent), 30 shoemakers (6.0 per cent), but also 16 cooks (3.2 per cent) and 15 bakers (3.0 per cent), 15 musicians (3.0 per cent), and, finally, of bricklayers and tailors 14 (2.8 per cent) each; among the 85 female slaves that escaped, traditional household tasks prevailed, with laundresses (17.6 per cent), seamstresses (14.1 per cent), knitters (11.8 per cent), vendors (10.6 per cent) and

---

[130]   Shell's use (1994a) of Winthrop Jordan's famous phrase of 'an unthinking decision' is in this respect quite on the mark. The discussions captured in the Chavonnes Report (1717) appear to have finally closed the door to a more European immigrant-based colony.

[131]   As Bonaire and Aruba were still WIC dependencies of Curaçao and were developed relatively late into the nineteenth century, they will not be further discussed here. The other Dutch Caribbean islands (St. Eustatius, St. Maarten and tiny Saba) had a small-scale plantation culture along West Indian lines.

[132]   As a history of slavery on Aruba puts it most directly, they were 'slaves without plantations' (Alofs 1996).

[133]   The most likely destination was Coro, on the Venezuelan coast. Since this kind of marronage always took place by boat, it is no wonder that sailors and fishermen were well represented here. For more on this maritime marronage, see Rupert 2006.

domestic slaves (9.6 per cent) all looking to improve their condition (Klooster 1994:285). Besides showing the variety of slave labour, the list demonstrates that seemingly preferable working conditions were no guarantee for a slave's acquiescence; in fact, the lure of freedom might have been greater for those who had already received a taste of it.

This list mainly reflects slavery on Curaçao in the post-*asiento* era, after its economy underwent a dramatic transition. Between the 1660s and 1710s, a sizeable contingent of Company slaves was employed in the transit slave trade. The 'garden slaves' (*tuinslaven*) attending the Company plantations were primarily occupied with cattle breeding and the production of sorghum to feed the 'trade slaves' (*negotieslaven*) awaiting transport to arguably harsher and more monotonous labour conditions elsewhere. From 1700 to 1715, the WIC owned an average total of 618 slaves on the island, but after the *asiento* contracts fell to the English, following the Spanish Succession War, the Company reduced its slaves to 206 in 1718 and to only 181 in 1720 (Jordaan 1999:482).

It was fairly common for both the WIC and the VOC to downsize their slave holdings after large initial infrastructure and public works projects had been completed. Such slaves were usually sold on the private market or transported elsewhere. Over time, the share of private in relation to Company slaves residing in a colony therefore grew invariably larger. During the eighteenth century the number of VOC slaves at the Cape fluctuated between roughly 500 and 750, whereas the *freeburgher* slave holdings grew from less than a thousand in 1701 to more than 16,000 in 1795.[134] In Colombo (Ceylon) the Company slave population numbered 1,570 in 1685, many of them involved in the time-consuming (1659-1700) castle building project (Knaap 1981:96). Among these 1,570 VOC slaves were 185 males, 348 females and 196 children between the age of six and fourteen working on the fortifications. The remaining adult male slaves were saddled with a greater variety of tasks, ranging from working in the gardens (10), the gunpowder mills (20), the bleaching works (27), as stonemasons (8), carrying water (12), tending to the VOC stables (19) and to the armoury (17), with 11 of them given the responsibility to clean the guns; furthermore, there were 37 slaves assisting the head carpenter, while the blacksmith 'employed' 21 of them. The Company was also 'burdened' by unproductive slaves: 47 patients in the slave hospital staffed by 8, 24 pregnant slaves, 12 preparing for delivery and 40 females recovering from childbirth who were restricted to weaving mats; 17 slaves were blind, paralyzed or 'insane' and 245 young children and 'sucklings' were clearly also of little use (Knaap 1981:97-8).

---

[134]   Van Duin and Ross 1987:9, 113-5. Van Duin and Ross (1987:9) state that to replenish this small number of Company slaves throughout the eighteenth century approximately 3,000 slaves were imported from Madagascar and the East African coast.

But the situation on Curaçao during the 1710s was more complex. Slaves continued to arrive from Africa, but there were hardly any buyers available.[135] In the first half of 1715, an average of 64 trade slaves awaited further sale; this number rose to an average of 339 in the second half of that year and peaked at 931 slaves in April 1716, before gradually going down to a more manageable size at the end of 1717 (Jordaan 1999:482). Combined with the already precarious food situation, caused by recent droughts, this led to substantial tensions on the island.[136] Looking for solutions, the governor attempted a haphazard 'plantation-experiment' on Aruba and to send slaves to Bonaire as well (Jordaan 1997), perhaps more with the intent to ease the pressure on Curaçao than honestly believing that decent profits could be made.

At a certain point the slave-to-food ratio on the island became so unstable that old and sick slaves were manumitted and were 'free' to fend for themselves. Apparently, the material costs to maintain such slaves had become higher than the economic returns of their labour, and any paternalist ideology went quickly out the door. There are more cases of manumission as a cost-effective strategy among Dutch colonists. For example, when Batavia was struck by a leprosy epidemic in the 1670s, owners parted with their slaves at such an alarming rate that around 1684 a total of 1,366 people were dependent on poor relief from the church, an estimated seventy to eighty per cent of them single women and their children (Niemeijer 2000:181). And in New Amsterdam, the WIC granted freedom to its first generation of loyal slaves, those that helped build the foundations of Manhattan and worked its Company gardens, but freedom came with such stipulations that manumission seemed more like a calculating than a truly honourable deed (Berlin 1996; Wagman 1980). While the letting go of an old or incapacitated slave is likely as old as the institution of slavery itself, large-scale manumissions for reasons of – relative – profitability have, as far as I know, seldom occurred in plantation economies where slave labour was dearest.[137]

Individual manumission was, of course, often the result of intimate bonds and long-standing relationships between masters and slaves. Such bonds had a better chance of developing and thriving in the closed settings of the private European households where domestic slaves spent most of their days. Their actual tasks may not have differed much from those performed by servants

---

[135]   This episode – slaves arriving, but no buyers and no food available – shows remarkable resemblance to the situation in Dutch Recife around 1645.

[136]   Jordaan (1999) gives a fascinating in-depth account of these conditions, connecting them – quite convincingly – to the slave rebellion of trade slaves on the St. Maria plantation in 1716.

[137]   Suriname witnessed regular manumissions of old and incapacitated slaves, but to prevent this from becoming a nuisance to society specific limitations were set in 1733, and from 1788 on, slave owners had to pay one hundred guilders for a manumission letter. I thank Henk den Heijer for drawing my attention to this.

and maids in Europe, but their legal status did and with it their vulnerability in face of their master and mistress. Depending on the personal whims of their owners, the fortune of domestic slaves fluctuated between the extremes of freedom and upward social mobility on the one hand, or chronic mental and physical abuse and death on the other. As they were considered part and parcel of the households, their social isolation could be quite debilitating.

Domestic slavery was perhaps the central feature of Dutch colonial society in the Indian Ocean World. Table 5.15 gives an idea of the preponderance of slavery among the free households of some of the major colonial towns in the VOC domain.

Table 5.15 Free households and their private slave holdings in selective VOC towns

Colonial town	Year	Without slaves	1-2 slaves	3-10 slaves	11+ slaves	Average number of slaves (and % of) average size of total household	
Fort Cochin	1760	23	46	107	30	6,18	(62.4%)	9,90
	1790	39	69	100	33	5,39	(56.1%)	9,61
Colombo	1694	103	117	144	45	4,31	(53.4%)	8,07
- Fort	1694	33	47	63	18	4,74	(54.9%)	8,64
- Town	1694	70	70	81	27	4,03	(52.4%)	7,69
Jaffnapatnam	1694	37	31	43	16	4,73	(52.5%)	9,00
- Fort	1694	16	22	27	10	4,76	(55.3%)	8,62
- Town	1694	21	9	16	6	4,68	(49.2%)	9.52
Kota Ambon	1694	240	195	170	68	4,26	(60.2%)	7,08
Malacca (town)	1680	422	191	102	19	1,54	(35.5%)	4,34
- Fort	1677	n.a.				6,34	(64.5%)	9,83

Sources: Fort Cochin: Wolff 1992:50-1, 71-2; Colombo: Knaap 1981:88, 93; Jaffnapatnam: Vos tot Nederveen Cappel 1978:308-15; Kota Ambon: Knaap 1991:121, 124; Malacca: Ketelaars 1985:69-71.

If we focus on the households of European background or on those belonging to the Company elite, the average slave holdings significantly increase. Of the 41 European *freeburgher* households of Malacca, for example, twelve possessed no slaves at all, but eight had more than ten (Ketelaars 1985:71), while the households within the fort were all Dutch/European. Households headed by European (or castizo) men married to European women – a clear sign of elite status – owned an average of 10.6 slaves in Colombo and 20.6 slaves – and 0.92 children – in Kota Ambon (Knaap 1981:94, 1991:123). Colombo's European female-headed households contained on average 13.4 slaves, although this figure was admittedly a bit skewed: two widows of important Company officials were the town's largest slave owners with 55 and 60 slaves respectively, outdoing even the 47 slaves belonging to the governor of Ceylon,

Thomas van Rhee.[138] The governor of Ambon, Nicolaas Schaghen, possessed an exceptionally high number of slaves, 92 in total (Knaap 1991:123), while his colleague Van Angelbeek in Cochin during the 1790s owned 71 slaves. But according to Singh (2007:107) 'it can be speculated that not all of them were employed in his household within Fort Cochin[; m]any must have been lent out to others to work in the gardens and plantations'.

While some of the larger private slave holdings hired out slaves for profit or participated in the local slave trade, it can be surmised from these figures that most European households contained more domestic labour than was strictly necessary. In some cases this may have resulted in a lighter overall work load for the slaves, or more 'uneconomic' and 'eccentric' tasks, such as playing in a private orchestra. To emphasize their social status in the colonial world, the local European elite apparently did not shy away from conspicuous consumption, in sharp contrast with the Calvinist 'embarrassment of riches' that Simon Schama (1987) discerned in the seventeenth-century Dutch Republic.[139]

Slavery and social relations in the Dutch colonial sphere

The belief that European colonists in the tropics were easily corrupted by greed, luxury and slavery has been widely disseminated since the early days of travel writing. A recent analysis (Van den Boogaart 2000) cleverly demonstrates early Dutch concerns that Europeans would degenerate as a result of the exotic climate and guilty pleasures of Asia, including their dependence on servile labour. Nicolaus de Graaff's oft-cited comment that the wives of VOC officials 'are waited on like princesses, and some have many male and female slaves, who have to be alert as watchdogs day and night' had – certainly from a metropolitan perspective – a very negative sound to it.[140] Moreover, judging from the scattered anecdotal evidence, these wives were often susceptible to

---

[138] Knaap 1981:94. Without these two, Knaap (1981:95) puts the average slave holdings of European female-headed households at 6.1.

[139] Of course, Schama was careful enough to point out that this embarrassment quickly disappeared as the Dutch Republic came of age. Wealthy Dutch burghers returning to the metropolis sometimes brought back slaves as their domestic servants and included these exotic status symbols in paintings by Dutch masters. See also Oostindie and Maduro 1986 and Blakely 1993. In 1689, according to Boomgaard (2004:86), 'the Governor-General was highly critical of those Europeans in Batavia who owned slaves purely for reasons of "splendour, exuberance, pride and improper display of wealth".' Campbell (2004a:xix) suggests that this conspicuous consumption of 'uneconomic slaves' sometimes resulted in the financial ruin of the slaveowners.

[140] Knaap 1981:93. Knaap (1981:93) suggests that, owing to the presence of many households with no or only a few slaves, 'descriptions of women living like princesses should be treated with caution', yet he himself gives fairly high average slave holdings for the European households. Ketelaars (1985:72) points out that De Graaff was singling out the wives of Company servants and that his comments might therefore have more validity than Knaap submits.

Het oude slavenhuis van La Cana, Cuba

power abuse, with their private slaves as the prime victims.[141] Since domestic slavery was so prevalent in these colonial societies, it logically follows that the female head of the household carried the main burden for managing these slaves. But perhaps the brunt of contemporary criticism was also reserved for her because she constituted the most 'exotic' (read: racially mixed) element in the European power structure; in other words, it may have been psychologically convenient to blame cruelty and overindulgence strictly on the Asian character of colonial society.[142]

The dearth of European women was a crucial problem in European colonial expansion in general, but particularly so in the VOC domain. For example, the town of Malacca counted a total of 558 European men in 1678, but only 26 European women, of whom 24 were married to Company servants (Ketelaars 1985:68). Cochin in 1760 had 89 European men, but no women; thirty years later the VOC-controlled town numbered 152 males from Europe against only three females (Wolff 1992:71-2). Elsewhere the situation was hardly different. Consequently, the highly imbalanced sex ratios could only be overcome by appealing to local women and racial intermixture developed almost hand in hand with the colonization process.[143] The stock of young native and mestizo women rose dramatically and through them the mixed outlook of VOC settlements became even more pronounced (Knaap 1981; Singh 2007:105-8). Of course, there was plenty of interracial mixing in the American colonies as well. But what set the Asian developments apart was that by marrying Company servants and *freeburghers*, native and mestizo women and their legitimate offspring joined the ranks of the colonial elite.[144] To emphasize her newly acquired 'European' identity, it is quite conceivable that the mestizo wife sometimes acted the part, by treating her domestic slaves, who often had a similar ethnic background, in an extremely deprecating manner.

This tension within the household may have been further exacerbated by

---

[141] Willem van Hogendorp's novel *Kraspoekol* (1780) is perhaps the most famous example of this; see Reid (1983a:25) for this argument. Oosterhoff (1985:56) mentions the case of a Dutch *freeburgher* wife, Engelken Davitsz, at Zeelandia, who had killed one of her female slaves and was accordingly sentenced to death in 1654 by strangling. This was an exceptionally severe punishment and the women in question retracted her earlier confession saying she had done so to escape torture and because she had been told 'that it would only concern a fine and that she could not be sentenced to death because of a (female) slave', in: Blussé, Milde and Ts'ao Yung-ho 1996:352-3

[142] For a recent discussion of the European representation of Asian women in contemporary travel literature, see Van de Walle 2001.

[143] Knaap (1991:111) mentions that '[a]s early as 1607, Adm. Cornelis Matelief allowed Dutch men to officially marry Ambonese and other Asian women'. Elsewhere (1981:90) he states that 'if only free males are taken into account, Colombo was much less of an 'ethnically mixed town' than colonial settlements of the period are sometimes considered to be'.

[144] Although Reid (1983a:18) claims that the Dutch and British were less inclusive than the Portuguese in this matter, and resisted to incorporate the descendants of slaves into the white caste; see also Reid (1983b:173-5).

the fact that female slaves were not excluded from marrying European men either. Yesterday's slave could be today's concubine and tomorrow's wife. Falling into favour with her European master or one of his friends, she could – after the required manumission and conversion to Christianity – legally marry him and acquire the coveted European status (Ketelaars 1985:61, 67). The Bali slave trade was particularly notorious for providing both Chinese and European men with desirable concubines and potential future marriage partners. Consequently, choice female slaves often commanded higher prices than their male counterparts on Asian slave markets – in contrast with the Americas, where strong adult men were preferred for the hard field labour on the plantations.

Considering the substantial social mobility involving a marriage between a master and his former slave, it is not difficult to conceive that under the circumstances most of these women considered themselves 'lucky' and submitted rather willingly to such an ordeal. There do not appear to be many scholarly discussions about the history of the sexual abuse and rape of these concubine slaves in the Indian Ocean World, a most sensitive topic in the historiography of slavery in the Americas. In the New World, even in the best-case scenario in which a female slave was manumitted together with her children and generously taken care of by her former master, there were – outside the Iberian colonies – very few cases of legally sanctioned marriages between the two as it was by and large legally prohibited. In the American colonies, the ranks of white Europeans were generally closed to former slaves.

In Degler's (1972) classic but controversial study comparing race relations in Brazil and the US South, he characterized the former as more flexible and lenient because of the so-called 'mulatto escape hatch': light-skinned African Americans of considerable means and education and with well-established social connections were able to escape the black mass and perhaps enter the dominant caste. Elsewhere, in various parts of the former Spanish Americas, *'mestizaje'* – not white, not red, not black, but a mixture of them – is often proclaimed to be the core national identity. To some extent these are highly romanticized and nationalistic representations that emerged only after emancipation and decolonization. At the same time these Iberian-American colonies do mirror some of the demographic dynamics of the Indian Ocean World, with more sizeable indigenous populations and, perhaps as a result thereof, a greater tolerance for interracial mixing and a better treatment of slaves. At the risk of resurrecting an awkward term, one could perhaps state that Asian women, by marrying Dutch or European men, benefited from a 'mestizo escape hatch'. But we should be extremely cautious in bringing uniquely American concepts of race into a discussion on the Indian Ocean World. The various ethnic groups serving as slaves to the Dutch and other Europeans in Asia were generally represented by much larger non-slave populations and were subsequently unburdened by a stigma of slavery or a somatic-norm image from which they felt pressured to escape.

The key to unlocking race relations in the Americas – it has been suggested before – is rooted in the legal and social positions accorded to Free Blacks and mulattos. In the plantation colonies of the greater Caribbean, the large black majorities and the small European master class in time forced the creation of a three-caste system, with an intermediate buffer group of loyal house slaves, Free Blacks and free mulattos who sometimes aided, but were never fully accepted by the white elite. On Curaçao, the relative size of the Free Black/ mulatto population expanded dramatically during the eighteenth century, largely because of the island's diminished role in the transatlantic slave trade. The very small group at the turn of the century grew to respectively 540 people in 1742 and 3,714 (17.7 per cent) in 1789, a much higher percentage than on any other Caribbean island (Klooster 1999:508). This process continued into the nineteenth century when, even before the abolition of slavery, Free Blacks and mulattos had become the dominant identity, amounting to 32.2 per cent in 1817 and 43.5 per cent of the island population in 1833 (Klooster 1994:288). As the slave-free dichotomy became increasingly vague, white residents began invoking modern pseudoscientific ideologies of race to ensure that, if no longer slaves, Free Blacks were still considered outsiders to the established order (Oostindie 2000:56-9).

Where the European colonial population was stronger and the sex ratios more balanced, as in the settlement colonies of North America and South Africa, over time a more rigid line was drawn between whites and blacks, ultimately leading to tragic legal constructions such as Jim Crow segregation and apartheid to prevent, or at least tightly channel, interracial contact. Over the past two decades historians have begun unearthing what Gary Nash (1995) has called the 'hidden history of mestizo America', to show that more social openness and flexibility existed in earlier times. But their strenuous mining of the earliest colonial sources only appears to confirm that such mixed relationships quickly became taboo in North America. They also point out that racial exclusivity grew ever stricter over time, as the white settler population continued to increase and the abolition of slavery allowed a much more virulent type of racism to develop.

As a consequence of this strong racial identification of American slavery, the multiple identities of slaves, blacks and Africans became closely intertwined and were – in most cases – immediately visible. Over time it helped create a resilient group identity that is still very much alive today, albeit in various gradations. Naturally, this has great implications for the historic development of slave community and culture, the frequency of slave resistance and rebellion, and ultimately for the willingness to remember and identify with a past of slavery.

In the Indian Ocean World such empowerment in the face of adversity was noticeably absent among the slaves. Slavery and freedom were never as strongly opposed as in the Americas anyway, with many intermediate categories that were nearly indistinguishable from slave status. In fact, the predominance of domestic slavery in European colonial households presented the individual slave with opportunities to 'work the system' to his or her personal advantage, opportunities that may never have sprung up had they not become slaves in the first place. Furthermore, manumission did signify, in decided contrast with the Americas, a clear break with the slave 'community'. The lack of one specific racial, ethnic or religious identity that was imprinted on either the slave or the master prevented the growth of a common culture and solidarity among slaves.[145] The slave rebellion at the Cape in 1760, for example, was primarily rooted in the religious (Muslim) and ethnic (Bugis) background of the participants, who formed quite a uniform group considering that the Cape Colony has been labelled the most diverse slave society in the world (Koolhof and Ross 2005). In whatever form, shape or gradation freedom eventually came – through individual manumission, by flight, or in a general emancipation – the ex-slave of the Indian Ocean World gradually disappeared in its massive, motley crowd. Therein rests the key explanation as to why the history of slavery in the Indian Ocean World has been neglected thus far. If we want to get a fuller picture of Dutch colonial slavery, it is entirely up to the historians to unravel this story, because no one else will.

Epilogue; A slow death to slavery

The prohibition of the international slave trade, exactly two centuries ago, signalled an important watershed in European colonial history. Though the British-led measure did not immediately halt all transoceanic transports of slaves – particularly to Cuba, Brazil and the French Mascarenes – it nevertheless criminalized such voyages and made them punishable under international law. As a result, the transatlantic slave trade declined rapidly, was forced 'underground' and never recovered its pre-1808 volume.

But to the Dutch, the prohibition must have seemed somewhat of a non-event, considering the much more serious problems they were facing at the time. From the harsh realization after the Fourth Anglo-Dutch Naval War (1780-1784) that 'Britannia rules the waves', through the dissolution of the moribund Companies in the 1790s and the loss of national independence to revolutionary France, the Dutch state was in a downward spiral for everyone

---

[145]   Campbell (2004a:xx-xxi) points at the various obstacles against the development of slave class-consciousness in the Indian Ocean World.

to see. This weakness was effortlessly exploited by the United Kingdom, which took hold of almost all Dutch possessions during the 1790s and many of them – Malacca, Ceylon, India (Coromandel and Malabar Coast), Cape Colony and Guyana (Berbice, Essequibo and Demerara) – were never returned. If the phenomenal rise of the Dutch colonial empire had been intricately tied up with the war against Spain and Portugal, its dramatic decline was caused by military-political developments in Europe as well.[146]

Table 5.8 demonstrated that the Dutch transatlantic slave trade was already in serious decline decades before the 1808 prohibition. This bore a similarity to the waning years of the VOC, when the Dutch Indian Ocean slave trade quickly lost ground to foreign competition. Most slaves arriving at the Cape Colony were now carried by a variety of European vessels, and in Southeast Asia Chinese and indigenous merchants took over large shares of the human traffic. As Richard Allen (forthcoming) shows, the Dutch in South Asia were surpassed by French slavers and simultaneously condemned by the more progressive British.[147] In a sense the Dutch were ideally situated to take the pragmatic and self-interested road to abolition as suggested by the classic Williams thesis – and yet they showed no interest (Drescher 1994; Oostindie 1995). Instead, the British took the moral high road and were willing to commit, in Drescher's (1977) great phrase, 'econocide'.

The British returned some of the colonial possessions to the Dutch after the Napoleonic Wars but only on the condition that the new Kingdom of the Netherlands was seriously dedicated to the abolition of the international slave trade. The Dutch would even assist the British in suppressing the trade, with Paramaribo functioning as a location of one of the mixed commission courts overlooking possible violations of the 1808 law. Despite this commitment, slavers from Africa managed to disembark an estimated 4,300 slaves in Suriname between 1820 and 1825, with the largest volume (3,200) transported on French ships (see table 5.8).[148] Van Stipriaan's latest estimates suggest, based on a multitude of sources, that approximately 33,000 slaves entered Suriname between 1808 and 1830, of whom 8,000 arrived during the years of the British occupation ending in 1816 and 25,000 after that time.[149] But most of these slaves came

---

[146]   Although the peaceful manner in which the English overtook most Dutch possessions stands in stark contrast to the ways in which the Dutch 'feasted' on the Portuguese colonial empire during that nation's loss of independence to Spain (1580-1640).

[147]   Allen gives a refreshing take on abolitionism by looking at it from the more local perspective of British colonists in India. In the process, he complicates the traditional view of abolitionism as emerging solely from London or, otherwise, from the British Caribbean.

[148]   TSTD2: http://wilson.library.emory.edu:9090/tast/assessment/estimates.faces?permlink=1788958.

[149]   I thank Alex van Stipriaan for generously sharing his research notes with me. Most of his recent findings will soon be published in the journal *Aquandah*. In earlier work (1993:102-4, 314)

directly from other Caribbean colonies (mainly the French West Indies, but also British and Danish colonies) and entered Suriname legally. And if not constituting new slaves from Africa, they should not be counted towards the transatlantic slave trade. Even so, their arrival from various locations in the Atlantic World – driven by the ingenuity of regional slave traders – probably led to an even greater ethnic and cultural diversity of the African American population. The slave trade was truly a defining experience in the history of Suriname.[150]

Evidently, the prohibition of the slave trade had important consequences for the future of colonial slavery. In fact, one of the primary motivations behind the abolitionist measure was to cause a slow death to slavery itself. Unless planters began improving the working and living conditions of their chattel, slave populations were destined to decline. At the time, it was often wondered if such improvements could be made while keeping the institution profitable or the slaves under control. Despite its lengthy history, the institution of slavery finally went on the defensive. And in the shrunken colonial world of the Dutch this played itself out in several ways.

The plantation economy of Suriname was still completely dependent on slave labour and therefore stood to benefit most by reforming the system from within. Whether caused by humanitarian motives or sheer self-interest, ameliorative policies and improved medical care for slaves gave rather positive results. Slavery in nineteenth-century Suriname has aptly been described as 'an iron fist in a velvet glove' (Van Stipriaan 1993:369). Its slave population decreased from 59,923 in 1774 to 44,084 in 1813 and 36,484 in 1862, on the eve of abolition, but the natural growth rate gradually improved, with only a small decline of 3.5 per thousand slaves in the last decade of slavery (and a remarkable positive growth rate of 7.0 in the emerging cotton sector)[151] (Van Stipriaan 1993:311, 318). If the historically bad eighteenth-century reputation of Suriname as rendered by Voltaire and Stedman has recently been questioned from a demographic (Van Stipriaan 1993:313-4) and a cultural perspective (Oostindie 1993), the nineteenth-century colony was definitely comparable to most other plantation economies in the larger Caribbean.

In the East, the Dutch colonial presence was restricted to expansion within the Indonesian archipelago, as a result of which the previous 'triangular'

---

he already came – largely based on population data – to an estimate of around 12,000 slaves entering the colony between 1817 and 1826.

[150]   Because slaves coming from the Caribbean still received legal status, even though the slave trade with Africa was already prohibited, it is not inconceivable that slave traders legitimized their cargo by assigning the slaves a New World identity. The decreased supply of new slaves pushed up prices, which was an extra incentive for slave traders to 'go the extra mile'.

[151]   Van Stipriaan (1993:327-9) attributes this positive rate in the cotton sector to the geographic location of the plantations, the relatively better working conditions and perhaps also the background of the planters, many of whom were of British origins.

Table 5.15 Slaves emancipated in the Dutch colonial sphere, 1860-1863

Colony	Year	Number of slaves emancipated and their % of the total population	
Moluccas	1860	1,255	(< 1%)*
Sulawesi	1860	615	(< 1%)
Nusa Tenggara	1860	298	(< 1%)
Kalimantan	1860	9	(< 1%)
Java (+ Batavia)	1860	1,777	(< 1%)
Sumatra	1860	781	(< 1%)
Subtotal	1860	4,735	
Gold Coast	1873	? ? ?	
St. Maarten*	1863	1,878	
St. Eustatius	1863	1,138	
Saba	1863	710	
Aruba	1863	480	
Bonaire	1863	758	
Curaçao	1863	5,498	(28.7%)
Suriname	1863	36,484	(68.9%)

* Knaap suggests 514 slaves emancipated at Banda and 566 at Ambon, with the remainder likely coming from Ternate; clearly, for European colonial towns such as Kota Ambon or Neira Town, the percentage of these last remaining slaves was greater than one per cent of the total population. Hanna (1978:105) estimated a total of 1,122 *perk* slaves emancipating on the Banda Islands in 1860, not including the house slaves, which would – given an estimated total population of 6,333 in 1854 – come to 17.7 per cent.

Sources: Southeast Asia (Indonesia): Knaap 1995:200-1; Dutch Caribbean islands: Goslinga 1990:282 gives a total of 11,715 slaves; Oostindie (1995:158) gives a lower total of 11,654 emancipated slaves for all Dutch West Indian islands; Curaçao: Renkema 1981:337; Suriname: Van Stipriaan 1993:28; Oostindie (1995:158) gives a slightly lower number of 33,621 emancipated slaves.

Dutch Indian Ocean slave trade was broken too. The official prohibition of the regional Southeast Asian slave trade in 1811 had undeniable effects on the export economies of Bali and Makassar in particular. Though slave trading continued in more indigenous-controlled areas,[152] the pivotal market of Batavia was forever lost. The total slave population of Batavia and its hinterland (Ommelanden) rapidly declined from 32,906 in 1789 (Raben 1996:

---

[152]   Schulte Nordholt 1996:167. The Dutch colonial officials were afraid that an all-too strict prohibition of the indigenous slave-trading networks would create great conflicts with the local rulers and merchants profiting from this enterprise. See Sutherland 1983:273. Dutch concerns about indigenous slavery, whether based on a sincere 'ethical policy' or as a subterfuge for further colonial expansion throughout Indonesia, remains beyond discussion here, since it happened – in theory at least –outside the Dutch colonial sphere. See, for example, Schulte Nordholt 1996:170, 210 on Dutch anti-slavery attitudes towards Balinese society.

Appendix) to 7,556 in 1850 (*Koloniaal Verslag* 1850:4). How insignificant the institution of slavery in the Dutch East Indies had become by the time of emancipation can easily be assessed from table 5.16.

Considering the largely domestic nature of Dutch slavery in Southeast Asia, the economic effects of abolition were minimal in comparison with the American plantation colonies. It is quite credible that many of the 'house slaves' continued the same domestic tasks under different legal titles. Terms and conditions of servitude had always been ambiguous in the Indian Ocean World and there is no reason to believe this suddenly changed. The increased Dutch dominance over Java and its rapidly growing population – partly assisted by slave soldiers from Bali and contract soldiers from Elmina – offered sufficient opportunities for other, more indirect forms of labour control.[153] The most striking example of this was the infamous Cultivation System (Cultuurstelsel, 1830-1870), which eventually generated more sugar than Suriname, and did so without the labour of 'true' slaves. In one of the greater ironies of Dutch colonial history, coerced and indentured Javanese labour enabled the Dutch government to both financially compensate plant-ers in Suriname for the loss of their enslaved property and supply them with a radically new labour force (see Chapter VI). How minute the actual change in labour conditions was, can perhaps best be judged by considering that the Dutch equivalent of Harriet Beecher Stowe's *Uncle Tom's cabin* (1852), Multatuli's *Max Havelaar* (1859), concentrated on the lot of the Javanese under this new production system, not on legally defined slaves.

Only on the Banda islands, where *perk* slaves had always toiled under more plantation-like conditions, did the abolition of slavery cause some important adjustments. As table 5.14 revealed, the transition from slaves to other forms of (semi-)coerced labour was already under way before the final emancipation in 1860. According to Hanna (1978:110), the workforce on the nutmeg *perken* immediately after the official abolition consisted of 1,542 peo-ple, classified as 215 exiles (179 men, 36 women), 360 vagabonds (all men) and 967 contract coolies (805 men, 162 women). Many of the former *perk* slaves would – after a short 'flight' from the plantation – eventually return to their old work and, considering their experience and know-how, they were prob-

---

[153] Nieboer's (1900) classic land-labour theory, arguing that the rise and fall of slavery is con-nected to the availability of free natural resources and the population density to work these with, may explain why the decline of slavery on Java was set in motion before the official abolition of the system in 1860. Nieboer's theory was strongly influenced by nineteenth-century English economists (Wakefield, Gibbons); see his influence on Boomgaard 1991 and Reid (1983a:35) who states that 'traditional systems of bondage and obligation were redefined to the exclusion of those relationships closest to chattel slavery, which had in any case become expensive and unnecessary by this time. [...] Corvée and debt bondage became the dominant forms of labour in the nineteenth century.'

ably rewarded with positions as overseers among the new indentured labour force (Hanna 1978:105). The workforce on the *perken* did decidedly become more male after this transition, a development that mirrors the plantations in the Americas where many former slaves sought to restore more 'traditional' family patterns and labour divisions.

The lacklustre Dutch support of the abolitionist cause has been superbly discussed in recent times (Drescher 1994; Oostindie 1995) and needs no elaborate commentary here. The fascinating paradox permeating most of these contributions – that the famously tolerant Dutch were so noticeably absent from the fight to abolish what by late eighteenth-century moral standards was regarded as an inhumane system – was generally resolved by concluding that the Dutch state no longer served as an exemplary nation. The colonial empire of the Dutch had shown severe cracks and this was only a confirmation of their weakened position in Europe. And yet, such an explanation will not entirely suffice, because the (invented) tradition of freedom and tolerance as typically Dutch characteristics somehow persisted into the twentieth century.

The fruitful suggestion of Drescher (1994) and others to instead go back in time and look for anti-slavery opinions in the Dutch Republic during its glorious Golden Age delivered little conclusive evidence. The general consensus remains that the emergence of an anti-slavery movement was a relatively modern affair, situated somewhere in the mid-eighteenth century – when Dutch decline was already in progress.[154] David Brion Davis and other historians after him (Bender 1992) professed that one of the forces behind the rise of abolitionism was the increased transatlantic communication, in Davis' case particularly embodied in the international community of Quakers. If so, it may perhaps serve as an additional explanation for the Dutch inactivity on this front. The admittedly small Dutch colonial populations never established the strong bonds of empire as the English and the French did. And if the relative distance and rate of communication between the metropolis and the colonial periphery is indeed crucial in determining the spread of anti-slavery opinions, then the Dutch situation was certainly far from promising.

In a chapter that perhaps raised more questions than it answered it might be fitting to finish with a few final ones, in an attempt to get to the heart of the comparison. If the institution of slavery in the VOC domain was by and large embraced during the 1610s, when slaves were already transported by the Dutch to the Banda Islands and new-found Batavia,[155] then why did the

---

[154]   More than any other scholar, David Brion Davis has pursued the intellectual history of slavery and abolitionism.

[155]   Pieter van Dam (Stapel 1929:653 n.1) mentioned a resolution of 17-8-1616 to acquire slaves at Madagascar. Governor general Gerard Reynst pressed several times between 1614 and 1615 to

Een van de slavinnen van de radja van Boeleleng

board members of the WIC – who surely must have been aware of these developments – still entertain some moral doubts regarding the Angolan slave trade in one of their first meetings in 1623? Was it because they specifically discussed a form of slave trading for profit that diverged from the more traditionally accepted practice of enslaving war captives? Was it because slavery in the New World was – by this time – already considered more exploitative and crassly materialistic than its counterpart in the Indian Ocean World? Or did it stem from a more self-conscious fear that participation in the transatlantic slave trade would always originate and lead back to the metropolis itself, thereby diminishing the convenient distance between what was morally acceptable at home and what was considered necessary and useful in the colonies? To keep that distance as wide as possible – between a carefully moulded public image at home and the sordid and self-interested acts abroad – may be typical of human nature.

Appendix

Table 5.11 References

General: Vink 2003b:148, 155; see table 5.9 in this chapter.
Zeelandia (Formosa/Taiwan): Oosterhoff 1985:55. Van Veen (1996:74) estimates the Chinese population on the island at 15,000 around 1650, while Oosterhoff (1985:55) suggests 20,000, but with 15,000 in the rural areas, so perhaps Van Veen excluded the merchants and Chinese residents of Zeelandia. Van Veen (1996:77) also gives the number of Formosean villages under VOC control: 351 in 1650, with 63,861 residents.
Kota Ambon: Numbers are drawn from personal calculations based on the figures rendered by Knaap (1991:119-25); Knaap and Sutherland (2004:163) give a rough estimate of between 10-20 per cent slaves among the indigenous Ambonese population – thus outside Kota Ambon – during this period.
Banda Islands: 1638: Hanna (1978:66), based on the journals of German soldier-merchant Johan Sigmund Wurffbain; 1687: Van Goor (1994:113) mentions 678 Company personnel and 168 European and 265 mestizo *freeburghers*; here I have, recklessly perhaps, assumed that all Company personnel belonged to the European caste; 1854: Hanna (1978:110-1). There were 1,182 *perk* slaves and 708 house slaves, with additional labour coming from groups such as free native workers (942) and exiles (980), a logical development as the slave trade had been 'legally' closed for several decades.
Makassar: Sutherland 1986:41-2.
Batavia: 1632: Raben 1996:86, table 4.2. I have included all 1,730 Company servants in the European category although a decade earlier (Raben 1996:84, table 4.1) there were a substantial number of 'black' VOC employees as well as the separate categories of

acquire Malagasy slaves to help in the construction of forts at the Moluccas (Coolhaas 1960:43-6).

242   *Rik van Welie*

Japanese and Chinese Company personnel. Of the non-European free population of Batavia in 1632, 2,390 people were of Chinese background. All other population figures for Batavia are from Raben (1996:89, table 4.4 and Appendix); the European population consists of all Europeans and mestizos; 1850 numbers for Batavia, Java and Madura from *Koloniaal Verslag* (1850:4).
Malacca: Ketelaars 1985:61;
Silida: Böeseken 1977:68;
Colombo: Raben (1996:104) and I have divided the 94 unknown Europeans and mestizos equally among the fort and the town population, although the fort population may have had a greater weight here. Knaap (1981:88-94) gives slightly different numbers than Raben, likely caused by some differences with regard to unspecified categories. The surrounding population of Colombo under VOC jurisdiction in 1683 is based on Raben (1996:301, Appendix 1); there was likely a small group of Europeans/mestizos residing there as well, but they cannot be distilled from the information Raben gives here.
Galle: Wagenaar 1994:36, 46. For the European category I have excluded the non-European VOC servants of the so-called Eurasian group as well as the six indentured labourers and forty convicts, as they were probably of non-European origins, see Wagenaar 1994:59.
Jaffnapatnam: Vos tot Nederveen Cappel 1978:308-15.
Cochin: Wolff 1992:50, 71-2.
Mauritius: Moree 1998:91.
Cape Colony: All calculations taken from Van Duin and Ross (1987:112-26), except Cape Town in 1731, which came from Worden, Van heyningen and Bickford-Smith (1998:26, 50); note that in the last figure other forms of coerced labour, such as 'kettinggangers', 'gecondemneerden' (convicts) or 'indigenous servants', are not included.

Table 5.12 References

Gold Coast: Numbers for 1645 based on the report by Ruychaver (1-12-1645) as discussed by Ratelband (1953:lvii-xci), including the personnel on four coastal vessels based at Elmina; eighteenth-century figures based on Goslinga (1985:51, 57) and Feinberg (1989:35, 65, 85), who estimates an average of 253-257 European WIC personnel between 1700-1760, and states that there is no consistent information on the numbers of visiting traders, seamen or people waiting to go to the New World. Den Heijer (1997:81) suggests an average of European WIC personnel (including the coastal vessels) fluctuating between 180 and 380 for the period 1674-1740.
Dutch Brazil: Numbers for Pernambuco are tentative estimates based on various scholars, given in Schalkwijk (2005:48-9), with the Europeans divided into 30,000 Portuguese, 12,000 Dutch-Europeans and 1,500 Jews. Estimates suggest another 25,000 in the *capitanias* of Itamaracá, Paraíba, Rio Grande do Norte and Ceará; numbers for 1645-1646 are restricted to the small coastal area, after the revolt broke out, and therefore contain hardly any Portuguese, even fewer Brazilians and no plantation slaves. These numbers are cited in Enthoven (2006:155). Gonsalves de Mello (2001:114-5, note 122) gives a lower number for the European soldiers, sailors and civil personnel: a total of 3,050 against Enthoven's 4,225.
Suriname: 1683 numbers in Hoogbergen (1992:9) and Van Goor (1994:118), who also

estimated 9,400 Native Americans; Enthoven (2006:160) gives lower numbers, respectively 3,332 slaves (83.6 per cent) and 652 whites (16.4 per cent), but this is based on those paying poll and land taxes and may not include the total population of the colony; 1738 slave population is based on Hoogbergen's (1992:10) figure for 1728 and his estimated growth of the slave population after that time, while the white and Free Black population figures are taken from Van Lier (1977:71); 1795 slave population listed in Van Stipriaan (1993:311), but the white and Free Black/mulatto population are from 1791 (Van Lier 1977:70; Goslinga 1985:364). Van Stipriaan (1993:314) gives a total free population in 1795 of 4,953 and it would not be unreasonable to think that this growth of 293 people over four years was largely made up of Free Blacks and mulattos (numbers seem to correspond with Van Lier here); 1830 numbers are taken from Van Lier (1977:23, 71); Van Stipriaan (1993:311) gives a slave population of 46,879 for 1836, which seems reasonable when looking at Van Lier's figures.

Paramaribo: figures for 1791 from Van Lier (1977:23, 71) – although the number of 8,000 slaves in Paramaribo seems very high when compared with the low number of Van Stipriaan (1993:311); for 1850 from *Koloniaal Verslag*: the division between free European and free non-European is arguably a guesstimate: the total free population of Paramaribo is estimated at 10,199 and given that there were 2,202 free people outside of Paramaribo, most of them likely of European origins, an estimate of 3,500 Europeans in Paramaribo seems reasonable. Plantation figures are from same sources and the choice was made (see 1791) to exclude all Free Blacks and mulattos from this count. Like in Van Stipriaan's numbers, the military personnel was often excluded from these population figures, even though they could amount to 1,950 in 1774.

Berbice: 1720: Enthoven (2006:157-8), 1762: Netscher (1888:191), cited in Koulen (2006:41-2, note 16), including 244 'Indian' slaves; 1796: Goslinga (1985:439) and Enthoven (2006:157-8).

Essequibo and Demerara: Van der Oest 2003:329; Enthoven 2006. Den Heijer (1997:347) gives 931 slaves and 112 Europeans at Essequibo around 1700, which is remarkably higher than the numbers of Van der Oest; Goslinga (1985:439) arrives at 21,259 slaves for 1790, which sounds plausible given the heavy British imports in the 1790s; the split between Essequibo and Demerara was with regard to 1769 (4,543/5,967) and 1796 (8,000/20,000).

Tobago (Nieuw Walcheren): Roos 1992:113.

Curaçao: 1720 in Goslinga 1985:102; Van Goor 1994:119; Klooster (1999:508) gives the number of Free Blacks (48), although suggesting that they made up 5.6 per cent of the island population seems off the mark and he must have been considering the free population only: in 1709 the free white population of Willemstad was 687 (Rupert 2006:147), adding the 233 WIC personnel and military from 1720 (Goslinga 1985:103), one comes close to Klooster's percentage. For the free white population of Curaçao in 1720 Van Goor (1994:119) states that there were 220 employees of the WIC and 500 *freeburgher* families and that we should multiply this number by 3 to 4, which would mean around 2,000 European colonists – I have chosen the factor 3, based on Rupert (2006:147); 1789 in Klooster (1994:289, 1998:61). Klooster logically assumes that free servants (846) were all white, as the free non-white population (3,714) was listed as a separate category. These numbers are slightly different from Enthoven (2006:159), who calculates 3,814 Europeans and 2,450 Free Coloured people and Van Goor (1994:119) who gave lower figures; 1825 figures from the Verveer Report (1825)

cited in Coomans-Eustatia, Coomans and Van der Lee (1998:199); 1833 figures from Teenstra (1836:164, table A.
Bonaire: 1720: Goslinga 1985:102; 1806: Goslinga 1990:130; 1833: Teenstra (1836:190, table B) and 400 government slaves added, although only around 150 were active labourers, the rest was old, weak, sick or too young, see Lemmers 1998:170-2, 178.
Aruba: 1816: Enthoven 2006:158; 1833 in Teenstra 1836:196, table C.
St. Eustatius, St. Maarten and Saba: Goslinga 1985:131, 138, 152, 1990:154.
New Netherland: Jaap Jacobs 1999: 67, 253, 267-8. Jacobs (1999:417, note 13) considers Van den Boogaart's estimate (1986) of a total population of 6,030 in 1664 too low, especially because he hardly takes into account natural growth, and this was certainly the case with family migration to a moderate climate. For the black and slave population estimates for New Amsterdam, see Harris (2003:21-2) among others. Of course, such figures could quickly change, for example with the arrival of 290 slaves from Africa just before the British takeover, even though most of these slaves were sold to the Chesapeake tobacco plantations. Native American populations are excluded from these estimates, although some lived in and around Dutch colonial communities.

Bibliography

Allen, Richard B.
2004   'The Mascarene slave-trade and labour migration in the Indian Ocean during the eighteenth and nineteenth centuries', in: Gwyn Campbell (ed.), *The structure of slavery in Indian Ocean Africa and Asia*, pp. 33-50. London: Frank Cass.
forthcoming   'Suppressing a nefarious traffic; Britain and the abolition of slave trading in India and the Western Indian Ocean, 1770-1830', *William and Mary Quarterly*.

Alofs, Luc
1996   *Slaven zonder plantage; Slavernij en emancipatie op Aruba, 1750-1963*. Oranjestad: Charuba.

Amussen, Susan Dwyer
2007   *Caribbean exchanges; Slavery and the transformation of English society, 1640-1700*. Chapel Hill: University of North Carolina Press.

Armstrong, James C.
1979   'The slaves, 1652-1795', in: Richard Elphick and Hermann Giliomee (eds), *The shaping of South African society*, pp. 75-115. Middletown: University of Connecticut Press.
1983-84   'Madagascar and the slave trade in the seventeenth century', *Omaly Sy Anio* 17-20:211-33.

Barendse, R.J.
1995   'Slaving on the Malagasy coast, 1640-1700', in: Sandra Evers and Marc Spindler (eds), *Cultures of Madagascar; Ebb and flow of influences*, pp. 137-55. Leiden: International Institute for Asian Studies (IIAS).

Bender, Thomas (ed.)
1992   The antislavery debate; Capitalism and abolitionism as a problem in historical
            interpretation. Berkeley: University of California Press.
Berlin, Ira
1996   'From creole to African; Atlantic creoles and the origins of African-
            American society in mainland North America', William and Mary Quar-
            terly 53-2:251-88.
1998   Many thousands gone; The first two centuries of slavery in North America.
            Cambridge: Harvard University Press.
Biewenga, Ad W.
1999   De Kaap de Goede Hoop; Een Nederlandse vestigingskolonie, 1680-1730.
            Amsterdam: Prometheus/Bert Bakker.
Blackburn, Robin
1997   The making of New World slavery; From the baroque to the modern, 1492-
            1800. New York: Verso.
Blakely, Allison
1993   Blacks in the Dutch world; The evolution of racial imagery in a modern soci-
            ety. Bloomington: Indiana University Press.
Blussé, J.L., W.E. Milde and Ts'ao Yung-ho (eds)
1996   De dagregisters van het kasteel Zeelandia, Taiwan (1629-1662); Vol. III:
            1648-1655. Den Haag: Instituut voor Nederlandse Geschiedenis. [Rijks
            Geschiedkundige Publicatiën, Grote Serie 233.]
Böeseken, A.J.
1977   Slaves and free Blacks at the Cape, 1658-1700. Cape Town: Tafelberg.
Boogaart, Ernst van den
1986   'The servant migration to New Netherland, 1624-1664', in: P.C. Emmer
            (ed.), Colonialism and migration; Indentured labour before and after slavery,
            pp. 55-81. Dordrecht/Boston/Lancaster: Nijhoff.
1992   'The trade between Western Africa and the Atlantic world, 1600-90;
            Estimates of trends in composition and value', The Journal of African
            History 33:369-85.
2000   Het verheven en verdorven Azië; Woord en beeld in het Itinerario en de Ico-
            nes van Jan Huygen van Linschoten. Amsterdam: Het Spinhuis, Leiden:
            KITLV Uitgeverij.
Boogaart, Ernst van den and Pieter C. Emmer
1979   'The Dutch participation in the Atlantic slave trade, 1596-1650', in:
            Henry A. Gemery and Jan S. Hogendorn (eds), The uncommon market;
            Essays in the economic history of the Atlantic slave trade, pp. 353-75. New
            York: Academic Press.
Boomgaard, Peter
1991   '"Why work for wages?"; Free labour in Java, 1600-1900', in: Economic
            and Social History in the Netherlands II, pp. 37-56. Amsterdam: The Neth-
            erlands Economic History Archive.
2004   'Human capital, slavery and low rates of economic and population
            growth in Indonesia, 1600-1910', Slavery and Abolition 24-2:83-96.

Campbell, Gwynn (ed.)
2004a   *The structure of slavery in Indian Ocean Africa and Asia.* London: Frank
             Cass.
2004b   *Abolition and its aftermath in Indian Ocean Africa and Asia.* London: Frank
             Cass.
Christopher, Emma
2006   *Slave ship sailors and their captive cargoes, 1730-1807.* Cambridge: Cam-
             bridge University Press.
Christopher, Emma, Cassandra Pybus and Marcus Rediker (eds)
2007   *Many middle passages; Forced migration and the making of the modern
             world.* Berkeley: University of California Press.
Coolhaas, W.Ph.
1960   *Generale missiven van Gouverneurs-Generaal en Raden aan Heeren XVII
             der Verenigde Oostindische Compagnie; Deel I: 1610-1638.* 's-Gravenhage:
             Nijhoff.
Coomans-Eustatia, Maritza, Henny E. Coomans and To van der Lee (eds)
1998   *Breekbare banden; Feiten en visies over Aruba, Bonaire en Curaçao na de
             Vrede van Munster, 1648-1998.* Bloemendaal: Stichting Libri Antilliani.
Cooper, Frederick, Thomas C. Holt and Rebecca J. Scott
2000   *Beyond slavery; Explorations of race, labour and citizenship in postemancipa-
             tion societies.* Chapel Hill: University of North Carolina Press.
Crosby, Alfred W.
1972   *The Columbian exchange; Biological and cultural consequences of 1492.*
             Hartford: Greenwood Press.
Curtin, Philip D.
1969   *The Atlantic slave trade; A census.* Madison: University of Wisconsin
             Press.
Daalder, Remmelt, Andrea Kieskamp and Dirk Tang (eds)
2001   *Slaven en schepen; Enkele reis, bestemming onbekend.* Leiden: Primavera
             Pers.
Davis, David Brion
2000   'Looking at slavery from broader perspectives', *The American Historical
             Review* 105:452-66.
Deerr, Noel
1950   *The history of sugar.* Vol. II. London: Chapman and Hall.
Degler, Carl N.
1972   *Neither black nor white; Slavery and race relations in Brazil and the United
             States.* New York: Macmillan.
Doortmont, Michel R. and Jinna Smit (eds)
2007   *Sources for the mutual history of Ghana and the Netherlands; An anno-
             tated guide to the Dutch archives relating to Ghana and West Africa in the
             Nationaal Archief, 1593-1960s.* Leiden: Brill.
Drescher, Seymour
1977   *Econocide; British slavery in the era of abolition.* Pittsburgh: University of
             Pittsburgh Press.

1994   'The long goodbye; Dutch capitalism and antislavery in comparative perspective', *The American Historical Review* 99:44-69.

Duin, Pieter van and Robert Ross
1987   *The economy of the Cape Colony in the eighteenth century*. Leiden: Centre for the History of European Expansion. [Intercontinenta 7.]

Dijk, Wil O.
2006   *Seventeenth-century Burma and the Dutch East India Company, 1634-1680*. Singapore: Singapore University Press.

Ebert, Christopher
2003   'Dutch trade with Brazil before the Dutch West India Company, 1587-1621', in: Johannes Postma and Victor Enthoven (eds), *Riches from Atlantic commerce; Dutch transatlantic trade and shipping, 1585-1817*, pp. 49-75. Leiden: Brill.

Eldredge, Elizabeth A.
1994   'Delagoa Bay and the hinterland in the early nineteenth century; Politics, trade, slaves and slave raiding', in: Elizabeth A. Eldredge and Fred Morton (eds), *Slavery in South Africa; Captive labour on the Dutch frontier*, pp. 127-65. Boulder, CO: Westview.

Eldredge, Elizabeth A. and Fred Morton (eds)
1994   *Slavery in South Africa; Captive labour on the Dutch frontier*. Boulder, CO: Westview.

Eltis, David
1993   'Europeans and the rise and fall of African slavery in the Americas; An interpretation', *The American Historical Review* 98:1399-423.
1994   'The relative importance of slaves and commodities in the Atlantic trade of seventeenth-century Africa', *The Journal of African History* 35:237-49.
1999   'Slavery and freedom in the early modern world', in: Stanley L. Engerman (ed.), *Terms of labor; Slavery, serfdom and free labor*, pp. 25-49. Stanford: Stanford University Press.
2000   *The rise of African slavery in the Americas*. Cambridge: Cambridge University Press.
2001   'The volume and structure of the transatlantic slave trade; A reassessment', *William and Mary Quarterly* 58-1:17-46.

Eltis, David, S.D. Behrendt, H.S. Klein and David Richardson (eds)
1999   *The trans-Atlantic slave trade; A database on CD-ROM*. New York: Cambridge University Press.

Emmer, Pieter C.
1972a   'De slavenhandel van en naar Nieuw-Nederland', *Economisch- en Sociaal-Historisch Jaarboek* 35:94-147.
1972b   'The history of the Dutch slave trade; A bibliographical survey', *The Journal of Economic History* 32:728-47.
1998   *The Dutch in the Atlantic economy, 1580-1880; Trade, slavery and emancipation*. Aldershot: Ashgate.
2000   *De Nederlandse slavenhandel, 1500-1850*. Amsterdam: Arbeiderspers.
2006   'Nederland als leerling; De buitenlandse invloeden op de opkomst en neergang van de Nederlandse slavenhandel en slavernij', in: Wim van

Noort and Rob Wiche (eds), *Nederland als voorbeeldige natie*, pp. 41-52. Hilversum: Verloren.

Enthoven, Victor
2003   'Early Dutch expansion in the Atlantic region, 1585-1621', in: Johannes Postma and Victor Enthoven (eds), *Riches from Atlantic commerce; Dutch transatlantic trade and shipping, 1585-1817*, pp. 17-47. Leiden: Brill.
2006   'Dutch crossings; Migration between the Netherlands and the New World, 1600-1800', *Atlantic Studies* 2-2:153-76.

Feinberg, Harvey M.
1989   *Africans and Europeans in West Africa; Elminans and Dutchmen on the Gold Coast during the eighteenth century*. Philadelphia: American Philosophical Society. [Transactions of the American Philosophical Society 79-7.]

Finley, M.I.
1968   'Slavery', in: *International encyclopedia of the social sciences*, Vol. 14, pp. 307-13. New York: Macmillan/Free Press.

Foner, Laura and Eugene D. Genovese (eds)
1969   *Slavery in the New World; A reader in comparative history*. Englewood Cliffs: Prentice Hall.

Fox, J.
1983   '"For good and sufficient reasons"; An examination of early Dutch East India Company ordinances on slaves and slavery', in: Anthony Reid (ed.), *Slavery, bondage and dependency in Southeast Asia*, pp. 246-62. St. Lucia: University of Queensland Press.

Frederickson, George M.
1981   *White supremacy; A comparative study in American and South African history*. New York: Oxford University Press.

Galen, Stephan van
2008   *Arakan and Bengal; The rise and decline of the Mrauk U kingdom (Burma) from the fifteenth to the seventeenth century*. PhD thesis University of Leiden.

Gelderen, Martin van
1992   *The political thought of the Dutch Revolt, 1555-1590*. Cambridge: Cambridge University Press.

Gemery, Henry A. and Jan S. Hogendorn (eds)
1979   *The uncommon market; Essays in the economic history of the Atlantic slave trade*. New York: Academic Press.

Gonsalves de Mello, José Antonio
2001   *Nederlanders in Brazilië (1624-1654); De invloed van de Hollandse bezetting op het leven en de cultuur in Noord-Brazilië*. Zutphen: Walburg Pers. [First edition in Portuguese 1947.]

Goor, J. van
1994   *De Nederlandse koloniën; Geschiedenis van de Nederlandse expansie 1600-1975*. Bilthoven: Sdu Uitgevers.

Goslinga, C.Ch.
1971   *The Dutch in the Caribbean and on the Wild Coast, 1580-1680*. Assen: Van Gorcum.

1985   *The Dutch in the Caribbean and the Guianas, 1680-1791.* Assen: Van Gor-
              cum.
1990   *The Dutch in the Caribbean and in Surinam, 1791/5-1942.* Assen: Van Gor-
              cum.

Guha, Sumit
2005   'Slavery, society, and the state in Western India, 1700-1800', in: Indrani
              Chatterjee and Richard M. Eaton (eds), *Slavery and South Asian history*,
              pp. 162-86. Bloomington: Indiana University Press.

Hanna, Willard A.
1978   *Indonesian Banda; Colonialism and its aftermath in the nutmeg islands.*
              Philadelphia: Institute for the Study of Human Issues (ISHI).

Harris, Leslie M.
2003   *In the shadow of slavery; African Americans in New York City, 1626-1863.*
              Chicago: University of Chicago Press.

Hatfield, April Lee
2003   *Atlantic Virginia; Intercolonial relations in the seventeenth century.* Phila-
              delphia: University of Pennsylvania Press.

Heijer, Henk den
1997   *Goud, ivoor en slaven; Scheepvaart en handel van de tweede Westindische
              Compagnie op Afrika, 1674-1740.* Zutphen: Walburg Pers.
2003   'The West African trade of the Dutch West India Company, 1674-1740',
              in: Johannes Postma and Victor Enthoven (eds), *Riches from Atlantic
              commerce; Dutch transatlantic trade and shipping, 1585-1817*, pp. 139-69.
              Leiden: Brill.
2006   (ed.) *Expeditie naar de Goudkust; Het journaal van Jan Dircksz Lam over de
              Nederlandse aanval op Elmina, 1624-1626.* Zutphen: Walburg Pers.

Heywood, Linda M. and John K. Thornton
2007   *Central Africans, Atlantic Creoles, and the foundation of the Americas, 1585-
              1660.* Cambridge: Cambridge University Press.

Hoetink, Harry
1967   *The two variants in Caribbean race relations; A contribution to the sociology
              of segmented societies.* London: Oxford University Press.

Hoogbergen, Wim
1992   *'De bosnegers zijn gekomen!'; Slavernij en rebellie in Suriname.* Amster-
              dam: Prometheus.

Israel, Jonathan and Stuart B. Schwartz
2007   *The expansion of tolerance; Religion in Dutch Brazil (1624-1654).* Amster-
              dam: Amsterdam University Press.

Jacobs, Els M.
2006   *Merchant in Asia; The trade of the Dutch East India Company during the
              eighteenth century.* Leiden: CNWS Publications.

Jacobs, Jaap
1999   *Een zegenrijk gewest; Nieuw-Nederland in de zeventiende eeuw.* Amster-
              dam: Bert Bakker.

Jonge, J.K.J. de
1862   De opkomst van het Nederlandsch gezag in Oost-Indië. Deel I. 's-Gravenha-
        ge: Nijhoff.
1864   De opkomst van het Nederlandsch gezag in Oost-Indië. Deel II. 's-Graven-
        hage: Nijhoff.
1865   De opkomst van het Nederlandsch gezag in Oost-Indië. Deel III. 's-Graven-
        hage: Nijhoff.
Jordaan, Han
1997   'De eerste slaven op Aruba; Het plantage-experiment van 1715', in: Luc
        Alofs, Wim Rutgers and Henny E. Coomans (eds), Arubaans akkoord;
        Opstellen over Aruba van vóór de komst van de olie-industrie, pp. 117-26.
        Bloemendaal: Stichting Libri Antilliani.
1999   'De veranderende situatie op de Curaçaose slavenmarkt en de mis-
        lukte slavenopstand op de plantage Santa Maria in 1716', in: Henny
        E. Coomans, Maritza Coomans-Eustatia and Johan van't Leven (eds),
        Veranderend Curaçao; Collectie essays opgedragen aan Lionel Capriles ter
        gelegenheid van zijn 45-jarig jubileum bij de Maduro & Curiel's Bank N.V.,
        pp. 473-501. Bloemendaal: Stichting Libri Antilliani.
2003   'The Curaçao slave market; From asiento trade to free trade, 1700-1730',
        in: Johannes Postma and Victor Enthoven (eds), Riches from Atlantic
        commerce; Dutch transatlantic trade and shipping, 1585-1817, pp. 219-57.
        Leiden: Brill.
Kessel, I. van (ed.)
2002   Merchants, missionaries and migrants; 300 years of Dutch-Ghanaian rela-
        tions. Amsterdam: KIT Publishers.
Ketelaars, A.P.M.
1985   Van inheemse stapelmarkt tot tweederangs koloniale stad; Een geschiede-
        nis van Malakka van 1403 tot omstreeks 1690. PhD thesis University of
        Utrecht.
Klein, Herbert
2004   'The Atlantic slave trade to 1650', in: Stuart B. Schwartz (ed.), Tropical
        Babylons; Sugar and the making of the Atlantic world, 1450-1680, pp. 201-
        36. Chapel Hill: University of North Carolina Press.
Klooster, Wim
1994   'Subordinate but proud; Curaçao's free blacks and mulattoes in the
        eighteenth century', New West Indian Guide 68:283-300.
1997   'Slavenvaart op Spaanse kusten; De Nederlandse slavenhandel met
        Spaans Amerika, 1648-1701', Tijdschrift voor Zeegeschiedenis 16:421-40.
1998   Illicit riches; Dutch trade in the Caribbean, 1648-1795. Leiden: KITLV
        Press. [Caribbean Series 18.]
1999   'Van zoutwaterslaven tot creolen; Curaçao's zwarten en mulatten
        ten tijde van de West-Indische Compagnie', in: Henny E. Coomans,
        Maritza Coomans-Eustatia and Johan van 't Leven (eds), Veranderend
        Curaçao; Collectie essays opgedragen aan Lionel Capriles ter gelegenheid
        van zijn 45-jarig jubileum bij de Maduro & Curiel's Bank N.V., pp. 505-15.
        Bloemendaal: Stichting Libri Antilliani.

2003   'Curaçao and the Caribbean transit trade', in: Johannes Postma and
               Victor Enthoven (eds), *Riches from Atlantic commerce; Dutch transatlantic
               trade and shipping, 1585-1817*, pp. 203-18. Leiden: Brill.

Knaap, Gerrit J.
1981   'Europeans, mestizos and slaves; The population of Colombo at the
               end of the seventeenth century', *Itinerario* 5:84-102.
1987   *Kruidnagelen en christenen; De VOC en de bevolking van Ambon, 1656-
               1696.* Leiden: KITLV Uitgeverij. [Verhandelingen 125.]
1991   'A city of migrants; Kota Ambon at the end of the seventeenth century',
               Indonesia no. 51:105-28.
1995   'Slavery and the Dutch in Southeast Asia', in: Gert Oostindie (ed.), *Fifty
               years later; Antislavery, capitalism and modernity in the Dutch orbit*, pp.
               193-206. Leiden: KITLV Press. [Caribbean Series 15.]
2006   'Kasteel, stad en land; Het begin van het Nederlandse imperium in de
               Oost', *Leidschrift* 21-2:17-30.

Knaap, Gerrit J. and Heather Sutherland
2004   *Monsoon traders; Ships, skippers and commodities in eighteenth-century
               Makassar.* Leiden: KITLV Press. [Verhandelingen 224.]

Kolchin, Peter
1987   *Unfree labor; American slavery and Russian serfdom.* Cambridge: Harvard
               University Press.

Koloniaal Verslag
1850   *Koloniaal verslag; Bijlage C van de Handelingen der Staten-Generaal.*
               's-Gravenhage: Algemeene Landsdrukkerij.

Koolhof, Sirtjo and Robert Ross
2005   'Upas, September and the Bugis at the Cape of Good Hope; The context
               of a slave's letter', *Archipel* 70:281-308.

Kopytoff, Igor and Suzanne Miers (eds)
1977   'African "slavery" as an institution of marginality', in: Igor Kopytoff
               and Suzanne Miers (eds), *Slavery in Africa; Historical and anthropological
               perspectives*, pp. 3-81. Madison: University of Wisconsin Press.

Koulen, Paul
2006   'Kyk-Over-Al; Genealogische bronnen en Guyana', *Wi Rutu; Tijdschrift
               voor Surinaamse Genealogie* 6-2:19-43.

Lemmers, Alan
1998   'De ezels van Bonaire; Enkele teruggevonden documenten met betrek-
               king tot de vroeg negentiende-eeuwse geschiedenis der Beneden-
               windse eilanden', in: M. Coomans-Eustatia, Henny E. Coomans and To
               van der Lee (eds), *Breekbare banden; Feiten en visies over Aruba, Bonaire
               en Curaçao na de Vrede van Munster, 1648-1998*, pp. 166-74. Bloemendaal:
               Libri Antilliani.

Lequin, Frank
2005   *Het personeel van de Verenigde Oost-Indische Compagnie in Azië in de 18e
               eeuw, meer in het bijzonder in de vestiging Bengalen.* Alphen aan den Rijn:
               Canaletto. [First edition 1982.]

Lier, Rudolf van
1977   *Samenleving in een grensgebied; Een sociaal-historische studie van Suriname.*
             Derde, herziene druk. Amsterdam: Emmering. [First edition 1949.]
Loth, Vincent C.
1995   'Pioneers and perkeniers; The Banda Islands in the seventeenth cen-
             tury', *Cakalele* 6:13-35.
Lovejoy, Paul E.
1983   *Transformations in slavery; A history of slavery in Africa.* Cambridge:
             Cambridge University Press.
Manning, Patrick
1990   *Slavery and African life; Occidental, oriental, and African slave trade.* Cam-
             bridge: Cambridge University Press.
McCusker, John J. and Russell R. Menard
2004   'The sugar industry in the seventeenth century; A new perspective on
             the Barbadian "sugar revolution"', in: Stuart Schwartz (ed.), *Tropical
             Babylons; Sugar and the making of the Atlantic world, 1450-1680*, pp. 289-
             330. Chapel Hill: University of North Carolina Press.
Miers, Suzanne
2004   'Slavery; A question of definition', in: Gwyn Campbell (ed.), *The struc-
             ture of slavery in Indian Ocean Africa and Asia*, pp. 1-16. London: Frank
             Cass.
Mintz, Sidney W.
1985   *Sweetness and power; The place of sugar in modern history.* New York:
             Viking.
Mintz, Sidney W. and Richard Price
1992   *The birth of African-American culture; An anthropological perspective.* Bos-
             ton: Beacon Press. [First edition 1976.]
Moitt, Bernard (ed.)
2004   *Sugar, slavery, and society; Perspectives on the Caribbean, India, the Mas-
             carenes, and the United States.* Gainesville: University Press of Florida.
Moree, P.J.
1998   *A concise history of Dutch Mauritius, 1598-1710; A fruitful and healthy
             land.* London: Kegan Paul, Leiden: International Institute for Asian
             Studies.
Morgan, Philip D.
1998   *Slave counterpoint; Black culture in the eighteenth-century Chesapeake and
             Lowcountry.* Chapel Hill: University of North Carolina Press.
Morton, Fred
1994   'Slavery and South African historiography', in: Elizabeth A. Eldredge
             and Fred Morton (eds), *Slavery in South Africa; Captive labour on the
             Dutch frontier*, pp. 1-9. Boulder, CO: Westview.
Moutoukias, Zacarías
1988   *Contrabando y control colonial en el siglo XVII; Buenos Aires, el Atlántico y
             el espacio peruano.* Buenos Aires: Centro Editor de Américana Latina.

Nash, Gary B.
1995   'The hidden history of mestizo America', *The Journal of American History* 82:941-64.
Netscher, P.M.
1888   *Geschiedenis van de koloniën Essequebo, Demerary en Berbice, van de vestiging der Nederlanders aldaar tot op onzen tijd.* 's-Gravenhage : Nijhoff.

Nieboer, H.J.
1900   *Slavery as an industrial system; Ethnological researches.* The Hague: Nijhoff.
Niemeijer, Hendrik E.
2000   'Slavery, ethnicity and the economic independence of women in seventeenth-century Batavia', in: Barbara Watson Andaya (ed.), *Other pasts;*

            Gender and history in early modern Southeast Asia, pp. 174-94. Honolulu: University of Hawai'i Press.
2005   *Batavia; Een koloniale samenleving in de 17de eeuw.* Amsterdam: Balans.
Oest, Eric Willem van der
2003   'The forgotten colonies of Essequibo and Demerara, 1700-1814', in: Johannes Postma and Victor Enthoven (eds), *Riches from Atlantic commerce; Dutch transatlantic trade and shipping, 1585-1817*, pp. 323-61. Leiden: Brill.
Oosterhoff, J.L.
1985   'Zeelandia; A Dutch colonial city on Formosa, 1624-1662', in: Robert Ross and Gerard J. Telkamp (eds), *Colonial cities; Essays on urbanism in a colonial context*, pp. 51-63. Dordrecht: Nijhoff.
Oostindie, Gert
1993   'Voltaire, Stedman, and Suriname slavery', *Slavery and Abolition* 14-2:1-34.
1995   (ed.) *Fifty years later; Antislavery, capitalism and modernity in the Dutch orbit.* Leiden: KITLV Press.
1999   (ed.) *Het verleden onder ogen; Herdenking van de slavernij.* Amsterdam: Arena, Den Haag: Prins Claus Fonds.
2000   *Het paradijs overzee; De 'Nederlandse' Caraïben en Nederland.* Derde druk. Leiden: KITLV Press. [Caribbean Series 20.]
2003   'Squaring the circle; Commemorating the VOC after 400 years', *Bijdragen tot de Taal-, Land- en Volkenkunde* 159:135-61.
2008   'Slavernij, canon en trauma; Debatten en dilemma's', *Tijdschrift voor Geschiedenis* 121:4-21.
Oostindie, Gert and Emy Maduro
1986   *In het land van de overheerser; II Antillianen en Surinamers in Nederland, 1634/1667-1954.* Dordrecht: Foris. [KITLV, Verhandelingen 100.]
Paesie, Ruud
2008   *Lorrendrayen op Africa; De illegale goederen- en slavenhandel op West-Afrika tijdens het achttiende-eeuwse handelsmonopolie van de West-Indische Compagnie, 1700-1734.* Amsterdam: De Bataafsche Leeuw.

Patterson, Orlando
1982   *Slavery and social death; A comparative study.* Cambridge: Harvard University Press.

Peabody, Sue
1997   *'There are no slaves in France'; The political culture of race and slavery in the Ancien Régime.* New York: Oxford University Press.

Peters, Marion and Ferry André de la Porte
2002   *In steen geschreven; Leven en sterven van VOC-dienaren op de kust van Coromandel in India.* Amsterdam: Stichting Historisch Onderzoek in Woord en Beeld.

Pétré-Grenouilleau, Olivier
2004   'Les traits négrières, ou les limites d'une lecture européocentrique', *Revue d'Histoire Moderne et Contemporaine* 52-4:30-45.

Poeze, Harry A.
1986   *In het land van de overheerser; I Indonesiërs in Nederland, 1600-1950.* Dordrecht: Foris. [KITLV, Verhandelingen 100.]

Postma, Johannes M.
1990   *The Dutch in the Atlantic slave trade, 1600-1815.* Cambridge: Cambridge University Press.
2003a   'A reassessment of the Dutch Atlantic slave trade', in: Johannes Postma and Victor Enthoven (eds), *Riches from Atlantic commerce; Dutch transatlantic trade and shipping, 1585-1817*, pp. 115-38. Leiden: Brill.
2003b   'Suriname and its Atlantic connections, 1667-1795', in: Johannes Postma and Victor Enthoven (eds), *Riches from Atlantic commerce; Dutch transatlantic trade and shipping, 1585-1817*, pp. 287-322. Leiden: Brill.

Postma, Johannes M. and Victor Enthoven (eds)
2003   *Riches from Atlantic commerce; Dutch transatlantic trade and shipping, 1585-1817.* Leiden: Brill.

Price, Richard
2006   'On the miracle of creolization', in: Kelvin A. Yelvington (ed.), *Afro-Atlantic dialogues; Anthropology in the diaspora*, pp. 113-45. Santa Fe: SAR Press.

Priester, L.R.
1987   'De Nederlandse houding ten aanzien van de slavenhandel en slavernij, 1596-1863; Het gedrag van de slavenhandelaren van de Commercie Compagnie van Middelburg in de 18e eeuw'. MA thesis Erasmus Universiteit Rotterdam.

Raben, Remco
1996   *Batavia and Colombo; The ethnic and spatial order of two colonial cities, 1600-1800.* PhD thesis University of Leiden.
2008   'Cities and the slave trade in early-modern Southeast Asia', in: Peter Boomgaard, Dick Kooiman and Henk Schulte Nordholt (eds), *Linking destinies; Trade, towns and kin in Asian history*, pp. 119-40. Leiden: KITLV Press. [Verhandelingen 256.]

Ratelband, Klaas
1953   (ed.) *Vijf dagregisters van het kasteel São Jorge da Mina (Elmina) aan de Goudkust (1645-1647)*. 's-Gravenhage: Nijhoff.
2000   *Nederlanders in West-Afrika, 1600-1650; Angola, Kongo en São Tomé*. Zutphen: Walburg Pers.

Rediker, Marcus
2007   *The slave ship; A human history*. New York: Viking.

Reid, Anthony
1983a   'Introduction; Slavery and bondage in Southeast Asian history', in: Anthony Reid (ed.), *Slavery, bondage and dependency in Southeast Asia*, pp. 1-43. St. Lucia: University of Queensland Press.
1983b   '"Closed" and "open" slave systems in pre-colonial Southeast Asia', in: Anthony Reid (ed.), *Slavery, bondage and dependency in Southeast Asia*, pp. 156-81. St. Lucia: University of Queensland Press.
1983c   (ed.) *Slavery, bondage and dependency in Southeast Asia*. St. Lucia: University of Queensland Press.

Reinders Folmer-van Prooijen, C.
2000   *Van goederenhandel naar slavenhandel; De Middelburgse Commercie Compagnie, 1720-1755*. Middelburg: Koninklijk Zeeuwsch Genootschap der Wetenschappen.

Renkema, W.E.
1981   *Het Curaçaose plantagebedrijf in de negentiende eeuw*. Zutphen: Walburg Pers.

Roos, Doeke
1992   *Zeeuwen en de Westindische Compagnie (1621-1674)*. Hulst: Van Geyt.

Ross, Robert
1983   *Cape of torments; Slavery and resistance in South Africa*. Boston: Routledge.
1986   'The Dutch on the Swahili Coast, 1776-1778; Two slaving journals, part I', *International Journal of African Historical Studies* 19:305-60.
1988   'The last years of the slave trade to the Cape colony', *Slavery and Abolition* 9-3:209-19.
1995   'Book review, Elizabeth A. Eldredge and Fred Morton (eds), *Slavery in South Africa; Captive labour on the Dutch frontier* (Boulder, 1994)', *The Journal of African History* 36:511-2.

Rupert, Linda M.
2006   *Inter-imperial trade and local identity; Curaçao in the colonial Atlantic world*. PhD thesis Duke University, Durham, NC.

Santen, H.W. van
1982   *De Verenigde Oost-Indische Compagnie in Gujarat en Hindustan, 1620-1660*. PhD thesis University of Leiden.

Schalkwijk, Frans L.
1998   *The Reformed Church in Dutch Brazil (1630-1654)*. Zoetermeer: Boekencentrum.

Schama, Simon
1987   *The embarrassment of riches; An interpretation of Dutch culture in the
              Golden Age.* New York: Knopf.
Schmidt, Benjamin
2001   *Innocence abroad; The Dutch imagination and the New World, 1570-1670.*
              Cambridge: Cambridge University Press.
Schouten, Wouter
1676   *Aenmercklijke voyagie gedaan door Wouter Schouten naar Oost-Indiën.*
              Amsterdam: Jacob van Meurs and Johannes van Someren.
Schulte Nordholt, Henk
1996   *The spell of power; A history of Balinese politics, 1650-1940.* Leiden: KITLV
              Press. [Verhandelingen 170.]
Schwartz, Stuart B. and Johannes Postma
2003   'The Dutch Republic and Brazil as commercial partners on the West
              African coast during the eighteenth century', in: Johannes Postma and
              Victor Enthoven (eds), *Riches from Atlantic commerce; Dutch transatlantic
              trade and shipping, 1585-1817,* pp. 171-99. Leiden: Brill.
Scott, James
1985   '*Slavery, bondage and dependency in Southeast Asia;* A review', *Indonesia*
              no. 39:141-3.
Scully, Pamela
1997   'Book review, Elizabeth A. Eldredge and Fred Morton (eds), *Slavery
              in South Africa; Captive labour on the Dutch frontier* (Boulder, 1994)', *The
              International Journal of African Historical Studies* 29:607-8.
Shell, Robert C.-H.
1994a   *Children of bondage; A social history of the slave society at the Cape of Good
              Hope, 1652-1813.* Hanover: Wesleyan University Press.
1994b   'The tower of Babel; The slave trade and creolization at the Cape,
              1652-1834', in: Elizabeth A. Eldredge and Fred Morton (eds), *Slavery in
              South Africa; Captive labour on the Dutch frontier,* pp. 11-39. Boulder, CO:
              Westview.
Singh, Anjana
2007   *Fort Cochin in Kerala, 1750-1830; The social condition of a Dutch community
              in an Indian milieu.* PhD thesis University of Leiden.
Sluiter, Engel
1997   'New light on the "20 and odd Negroes" arriving in Virginia, August
              1619', *William and Mary Quarterly* 54-2:395-8.
Stapel, F.W. (ed.)
1929   *Pieter van Dam; Beschryvinge van de Oostindische Compagnie.* Eerste Boek,
              Deel II. 's-Gravenhage: Nijhoff.
1939   *Pieter van Dam; Beschryvinge van de Oostindische Compagnie.* Tweede
              Boek, Deel III. 's-Gravenhage: Nijhoff.
Stern, Philip J.
2006   'British Asia and British Atlantic; Comparisons and connections', *Wil-
              liam and Mary Quarterly* 63-4:693-712.

Stipriaan, Alex van
1993   *Surinaams contrast; Roofbouw en overleven in een Caraïbische plantageko-
           lonie, 1750-1863.* Tweede druk, Leiden: KITLV Uitgeverij. [Caribbean
           Series 13.]
1995   'Debunking debts, image and reality of a colonial crisis; Suriname at
           the end of the eighteenth century', *Itinerario* 19-1:69-84.
1996   'Suriname and the abolition of slavery', in: Gert Oostindie (ed.), *Fifty
           years later; Antislavery, capitalism and modernity in the Dutch orbit*, pp.
           117-41. Leiden: KITLV Press. [Caribbean Series 15.]
Stipriaan, Alex van and Ellen Bal
2002   'De VOC is een geloof; Kanttekeningen bij een populair Nederlands
           imago', in: Manon van der Heijden and Paul van de Laar (eds), *Rotter-
           dammers en de VOC; Handelscompagnie, stad en burgers (1600-1800)*, pp.
           213-43. Amsterdam: Bert Bakker.
Stowe, Harriet Beecher
1852   *Uncle Tom's cabin; Or life among the lowly.* Boston: Jewett.
Sutherland, Heather
1983   'Slavery and the slave trade in South Sulawesi, 1660s-1800s', in: Antho-
           ny Reid (ed.), *Slavery, bondage and dependency in Southeast Asia*, pp. 263-
           85. St. Lucia: University of Queensland Press.
1986   'Ethnicity, wealth and power in colonial Makassar; A historiographical
           reconsideration', in: Peter J.M. Nas (ed.), *The Indonesian city; Studies in
           urban development and planning*, pp. 37-55. Dordrecht: Foris.
Tannenbaum, Frank
1947   *Slave and citizen; The Negro in the Americas.* New York: Knopf.
Teenstra, M.D.
1836   *De Nederlandsche West-Indische eilanden in derzelver tegenwoordigen toe-
           stand.* Amsterdam: Sulpke.
Terpstra, H. (ed.)
1955   *Itinerario; Voyage ofte schipvaert van Jan Huygen van Linschoten naer Oost
           ofte Portugaels Indien, 1579-1592.* Deel 1. 's-Gravenhage: Nijhoff.
Thornton, John K.
1998a   *Africa and Africans in the making of the Atlantic world, 1400-1800.* Cam-
           bridge: Cambridge University Press. [First edition 1992.]
1998b   'The African experience of the "20 and odd Negroes" arriving in Vir-
           ginia in 1619', *William and Mary Quarterly* 55:421-34.
Unger, W.S.
1961   'Bijdragen tot de geschiedenis van de Nederlandse slavenhandel II',
           Economisch-Historisch Jaarboek 28:3-148.
Van der Kraan, A.
1983   'Bali: Slavery and slave trade', in: Anthony Reid (ed.), *Slavery, bondage
           and dependency in Southeast Asia*, pp. 315-40. St. Lucia: University of
           Queensland Press.
Van de Walle, An
2001   '"Soete dieren en stinkende swartinnen"; Beeldvorming en represen-
           tatie van de Oost-Indische vrouw in de Nederlandse reisliteratuur',

in: Jan Parmentier and Sander Spanoghe (eds), *Orbis in orbem; Liber amoricum John Everaert*, pp. 475-502. Gent: Academica Press.

Veen, Ernst van
1996   'How the Dutch ran a seventeenth-century colony; The occupation and loss of Formosa, 1624-1662', *Itinerario* 20-1:59-77.

Vink, Markus P.M.
2003a   A work of compassion?; Dutch slavery and slave trade in the Indian Ocean in the seventeenth century. Paper presented at 'Seascapes, Littoral Cultures, and Trans-Oceanic Exchanges', Washington DC.
2003b   '"The world's oldest trade"; Dutch slavery and slave trade in the Indian Ocean in the seventeenth century', *The Journal of World History* 14-2:131-77.
2007   'Indian Ocean studies and the "new thalassology"', *The Journal of Global History* 2:41-62.

Viotti da Costa, Emilia
1994   *Crowns of glory, tears of blood; The Demerara slave rebellion of 1823.* New York: Oxford University Press.

Vos, Jelmer
2008   The slave trade from the Windward Coast; The case of the Dutch, 1740-1805. Paper presented at 'African Economic History Workshop', London School of Economics and Political Science.

Vos, Jelmer, David Eltis and David Richardson
2008   'The Dutch in the Atlantic world; New perspectives from the slave trade with particular reference to the African origins of the traffic', in: David Eltis and David Richardson (eds), *Extending the frontiers; Essays on the new transatlantic slave trade database*, pp. 228-49. New Haven: Yale University Press.

Vos tot Nederveen Cappel, H.A.E.
1978   'De dienaren van de V.O.C. teelden in Ceylon vele kinderen bij Europese, Mestiesen, Castiesen, Toepassen, Swarte, Bandanese, Maleise en Singalese vrouwen', *Gens Nostra* 33:308-15.

Wagenaar, Lodewijk
1994   *Galle, VOC-vestiging in Ceylon; Beschrijving van een koloniale samenleving aan de vooravond van de Singhalese opstand tegen het Nederlandse gezag, 1760.* Amsterdam: De Bataafsche Leeuw.

Wagman, Morton
1980   'Corporate slavery in New Netherland', *The Journal of Negro History* 65-1:34-42.

Ward, Kerry R.
2001   *'The bounds of bondage'; Forced migration from Batavia to the Cape of Good Hope during the Dutch East India Company era, c. 1652-1795.* PhD thesis University of Michigan, Ann Arbor.

Wättjen, Hermann
1921   *Das holländische Kolonialreich in Brasilien; Ein Kapitel aus der Kolonialgeschichte des 17. Jahrhunderts.* Haag: Nijhoff, Gotha: Perthes.

Westra, Piet and James C. Armstrong (eds)
2006   *Slave trade with Madagascar; The journals of the Cape slaver Leijdsman, 1715.* Cape Town: Africana Publishers.
Wolff, Marianne
1992   'Cochin; Een mestiese samenleving in India'. MA thesis University of Leiden.
Worden, Nigel
1985   *Slavery in Dutch South Africa.* Cambridge: Cambridge University Press.
Worden, Nigel, Elizabeth van Heyningen and Vivian Bickford-Smith
1998   *Cape Town; The making of a city; An illustrated social history.* Hilversum: Verloren.

THIO TERMORSHUIZEN

Indentured labour in the Dutch colonial empire
1800-1940

Introduction

As the Atlantic slave trade and European colonial slavery withered and died in the nineteenth century, a new pattern of labour migrations emerged, connecting the world in both familiar and previously unseen ways.[1] The age of imperialism witnessed the organization of a new type of overseas contract labour, to some extent intended as a substitute for the abolished trade in enslaved Africans. Indentured labourers, mostly from Asia, were caught up in the carousel of world capitalism. Many volunteered with high hopes, enticed by what would turn out to be lies and deceit. Driven by a mixture of hope and desperation they would enter a world previously unimagined.

Indentured labour was not a new concept. Since the sixteenth century, thousands of European migrants travelling to the New World had signed a similar contract, binding them to their employer for a number of years, during which their debts were paid off, often including the cost of their journey. After completing their period of indenture these white labourers became free and were often in a position to make a good life for themselves. The line dividing these early servants and free European migrants was usually a thin one. For the nineteenth-century Asian indentured labourer, however, the image becomes more diffuse. Although conditions were particularly harsh in the period up until 1900, there were stark contrasts between regions and groups of migrants. While many led a hard life, often ending in premature death far away from their homes in an alien and often inhospitable environment, others managed to exceed the standard of living they had attained in

---

[1]   I would like to thank Peter Boomgaard, Pieter Emmer, Maurits Hassankhan, Rosemarijn Hoefte and Gert Oostindie for their valuable comments on early drafts of this chapter.

their home country. Over time, however, conditions did generally improve. While indentured labour may initially have been, in Hugh Tinker's famous but contested phrase, 'a new system of slavery', the system certainly became more just in the twentieth century.[2]

This chapter does not aim to present an all-encompassing survey of indentured labour recruitment and deployment in the Dutch colonial empire, much less does it intend to write the full history of the position of the descendants of these early migrants in their present societies. Instead, it aims to shed light on extant empirical evidence on indentured labour migrations within the Dutch empire from circa 1800 until 1940.

The first two sections will discuss the concept of indenture and the Javanese precursors of the eventual indentured labour system. A study of indentured labour automatically implies a study of migratory labour, as the majority of workers came from non-Dutch regions, notably British India and China. The third section will address these areas of recruitment, while the final section focuses on the destination areas, principally Suriname, Sumatra's East Coast (SEC) and other parts of the Outer Islands of the Dutch East Indies. Attention will also be given to regions such as Malaysia, New Caledonia and Australia, where indentured Dutch colonial subjects – primarily Javanese – were sent.

This chapter does not discuss larger debates on the meaning and development of indenture within the Dutch empire, but is based on secondary literature and focuses specifically on demographic figures, migratory routes and destinations, besides early working and living conditions.

On 'indenture'

The terms 'indentured labour' and 'contract labour' have been used interchangeably up until this point since contract is key to the concept of indenture.[3] Yet the concept of contract labour contains all forms of work submitted to certain stipulations written on paper or agreed to verbally. This is different from indentured labour, which always involves a formal written contract signed for an extended period of time. In the Dutch colonial case, the contracts were made for three to five years.

Another important dimension of indentured labour, in definition and in

---

[2] Hugh Tinker is the author of *A new system of slavery: The export of Indian labour overseas 1820-1920*. Published in 1974, this book played a key part in the historic discussion regarding indentured labour in British India.

[3] The term 'indenture' is originally derived from 'a document in duplicate having indented edges'. This is 'a contract binding one party into the service of another for a specified term' (*American heritage dictionary* 2000).

practice, involves force. Indentured labour as understood in this study is bonded labour. In a general sense, contract labour may include free labour, where one can 'enter' or 'leave' a contract without being prosecuted by criminal law. But this was not the case for indentured labourers who broke their contracts. Moreover, they were not free to move from one employer to the other (Bates 2001:10). In the Dutch East Indies such restrictions (and rights as well) were established with the Coolie Ordinance that was introduced in 1880. The most far-reaching clause of this ordinance was the penal sanction (*poenale sanctie*), which made criminal prosecution of indentured labourers possible.[4] Colonial employers were thus able to control (or subjugate) their workers. The penal clause also applied to other indentured labourers in the Dutch colonial sphere, including Suriname. Penal sanctions would remain linked to the concept of 'indenture' until 1931, when they were gradually abolished.[5] 'Free' labour – usually also involving some form of contract – became more prominent after 1931, although in many instances it had already been introduced, especially in various regions of the Outer Islands of the Dutch East Indies.

The establishment of a penal clause reveals yet another aspect of indentured labour, that is the level of government interference. Authorities were involved in one way or another, usually providing the legal framework for the recruitment of indentured labour and the parameters of this labour system, as was the case with the introduction of the aforementioned Coolie Ordinance. Finally, indentured labour as discussed here is characterized by its migratory character: indentured labourers came from afar to perform tasks that the local population was unable or unwilling to take on.

---

[4]   The Coolie Ordinance stated, among other things, that workers employed from elsewhere (either other islands of the Dutch East Indies or foreign countries) had to be in the possession of a written contract. These contracts were to last up to three years and held a penal sanction. Workers who refused to work or who 'deserted', were liable to a punishment of up to three months of forced labour. A second offence was punishable by forced labour ranging from three to twelve months. The Coolie Ordinance of 1880 only applied to Sumatra's East Coast (SEC). As a result, up until 1885, when the first Javanese arrived on SEC, the ordinance almost exclusively applied to Chinese labourers. Heijting (1925:7) mentions that these Chinese workers were familiar with the penal sanction, as similar stipulations existed in British Malaya and the Straits Settlements.

[5]   Plans for the abolition of the penal sanction were discussed by Dutch authorities in the 1910s, but a real commitment for change was only made in 1928. The new Coolie Ordinance of 1931 stipulated that gradually the percentage of 'contract labourers' and 'non-contract labourers' had to shift in favour of the latter category. There were several reasons for this policy change, including pressure from the United States. In the end, however, the change actually benefited the enterprises, since the economic world crisis forced them to dismiss a substantial number of workers. 'Free workers' had no multi-year contracts like 'penal sanction workers' and could be dismissed more easily. For a detailed account of the history of the Coolie Ordinance and the penal clause, see Langeveld 1975:1-12.

'Indentured labour' remains a contested term among historians since there were various 'systems' under which labourers were recruited and employed in different colonial settings. For instance, the so-called *kangani* and *maistry* systems under which many British Indians ventured overseas demonstrate grey areas between 'bonded' and 'free' labour. Some authors, such as Bates (2001:25) and Bhagwanbali (1996:16-9), make a distinction between *kangani* (and/or *maistry*) on the one hand and the indentured labour system on the other. Others, such as Northrup (1995:10-1), acknowledge certain differences, but hesitate to classify these variants as altogether different from indenture. The 'credit ticket' system used by many Chinese to travel to the Straits Settlements (present-day Malaysia) and then to the Dutch East Indies, is another example of a system sharing some characteristics with indentured labour. For present purposes, and following many other authors, such similar systems have been brought together here under the umbrella of indentured labour.

Before indenture: bonded and 'free' labour in the Dutch empire, 1800-1860

Slavery

Slavery had existed in the Indonesian archipelago since ancient times and should thus be differentiated from European colonial slavery. However, there was no such thing as specific 'slave labour', slaves of both sexes worked and lived among free subjects, the treatment of slaves was often characterized as relatively mild and manumission rates were high.

Following the Portuguese example, the Dutch East Indies Company (VOC) took advantage of the existence of slavery on its arrival in the archipelago. Slavery, and hence also the regional slave trade, were crucial in all major Dutch colonial settlements. Yet the importance of colonial – as opposed to local – slavery was restricted to the urban environment and was actually withering in the nineteenth century. By 1860, when slavery ended in the Dutch East Indies, the number of slaves emancipated was a mere 4,735 of a population of many millions.[6]

In the Dutch Caribbean, however, slavery was the backbone of the entire economy, with enslaved Africans and their descendants forming the majority of the population. On emancipation in 1863, Suriname's 36,484 slaves (on a

---

[6] Knaap 1995:200. See also Chapter V in this book. The prohibition of slave ownership only applied to slaves owned by Europeans and Chinese in areas under direct Dutch control. In the autonomous, self-governing and indirectly ruled areas indigenous slavery continued. See Knaap 1995:201; Reid 1993:77.

population of about 50,000[7]) were freed as well as 11,211 (on a population of more than 30,000) on the Antillean islands (Goslinga 1990:303).

'Obligatory' labour

Besides slavery and convict labour[8] other forms of bonded labour existed in the Indonesian archipelago. On Java it was common practice for aristocratic rulers, the *priyayi*, to levy tributes from their subjects, often in the form of manual labour. The VOC made use of these existing social labour duties, which in the Dutch colonial context came to be known as *corvée* or *heerendiensten*. As the new 'sovereigns', the Dutch felt they could lay claim to these ancient Javanese rights. Well into the nineteenth century the Dutch East Indies government claimed the right to such uncompensated labour for the construction of roads, bridges, fortifications, waterways and public buildings.

The Cultivation System, 1830-1870

In 1830 Governor General Johannes van den Bosch implemented the so-called Cultivation System (*Cultuurstelsel*) on Java.[9] This general term is somewhat misleading, as its implementation and practical organization differed from region to region and from village to village. The system developed into a series of local arrangements operating on some basic 'ground rules', of which the forced labour of Javanese peasants was crucial.

A taxation called land rent (*landrente*) and traditional lines of authority were central to the Cultivation System.[10] Every village was to use one-fifth of its land for the cultivation of export crops for the European market. These crops were to be delivered to the government or to government contractors, while the village would receive either remission of land rent or monetary payment.[11]

---

7   Excluding Amerindians and Maroons. See Goslinga 1990:303.
8   This form of forced labour was introduced in 1828. Prisoners were often used as bearers on military expeditions. See Knaap 1995:202.
9   A long debate preceded the decision to implement the Cultivation System on Java. Its chief purpose was the production of commodities for the world market. King Willem I could instead have chosen a system based on slave labour, which already existed in the Dutch West Indies at the time, but Van den Bosch was able to convince him that his system was a better solution since slave labour was more costly. See Emmer 1995:214.
10   Land rent was introduced during the British interregnum and later adopted by the Dutch. According to its principles, the sovereign, as owner of all land, rented the land to village chiefs, who for their part were responsible for dividing the land among the villagers, who communally were responsible for paying the tax. Before 1830, this was generally paid in the form of money. For more details, see Van Niel 1992:5-28.
11   If the total value of the produce failed to meet the land rent, this then had to be made up by the village in either cash or kind.

Traditional patterns of authority made the system viable. Following the tradition of obligatory labour by Javanese peasants for the nobility, they were now forced to work for the Dutch through the Javanese elite in the production of crops for the export trade.[12] The village chief in particular held an important intermediary position, organizing the daily allocation of forced labour. While the peasants probably did not make any distinction between the different tasks they were forced to perform as part of their social obligations, the Dutch government regarded this cultivation service as different from *corvée* or forced labour.[13] Van Niel points out that from 1837 onwards in order to 'maintain some sense of equity in the heavy labour burdens imposed on the Javanese peasantry', individual peasants were generally paid (some) monetary wages instead of the village chief. Other obligations, such as *corvée* and village services, were not being paid for, but it was often difficult to clarify what type of work was being done in what category.[14]

Between 1836 and 1860, on average approximately 60 to 75 per cent of all Javanese peasant households were forced to work in cultivation services.[15] After 1860 this percentage gradually dropped, as the system fell into disrepute and was finally abolished. Reliable numbers are difficult to establish, if only because scholars provide widely divergent estimates of Java's total population. Boomgaard (1989:163-7) mentions that most present-day scholars in the field have used the so-called 'bad' benchmark years of 1815 (the first census for the entire island) and 1850. In both years the under-recording of people was a (particularly) serious problem. Boomgaard and Gooszen

[12]   In exchange for their cooperation, the Javanese elite received all kinds of benefits, such as a substantial salary and a percentage of the value of crops produced in their district. See Van Niel 1992:111.

[13]   Van Niel 1992:111. Sometimes (even before 1830) a division of labour occurred: some peasants of a certain village would perform mostly *corvée* duties, while others worked the land. Wage labour did exist – for instance, some peasants worked as day labourers for other villagers – but the rate of pay was generally not enough for subsistence. Despite this, some landless people hired themselves out for *corvée* to others and were almost continuously employed in this way. See Van Niel 1992:211-8.

[14]   Van Niel (1992:116-8) describes how the cultivation of different crops led to various forms of payment. Tasks performed in relation to cultivation services, such as processing plants and transport, were compensated separately and individually. Ideally, these duties should have been performed by 'free' labourers, but there were few of these on Java. As a consequence, the labourers were delivered through the channels of village and supra-village administration. This practice would only gradually begin to change after 1860.

[15]   Van Niel (1992:111) estimates that about 65 to 70 per cent of agricultural households worked in government cultivations during the system's existence. Dros (1991:139) mentions 65 to 75 per cent for the period between 1837 and 1851. Elson (1994:90, 111, 185) gives similar percentages for the period between 1836 and 1852 (with percentages gradually dropping thereafter to around 40 percent in the late 1860s). Boomgaard (1990:126) gives an average percentage of households employed for five residencies in the period 1835 to 1870, indicating that four of these residencies (slightly) exceeded the 50 percent mark.

(1991:182) conclude that in 1850 Java's population must have been around fourteen million.[16] They stress, however, that even this number is unreliable, given the many flaws relating to censuses, particularly in the early nineteenth century.[17] Given these figures, it seems fair to estimate that around 1850 between eight and eleven million Javanese were involved in the Cultivation System, part-time, alongside *corvée* and subsistence agriculture. This number would increase in later years with the general population growth.

Labour on Java after 1870

Historians disagree about the impact of the Cultivation System on Java's over-all economic (labour) development.[18] In the 1850s, when the system was still in full operation, the colonial government supplied workers to the sugar factories with the help of the village chiefs. Besides these forced labourers, factories also employed a growing number of (voluntary) wage labourers, both skilled and unskilled.[19] Most of these were peasants with little or no land and included women and children. A large number came from the region surrounding the factories (Elson 1986:149). Still others were migrants or seasonal workers.

After 1860 the colonial government on Java gradually withdrew from the recruitment of labour, leaving private enterprise to take its place. Initially, labour recruitment and organization remained much the same, however, with village chiefs retaining their position as middlemen for the delivery of workers to the factories. Only after 1872 factories came to depend solely on 'free wage labour' (Elson 1986:159). A large part of the workforce consisted of seasonal labour, especially in the sugar industry, Java's main export asset. Most workers in this industry were employed on an irregular daily basis, making it very

[16]   Boomgaard and Gooszen give the following estimates: 7.5 million for 1900, 14 million for 1850, 30.4 million for 1900, 37.1 million for 1920, 40.9 million for 1930 and 47.5 million for 1940. However, only the figure for 1930 is truly reliable, according to Boomgaard. As far as other estimates are concerned, Elson (1994:25, 279) uses the Cultivation Reports (*Kultuur Verslagen*), citing a population number of 'around 6 million' for 1830, 7,292,349 for 1850 and 13,582,391 for 1870, while adding that the population estimate for 1830 is 'conjectural and almost certainly significantly underestimate(s) the true count'.Van Niel (1992:85) discusses population numbers given by Breman and Peper, whose estimates are 12,5 million and 13,1 million respectively for 1850. Van Niel states that Breman's numbers are probably more accurate, considering the frequent under-reporting in the Cultivation Reports.

[17]   For a discussion of the causes of under-recording in the nineteenth century, see Boomgaard 1991:14-6.

[18]   Boomgaard (1991) notes that the Cultivation System 'must have delayed the spread of free wage-labour because enterprises had easy access to compulsory labour and [...] because most peasants were kept too busy to go in search for more remunerative activities'.

[19]   The percentages of these workers differed from region to region and from factory to factory. In some areas, such as Surabaya, Cirebon and Kediri, voluntary workers made up a 'sizeable proportion' of factory labourers. See Elson 1986:145-6.

difficult to estimate the number of wage workers on Java prior to 1940.[20]

Data regarding the total number of free wage workers in Java's industrial sector are thus few and far between, especially for the nineteenth century (Boomgaard 1989:131). While for some industries a few early figures or estimates are available, for others they are utterly lacking.[21] Information on the aggregate number of workers in the twentieth century is largely derived from official population counts. According to the 1905 census the total number of workers in Java's manufacturing industry was 538,682.[22] The 1930 census indicated the total number of workers in this industry to be 1,698,924. In both cases, however, workers employed in Western estate and mining factories were not included (Segers 1987:28). According to Segers, the number of workers employed in these estate factories for the whole of the Dutch East Indies was about 108,000 in 1930 and approximately 235,000 in 1940.[23]

The indentured labour trade: supply and recruitment

Three major zones of recruitment dominated the migration of indentured labour within or into the Dutch colonial empire: China, British India and Java. Each of these three areas will be discussed separately here, with a focus on figures, gender and recruitment methods.

China

In the early 1840s the Chinese indentured labour trade, or the 'pig trade' as it was unflatteringly called, commenced. Largely due to British pressure, the Chinese government was forced to open several of its harbours for the trans-

---

[20]   Colin Brown (1994:78) estimates that prior to the Second World War, the sugar industry must have employed at least 250,000 and perhaps as many as 1,000,000.

[21]   Boomgaard (1989:118, 121, 125, 131) gives for instance an estimate of 52,500 workers in the sugar industry in 1880. Of these, 11,500 were permanently employed, while 41,000 worked only during the harvesting season. By comparison, in 1820 the total number was approximately 12,000. Segers (1987:137, 140-1) gives estimates of workers in the sugar industry for the 1920s and 1930s. In 1930 the total number of permanent and temporary workers in this industry was about 175,000. Complete surveys of numbers of employees in the petroleum industry are provided for the first time in 1909 (9,414 workers in total; Segers 1987:17). For figures regarding workers in the petroleum industry in the 1920s and 1930s, see Segers 1987:151-2. For other industries, see Segers 1987:126-200.

[22]   For an overview of employment in the manufacturing industry in 1905 and in 1930, see Segers 1987:64, 82.

[23]   Industrial establishments not registered under factory are not included. See Segers 1987:29. Elson (1986:157-8) provides two tables, one regarding the number of days worked by forced labourers per region between 1862-72 and one for factories using forced labourers in the same period.

port of recruited labourers to the overseas colonies.[24] The Chinese indentured labour trade was part of a much greater migration from China in the nineteenth and twentieth centuries, numbering in the millions.[25]

The total number of Chinese indentured labourers recruited and shipped is unknown. According to one source those moving between continents – the US not included – numbered 386,901 between 1841 and 1910.[26] Another great number of recruits remained in Asia, venturing to places such as Malaysia and the Dutch East Indies. The latter received probably as many as 200,000 to 300,000 Chinese labourers in a time span of about seventy years (1863-1932), although the exact figure remains elusive (for more details see above). Suriname was the destination of approximately 3,000 recruits.[27]

Recruitment

At first the Chinese coolie trade was almost indistinguishable from the slave trade. Regulations were absent and, as Emmer (2007:61) describes it, 'every ship that could float could be used to transport Chinese labourers'.[28] Out of desperation there was always an ample supply of people willing to work overseas. Floods, famine, tribal and ethnic struggle were some of the problems plaguing China's rural population. In addition, the growth of the nation's population was a particularly important motivating factor.[29] Many Chinese peasants flocked to the cities, where Western enterprises and their

[24]   Experiments with Chinese labourers went as far back as 1806, when 192 Chinese arrived in British Trinidad. See Look Lai 2004:5. The two 'open' harbours were Hong Kong (British) and Macao (Portuguese) (Ankum-Houwink 1985:182).
[25]   Between 1847 and 1874 approximately 1.5 million Chinese emigrated, amounting to 0.3 per cent of the total population at that time (Emmer 2004:89).
[26]   Northrup 1995:44, 156-7. The number of Chinese migrating to Suriname is included in this figure (2,979, according to Northrup). Northrup (1995:10-2) limits his study to *intercontinental* indentured labour, thus excluding the huge group of Chinese indentured labourers employed in Southeast Asia (including the Dutch East Indies). He also excludes Chinese labourers going to California, since they were not in a true sense 'indentured', although the debate surrounding this issue is still without conclusion. Blussé (1988:43) refers only to contract labourers in a general sense and therefore arrives at considerably higher numbers. His estimates are as follows: approximately 200,000 Chinese contract labourers went to Peru and the Caribbean in the period between 1847 and 1880; 300,000 were employed in California in the same period and South-Africa, Hawaii and the Dutch East Indies together make up for about 500,000 Chinese contract labourers for the period from 1860 to 1930.
[27]   Different authors give different numbers. It seems that Look Lai has made a (typographical) error by giving a total number of Chinese indentured labourers of '2,645' on p. 8, while his table adds up to 2,945 (2004:8, 21-3). Northrup (1995:156) is less specific about the period in which Chinese labourers entered Suriname, as he gives the total decennial influx between 1851 and 1880.
[28]   See also Ankum-Houwink 1985:182.
[29]   The Chinese population tripled between 1650 and 1850 (Emmer 2004:89).

Sugar estate Mariënburg, Suriname

hired Chinese recruiters – *crimps* – had free play, taking advantage of their destitute condition. Some were tricked, others simply kidnapped.[30] Prisoners of war and debtors were also delivered to these firms.

Moreover, there was a continuous demand for labour from colonial employers all over the world. From the perspective of these employers, the Chinese market offered plenty of opportunities. The Chinese had a solid reputation as hard workers and the introduction of fast Western ships for transporting the labourers after 1842 made it far cheaper to transport them to their intended destinations.

During the 1850s knowledge of the malpractices associated with the Chinese indentured labour trade led to an expression of outrage in the Western press. The abolition movement in the United Kingdom had continually been alert to the abuse this new labour system could entail. As a result, the British began to formulate a coherent policy regarding the trade. In 1860 a treaty with regulations concerning the recruitment of Chinese labourers was signed by the English, French and Chinese governments. The principles laid down in the treaty also applied to the Dutch (Ankum-Houwink 1985:182). Although the extent of the mistreatment diminished in the following years as a result of the imposed regulations, abuse of the system would continue. In the wake of new incidents the trade was officially abolished in 1874 (Northrup 1995:58; Van den Boogaart and Emmer 1986:9). But this was not the end of Chinese labour migration, since Western companies would continue to find ways to recruit new, often impoverished labourers.[31] Many of these recruits made their way to the Dutch East Indies.

'Dutch' recruitment

In the Dutch East Indies the recruitment of Chinese coolies for the tin island of Bangka was underway as early as 1810. Recruitment went via the British Straits Settlements and was in the hands of Chinese tradesmen. At that time,

---

[30]   Many Chinese who volunteered for overseas indenture were indeed quite desperate. Northrup (1995:58) notes: 'An eyewitness at Amoy in 1852 wrote of "the care with which the poor fellows take to conceal any little physical defect [...] men of advanced years pick out their grey hairs [...]; boys try to appear as men [...] and no one is under 19 or over 33 according to their own account". The following account was given by a Chinese labourer: "They were beguiled on board the barbarian ship as contract labourers by emigration agents and confined to the hold [...]. After the ship sailed, the said barbarians gave each man in the hold a contract of servitude. If he did not accept he was flogged. [Then] the said barbarians suddenly seized all of them, brought them on deck and cut off their cues [queues]. More than ten who were sick in bed and could not walk were immediately killed and thrown into the ocean"'. (Quoted in Northrup 1995:56.)

[31]   Apart from the Chinese migrating to the Outer Islands in the Dutch East Indies, many more Chinese were transported elsewhere around the world. Some emigrated with the permission of the Chinese government. For example, during the First World War at least 140,000 Chinese were sent to France, mostly for support roles such as burying the dead. See Northrup 1995:59.

no Coolie Ordinance existed – the ordinance was only established in 1880 and then only for Sumatra's East Coast. In many other respects, however, Chinese labour was bonded. Daily practices on Bangka (and elsewhere) were controlled by so-called kongsis (cooperative organizations). Chinese workers had to pay off the costs made for their recruitment and transport; only then were they free to leave the mine or plantation.[32]

The first transport of Chinese labourers to Suriname occurred in 1853 with the arrival of eighteen men. This was organized by the colonial authorities in the Dutch East Indies. The second group was recruited in China five years later. As of 1862, recruitment was handed over to private enterprise.[33] 1865 saw the installation of the Immigratie Maatschappij (Immigration Society): a Hong Kong-based company recruiting labourers for employers in the Dutch colonial territories. Between 1865 and 1869 2,000 Chinese were thus transported to Suriname. Recruitment from Hong Kong ended, however, following the British closure of the harbour in 1869. In 1873 and 1874 the Dutch government delivered another 100 Chinese to Suriname. They would be the last Chinese migrants arriving in the colony under the indenture system.

Before 1888 the recruitment of labourers for plantations in the Dutch East Indies was handled by Chinese tradesmen or brokers. They recruited their workers in the British Straits Settlements, often employing dubious methods.[34] For the planters in the Dutch colony circumstances were far from ideal because they had to compete with the tin mines and plantations in Malaysia for the often scarce labour supply provided by these brokers.[35] Also, as a result of this competition, premiums payed to brokers rose to great heights (Breman 1987:40). As of 1888 things changed, with transports to the Indonesian archipelago now being handled directly from China (Van Klaveren 1997:112). This migration was organized by Dutch private companies that had received per-

---

[32]   The kongsi system operated on the principle that its members shared both the profits and losses of the labour. A kongsi would receive advances and was paid per *pikul* of tin by the Dutch East Indies government. These payments were low (about 15.5 guilders per *pikul* of tin) and thus resulted in huge profits for the colonial government (approaching 100 per cent). One could say that the kongsi system in some ways resembled the function of Javanese villages during the Cultivation System, although in the former the cooperation was voluntary. See Somers Heidhues 1992:32, 37-41; Kaur and Diehl 1996:108.
[33]   A compromise between liberals and proponents of state interference came about with the introduction of a subsidies scheme for private recruiters. See Ankum-Houwink 1985:183.
[34]   According to Hayashi (2002:5), the labour (or 'coolie') trade from the Straits Settlements was in the hands of private recruitment agencies which were controlled by 'Chinese secret societies'. The commissions paid to these agencies were very high, urging Sumatra's East Coast planters to find other ways to fulfil their labour demands.
[35]   Breman 1987:28. Another reason for the difficulty in obtaining enough workers was Deli's bad reputation. This (among other things) had to do with Sumatra's East Coast workers being paid task wages instead of a daily wage, as was the case in Malaysia.

mission from the Chinese authorities for recruitment.[36] It is interesting to note that this agreement was reached independently of the Dutch authorities.[37]

The system set up by the companies in China made use of *laukeh* (veterans) or *kheh-thau* (intermediaries). These were trusted labourers in the Dutch East Indies who were sent back to China to recruit new workers.[38] The *kheh-thau* had a close connection to the plantation elite[39] and were sent to China with letters of introduction in order to recruit labourers. Plantation owners were warned that these former labourers almost certainly would become professional recruiters over time, which would lead to the same problems – regarding supply and premiums - they had faced when dealing with professional agencies in the Straits Settlements (Breman 1987:42-3).

The *laukeh* system delivered mixed results. It was successful in some regions of the Outer Islands (such as the tin island of Belitung, and unsuccessful in other regions (notably Bangka – see also above).[40] On Sumatra's East Coast the system was unsatisfactory since it was unable to provide the number of labourers needed there. Gradually, the costly recruitment of labourers in China came to a standstill and Javanese recruitment – and consequently labour – would take its place.

Gender

The vast majority of Chinese recruits to Dutch colonies were young men. From 1888 onwards, when direct recruitment started, they often came from the southern provinces of China and had agricultural backgrounds.[41] In many cases they had gone to the cities, where they had fallen into debt. Some married before leaving, dreaming of returning one day to their native villages 'loaded with riches, so they could buy more land and expand their families'

---

[36]   Only the larger companies were involved. Smaller plantations not aligned to the Planters Association (DPV, Deli Planters Vereeniging) still had to rely on labour from Malaysia. See Breman 1987:43.

[37]   Breman (1989:53) states that this was proof of the 'supra-national character of plantation capitalism'.

[38]   Langeveld (1975:13) notes that this system was more humane: abuse and coercion were less prevalent than under the broker system. Breman (1987:40-2) mentions that shortly after 1900 it was the intention of SEC-based companies involved in the recruitment in China (which were organised under the umbrella of the DPV to send five per cent of the labourers back as *laukeh* or *kheh-thau*.

[39]   Often they held a special position, such as that of shopkeeper, grocer or (semi-)skilled labourer (Breman 1987:42).

[40]   For years, Bangka was unable to recruit enough labourers via this system, leading to a dimished tin production on the island. See Somers Heidhues 1992:113, 133-4.

[41]   The Chinese that were recruited in Malaysia before 1888 were of mixed backgrounds. For obvious reasons, planters preferred labourers with an agricultural background. Direct recruitment after 1888 made this possible (Breman 1987:41).

waning fortunes' (Emmer 2007:61; Northrup 1995:54).

Relatively few Chinese women emigrated, partly due to social and legal constraints in China and also due to the lack of interest in female labourers among planters in the receiving countries, especially on Sumatra's East Coast (Breman 1987:76). As a result, the typical workers' society in the Dutch East Indies (such as Sumatra's East Coast, Bangka and Belitung) was characterized by an overwhelming gender imbalance. This would gradually change as the number of Javanese, and subsequently also of Javanese women, increased. The Chinese migrant population would remain predominantly male, however. In 1912, on Sumatra's East Coast, there were only 7,000 Chinese women working alongside 93,000 Chinese men (Stoler 1995:31). Wertheim writes (1993:269) in this respect: 'For most of the labourers, many of whom had been cheated into signing a contract, working on a Delhi plantation meant lifelong bondage made even harsher by the nearly exclusively male composition of the frontier society'.

According to Look Lai's figures, there were no women on board the ships sailing to Suriname in the 1850s, nor in the 1870s. An exception was the *Tricolor*, that arrived in Suriname on 29 July 1865, disembarking 120 women – 41 per cent of the total number of 286 occupants.[42] According to Northrup (1995:75) between 1865 and 1869 14.7 per cent of Chinese indentured labourers in Suriname were women. Since no Chinese workers arrived on ships between 1860 and 1864, it is likely that this figure applied to the entire Chinese coolie trade to Suriname, which was more or less confined to the years 1865-1869.

British India

From the 1870s the Indian subcontinent became the world's greatest source of indentured labour. Between 1834 and 1917, in addition to many more millions of 'free' migrants, up to 1.5 million indentured British Indians left for overseas destinations.[43] About 500,000 of them were shipped to the Caribbean (Emmer 2004:90). Between 1873 and 1917 almost 35,000 of these came to Suriname.[44]

[42]   This shipment also had an unusually high mortality rate of forty per cent: 475 Chinese embarked, 286 arrived. Other shipments (where numbers are available) never came close to this percentage (Look Lai 2004:22-3).
[43]   Judith Brown 2006:30. Bhagwanbali (1996:78) writes that 1.16 million British Indians left their country as indentured labourers. According to Emmer (2004:89) 1.25 million British Indians left under indenture. Northrup (1995:60, 63) gives a figure of 1.3 million. During the greater part of the 1840s Indian migrants signed contracts only after arriving at their destination. In 1847 the signing of contracts prior to departure was introduced. The total number of Indians venturing overseas (indentured and non-indentured) in the nineteenth century was much greater: approximately 20 million (6.7 per cent of the nation's population).
[44]   Bhagwanbali (1996:78) cites Brij V. Lal, arriving at a total of 34,000. Northrup (1995:156-7)

Recruitment

In 1829 the first indentured British Indians arrived in the British colony of Mauritius. Nine years later British Guyana would receive its first small batch. Reports of abuses connected to the recruitment in India thwarted further trade for a few years, but from the mid-1840s a regular supply of indentured labourers were sent to a number of British colonies (Northrup 1995:24). Several authors, most notably Hugh Tinker in *A new system of slavery* (1974:xiv-xv), have argued that the British Indian indentured trade was a continuation of slavery under a new guise.

More recently, some scholars have begun to assess things differently. Central to their argument is the fact that although personal circumstances may have contributed to their decision, most British Indians signed a contract of their own free will. Despite the lack of reliable data on motives for migration, it seems that many workers were pressurized into signing by the harsh conditions prevailing in India. Bhagwanbali (1996:79) cites a few possible factors, most notably high unemployment and low wages, which in themselves were a result of British policies. He and Emmer conclude that overpopulation was not such an important factor – even though the nineteenth century saw rapid population growth[45] – whereas India's incorporation into the British Empire was. As a result, the size of landholdings increased, pushing many small farmers off their lands. As they often became indebted to the large landowners, many of them finally chose to emigrate (Emmer 2004:89; Bhagwanbali 1996:78-87).

Finally, a number of 'positive' factors influenced the decision to emigrate. Most migrants expected to become prosperous and return within a short time. Such false expectations were primarily the result of the deceptive images created by the *arkatia* or recruiters 'on the ground' (Hoefte 1998:34-5; Bhagwanbali 1996:87-9).

'Dutch' recruitment

Only after 1872, when a treaty with the British was ratified, were the Dutch able to recruit labourers from India.[46] This treaty on labour trade only applied

---

and Hoefte (1998:61) are more precise; the former arrives at a total of 34,503 and Hoefte at 34,304. Hoefte (1998:62, 207-8) also gives the annual number of British Indian migrants.

[45]   India's population grew from approximately 120 million in 1800 to 285 million in 1900 (Bhagwanbali 1996:84).

[46]   A long negotiation process had preceded this agreement. The intent of the treaty was to make the recruitment of Indian indentured labour the responsibility of both the British and Dutch (colonial) governments, preventing interference by private enterprise. See Bhagwanbali 1996:53.

to Suriname. Later attempts to secure Indian labour for the Outer Islands of the Dutch East Indies would fail.[47] Central to the treaty was that right from the start the trade would be coordinated and regulated by the British authorities.

The organizational set-up was identical for every country – France, Denmark and the Netherlands – that was allowed to recruit labour in India. The Dutch consul in Calcutta acted as 'Emigration Agent' and was answerable to the British authorities. He was responsible for recruitment and received requests for labour from Suriname. He was also responsible for appointing personnel in charge of organizing the indentured labour trade, such as medical staff, clerks and guards.[48]

As stipulated in the treaty, the Dutch could use the harbours of Madras, Bombay and Calcutta for the gathering and shipping of labourers. In practice, only the harbour at Calcutta in the north-east of India was used, partially due to the fact that the Dutch Emigration Agent was located in that city. Moreover, compared to Madras and Bombay, Calcutta was closest to the most favoured area of recruitment in the north-east provinces of India.[49] Most migrants came from inland villages in the United Provinces, Oudh, Punjab, Bihar and Central India (Bhagwanbali 1996:73).

The Emigration Agent was not directly involved in recruiting 'on the ground'. For that purpose, he appointed subagents, who in turn enlisted the *arkatia* or recruiters. They formed the backbone of the recruiting machinery. Each *arkatia* had to be in possession of a license that the Emigration Agent had to apply for at the British Protector of Emigrants (Bhagwanbali 1996:44, 68).

As in China, malpractice in British India became widespread within recruitment practices. British control may have prevented the worst excesses, but despite governmental regulations there are reports from migrants claiming to have been deceived by their recruiters.[50]

---

[47]   In 1876 the Dutch colonial authorities, urged by planters, started negotiations with the British. However, the Governor General of the Dutch East Indies decided against it when the British demanded the appointment of a British agent in Deli. New negotiations in 1883 and 1888 failed. See Breman 1987:40.

[48]   These appointments required the approval of the Governor of Suriname (Bhagwanbali 1996:58).

[49]   Bhagwanbali (1996:58) notes that since these provinces were the most densely populated, they were the preferred hunting grounds of recruiters.

[50]   After signing a contract – five years for Suriname – migrants were led before a magistrate who asked them if they were leaving the country voluntarily and if they understood their contract. In practice, however, these regulations could be circumvented by unscrupulous *arkatia*. See Hoefte 1999:34-5.

Gender

When looking at the composition of the Indian recruits, some interesting aspects can be gleaned. Although most migrants came from the margins of Indian society, as a whole they represented a cross section of the population. Artisan and high castes made up almost a third of all Indian migrants.[51] Approximately 15.4 per cent of those travelling to Suriname belonged to the highest caste, the Brahmans. They were not wanted by the plantation owners, who believed this group had difficulty adapting to the plantation regime. But the *arkatia* paid no heed to the planters' demands and Brahmans did venture overseas. They may also have experienced fewer impediments to emigrate due to their high standing (Bhagwanbali 1996:86).

Most of the migrants were young men. Only one third brought their families along (Bhagwanbali 1996:156). Plantation owners in Suriname were not interested in attracting female labourers, preferring physically strong males. However, women were also needed, if only to prevent social unrest.[52] According to British stipulations the number of female recruits in relation to male migrants had to be 40:100 – thus 28.5 per cent of the contract workers migrating to Suriname had to be women.[53] Bhagwanbali (1996:98) states that this demand, which previously had been as high as 33 per cent, was probably the result of British experiences with Chinese indentured labourers, who had become demoralized as a result of the lack of women.

The recruiters in India experienced great difficulty in reaching this quota,

---

[51] Northrup (1995:68) asserts that while most were led by desperation, the high percentage of high caste workers indicates that ambition may well have been an important migration factor for British Indians. He points out that ship records from the Madras Presidency to Natal in the period 1860-1902 show that 14.6 per cent of the British Indians migrating to South Africa consisted of the lowest class (Pariah, or Untouchables), indicating that the rest were of higher castes. According to Roopnarine (2007:66-7), some Indian migrants probably lied about their caste in a bid to improve their status in the Caribbean. These practices were not widespread however, since usually it was quite difficult to keep one's real status from fellow countrymen and on the deception being revealed ridicule and even beatings were likely to follow.

[52] Hoefte 1987:86. Emmer (1985:245-66) states that British Indian female migrants often benefited from coming to Suriname. They were provided with an opportunity to improve their existence in more than a material sense, as they often enjoyed more freedom and greater independence than had been possible in India.

[53] There is some confusion surrounding this issue. Emmer (1985:249) notes that this rule was applied after 1860, while Northrup (1995:77) mentions the year 1868. Dalhuizen, Hassankhan and Steegh (2007:103) state that the 40:100 ratio was established in the British-Dutch Treaty that was ratified in 1872. According to Emmer (1985:249), the proportion of women had to be forty per cent, while others, such as Northrup, Hoefte (1987:58, 1998:31) and Dalhuizen, Hassankhan and Steegh (2007:103) note that the ratio had to be 40 women for every 100 men, resulting in a percentage of 28.5. Bhagwanbali (1996:98) sticks to the 'old' regulation of 50 women per 100 men or 33 per cent, which, according to Northrup, was enforced prior to 1868 and is mentioned by both Hoefte (1987:56) and Dalhuizen, Hassankhan and Steegh (2007:103).

one reason being the relative lack of single women in India. Yet a large proportion of the women migrants consisted of single women.[54] Contemporaries
stated that these were primarily widows, prostitutes and outcasts (Hoefte
1987:57; Bhagwanbali 1996:97). Initially, the gender rules were not strictly
enforced and ships bound for Suriname would depart with fewer women
than was officially required. Deficits, however, had to be made up for
over time. And indeed, over the entire period approximately one third of
the migrants shipped to Suriname were women (Bhagwanbali 1996:156),
although at Mariënburg, the largest plantation, the average proportion of
British Indian women arriving between 1897 and 1918 amounted to just less
than 26 per cent.[55]

Java

In contrast to the Dutch position in China and British India, the Dutch on
Java were able to organize labour recruitment themselves. Here I will follow
the generic use of the term 'Javanese' in the literature, which is to say that it
refers to all labourers recruited on the island of Java, despite a minority of
these being recent immigrants.

It is difficult to arrive at an accurate estimate for the total number of
Javanese labourers venturing overseas between 1890 and 1940. Even for
Sumatra's East Coast, which is well documented, figures on the total immigration from Java are incomplete. From the available data[56] it can be estimated that close to a million Javanese went to Sumatra's East Coast (for estimates
and calculations see the subsection 'Javanese' under 'Destinations). The great
majority of these immigrants came with indentured contracts. A considerable
number also went to other parts of the Outer Islands and Malaysia, bringing
the total figure for Javanese migrants to well over a million. Upon expiry of
their contract, the greater part of these labourers would return home. The
number of Javanese migrating to Suriname, 33,000, made up only a very
small portion of this total.

---

[54]   Except for a few years single women were in the majority. For exact numbers, see
Bhagwanbali 1996:96.
[55]   Only in five years was the required percentage achieved. See Hoefte 1987:58.
[56]   The aggregate recruitment figure on Java between 1902 and 1907 gives a yearly average of
12,657 and between 1917 and 1927 of 33,155. Taking into account that demand increased after
1910, the average number for the period between 1902 and 1907 is extended to the period up until
1910. If we take for the period 1911-16 the second, higher average, this all adds up to a yearly
average of 25,563 between 1902 and 1927. This happens to compare nicely with the available
figure of 295,409 for labour migration from Java to Sumatra's East Coast between 1920 and 1930.
See Houben 1999b:42; Langeveld 1975:15; and for the latter data, Gooszen 1999:116.

Recruitment: set-up

In the latter part of the nineteenth century, Java gradually became a centre of labour recruitment. Initial experiments with Javanese indentured labourers started in 1875, when a group was sent to Sumatra's East Coast. In 1890 the first Javanese indentured labourers were sent to Suriname. In the early twentieth century the flow of these indentured migrants expanded rapidly, as the streams of British Indians and Chinese (respectively to Suriname and Sumatra's East Coast) slowly diminished. The Dutch government was in favour of Javanese immigration for both economic and ethical reasons, since one of its goals was to relieve the population pressure on Java in an effort to 'improve' its peasant populace. Indentured migration was seen as one way of reaching this goal.

It is assumed that the recruitment system set up on Java was superimposed on older, more informal networks in existence for centuries. Already in pre-colonial times the Javanese were quite mobile. As a result, many Javanese communities had emerged outside Java. The recruiters on the island made use of these old networks to entice people to sign up for work in the overseas colonies (Houben 1999b:27-8).

In the course of time the recruitment process on the island underwent several developments and changes of direction. Up until 1910, recruitment for firms in the Outer Islands (mainly Sumatra's East Coast) was completely in the hands of professional commercial agencies.[57] In 1910 the planters' associations on Sumatra's East Coast, unhappy with some aspects of the agencies' work, began setting up their own recruitment enterprises. The principal reason for taking this step was the increased demand for labour and the high prices charged by the commercial firms.[58]

A number of planters joined together to form the Algemeen Delisch Emigratie-Kantoor (ADEK, General Deli Emigration Office), formerly the Soesman Agency. Recruitment for Suriname was also directly handled by ADEK for the colonial government (Houben 1999b:34-9). In practice, the ADEK system was more or less a continuation of the old commercial system, including all of its shortcomings. During the 1910s and early 1920s competition to sign up labourers mounted as both commercial and privately owned recruitment organizations struggled to recruit workers. In 1931, after the abolition of the penal clause, the Zuid-West Sumatra Syndicaat (ZWSS, South

[57] Around 1900 two of these agencies controlled the lion's share of the labour supply: Soesman based in Semarang and Falkenberg & De Haas in Batavia.
[58] It was a colonial official who gave the first impetus: labour inspector D.G. Stibbe, who foresaw great problems if the labour supply was not increased through a different recruiting system. According to sources cited by Engelen (1993:16) due to the monopoly of recruiting agents of the commercial agencies, they could ask high prices for 'their' labourers.

Chinese coolies and their overseers, Deli

West Sumatra Syndicate) was set up. It was intended to provide the companies in the Outer Islands – except Sumatra's East Coast – with labourers. It also managed the supply of Javanese labour to regions outside the archipelago, such as New Caledonia and Suriname.[59]

Recruitment: 'regular','laukeh' and 'free'

Over the years, several methods of recruitment were used. 'Regular' recruitment, used by both commercial agencies and planters' associations, made use of henchmen (*handlangers*) and 'recruiters'. The henchmen, in most cases Javanese, handled the actual recruiting, while higher up in the hierarchy the European 'recruiters' were the ones in charge. Both groups were by government order obliged to be in possession of a permit. But in practice, henchmen often operated without one. This was for the most part no hindrance to their activities since government regulations were hardly ever enforced.[60]

Recruiters had trouble finding enough Javanese willing to sign a contract as a result of reports of deception and fraud continuing to appear in newspapers and official documents. It is uncertain how widespread these malpractices were on Java. Houben (1999b:32) argues that they existed, certainly from 1910 onwards, when the demand for labourers in the Outer Islands grew rapidly.[61] Engelen (1993:9) describes how officials 'further down the line' often participated in these malpractices. The depot masters, responsible for registering the recruits in the places of assembly, sometimes forged documents in order to sell labourers to recruiters of other agencies, while (European) doctors and other officials sometimes failed to carry out or enforce the rules and regulations enacted by the government. Some doctors had, for instance, signed medical certificates for people they had not even examined.[62]

The *laukeh* system was another form of labour recruitment on Java, operating in basically the same way as in China. A trusted labourer was sent back to Java by his employer in the Outer Islands (in most cases Sumatra's East Coast) to recruit acquaintances and family members. According to Engelen (1993:27), this system was preferred by both employers and employees

---

[59]   In 1939 Javanese labourers found their way to Suriname via the ZWSS for the first time in ten years. One year earlier, the ZWSS sent forty workers to British Malaya at the request of an oil palm plantation in Johore. See Hayashi 2002:18-21.

[60]   For a more detailed account of the (mal)practices involving permits and such, see Engelen 1993:2-3. In 1914 a new recruitment ordinance was issued, stating that henchmen were no longer required to hold a permit.

[61]   Apart from in 1910, spectacular rises in labour demand occurred between 1915 and 1920 and between 1923 and 1929.

[62]   For a description of the various ways in which some officials and doctors avoided complying with the regulations, see Engelen 1993:7-11.

(*coolies*) since the extent of deceit involved was limited. Labourers signed on generally knowing more or less what they could expect. Unfortunately, however, the *laukeh* system could not provide nearly enough of the labourers required. Between 1917 and 1927 only 41,283 Javanese were recruited in this way, amounting to little more than ten per cent of the total labour supply for that period.[63] This meant that the 'regular' forms of labour recruitment remained dominant.

However, a new form of recruitment emerged after 1910, coexisting with the 'regular' and *laukeh* recruitment practices. It became known as 'free recruitment' and deviated from the other two in one important aspect: long-term labour contracts were not signed on Java itself. This was a violation of the Recruitment Ordinance of 1909, stating that Javanese were prohibited from travelling abroad to work without having agreed upon a contract before embarking.[64] To circumvent this government regulation, labourers on Java signed a contract for the duration of the journey (eight or fourteen days), arriving in the Outer Islands a free man (or woman) and thus able to decide then and there if they wanted to sign a 'real' contract.[65]

In 1927 the Recruitment Ordinance was reformed, making it possible to sign labour contracts outside Java without previously engaging in temporary 'journey contracts' (Engelen 1993:1, 29, 34-6). The colonial government – reluctantly at first – argued that in the long run 'free recruitment' was the only way to establish a Javanese population on Sumatra that would be able to act as a permanent local labour reservoir. After 1927 employers thus had four options to obtain labour: commercial agencies (until 1930), their own recruitment organizations, *laukeh* and free recruitment. The last form of employment was the only one without an indentured contract (Engelen 1993:36).

By the mid-1920s about ten per cent of the total labour force of 250,000 on East Sumatra consisted of 'free' labourers, while the remainder were indentured. The larger part of this 'free' group of 25,000 had signed a new contract after their period of indenture had expired. Under the new law they were now able to sign a 'free' contract. As a result of the abolition of the penal sanction in 1931 the number of 'free labourers' would substantially increase (Houben 1999b:39-41).

---

[63]   I have added the aggregate figure for this period given by Langeveld (1975:15) and compared this to the total *laukeh* recruitment for the same period.

[64]   Javanese were allowed to go to Sumatra (and possibly other areas) as free colonists, as long as they were not employed by planters after their arrival. See Engelen 1993:25.

[65]   This was a problem, as many Javanese wished to go to the Outer Islands as free men. For more details, see Engelen 1993:25.

Rules and regulations: the colonial authorities

As can be inferred from the section above, the role of the (colonial) Dutch government in recruiting Javanese indentured labour was not without significance. While the authorities did not interfere with the actual recruitment or transport of labourers, they did provide the legal framework supporting the system.

Houben (1999b:32-4) concludes that the policy employed by the Dutch authorities held two contradictory elements. On the one hand, it facilitated the operation of the plantations by putting the Coolie Ordinance with the penal sanction in place, resulting in forced labour; on the other hand, it introduced regulations trying to exercise some control over labour conditions and combating its inherent evils. Regulations followed the British example in many cases, such as the issuing of permits, transport and medical care. The Recruitment Ordinance was enacted for this purpose.[66] The Labour Inspectorate (Arbeidsinspectie) was responsible for supervision. In actual fact, however, these efforts often fell short and abuse of the system continued.

Gender

Although most recruits were men, the Javanese, in contrast to the Chinese, often brought their families along with them overseas, resulting in the presence of more women (Hoefte 1990:12). Among the Javanese in Suriname, the male-female ratio was more even than among the British Indian labour population. Between 1897 and 1930 at Mariënburg the average proportion of Javanese women was 31.5 per cent. After the First World War, the Dutch government encouraged the emigration of Javanese families to Suriname. In the period between the First and the Second World War, the number of women arriving from Java sometimes exceeded that of men. According to Hoefte (1987:59), 37 per cent of all Javanese émigrés to Suriname were women.

Destinations

This section will look at the labour movements to Sumatra's East Coast, the Outer Islands and Suriname. It will examine why indentured labourers were attracted to these places and analyse the various outcomes of the interplay between supply and demand. It will discuss the number of people involved

---

[66]   For instance, for married women no work agreements could be made without the consent of their husbands. Recruitment agents had to keep records of their recruits and these were to be sent to the colonial administration; there were also regulations concerning transport and medical care.

in labour migration in each period and also look at how many repatriated and how many never returned. Finally, the legacy of these labour immigrants and their lasting demographic impact on Sumatra's East Coast, the Outer Islands and Suriname will be touched upon.

Sumatra's East Coast

In 1863 pioneer and plantation owner Jacob Nienhuys introduced tobacco to Sumatra's East Coast. Over the following sixty years, the plantation society on Sumatra would gradually expand, finally encompassing an area three times the size of the Netherlands. In 1925 SEC accounted for 33 per cent of the total export value of the Dutch East Indies.[67] Since the local population of Bataks and Malays were too few in number to meet labour demands, the workforce was drawn from other sources.

The labour force

At first, Chinese labour was supplied via the Straits Settlements, but Sumatra's plantation owners urged the Dutch colonial authorities to engage in talks with the British – in 1876 and again in 1883 – to allow the recruitment of labour in British India. The British agreed on the condition that a British representative was stationed in Deli to ensure working conditions were satisfactory. The Dutch Governor General opposed this as he felt this would lead to meddling in domestic affairs. As a result, no official agreement was reached concerning British Indian labour recruitment. But British Indians still travelled to Sumatra. Between 1881 and 1902 their number working on SEC neared 2,000.[68]

Prior to 1900, a considerable amount of the workforce on SEC consisted of Chinese. Before 1880 Chinese coolies arriving on Sumatra's East Coast signed contracts for one year only, but as imposed by the Coolie Ordinance of that year these would become three-year contracts.[69] Apart from these 'contract coolies', or indentured workers, there were also 'day coolies', who worked on a daily and casual basis.[70] As previously mentioned an agreement was reached in 1888 between the Chinese government and a conglomerate of enterprises regarding the recruitment of Chinese labourers in China itself.

---

[67]   See Houben (1999a:2) for export figures between 1898 and 1940.
[68]   Breman (1989:60) gives the composition of the plantation workforce for this period.
[69]   Breman 1989:41. At first, no reason was given for this extension. Planters later argued that only after three years had the worker repaid his debt (advance money and transportation costs) and contributed enough in terms of labour to give the planter a reasonable profit.
[70]   A distinction should be made between this group and 'free workers', a category that would emerge in later years. Free workers did sign a contract, but were not subject to the penal sanction.

This ensured a much greater flow of labour from the country to SEC (Breman 1989:53). Only after 1900 would Javanese labourers start to arrive in the region, often bringing their families along and hence changing the landscape of the society established there.

Number of indentured labourers and periods of recruitment

Early figures for Sumatra's East Coast are incomplete. The number of (contract) labourers fluctuated in accordance with economic cycles. However, information concerning the number of labourers on SEC is available for the post-1880 period. In 1881 almost 18,000 indentured contract workers were employed, next to approximately 3,500 'day coolies'. In 1900 the total number of workers on SEC was close to 100,000. Ten years later, this had increased to a figure somewhere between 108,000 and 125,000, depending on the source.[71] In 1929 an all time high was reached with well over 300,000 workers employed. Throughout the Outer Islands, SEC included, the total number of workers employed in that year reached the half million mark.[72]

Table 6.1 Coolie population on SEC in selected years, 1881-1931

Year	Chinese	Javanese	Total (all workers)
1881	15,500	1,887	22,757
1891	54,715	15,850	83,933
1901	54,489	29,457	93,182
1910	46,619	58,518	108,130
1921	29,145	189,230	220,893
1929	26,819	272,718	302,703
1931	18,484	205,530	225,695

Sources: For 1881-1901, Breman 1989:60; for 1910-31, Lindblad 1999a:72.

Chinese

In the period 1888-1940 it is estimated that somewhere between 200,000 and 300,000 Chinese arrived on Sumatra's East Coast.[73] If the early period (1864-

---

[71]   Lindblad (1999a:72), citing Arbeidsinspectie records, arrives at lower aggregate numbers than Heijting (1925:106), who uses Colonial Reports (*Koloniale Verslagen*).
[72]   Houben 1995:96. Periods seeing considerable growth were 1880-1920 and 1924-29, while the periods 1921-23 and 1930-34 witnessed a decline in the number of contract workers. For an overview of the period 1881-1902, see Breman 1989:60; for 1910-39 see Lindblad 1999a:72.
[73]   According to Breman (1989:57) close to 90,000 Chinese went to SEC between 1888-1900, giving a yearly average of 6,923. Goedhart (2002:147) mentions a considerably lower number of 70,000 Chinese between 1883 and 1900. Van Langenberg (1977:48) notes that between 1888

1887) is included, then several tens of thousands more have to be added. After having reached its peak of nearly 60,000 workers in 1900, the Chinese workforce remained for the most part stable up until 1913, indicating that the yearly influx must have been (considerably) lower than during the twelve years before 1900. How much lower is speculative, since repatriation and (to a larger extent) mortality rates are incomplete.[74] After 1913 the number gradually dropped, followed by an irregular increase during the 1920s.[75] But after 1928 the number dropped sharply as a consequence of the world crisis from which SEC was not spared. The abolition of the penal clause in 1931 also meant that the number of indentured labourers declined. In 1932 only 905 indentured Chinese remained, while the 'free' Chinese labourers numbered 12,918 (Langeveld 1975:83). After 1932 no more indentured Chinese were employed in the region.[76]

Almost all of the Chinese workers were male, most were young and many had an agricultural background. Although many may have planned to return to China, in the early years, up until 1900, approximately only twenty per cent ever did. For some the failure to return was due to (lifelong) indebtedness, while others were satisfied with the new environment and the opportunities it provided. In addition, the high mortality among this group played a part in the low return rates, although mortality rates are unclear for the pre-1900

---

and 1902 'just over 100,000' labourers entered SEC, twenty per cent coming from the Straits Settlements and eighty per cent from China. According to Northrup (1995:61), the number of Chinese arriving on Sumatra between 1876 and 1901 totalled 86,000, with almost all going to the East Coast. Blussé (1988:45) states that between 1880 and 1920 over 100,000 Chinese were transported to Sumatra. My estimates for this forty-year period are considerably higher. Based on a yearly repatriation figure of on average twenty per cent (as cited by Breman for the period 1888-1900) and a population of (on average) approximately 55,000 between 1900 and 1913 (as cited by Heijting 1925:106), the number of Chinese coolies coming in had to be 156,000 during this period alone. In this, mortality has not even been taken into account. Mortality rates for the period 1908-13 for all coolies on SEC fluctuated between 1,997 and 3,182 per cent. Rates for the beginning of the century are considerably higher: circa six per cent for all coolies. Taking four per cent as a safe intermediary figure for the entire period, this would mean that on average 2,200 Chinese died every year. Over the thirteen-year period this would have meant 28,600 died. Added to the total of 156,000, this would have meant that over 180,000 arrived between 1900 and 1913. After 1913 the total number of Chinese decreased almost every year, while the mortality rate also declined, indicating that the influx must have lowered considerably. See also Van Klaveren 1997:114-7.

[74] The number of Chinese labourers leaving SEC was nearly 20,000 (about twenty per cent) for the period 1888-1900. Van Klaveren (1997:114) concludes that mortality rates for SEC are only given for the post-1908 period and that with regard to these figures no distinction was made between different groups of indentured labourers. See also Breman 1992:57.

[75] In 1928 the number was 30,313. See Lindblad 1999a:72. Both Lindblad and Langeveld cite numbers for the periods 1910-38 and 1912/13-39. Often these numbers do not entirely correspond.

[76] The number of 'free' Chinese workers gradually declined to a mere 8,598 in 1939 (Langeveld 1975:84).

period, with speculations ranging from 33 per cent (Breman's (1992:45) highest estimate) to 7.4 per cent (in one hospital, Van Klaveren (1997:115)). After 1900, as a result of better medical care, mortality rates for both Chinese and Javanese labourers declined sharply. Noteworthy is the fact that the Chinese had a far higher mortality rate than the Javanese, however, a difference that continued up until at least 1928, probably to a great extent as a result of their lack of immunity to local diseases (Van Klaveren 1997:118-21).

Javanese

The number of Javanese recruited for Sumatra in the late nineteenth and twentieth century must have amounted to somewhere in the region of 700,000 to one million.[77] On the basis of the available data this must be seen as a conservative estimate.[78]

The first experiment with Javanese indentured labour for SEC was conducted in 1875. Employers were not content with these migrants, however, who were considered lazy and unsuitable for work on the tobacco plantations. Nonetheless, as worries about the future of the Chinese labour supply were mounting – due to the Chinese government threatening to take action unless working conditions were improved – the eyes of the planters once again turned to Java. Since the introduction of new crops, the wage system had also changed from task to daily wages. The latter was more suited to the Javanese, who according to the planters had never reacted to the incentive of a higher reward for a greater effort. Adding to the appeal of the Javanese worker was

[77]   Gooszen (1999:38) gives a figure of 736,049 migrants from Java to Sumatra between 1900 and 1930. These were not all labourers, however, since this number also included other migrants, such as colonists. Emmer and Shlomowitz (1997:125) propose 'a very rough estimate' of 700,000 Javanese indentured labourers going to locations in the Dutch East Indies (mainly SEC) from the late nineteenth century until the 1930s. They add that approximately 100,000 indentured Javanese went to locations outside the Dutch East Indies from the late nineteenth century until the 1930s.

[78]   By 1917 over 170,000 Javanese workers had already populated the region. Between 1917 and 1930 another 490,000 were recruited on Java for SEC's plantations, while in the same period 230,000 returned to Java. Since repatriation rates were high (although unknown for the period up until 1917) an additional number of labourers for the pre-1917 period must be added to this figure. Between 1917 and 1930 the repatriation percentage in some years far exceeded the number of incoming labourers. In other years it fluctuated around thirty per cent. Even when taking the lowest repatriation percentage available, twenty per cent for 1917, this would mean that one fifth of 170,000 must be added, thus 34,000. Adding this to the figures mentioned, this would result in at least 700,000 indentured Javanese (and, in later years, 'free') workers migrating to SEC. Mortality (and indeed fertility, which must have been low considering the low ratio of women) has not been taken into account here. See Langeveld 1975:15, 18. The numbers in Langeveld's tables are added up, giving the total number recruited as 489,708 between 1917 and 1930. Repatriation percentages are also derived from the tables.

his more 'docile' nature and the lower cost. Since Javanese women were also encouraged to migrate, on average the wages became even lower, as women were paid less than men. As a result, the previously negligible female population on SEC increased substantially (Breman 1989:61-3; Lindblad 1999a:73).

British Indians

Besides Chinese and Javanese, small numbers of British Indians from South India (Klings) also came to SEC. Only a few scholars mention their presence there. Between 1881 and 1901, the number of British Indians on Sumatra's East Coast increased to 4,140 (Breman 1992:44). After 1902 their numbers apparently remained quite stable – in 1912 and 1913 fluctuating around 4,200 before gradually declining in the latter period. During the 1930s on average only about 500 British Indians ('free' labourers) worked on Sumatra's East Coast plantations on a yearly basis (Langeveld 1975:83-4).

The 'other' Outer Islands

When looking at indentured labour, attention has almost exclusively been focused on Sumatra's East Coast (Lindblad 1999b:79). Therefore it is easy to forget that SEC only made up part of the entire (indentured) labour migration to the Dutch East Indies. Fifteen other regions in the Outer Islands were to a greater or lesser extent affected. Data regarding these territories are scarce, but an attempt is made here to summarize the available information, especially regarding the number of indentured labourers going to these regions. Most of the material is derived from Houben et al (1999). Three regions are given special attention: Bangka and Belitung, Southeast Kalimantan and West Sumatra – partly due to their relative economic importance (Bangka and Belitung, Southeast Kalimantan) and partly because the data regarding these areas are more voluminous (West Sumatra).[79]

In 1913 Sumatra's East Coast was responsible for forty per cent of the total revenue generated on the Outer Islands (120 million guilders of a total of 320 million). Sixteen years later, in 1929, this had declined to one-third of the total revenue. The prospering economies on the other Outer Islands, particularly Bangka and Belitung, Southeast Kalimantan and Palembang, were responsible for this shift (Lindblad 1999b:83-4).

---

[79]   For absolute numbers of coolies in these and other (minor) regions, see Lindblad 1999b:101-7 (tables).

Bangka and Belitung: tin mining centre of the archipelago

Bangka and Belitung, two neighbouring islands off the coast of southeast Sumatra, are usually referred to as a single unit, primarily because of their shared economic importance as the centre of tin mining in the Dutch East Indies as well as in present-day Indonesia.[80]

On both islands Chinese (indentured) labour was of principal importance during the entire colonial period. On Bangka at most times 95 per cent of the indentured population consisted of Chinese.[81] After resistance from China against recruitment intensified, employers did begin to look to Java and other Indonesian islands for workers, although only relatively few were actually recruited: in 1927 320 Javanese contract labourers were employed on Bangka, in addition to 900 'free' Sundanese and Buginese workers. In 1936 all contract workers were Chinese, while of the free workers 614 were Javanese (Somers Heidhues 1992:115, 132). The penal sanction was never officially abolished on the island, but instead died a slow death with declining recruitment in the 1930s.[82] By 1931, on Belitung contracts under the penal clause were no longer

---

[80] In 1722 the VOC gained a trade monopoly on Bangka's vast tin deposits. This commodity was mined by Chinese kongsis via representatives of the Sultan of Palembang. After the British interregnum ended, the Dutch government took direct control over Bangka's mines. This implied for instance that the Dutch envoy (resident) on the island (after 1913 the Director of Mining) decided on matters such as the required number of labourers. On Belitung mining operations began considerably later. In 1852 a group of prospectors was granted a concession by the Dutch government for the mining of tin on the island. This concession was taken over by the Billiton Maatschappij in 1860. In 1892, when the agreement ended, the Dutch colonial government appointed three representatives to the corporation's board of directors, while at the same time laying claim to five-eights of its net profits. In 1928 both 'partners' formed a new corporation called the Gemeenschappelijke Mijnbouw Maatschappij Billiton (Billiton Joint Mining Company). There is also a third tin island: Singkep, considerably smaller than the other two. Mining there started in 1889, when the Singkep Company gained a concession from the Sultan of Lingga to mine tin deposits. In 1934 this company was taken over by the Billiton Joint Mining Company. See Kaur and Diehl 1996:97-100.

[81] As mentioned in the section on Chinese recruitment, labour for Bangka – as well as other regions in the Outer Islands, including SEC – was initially acquired via Chinese middlemen (coolie brokers) in Singapore. Later on private firms recruited directly in China. As of 1907, labourers were directly brought to the Outer Islands from Hong Kong. The *Holland-China Handels Compagnie* (Holland China Trading Company) brought Chinese coolies from Hong Kong to Mentok, Bangka's northwestern harbour. The recruitment process on Chinese soil was a clandestine activity, as Chinese officials strongly opposed it. Experiments involving *laukeh* failed on Bangka, whereas on Belitung they were – for unknown reasons – successful. A new labourer brought to the island via this system was usually free to change his workplace and join a *numpang* (the Belitung equivalent of the kongsi) after one year. The main difference between workers on Bangka and Belitung was that on the latter island they were considered 'free' after having paid off their recruitment costs. See Kaur and Diehl 1996:109-10; Somers Heidhues 1992:112-3.

[82] In 1930 workers on Bangka with more than five years of service were free to sign a contract without the penal sanction. As a result, the number of 'free' contracts rose in the following years,

Female workers threading tobacco, Deli

offered (Lindblad 1999b:87-8).

Since data are incomplete it is impossible to determine exactly how many indentured labourers travelled to the tin islands of Bangka and Belitung.[83] What we do know, is that the average number of workers employed on both islands was greatest in the period between 1906 and 1930.[84] According to accumulated data gathered by Lindblad, the contract worker population of Bangka amounted to around 20,000 between 1910 and 1928 before declining. Up until the late 1920s the number of 'free coolies' was exceptionally low on the island. After that time this figure drastically changed and by 1934 three of every four labourers were 'free'.[85]

Belitung reached a maximum (on average) of 19,582 workers between 1921 and 1925. The number of contract labourers on the island rose from 14,528 in 1910 to as many as 20,370 in 1921. After this period, the number of contract labourers declined, while free workers were on the rise as of 1925. After 1932 apparently no more contract coolies were employed on Belitung (Lindblad 1999b:103).

From 1929 onwards the international economic crisis wreaked havoc among the businesses on Bangka and Belitung. As a result, labour recruitment gradually came to a halt.[86] A great many Chinese returned home, while others went to Java or Sumatra.[87] In 1936 the importation of Chinese labourers commenced once again, but would remain limited until 1940, when 1,877 Chinese workers were imported. By the late 1930s, Javanese free labourers had begun to join Bangka's workforce (Somers Heidhues 1992:112, 132). On Belitung the decline was even more drastic: in 1933 only 4,000 Chinese tin

---

partly strengthened by the fact that locally recruited labour was not subject to the sanction. The number of 'penal sanction' labourers thus decreased, both in terms of percentages and (later) in absolute numbers. In 1940 the number of indentured workers actually increased as a result of the rising influx from China. See Somers Heidhues 1992:116.

[83]   As stated by Kaur and Diehl: 'Often different sources give different figures without stating whether these are annual averages, end of production year or end of financial year figures' (Kaur and Diehl 1996:111).

[84]   More information is available for the period between 1910 and 1938. Kaur and Diehl give an average number of employed workers, while Somers Heidhues (1992:116) makes the distinction between 'free' and 'penal sanction' (indentured) workers for a number of years. Besides giving information regarding labourers on Bangka and Belitung (1866-1938), Kaur and Diehl (1996:97-100) also shed some light on the situation on Singkep, the smallest and most under-researched tin island.

[85]   Lindblad 1999b:87-8. For a complete overview of the importation of coolies to Bangka, see Somers Heidhues 1992:112. For data regarding the number of coolies employed between 1910 and 1938, see Lindblad 1999b:103.

[86]   In 1929 6,715 coolies were brought to Bangka, while in the following years this influx diminished, coming to a complete stop in 1933 (Somers Heidhues 1992:112).

[87]   A second wave of a 'few thousand' Chinese people repatriated after the Second World War. For more details on the reasons for repatriation and the laws that Bangka's Chinese were subjected to, see Somers Heidhues 1992:219-20.

miners remained (Somers Heidhues 1992:178-9).

On both islands the workforce almost exclusively consisted of men. The strains of mine labour and the composition of the Chinese labour force had everything to do with this.[88] But in 1920 the gender ratio among the non-mining Chinese population of Belitung was 1.6 males per 1 female, indicating that the Chinese outside the mines were a relatively settled group by that year.[89]

Southeast Kalimantan: oil and 'freedom'

As of the late nineteenth century, labourers were recruited to work on Southeast Kalimantan, with at least 75 per cent coming from Java. The Chinese – who were almost exclusively employed in coal mining and the oil industry – made up circa ten to fifteen per cent of the entire workforce.[90] In this region, the number of 'free' coolies (without penal sanction) was relatively high. Employers in the oil industry preferred free contracts, due to the nature of the work, such as the construction of pipelines in remote areas, which precluded close surveillance. As a result, semi-skilled labourers, who were relatively thin on the ground, had to be bonded in other ways, such as through higher wages (Lindblad 1999b:84-5, 87).

Data on the number of labourers on Southeast Kalimantan are, as elsewhere, incomplete. Between 1911 and 1929 the total figure (both indentured and 'free' workers) rose from 11,637 to 36,340 before (drastically) declining in the following years. Between 1911 and 1920 the number of contract labourers under the penal clause lay somewhere around 8,500. This category of workers reached a highpoint of 16,675 in 1927. After that time, numbers dropped, with only 58 workers still falling under the penal clause in 1938. The number of 'free' workers increased correspondingly from 1,593 in 1917 to 24,627 in 1929. On Southeast Kalimantan gender ratios followed familiar lines: Chinese coolies were virtually all male, although marked differences can be seen between the types of enterprise.[91]

---

[88]   Lindblad 1999b:87-8. According to Somers Heidhues (1992:150) on Bangka in 1897 circa 3,000 of the 15,000 coolies (twenty per cent) were married (to local women), although this probably included miners who were born locally, since in 1905 ninety per cent of the Chinese contract coolies were unmarried.

[89]   For more details regarding these figures, see Somers Heidhues 1992:150, 175-9.

[90]   The remainder of the workforce (about ten to fifteen per cent) came from other areas in the Outer Islands. After 1930 the composition changed, with the percentages of Javanese and Chinese dropping to respectively seventy and five per cent in the late 1930s. The segment of locals and 'others' increased to approximately 25 per cent. See Nierop 1999:159.

[91]   Between 1910 and 1920, the ratio of men to women was 10:1 in the mine and oil industry, while in the rubber industry this figure was about 3:1. In 1929 the ratio of Javanese men to women was around 12.5 to 1. See Nierop 1999:159-60, 171.

West Sumatra: the Ombilin coal mines

In 1868 a rich coalfield was discovered near the Ombilin River in West Sumatra. The state mines established there, usually referred to as Ombilin Mines, became the largest coal producer in the Netherlands East Indies. Four kinds of labourers were employed in the mines: convicts, contractual (indentured) labourers, 'free' and casual workers. Contract workers were recruited on Java, while the 'free' coolies were (before 1930) former contract workers, thus (in most cases) also Javanese. Casual workers were recruited locally. The proportion and number of these labourers varied considerably over the years (Van Empel 1999:179, 182-3). Although they were the dominant industry, Ombilin Mines were not West Sumatra's only employer. In 1929 over 25,000 labourers worked throughout the region.[92]

As was generally the case, the labour force in the mines consisted almost exclusively of men. Between 1905 and 1930, women only made up about five per cent of the coolie population.[93] The shift from indentured to 'free' labour occurred swiftly in this region. By 1933 very few workers still toiled under the penal sanction (Lindblad 1999b:91).

Other regions

In Palembang, on Sumatra's Southeast Coast, between 1920 and 1929 the number of coolies increased enormously. In the former year, only about 10,000 contract labourers were present in the area, while nine years later this figure had quadrupled. Here, the proportion of 'free' coolies was strikingly large, long before the penal sanction's abolition – roughly fifty per cent by the early 1920s and 65 per cent by 1930. The nature of work within the oil industry explains this seemingly remarkable fact. It also explains the relatively high number of men. On the agricultural estates the differences were considerably less pronounced (Lindblad 1999b:84-5).

On Aceh, on the northern tip of Sumatra, aggregate figures for contract labourers were as high as 15,000 in 1917. Ten years later, this number had exceeded the 20,000 mark. Although the oil industry preferred 'free' coolies – as in Palembang and Southeast Kalimantan – in the 1920s the majority of the workers on rubber and palm estates were indentured. Gender ratios were

[92]   Coffee and copra estates were also in operation on West Sumatra. See Lindblad 1999b:91, 101, 104 (tables).
[93]   In the vicinity of the mines the percentage of women was higher, as women contract coolies generally did not sign any new contracts when they got married. The colonial authorities made an effort to increase the number of women workers to prevent, or alleviate, unrest among the male population. By 1925, the percentage of women living at the mines (most were not employed there) climbed to about 25 per cent. See Van Empel 1999:184.

around 3:1 in the late 1920s and 1930s (Lindblad 1999b:89-90).

Lampung, the utmost southern province of Sumatra, is best known for the 'colonization' programme instigated there from 1905 onwards. These colonization efforts by the Dutch government were meant to relieve the population pressure on Java, but also, and perhaps more so, served to provide regional enterprises with labour. The 'colonist Javanese' migrating to Lampung were not indentured, although some signed contracts upon arrival. In a way, 'guided' labour migration and 'free' colonization met each other halfway here. The colonists were not recruited in the 'normal' way, but selected by their village chiefs. Often, these *lurah* used their position to get rid of anyone deemed unfit to remain in their village, such as the elderly and petty criminals (Heeren 1967:14).

The first (experimental) colonization phase ended in 1911. At that time, 4,818 Javanese were still in Lampung. Only later, in the 1930s, would the number of 'transmigrants' to Lampung and other parts of South Sumatra become substantial. Between 1933 and 1941 over 220,000 'free' Javanese crossed the sea to settle in Lampung and other parts of South Sumatra. On the eve of the Second World War, 175,000 people of Javanese descent were living there. Not surprisingly, as early as the 1920s Lampung boasted a very high percentage of 'free' coolies, which had reached circa fifty per cent by 1928. In 1931 the abolition of the penal clause only affected about thirty per cent of the total workforce. Since colonization by families was preferred, the gender ratio was not too extreme, at 2.5:1 or less (Lindblad 1999b:93-4).

Suriname

After the abolition of the African slave trade imposed by the British in 1807 and anticipating the actual abolition of slavery (eventually enacted in 1863 in the Dutch territories), the Dutch government started facing the problem of attracting additional labour as of the 1840s. In 1845 a number of Dutch farmers were brought in, followed by Portuguese from Madeira (1853-1854, 1863-1864) and 1,500 Free Blacks from Barbados. Between 1872 and 1874 ninety European labourers arrived.[94] As none of these schemes became successful, colonial government and private enterprise turned to the recruitment of Asian indentured labour. In total, approximately 70,000 indentured labourers would arrive in Suriname between 1853 and 1939, with the overwhelming majority coming from British India (about 35,000) and Java (about 33,000) (Hoefte 1987:55).

By 1940, there were 42,538 British Indians in Suriname, making up thirty per cent of the total population. The Javanese numbered 31,681 in that year

---

[94]   Hassankhan 1995:61; Hoefte 1990:1. Many of the last group of Madeirans died.

(22 per cent of the population).[95] Due to both negative and positive factors most of these migrants would remain in Suriname. Some were ashamed to return home having failed to realize their high hopes. Others gave up their right to a free return passage in exchange for money and still others became tired of waiting for a ship to take them back. Among the positive factors was the fact that many former contract labourers managed to improve their position in Suriname while others – especially single British Indian women – were able to enjoy their freedom after indenture had ended.

Chinese

The importation of Chinese indentured labourers into Suriname cautiously began, under government supervision, in 1853.[96] Eighteen Chinese were recruited on Java, with fourteen surviving the voyage to the Caribbean.[97] In 1858 another group of 500 Chinese arrived, this time directly from China (the harbour of Macao).[98] Another 2,000 Chinese were shipped to the colony by private enterprise between 1865 and 1869. After that time, Chinese indentured trade was prohibited so that from China no more labourers were brought to Suriname.

This abrupt end to the influx of Chinese was not regretted by the plantation owners, who had been discontent with this labour supply, due to the fact that it was costly and never supplied substantial numbers of labourers.[99] In addition, Chinese labourers were not eager to 're-engage' (sign new con-

[95]   The total number of British Indians in Suriname remained relatively stable during the entire period, numbering 16,004 or 24 per cent of the colony's total population in 1896. In 1905 this figure had increased to 18,944, still 24 per cent. The Javanese population, on the other hand, increased rapidly after 1896, from 667 (one per cent) in that year to 6,330 (eight per cent) in 1905, to 31,681 (22 per cent) in 1940. For all figures between 1896 and 1940, see Hoefte 1998:79.
[96]   Contrary to Chinese migration movements in Southeast Asia and North America, Chinese migration to the Caribbean remains a topic that, in the words of Andrew R. Wilson (2004:xv), is 'poorly understood and largely un-chronicled'.
[97]   Man A Hing 1993:51-2; Look Lai 2004:21. Ankum-Houwink (1985:183) writes that fifteen Chinese survived the voyage, while four died in Suriname before the end of their indenture. Apparently, these first indentured labourers were treated more or less like slaves by the planters despite their (five-year) contracts. After these contracts had expired, only three could be convinced to stay.
[98]   Look Lai 2000:32. According to Ankum-Houwink (1985:183) the contracts of this group were actually changed while the ship was already on its way to Suriname. The planters wanted the contracts changed and the government succumbed to their demands. Among the changes were stipulations regarding payment (by task instead of by month), the possibility to return workers who did not live up to expectations and the right of supervisors to withhold part of the payment when tasks were not performed according to their standards.
[99]   Northrup 1995:28; Hassankhan 1995:62. Apparently, the planters had asked for over 4,000 indentured labourers in the second half of the 1860s. Only 2,000 were actually delivered. See Ankum-Houwink 1985:183.

tracts). The last 115 indentured Chinese arrived from Java between 1872 and 1874.[100] In total, just under 3,000 Chinese indentured labourers were shipped to Suriname between 1853 and 1874. The endeavour could hardly be called a success, as the intention had been to bring approximately 25,000 indentured Chinese during the ten-year period of Staatstoezicht (State Supervision) alone.[101] Approximately one third of the Chinese indentured labourers in Suriname returned to either China or the Dutch East Indies (Man A Hing 1993:55). The lack of Chinese women in Suriname was an important factor for this repatriation.[102] Between 1865 and 1869, 14.7 per cent of the Chinese indentured labour population in the colony consisted of women (Northrup 1995:28). Since no indentured Chinese women arrived prior to or since that period, one may conclude that this must have been the figure for the entire Chinese coolie trade to Suriname.[103]

Percentages regarding mortality rates among Chinese contract labourers in Suriname are known for the period between 1870 and 1881. According to the available data mortality was (somewhat) higher than three per cent for most of these years.[104] In comparison with estimates from SEC (see above) this number does not seem very high, but in common with Sumatra's East Coast, reliable data regarding mortality rates for Suriname are either lacking or unreliable.

British Indians

On 8 September 1870, after laborious negotiations with the British government, the Netherlands received permission to recruit Indian labourers in British India.[105] But mortality among the first groups of British Indians was

[100]   They were imported for sugar plantation De Resolutie in the Commewijne District.

[101]   In the twenty years between 1853 and 1874, according to Look Lai (2004:8, 21-3), around 2,945 Chinese indentured labourers set foot on Suriname's soil. Northrup (1995:28, 156) gives a somewhat higher figure, concluding that 2,979 indentured Chinese arrived in the West Indian colony. He is less specific about the period in which they arrived, as he gives the total decennial influx between 1851 and 1880. Most Chinese (2,015) came to Suriname in the latter part of the 1860s.

[102]   The Chinese population did not grow (despite free migration after 1874) and consisted of only 1,160 people in 1905. This is mainly attributed to the fact that most Chinese men married local women. Their offspring were not classified as Chinese (Tseng 1991:17).

[103]   Look Lai (2004:21-4) gives an account of the entire list of vessels transporting Chinese coolies to the Caribbean between 1853 and 1884. According to his data, the only ship carrying a substantial number of women was the *Tricolor*, arriving in Suriname in 1865, carrying 120 women (41 per cent of all workers on board).

[104]   In 1875 the mortality rate was as high as 5.1 per cent. For all (available) data for the period 1870-81, see Lamur and Vriezen 1985:174-5.

[105]   These negotiations had been instigated by the Colonial States (local parliament) of Suriname and planters. See also above.

alarmingly high, leading to the suspension of the trade by the British in 1875. Two years later the trade was resumed. Beginning in 1873 and ending in 1917, approximately 35,000 British Indian indentured labourers arrived.[106]

Despite numerous advantages[107] the British Indians as a group also posed problems for the Dutch colonial authorities. Their greatest worry was the danger that with a continued large influx of Indian migrants, who retained their English nationality, a large proportion of Suriname's population would eventually be British.[108] After 1917 no more indentured British Indians arrived in the colony. By that time the Dutch had found another source of labour: the Javanese.

Between 1878 and 1947 circa 34 per cent of all British Indians repatriated, a percentage similar to that of the Chinese.[109] The caste system made it especially difficult for higher caste British Indians to return, as they had in all likelihood lost their elevated status by crossing the 'black waters'. This could be further exacerbated by marrying lower caste members, as some had done (Hoefte 1998:63). But there were also positive factors for staying. In general, Indian workers were able to considerably increase their standard of living by moving to the Caribbean. Their general well-being also improved, as can be derived from lower average mortality rates in the destination areas (Emmer 2004:85). Emmer adds that for British Indian women, Suriname provided more freedom and an escape from a culture hostile to single women (Emmer 1985:250). For those migrants reaping the benefits of their new home, the possibility to return to India offered little appeal.

As stated above, the British had stipulated that at least 33 and later 28.5 per cent of the British Indians leaving for Suriname had to be women. A more equal gender ratio in the workforce also seemed to be in the interest of Suriname's planters, as they had had bad experiences with Chinese men due to the lack of women in their group. Although data are not conclusive, the

---

[106] From 1877 onwards workers had a choice between performing task labour or working a seven-hour day. In practice, however, labourers rarely worked for only seven hours per day. See Emmer 1984:100. For an overview of the immigration of British Indians (and Javanese) into Suriname between 1873 and 1942, see Hoefte 1998:62. Emmer (1985:262) gives an overview of the number of indentured British Indians in Suriname between 1873 and 1916.

[107] According to Northrup (1995:28) the Chinese had a better reputation than the British Indians: 'viewed as less reliable than the Chinese, Indian labourers could be obtained in steady lots at predictable prices through arrangements worked out with the British authorities'.

[108] Other disadvantages were the fact that being British subjects, the Indians were able to appeal to the British consul in Paramaribo against decisions made by the Dutch government and that the British could at any time decide to end migration from India, leaving Suriname vulnerable. See Hoefte 1990:6-7.

[109] For the period 1878-1947 Goslinga (1990:513) concludes that 11,690 of 34,024 British Indians repatriated – a percentage of 34.4. Hoefte (1998:63) notes that for the period 1878-1920 the repatriation percentage was 33.9.

percentages seem to have been achieved: between 1873 and 1916 the proportion of British Indian female migrants was in all likelihood approximately 33 per cent.[110]

Mortality rates of British Indians as well as Javanese (and Creoles) are incomplete or unreliable. According to Hoefte not all deaths were registered, drastically altering the overall mortality rate.[111] Emmer (1985:255, 263) has made calculations on basis of the available evidence for the period 1873-1916, concluding that the crude mortality rate for British Indians was 2.74 per cent. Lamur computed that between 1877 and 1921 this rate was 12.9 per 1,000 (or 1.3 per cent).[112] From these data we can infer that mortality rates were considerably lower in Suriname than in India, a difference partially explained by the atypical population structure in the colony which was a result of the fact that most migrants were young and relatively healthy.[113]

Javanese

The Dutch East Indian government prohibited the (labour) migration of its Javanese subjects to other countries. Only in extraordinary cases would the Dutch Governor General allow an exception to this rule (Hoefte 1990:7). Suriname was interested in acquiring Javanese labour for its plantations. After much deliberation, it was agreed that there would be an experiment with Javanese indentured labourers. They would sign five-year contracts, as was customary in the colony, and these contracts were modelled on those of the British Indians that had arrived earlier.[114]

In 1890, 94 Javanese were shipped from Java via Amsterdam to Suriname. Upon arrival, they did not seem to understand their contract, although it was 'explained' to them prior to signing.[115] Despite these unsteady beginnings,

---

[110]   Bhagwanbali 1996:156. Emmer (1985:262) lists the number of indentured British Indians in Suriname between 1873 and 1916. The number of women in this group is roughly one third. Many female recruits did not hail from the agricultural sector, as the agent for Suriname noted in 1878: 'Their number was considerably augmented by a batch of dancing-girls and women of a similar description with their male attendants. These people laughed at the idea of labouring as agriculturalists' (Emmer 1985:252).

[111]   According to Hoefte (1998:77), in the nineteenth and the beginning of the twentieth century mortality per ethnic group was not recorded in official reports. Strangely enough, Emmer (1985:261, 263) does give (exact) mortality figures for the entire period between 1873 and 1916 for the British Indians, on the basis of *Koloniale Verslagen* and reports by the British consul in Suriname.

[112]   Lamur cited in Hoefte 1998:77.

[113]   Emmer (1985:255) notes that mortality rates in Suriname and India in the period 1873-1916 were respectively 27.4 and 42.76 per thousand.

[114]   A special commission was appointed by the Dutch government in The Hague to investigate the possibility of Javanese labour migration. See Hoefte 1998:44-9.

[115]   Hoefte (1998:48) discusses one occasion where an 'overseer took the new labourers to the

Suriname's estate owners gradually came to the conclusion that the Javanese were 'more manageable' than the British Indians (Hoefte 1998:49). In the years up until 1939, many more Javanese would migrate to Suriname, mostly as indentured labourers. The total number of Javanese was slightly lower than that of the British Indians: circa 33,000. They arrived between 1890 and 1939.[116] After 1931 they were no longer indentured, but arrived as free labourers or colonists (or both). Averaged by year, most Javanese arrived after 1918, following the end of the British Indian influx (Hoefte 1998:62).

Approximately 28 per cent of the Javanese returned home, mostly before the Second World War.[117] Both positive and negative reasons contributed to the fact that the majority of Javanese – in common with other migrant groups – would remain in Suriname. However, more so than with other groups, the desire to one day return home would remain strong, especially among the older Javanese. As late as 1975 a small number of Javanese would still repatriate.[118]

The Dutch authorities made an effort to recruit Javanese women, having learned from the experiences with both the Chinese and British Indian men. In actual fact, even more Javanese than British Indian women would eventually arrive. In the period between the two World Wars, the number of Javanese women sometimes exceeded the number of men. In total 37 per cent of the Javanese group in Suriname were women (Hoefte 1987:59).

As is the case with the other ethnic groups, mortality rates are incomplete and/or unreliable. Calculations by Lamur indicate a crude mortality rate among Javanese indentured workers of 1.4 per cent for the period 1895 until 1933, thus slightly higher than among British Indian workers.[119]

---

highest official in the district of Beneden Commewijne, and the latter explained their obligations in no uncertain terms. Upon his remark that unwillingness to work was punishable by a term in jail, many "started to walk to the prison immediately".'

[116]   According to Hoefte (1998:61), the total number of Javanese migrating to Suriname was 32,962.

[117]   Repatriation figures differ from source to source. According to Dalhuizen, Hassankhan and Steegh (2007:109) up until 1954, 9,384 Javanese returned home of a total of 32,956, amounting to 28.5 per cent. Obviously, this percentage is lower (circa 23 per cent) if the post-Second World War period is not included. Figures cited by other authors do not cover the entire period. Goslinga (1990:513) covers 1878-1947 and gives a Javanese repatriation figure of circa 25 per cent for this period.

[118]   Several Javanese leaders in Suriname (Anton de Kom, Ideng Soemita and Paul Salem Somohardjo) made promises to the Javanese migrants to make their wish of returning to Java a reality. Somohardjo was instrumental in the return of several hundred Javanese to the Netherlands. Some of these later arrived in Indonesia. See Hoefte 1990:21.

[119]   Lamur cited in Hoefte 1998:77.

Javanese transmigrants disembark in Lampung on the journey to their new village

'Dutch' indentured labour on foreign shores

Apart from labourers moving in and between Dutch colonies, a number of 'Dutch' indentured workers also went to foreign regions.[120] Foremost, these were Javanese travelling to destinations such as Malaysia, New Caledonia and British North Borneo.[121] Between 1909 and 1939 nearly 60,000 of them migrated to these and other parts of the world, excluding those going to Suriname. Most, but not all, of these workers went under indenture.[122] About 25,000 returned to their home country. Data for most of these migration streams are incomplete at best.

Between 1909 and 1938 approximately 25,000 Javanese ventured to Malaysia, mainly during the 1910s, when on a yearly basis 'many thousands' went to the Straits Settlements and the Federated Malay States. They became an important ethnic group in the Pahang province, making up almost 25 per cent of the total labour population (Houben 1998:58-9). As a result of the contract coolie movements, by 1930 89,735 residents born on Java and 170,000 ethnic Javanese were living in Malaya (Hugo 1993:37). During the 1930s the labour movement increased and in 1947 the number of Java-born residents was 189,450. In 1947 Malaysia was also home to 62,400 Banjarese from South Kalimantan and 26,300 Sumatrans, alongside 20,400 born on Bawean and

---

[120]   From 1887 until 1897 the Dutch East Indies government prohibited all emigration of workers to countries with which it had no official recruitment agreements. This was made law in 1887 (*Staatsblad* 1887 no.7). During the following 25 years, until 1922, the supervision on recruitment was suspended (Vreede 1928:18). For information regarding numbers of Javanese contract labourers to 'foreign' countries and numbers of repatriates for the 1920s and 1930s, see *Indisch Verslag* 1933:185, 1935:191, 1940:251.

[121]   In the West, a few thousand inhabitants of Curaçao and Aruba found employment within the region, primarily on Cuba. After 1863 former slaves from Curaçao migrated voluntarily to countries in the region where they could find employment. Small numbers of Curaçaons went to places such as Costa Rica, Panama, Colombia, Santo Domingo, Suriname and Cuba. After the First World War, labour migration from Curaçao was massive and almost exclusively male dominated, with at times fifty per cent of the male population migrating to work in Cuba's cane fields. In 1919 a peak was reached with 1,900 men leaving Curaçao for Cuba. In total, circa 2,000 male labourers left the island. After 1921 most workers would gradually return. See Allen 2006b:82-3, 2006a:113. From Aruba, 4,072 labourers left for Cuba between 1917 and 1922, while the other major destination was Venezuela, where 3,901 workers went between 1891-1920. Over 1,500 labourers left Aruba for Curaçao and Suriname (302 between 1901 and 1905). See Pietersz 1985:63-71. These labour migrants, however, were 'free' workers, who for the most part signed short-term contracts. Some individual migrants did not sign a contract prior to departure and went abroad independently. No records are kept for this group (Pietersz 1985:63).

[122]   According to 'The Netherlands Indian Labourers Protection Ordinance' Javanese labourers were required to sign a contract under the supervision of a Dutch official. This contract was valid for no more than 900 days and was subject to a penal sanction. After expiry, these labourers were either sent back to Java or could continue working under 'verbal' contracts on a monthly basis. See Vreede 1928:18.

7,000 born on Celebes (Hugo 1993:37).

From the beginning of the twentieth century, the French colony of New Caledonia needed labourers for its plantations and nickel mines. During the 1920s and 1930s more than 15,000 Javanese left to work on the island. Most of them – nearly 8,000 – were sent by the ZWSS in the six years between 1933 and 1939 – 86 per cent of the total Javanese workforce leaving Java during the thirties.[123] They signed contracts for five years (Ward 1988:82). The 1946 census indicated that New Caledonia was home to 8,641 Javanese. Apparently, most Javanese contract labourers were not inclined to stay. 75 per cent (15,000) repatriated upon expiry of their contract (Maurer 2002:1). Roosman (1971:63) notes that after the Second World War, when they were freed from their contracts of indenture 'nostalgic Javanese flocked from the countryside to Noumea [the capital] to await repatriation'. Those remaining were later given the opportunity to acquire French nationality by way of naturalization. The Javanese population on the island would remain small, with only 2,900 in 1955 (Ward 1988:85) and in 1963 representing just four per cent of the total population of New Caledonia (Roosman 1971:71).

During the 1920s more than 7,000 Javanese went to British North Borneo (*Indisch Verslag* 1935:191), where their proportion of the total plantation workforce increased from 25 per cent in 1918 to forty per cent in 1928 (Houben 1998:58-9). A small number – a few hundred during the 1920s – of Javanese also went to Cochin China (*Indisch Verslag* 1935:191) and to Australia. Concrete numbers for Australia are unavailable, but it is certain that migration started in the 1870s and 1880s. It must have been a small group, considering the restrictive immigration policies implemented in the late nineteenth century to keep Australia 'white'. Some indication of scale is given by the fact that around 1900 circa 1,000 Indonesians were in Australia, mostly in Queensland and Western Australia (Coughlan 1992; Hoefte 1990:8).

Comparisons and conclusions

Recruitment

The history of indentured labour in the Dutch colonial sphere is multifaceted. As far as recruitment is concerned, the earliest labour migrants were in most cases Chinese, and this group would suffer the most. In contrast to the British Indians, the Chinese government left them unprotected and vulnerable, con-

---

[123]   For the numbers by year from 1922 onwards see *Indisch Verslag* 1933:185, 1935:191, 1940:251. Although it managed the labour supply for all the 'outer territories' beyond Java, with the exception of SEC, ZWSS' major clients were the Dutch government mines of Bukit Asam and Ombilin and the European agricultural companies of south and west Sumatra. See Hayashi 2002:20.

ditions which played into the hands of both private Dutch enterprises and the Dutch colonial government. In many ways, the organization of Chinese contract labour recruitment resembled the slave trade. The total lack of regulations, high mortality rates and the widespread use of force and even kidnapping were prime examples of this.

In comparison, the recruitment and transport of British Indians were much better organized. The Dutch government, like the British, was very concerned about being accused of continuing the slave trade under a new guise. Regulations put forward by the British were thus strictly followed. Some scholars disagree about the spread of abuse with regard to British Indian recruitment. However that may be, the situation does seem to have improved over the years.

Javanese recruitment probably held an intermediary position between Chinese and British Indian recruitment. On Java, as in other areas, abuse and malpractice by recruiters 'on the ground' were frequently reported and they probably increased after 1910, as demand for labour rose. Although administration and monitoring were improved, this was not sufficiently implemented to effectively combat the abuse (Houben 1999b:33-4). As with British India, on Java economic necessity was the prime motivator for migrating (Hoefte 1990:12).

The actual involvement of the Dutch (colonial) government in the recruitment of indentured labour is complex. In China recruitment was solely managed by either private recruiting agencies or, after 1888, by the planters' organizations themselves. In British India direct involvement was a fact, as the Dutch government engaged in successful negotiations with the British authorities regarding recruitment. The Dutch consul in Calcutta was responsible for the smooth operation of the entire process. On Java, in their own colony, the Dutch authorities did not directly intervene in the recruitment, a task left to private recruiting agencies and planters' associations.[124]

Indirectly, the Dutch authorities in both the East and West Indies played a vital role in upholding and maintaining the indentured labour system by adopting Coolie and Recruitment Ordinances from 1880 onwards. Although these were meant to serve the interests of both employers and employees, in practice they tended to favour the former, as in the enactment of the Coolie Ordinance's penal clause.

---

[124]   In the 1850s and 1870s the Dutch authorities did arrange the recruitment and transport of a small contingent of Chinese from Java to Suriname.

The (lasting) impact of indentured labour

With regards to scale, the demographics of Suriname are dwarfed by the
Dutch East Indies in all respects. The total influx of indentured labourers into
Suriname between 1851 and 1939 amounted to 70,000 labourers, not many
more than the aggregate number arriving in a single year on Sumatra's East
Coast (60,334 in 1929). However, the demographic impact on Suriname was
far more significant.

Despite the lack of data, it is certain that indentured labour migration did
have a lasting impact on Sumatra and other parts of the Outer Islands. In
1900 only 300,000 people lived in East Sumatra; in 1930 this number was 1.5
million. On Southeast Kalimantan the population nearly doubled between
1905 and 1930, from 770,000 to 1.3 million. In 1920 about fourteen to sixteen
million people lived on Sumatra. Ten years later this number had risen to
approximately eighteen million. The influx of contract labourers, and subsequently the natural growth among this group, was largely responsible for the
continued population increase.[125]

As the Depression struck the Outer Islands' economy between 1930 and
1934, almost half of SEC's coolies repatriated. This signalled the end of the
indentured labour system. Those who stayed mostly became 'free labourers', sometimes receiving a small parcel of land. This bound them to the land
now that the penal sanction was abolished and provided the planters with a
labour reservoir in the region.[126]

After 1932 a new shortage of labour forced the enterprises to recruit new
workers.[127] On the brink of the Second World War, SEC was home to over
200,000 Javanese labourers, almost all of them 'free'. The Chinese labour
presence in the region had all but vanished by that time. In 1938 only 9,604
Chinese labourers were employed (Lindblad 1999a:72). During the Second
World War many changes occurred; some plantations became occupied by
former labourers and local ethnic groups. During the 1950s the plantations
were 'nationalized' while recruitment on Java continued.[128] Between 1965 and
1968 the number of labourers on SEC decreased by 34 per cent, partly as a

[125]   Houben 1999a:4. According to the 1930 census, over 42 per cent of the total population of
northeast Sumatra were Javanese. Chinese made up ten per cent (with only a (very) small proportion working on the estates). See Sairin 1996:3-4.
[126]   Only married labourers who had worked for five years could receive land. See Stoler
1981:208.
[127]   This time, more families were recruited; the proportion of women on the plantation rose
from 25 per cent in 1933 to 37 per cent in 1937 (in 1913 this had been 22 per cent). See Stoler
1981:210.
[128]   In 1951 and 1952 almost 25,000 workers arrived from Java. More would follow in later
years: 55,000 between 1963 and 1965 (Stoler 1995:160).

result of the mass killings following the military coup of 1965.[129]

During the following years the number of estate workers on North Sumatra further declined.[130] The 1971 census showed that ten per cent of North Sumatra's populace (over 660,000 people) had lived in another province at some time.[131] Around 1980 labourers for the SEC plantations (and indeed other parts of Sumatra) no longer came from Java, but mainly hailed from the local Javanese community in North Sumatra (Stoler 1981:220). In 1980 at least half a million people of Javanese descent (still) depended on plantation activities (Sairin 1996:4; Stoler 1995:4). Transmigration schemes by the Indonesian government had little effect on North Sumatra. Between 1950 and 1997 only about 30,000 transmigrants, principally from Java, were relocated to this region, which by 2000 had a population of about 11.5 million (Hardjono 1977:28; Muhidin 2002:15, 53-4).

Dutch migration policies had a more profound impact on the demographic make-up of South Sumatra, specifically the region of Lampung.[132] In 1941, on the brink of the colonial demise, this province was estimated to be home to 511,400 people, over half of whom were Javanese (Hardjono 1977:20).

Today it is hard to disentangle the labour migration streams of the colonial past from more recent developments in this field. After independence, the Indonesian government continued the colonization scheme under the name of 'transmigration'. Between 1950 and 1972, 417,453 migrants were sent to the Outer Islands under government-sponsored programmes. Lampung received more than fifty per cent of this group (213,332) (Hardjono 1977:28). After 1972 this transmigration programme continued to bring over one million inhabitants from Java and other areas to the Outer Islands. Half of these went to Sumatra. In addition, circa 700,000 people migrated spontaneously to the Outer Islands without government assistance. Lampung became saturated during the 1980s and would no longer be the principal destination in the region.[133]

---

[129]   Stoler 1981:215. On the eve of the coup the workforce numbered almost 283,000; a year later this figure was reduced by 47,000. It is uncertain how many fled, were killed or dismissed. See Stoler 1995:163.

[130]   Between 1965 and 1977 this number declined from 282,804 to 119,006. For more details regarding the number and composition of estate labourers in the period 1965-78, see Stoler 1995:166.

[131]   Hugo 1980:108. Hugo adds that this census showed that two thirds of this ten per cent had lived in North Sumatra for over ten years. In 1971, the population of North Sumatra numbered 6,622,000. For these and other population figures for all provinces between 1961-2000, see Muhidin 2002:15.

[132]   In the period 1933-41 circa 222,585 migrants were resettled in these regions. See Muhidin 2002:54.

[133]   Other main destinations were various parts of South Sumatra and Riau. For all destinations and transmigration numbers between 1950 and 1972, see Hardjono 1977:28. For an overview of

On Bangka and Belitung tin mining continued following independence, with the influence of the Chinese (labour) community gradually declining over time, primarily as a result of repatriation. On the larger island of Bangka in 1930 the proportion of ethnic Chinese was 47 per cent of the population, while in 1971 this had declined to about 27 per cent. In 1981 only 21.3 per cent of Bangka's population consisted of ethnic Chinese (Somers Heidhues 1992:218). In 1979 the Chinese community on Belitung made up only about twelve per cent of the population, a figure that had been as high as 42 per cent in 1920, but had since decreased (Somers Heidhues 1992:178, 223). On both islands the Chinese legacy is evident by the presence of Chinese houses, shops, cemeteries and temples (Somers Heidhues 2007:70-1, 73).

While in the former East Indies the descendants of indentured migrants and colonists are today hard to distinguish from transmigrants arriving in the post-independence era, the situation in Suriname is quite different. Here, indentured labour migration had direct and far reaching consequences and its legacy is much more visible. In 1870, three years before the arrival of the first workers from India, the population numbered only about 50,000 people. Fifty years later, circa 56,000 labourers from India and Java had arrived and Suriname's population had increased to about 95,000 (Lamur 1993:48; Six-Oliemuller 1998:67).

These two Asian groups would fundamentally change Suriname's demographic make-up. Today Surinamese of Asian descent make up roughly half of the formerly 'African' nation. The Hindustani (formerly British Indian) segment of the population grew rapidly after the Second World War, primarily as a result of high fertility rates. In contrast, the Javanese population grew slowly in the 1950s, before expanding during the 1960s.[134] In 1972 former British Indians made up the largest ethnic group in Suriname with 37.6 per cent, while the Javanese constituted only 15.2 per cent of the population.[135] Despite the fact that almost forty per cent of the Hindustani community chose to migrate to the Netherlands after Suriname's independence in 1975, this group was still the largest ethnic segment of the population in 2004, even though its number had both proportionally and substantially declined. Of the

---

all destinations from 1969 until 1997, see Muhidin 2002:53-4. In 1980 Lampung was the residence of 4,625,000 people. In 1990 this number had increased to 6,018,000 (Muhidin 2002:15).

[134]   According to Six-Oliemuller (1998:23, 54), the desire to return to Java may have affected the fertility rate of Javanese in Suriname during the 1950s. It should be noted, however, that fertility had always been considerably higher among the British Indians than among the Javanese in Suriname.

[135]   With 31.4 per cent, the Creoles were the second largest group in 1972 (Choenni and Harmsen 2007:74).

Javanese, only about five per cent migrated to the Netherlands.[136] While their numbers increased between 1973 and 2004, the Javanese made up only 14.6 per cent of the total population in 2004, thus constituting the fourth largest ethnic group in Suriname.[137]

But perhaps the multi-faceted legacy of indentured labour migration in the Dutch colonial sphere is most strikingly characterized by the village of Tongar on West Sumatra. This village, located near Padang, was founded by Javanese repatriates from Suriname. Visiting the place gives one the impression, according to one observer, of being in the country of Suriname, as the village's infrastructure and architectural style resemble that of the former Dutch colony in the Western hemisphere (Cosijn-Mitrasing 1997:146-9). Here, in 'Desa Suriname', the legacies of colonial labour migration and colonization meet in the most profound way.

Bibliography

Allen, Rose Mary
2006a   'Constructing identity through inter-Caribbean interactions; The Curaçao-Cuban migration revisited', in: Jay B. Haviser and Kevin C. MacDonald (eds), *African re-genesis; Confronting social issues in the diaspora*, pp. 111-20. New York: UCL Press.
2006b   'Regionalization and identity in Curaçao; Migration and diaspora', in: Ruben Gowricharn (ed.), *Caribbean transnationalism; Migration, pluralization, and social cohesion*, pp. 79-98. Lanham: Rowman and Littlefield.
American heritage dictionary
2000   *American heritage dictionary of the English language*. Fourth edition. Boston, MA: Houghton Mifflin.
Ankum-Houwink, Joke
1985   'Chinese kontraktarbeiders in Suriname in de 19e eeuw', *Oso, Tijdschrift voor Surinaamse Taalkunde, Letterkunde, Cultuur en Geschiedenis* 4-2:181-6.
Bates, Crispin
2001   'Introduction; Community and identity among South Asians in diaspora', in: Crispin Bates (ed.), *Community, empire and migration; South Asians in diaspora*, pp. 1-45. Basingstoke: Palgrave.

[136]   In the late 1980s circa 20,000 Javanese from Suriname lived in the Netherlands (Houben 1998:63).
[137]   In 1972 and 2004 there were respectively 142,917 and 135,117 former British Indians in Suriname. The number of Javanese for these years were respectively 57,688 and 71,879. For all figures regarding the ethnic composition in these years, see Choenni and Harmsen 2007:74. For figures for 1964, see Six-Oliemuller 1998:50.

Bhagwanbali, Radjinder
1996   *Contracten voor Suriname; Arbeidsmigratie vanuit Brits-Indië onder het indentured-labourstelsel 1873-1916.* Den Haag: Amrit.
Blussé, Leonard
1988   'China overzee; Aard en omvang van de Chinese migratie', in: Pieter C. Emmer and Herman Obdeijn (eds), *Het paradijs is aan de overzijde; Internationale migratie en grenzen,* pp. 34-50. Utrecht: Van Arkel.
Boogaart, E. van den and Pieter C. Emmer
1986   'Colonialism and migration; An overview', in: Pieter C. Emmer (ed.), *Colonialism and migration; Indentured labour before and after slavery,* pp. 3-15. Dordrecht: Nijhoff.
Boomgaard, Peter
1989   *Children of the colonial state; Population growth and economic development in Java, 1795-1880.* Amsterdam: Free University Press.
1990   'Changing measures and measuring changes; Regional agricultural growth in Java, 1815-1875', in: Anne Booth, W.J. O'Malley and Anna Weidemann (eds), *Indonesian economic history in the Dutch colonial era,* pp. 111-35. New Haven: Yale University Southeast Asia Studies.
1991   '"Why work for wages?"; Free labour in Java, 1600-1900', in: *Economic and Social History in the Netherlands II,* pp. 37-56. Amsterdam: The Netherlands Economic History Archive.
Breman, Jan
1987   *Koelies, planters en koloniale politiek; Het arbeidsregime op de grootlandbouwondernemingen aan Sumatra's Oostkust in het begin van de twintigste eeuw.* Dordrecht: Foris. [KITLV, Verhandelingen 123.]
1989   *Taming the coolie beast; Plantation society and the colonial order in Southeast Asia.* Delhi: Oxford University Press.
1992   *Koelies, planters en koloniale politiek; Het arbeidsregime op de grootlandbouwondernemingen aan Sumatra's Oostkust in het begin van de twintigste eeuw.* Derde herziene druk. Leiden: KITLV Uitgeverij. [Verhandelingen 123.]
Brown, Colin
1994   'The politics of trade union formation in the Java sugar industry, 1945-1949', *Modern Asian Studies* 28:77-98.
Brown, Judith M.
2006   *Global South Asians; Introducing the modern diaspora.* Cambridge: Cambridge University Press.
Choenni, Chan and Carel Harmsen
2007   *Geboorteplaats en etnische samenstelling van Surinamers in Nederland.* Den Haag: Centraal Bureau voor de Statistiek. [http://www.cbs.nl/nl-NL/menu/themas/dossiers/allochtonen/publicaties/artikelen/archief/2007/default.htm].
Cosijn-Mitrasing, Ingrid
1997   'Een Surinaams plekje in het hart van Sumatra; Een reisverslag', *Oso, Tijdschrift voor Surinaamse Taalkunde, Letterkunde, Cultuur en Geschiedenis* 16-2:146-54.

Coughlan, James E.
1992   *The diverse Asians; A profile of six Asian communities in Australia.* Bris-
            bane: Griffith University, Centre for the Study of Australia-Asia Rela-
            tions.
Dalhuisen, Leo, Maurits Hassankhan and Frans Steegh (eds)
2007   *Geschiedenis van Suriname.* Zutphen: Walburg Pers.
Dros, Nico
1991   'Javanese labour relations in a changing rural economy, 1830-1870', in:
            Economic and Social History in the Netherlands III, pp. 133-54. Amster-
            dam: The Netherlands Economic History Archive.
Elson, R.E.
1986   'Sugar factory workers and the emergence of "free labour" in nine-
            teenth-century Java', *Modern Asian Studies* 20:139-74.
1994   *Village Java under the Cultivation System, 1830-1870.* Sydney: Allen and
            Unwin.
Emmer, Pieter C.
1984   'The importation of British Indians into Surinam (Dutch Guiana), 1873-
            1916', in: Shula Marks and Peter Richardson (eds), *International labor
            migration; Historical perspectives,* pp. 90-111. Hounslow: Temple Smith.
1985   'The great escape; The migration of female indentured servants from
            British India to Surinam 1873-1916', in: David Richardson (ed.), *Aboli-
            tion and its aftermath; The historical context, 1790-1916,* pp. 245-66. Lon-
            don: Frank Cass.
1995   'The ideology of free labor and Dutch colonial policy, 1830-1970', in:
            Gert Oostindie (ed.), *Fifty years later; Antislavery, capitalism and moder-
            nity in the Dutch orbit,* pp. 207-22. Leiden: KITLV Press. [Caribbean
            Series 15.]
2004   'A "spirit of independence" or lack of education for the market?;
            Freedmen and Asian indentured labourers in the post-emancipation
            Caribbean, 1834-1917', *Bulletin de la Société d'Histoire de la Guadeloupe*
            138-9:79-95.
2007   '"A new system of slavery?"; Een vergelijking tussen het vervoer
            van slaven en contractarbeiders in de negentiende eeuw', *Leidschrift*
            22-1:59-70.
Emmer, Pieter C. and R. Shlomowitz
1997   'Mortality and the Javanese diaspora', *Itinerario* 21-1:125-35.
Empel, Carin van
1999   'Dark mines; Labour conditions of coolies in the state coal mines of
            West Sumatra', in: Vincent J.H. Houben, J. Thomas Lindblad, Ellen
            Leenarts, Trudi Nierop, Carin van Empel and Jurrien van den Berg,
            *Coolie labour in colonial Indonesia; A study of labour relations in the Outer
            Islands, c. 1900-1940,* pp. 179-208. Wiesbaden: Harrassowitz.
Engelen, E.H.M.
1993   'Van beroepswerving tot vrije werving: achteruitgang, stilstand of ver-
            betering?; De belangen van Westerse planters en Javaanse koelies bij de
            werving voor ondernemingen in de Buitengewesten tussen 1910-1940'.
            MA thesis University of Leiden.

Goedhart, Adriaan
2002   Het wonder van Deli; Uit de geschiedenis van de cultures op Sumatra's Oost-
            kust. Alphen aan den Rijn: Albini.
Gooszen, Hans
1999   A demographic history of the Indonesian archipelago 1880-1942. Leiden:
            KITLV Press. [Verhandelingen 183.]
Goslinga, C.Ch.
1990   The Dutch in the Caribbean and in Surinam 1791/5-1942. Assen: Van Gor-
            cum.
Hardjono, J.M.
1977   Transmigration in Indonesia. Kuala Lumpur: Oxford University Press.
Hassankhan, Maurits S.
1995   'Immigratie van contractarbeiders voor en na de afschaffing van de
            slavernij; Voorwaarde tot en gevolg van de emancipatie', in: Lila
            Gobardhan-Rambocus, Maurits S. Hassankhan and Jerry L. Egger
            (eds), De erfenis van de slavernij, pp. 56-70. Paramaribo: Anton de Kom
            Universiteit van Suriname.
Hayashi, Yoko
2002   Agencies and clients; Labour recruitment in Java, 1870s-1950s. Amster-
            dam: International Institute for Asian Studies/International Institute of
            Social History.
Heeren, Hendrik Jan
1967   Transmigratie in Indonesië; Interne migratie en de verhouding van immi-
            granten/autochtonen speciaal met betrekking tot Zuid- en Midden-Sumatra.
            Meppel: Boom.
Heijting, Herman George
1925   De koelie-wetgeving voor de buitengewesten van Nederlandsch-Indië.
            's-Gravenhage: Van Stockum.
Hoefte, Rosemarijn
1987   'Female indentured labor in Suriname; For better or for worse?', Boletín
            de Estudios Latinoamericanos y del Caribe 42:55-70.
1990   De betovering verbroken; De migratie van Javanen naar Suriname en het
            rapport-Van Vleuten. Dordrecht: Foris Publications. [KITLV, Caribbean
            Series 12.]
1998   In place of slavery; A social history of British Indian and Javanese laborers in
            Surinam. Gainesville: University Press of Florida.
Houben, Vincent J.H.
1995   'Labour conditions on Western firms in colonial Indonesia; Outline of
            an approach', Jahrbuch für Wirtschaftsgeschichte 46:93-107.
1998   '"Nyabrang/overzee gaan"; Javaanse emigratie tussen 1880 en 1940', in:
            Pieter C. Emmer and Herman Obdeijn (eds), Het paradijs is aan de over-
            zijde; Internationale migratie en grenzen, pp. 51-65. Utrecht: Van Arkel.
1999a   'Introduction; The coolie system in colonial Indonesia', in: Vincent J.H.
            Houben, J. Thomas Lindblad, Jurrien van den Berg, Carin van Empel,
            Ellen Leenarts, Trudi Nierop, Coolie labour in colonial Indonesia; A study
            of labour relations in the Outer Islands, c. 1900-1940, pp. 1-24. Wiesbaden:
            Harrassowitz.

1999b   'Before departure; Coolie labour recruitment in Java, 1900-1942', in:
             Vincent J.H. Houben, J. Thomas Lindblad, Jurrien van den Berg, Carin
             van Empel, Ellen Leenarts, Trudi Nierop, *Coolie labour in colonial Indo-*
             nesia; A study of labour relations in the Outer Islands, c. 1900-1940, pp.
             25-42. Wiesbaden: Harrassowitz.

Houben, Vincent J.H., J. Thomas Lindblad Jurrien van den Berg, Carin van Empel,
Ellen Leenarts, Trudi Nierop
1999   *Coolie labour in colonial Indonesia; A study of labour relations in the Outer*
             Islands, c. 1900-1940. Wiesbaden: Harrassowitz.

Hugo, G.J.
1980   'Population movements in Indonesia during the colonial period', in:
             James J. Fox, Ross Garnaut, Peter McCawley and J.A.C. Mackie (eds),
             Indonesia; Australian perspectives, pp. 95-135. Canberra: Research School
             of Pacific Studies, Australian National University.
1993   'Indonesian labour migration to Malaysia; Trends and policy implica-
             tions', *Southeast Asia Journal of Social Science* 21-1:36-70.

Indisch Verslag
1932, 1934, 1939   *Indisch Verslag; II: Statistisch jaaroverzicht van Nederlandsch-Indië over*
             het jaar [...]. Batavia: Landsdrukkerij.

Kaur, Amarjit and Frits Diehl
1996   'Tin miners and tin mining in Indonesia, 1850-1950', *Asian Studies*
             Review; Journal of the Asian Studies Association of Australia 20-2:95-120.

Klaveren, Marieke van
1997   'Death among coolies; Mortality of Chinese and Javanese labourers
             on Sumatra in the early years of recruitment, 1882-1909', *Itinerario*
             21-1:111-25.

Knaap, Gerrit J.
1995   'Slavery and the Dutch in Southeast Asia', in: Gert Oostindie (ed.), *Fifty*
             years later; Antislavery, capitalism and modernity in the Dutch orbit, pp.
             193-206. Leiden: KITLV Press. [Caribbean Series 15.]

Lamur, Humphrey E.
1993   'De invloed van de (im)migratie op de demografische geschiedenis van
             Suriname', in: Lila Gobardhan-Rambocus and Maurits S. Hassankhan
             (eds), *Immigratie en ontwikkeling; Emancipatieproces van contractanten*,
             pp. 36-49. Paramaribo: Anton de Kom Universiteit van Suriname.

Lamur, Humphrey E. and Jean A. Vriezen
1985   'Chinese kontraktanten in Suriname', *Oso, Tijdschrift voor Surinaamse*
             Taalkunde, Letterkunde, Cultuur en Geschiedenis 4-2:169-79.

Langeveld, H.J.
1975   'Arbeidstoestanden op de ondernemingen ter Oostkust van Sumatra
             tussen 1920 en 1940 in het licht van het verdwijnen van de poenale
             sanctie op de arbeidscontracten'. MA thesis University of Amsterdam.

Lindblad, J. Thomas
1999a   'Coolies in Deli; Labour conditions in Western enterprises in East
             Sumatra, 1910-1938', in: Vincent J.H. Houben, J. Thomas Lindblad,
             Jurrien van den Berg, Carin van Empel, Ellen Leenarts, Trudi Nierop,

Coolie labour in colonial Indonesia; A study of labour relations in the Outer Islands, c. 1900-1940, pp. 43-78. Wiesbaden: Harrassowitz.

1999b   'New destinations; Conditions of coolie labour outside East Sumatra, 1910-1938', in: Vincent J.H. Houben, J. Thomas Lindblad, Jurrien van den Berg, Carin van Empel, Ellen Leenarts, Trudi Nierop, *Coolie labour in colonial Indonesia; A study of labour relations in the Outer Islands, c. 1900-1940*, pp. 79-108. Wiesbaden: Harrassowitz.

Look Lai, Walton
2000   'Origins of the Caribbean Chinese Community', *Journal of Caribbean Studies* 14-1/2:25-40.
2004   'The Chinese indenture system in the British West Indies and its aftermath', in: Andrew R. Wilson (ed.), *The Chinese in the Caribbean*, pp. 3-24. Princeton, NJ: Markus Wiener.

Man A Hing, William
1993   'De Chinese bevolkingsgroep; Een geïsoleerde groep?', in: Lila Gobardhan-Rambocus and Maurits S. Hassankhan (eds), *Immigratie en ontwikkeling; Emancipatieproces van contractanten*, pp. 51-67. Paramaribo: Anton de Kom Universiteit van Suriname.

Maurer, Jean-Luc
2002   Fragmented identities among Javanese youth in New Caledonia. Paper presented at the 13th annual workshop European Social Science Java Network 'Youth and identity', Marseille, 2-4 May.

Muhidin, Salahudin
2002   *The population of Indonesia; Regional demographic scenarios using a multiregional method and multiple data sources*. Amsterdam: Rozenberg.

Nierop, Trudi
1999   'Lonely in an alien world; Coolie communities in Southeast Kalimantan in the late colonial period', in: Vincent J.H. Houben, J. Thomas Lindblad, Jurrien van den Berg, Carin van Empel, Ellen Leenarts, Trudi Nierop, *Coolie labour in colonial Indonesia; A study of labour relations in the Outer Islands, c. 1900-1940*, pp. 157-78. Wiesbaden: Harrassowitz.

Northrup, David
1995   *Indentured labor in the age of imperialism, 1834-1922*. Cambridge: Cambridge University Press.

Pietersz, Jorge A.
1985   *De Arubaanse arbeidsmigratie 1890-1930; Drie studies over de trek van arbeiders in het Caraïbische gebied voor de Tweede Wereldoorlog*. Leiden: KITLV, Caraïbische Afdeling. [Antillen Working Papers 9.]

Reid, Anthony
1993   'The decline of slavery in nineteenth-century Indonesia', in: Martin A. Klein (ed.), *Breaking the chains; Slavery, bondage, and emancipation in modern Africa and Asia*, pp. 64-82. Madison: University of Wisconsin Press.

Roopnarine, Lomarsh
2007   *Indo-Caribbean indenture; Resistance and accommodation, 1839-1920*. Kingston: University of West Indies Press.

Roosman, Raden S.
1971   'The Javanese immigrant community in New Caledonia; A preliminary
              survey', *Te Reo; Proceedings of the Linguistic Society of New Zealand* 14:63-
              73.

Sairin, Sjafri
1996   'The appeal of plantation labour; Economic imperatives and cultural
              considerations among Javanese workers in North Sumatra', *Sojourn;
              Journal of Social Issues in Southeast Asia* 11-1:1-23.

Segers, W.A.I.M.
1987   *Changing economy in Indonesia; A selection of statistical source material
              from the early 19th century up to 1940; Vol. 8: Manufacturing industry 1870-
              1942.* Amsterdam: Royal Tropical Institute.

Six-Oliemuller, Blandine J.F.G.
1998   'Aziaten vergeleken; Hindoestanen en Javanen in Suriname 1870-1975'.
              MA thesis University of Leiden.

Somers Heidhues, Mary F.
1992   *Bangka tin and Mentok pepper; Chinese settlement on an Indonesian island.*
              Singapore: Institute of Southeast Asian Studies.
2007   'Poor little rich islands; Metals in Bangka-Belitung and West Kaliman-
              tan', in: Greg Bankoff and Peter Boomgaard (eds), *A history of natural
              resources in Asia; The wealth of nature,* pp. 61-79. New York: Palgrave
              Macmillan.

Stoler, Ann Laura
1981   'In de schaduw van de maatschappij; Een geschiedenis van plantage-
              vrouwen en arbeidsbeleid op Noord-Sumatra', in: *Socialisties-femi-
              nistiese teksten 5; Feminisme en antropologie,* pp. 202-20. Amsterdam:
              Feministische Uitgeverij Sara.
1995   *Capitalism and confrontation in Sumatra's plantation belt, 1870-1979.* Second
              edition, with a new preface. Ann Arbor: University of Michigan Press.

Tinker, Hugh
1974   *A new system of slavery; The export of Indian labour overseas 1830-1920.*
              London: Oxford University Press.

Tseng, Frank
1991   'De grote oversteek; Het lot van de Surinaamse Chinezen', *China Nu*
              16-4:16-8.

Van Langenberg, M.
1977   'North Sumatra under Dutch colonial rule; Aspects of structural
              change, part one', *Review of Indonesian and Malayan Affairs* 11-1:74-110.

Van Niel, Robert
1992   *Java under the Cultivation System; Collected writings.* Leiden: KITLV
              Press. [Verhandelingen 150.]

Vreede, A.G.
1928   *Rapport omtrent de arbeidstoestanden in en de werving van arbeidskrachten
              voor de Straits Settlements, de Federated Malay States en Ceylon.* Weltevre-
              den: Landsdrukkerij.

Ward, Alan
1988   'New Caledonia 1945-1955; Labour policy and immigration', in: John
               Connell, Michael Spencer and Alan Ward (eds), *New Caledonia; Essays in
               nationalism and dependency*, pp. 81-105. St. Lucia: University of Queens-
               land Press.
Wertheim, Wim F.
1993   'Conditions on sugar estates in colonial Java; Comparisons with Deli',
               Journal of Southeast Asian Studies 24:268-85.
Wilson, Andrew R.
2004   'New perspectives on the Caribbean Chinese', in: Andrew R. Wilson
               (ed.), *The Chinese in the Caribbean*, pp. vii-xxiii. Princeton, NJ: Markus
               Wiener.

HANNEKE LOMMERSE

Population figures

ASIA

VOC

Table 1. Total number of European and local employees of the VOC in Asia and the Cape Colony, 1700-1789*

Year	European	Local	Total	% Eur.
1700	13,481	723	14,204	95.0
1710	13,455	1,320	14,775	91.0
1720	16,451	1,361	17,812	92.4
1730	19,206	688	19,894	96.5
1740	19,983	2,139	22,122	90.3
1750	16,194	1,585	17,779	91.1
1760	18,811	0	18,811	
1770	20,858	0	20,858	
1780	17,167	0	17,167	
1789	19,003	687	19,690	96.5

Source: Lequin 2005:237.

* When reading this and all subsequent tables, the reader should be aware that the colonial category of 'Europeans' often included 'Europeanized' Eurasians and at times even Asians.

Table 2. Total number of employees in major VOC settlements inside Indonesia, 1700-1789

Year	Amboina	Banda	Batavia	Java's North-east Coast	Sumatra's West Coast	Ternate
1700	919	784	3,853	1,017	226	564
1710	856	733	3,468	1,101	390	656
1720	1,048	825	4,478	2,340	488	905
1730	1,049	873	4,999	1,619	711	823
1740	1,125	836	5,628	1,118	623	1,029
1750	949	587	6,306	0	449	0
1760	1,002	693	4,578	1,690	268	691
1770	1,149	610	5,822	1,852	290	838
1780	1,042	497	3,283	1,849	170	859
1789	1,085	608	4,410	2,603	132	866

Source: Lequin 2005:238-40.

- Totals include European and locally born Asians and Eurasians.
- For the selected years the share of Europeans in the total population oscillated between 90.3 and 96.5 per cent.

Table 3. Total number of employees in major VOC settlements outside Indonesia, 1700-1789

Year	Ceylon	Coromandel	Cape of Good Hope	Makassar	Malabar	Malacca
1700	2,966	514	544	834	690	468
1710	2,705	640	500	821	1,775	435
1720	2,804	454	800	770	1,297	582
1730	3,392	762	919	907	1,535	592
1740	3,212	701	1,141	2,261	2,342	648
1750	4,042	0	1,331	953	1,153	462
1760	3,904	1,091	1,354	818	875	526
1770	4,527	880	1,704	868	688	541
1780	3,784	775	1,687	902	949	477
1789	3,568	0	3,392	1,027	0	744

Source: Lequin 2005:240-3.

- Totals include European and locally born Asians and Eurasians.
- For the selected years the share of Europeans in the total population oscillated between 90.3 and 96.5 per cent.

Dejima

The total European population of Dejima never exceeded sixteen people over the entire 1700-1789 period. For annual listing see Lequin 2005.

Taiwan/Formosa

Van Veen (2003) provides some reliable population figures for the Dutch period. The European population increased from 336 in 1628 to some 707 in 1648, with an average of between 600-700 people. Van Lierop (1983) provides a total population of Castle Zeelandia in 1650 of 6,000, of whom some 1,800 were Europeans and 500 were slaves of unspecified origins. Between 1645-1650 the Chinese population experienced explosive growth, from 3,500 to 20,000 (Yao 2003 and Oosterhof 1985).

Malacca

There are few reliable population figures for the seventeenth century. For aggregate figures regarding VOC employees in the period 1700-1789, see table 3. Ketelaars (1985) provides detailed figures for 1675-1685.

Table 4. Population of Malacca, 1675 (excluding the local population)

Dutch	104
Mestizo/ Free Blacks/ Portuguese	1,463
Chinese	106
Moors	356

Malay/Javanese/ Buginese	597
Private slaves	1,409
In the fort:	
VOC employees and possible family members	674
Slaves of VOC employees	504
VOC-owned slaves	57
	5,324

Cochin/Malabar

For aggregate figures regarding VOC employees in the period 1700-1789, see table 3. Singh (2007) provides additional information on the ethnic composition of those living in households at Fort Cochin.

Table 5. Population in households of Fort Cochin, 1760 and 1790

	1760	1790
Total Europeans	93	155
Total white castizos		469
Total mestizos	415	180
Total indigenous people	257	214
Total slaves	1,275	1,299
Total population in households	2,040	2,317

Coromandel

For aggregate figures regarding VOC employees in the period 1700-1789, see table 3.

Ceylon/Sri Lanka

Raben (1996) provides detailed population figures for 1684 and 1694. In 1694 the total population was 4,764, of whom 1,412 are recorded as VOC employees without further specification. The remaining 3,352 inhabitants are divided according to residence (1,408 in the fort, 1,944 in town) and ethnicity. The major categories are mestizos (401), Europeans (386), Sinhalese (201) and Chetties (109). Slaves of unspecified origins (1,787) make up over half of the total.

Mauritius

Reliable figures for Dutch Mauritius (1598-1710) are not available. Figures provided by Moree (1998) indicate that the European population increased from a mere 25 in 1638 to some 170 in 1707. The number of slaves increased from around 50 in the early 1640s to 71 in 1707.

318 Hanneke Lommerse

Indonesia/Amboina

Population figures for the VOC period are scattered and pertain mainly to parts of Java and the Moluccas. For the post 1815-period more systematic and comprehensive censuses are available. Knaap (2004) provides detailed demographic figures for the latter part of the seventeenth century regarding the population of the government of Amboina, comprising the island of Ambon, the Lease islands (Haraku, Saparua and Nusalaut), southwest Seram and the western part of the Ambonese Moluccas (Buru, Ambelau, Manipa, Kelang and Boano).

The European population, other than VOC servants, mainly settled in Kota Ambon on the island of Leitimor. Knaap (2004) has specified the number of foreigners in Kota Ambon. For aggregate figures regarding VOC employees in the eighteenth century, see table 2.

Table 6. Number of foreigners in Kota Ambon, 1673-1692

Year	VOC servants	European burghers	Chinese burghers	Inland burghers	Total Kota Ambon
1673	1,198	748	9671,176	4,089	
1683	1,235	877	1,031	1,496	4,639
1692	1,266	1,932	1,147	874	5,219

Source: Knaap 2004:132.

For comparative purposes it should be borne in mind that the local population was many times this figure, as the following table illustrates.

Table 7a. Demographic growth of the indigenous population of the government of Amboina, 1671-1708

	1671	1692	1708
Ambon	19,338	21,071	21,140
Lease islands	15,973	21,288	21,343
Western islands	8,551	9,375	9,500
Southwest Seram	5,306	5,871	6,670
Total in government	49,168	57,605	59,653

Source: Knaap 2004:131.

Table 7b. Population of the government of Amboina, 1860-1930

Year	Europeans and those equal	Chinese	Arabs	Other Asians	Indigenous	Total
1860	1,132	373	69	680	123,416	125,670
1870	1,789	451	170		106,927	109,337
1880	1,451	499	288	14	277,880	n.a.
1890	2,132	995	660	4	247,100*	n.a.
1900	1,927	957	724	14	271,484*	n.a.

Year	Europeans and those equal	Chinese	Arabs	Other Asians	Indigenous	Total
1905	2,232	1,353	875	78	294,466	299,004
1920	2,635			2,843	271,879	277,966
1930	4,844	8,335		4,082	875,769**	893,030

Sources: Demographic figures for the year 1860 can be found in *Koloniaal Verslag* (KV) 1860, those for 1870 in KV 1871, for 1880 in KV 1882, for 1890 in KV 1892, for 1900 in KV 1902, for 1905 in KV 1907, for 1920 in KV 1923 and for 1930 in Indisch Verslag 1933.

*   guesstimate
**   including a rough estimate of 135,350 people

Indonesia/Batavia

Raben (1996) provides a total population for Batavia of 8,060 in 1632, of whom 2,724 were slaves. Of the total free population of 5,536, 1,730 were Company servants, all of European or Eurasian descent. The numbers of Chinese and free Mardijkers were 2,930 and 495 respectively. The Mardijkers were distinguished from the local population and were either free migrants, manumitted slaves of (South) Asian origin or their descendants. The great majority of Company servants and Chinese were men.

Raben (1996) provides detailed demographic figures for the period 1673-1797 regarding both the city of Batavia and environs (Ommelanden).

Table 8a. Total population of Batavia – inner city and the surrounding area (Ommelanden), 1673-1797

Year	Inner city	Surrounding area	Total
1673	17,740	9,311	27,051
1679	17,960	13,593	31,553
1689	20,051	45,550	65,601
1699	21,911	49,688	71,599
1709	20,544	55,581	76,125
1719	22,021	65,436	87,457
1729	23,701	78,957	102,658
1739	18,302	68,229	86,531
1749	14,141	77,015	91,156
1759	16,914	111,172	128,086
1769	15,444	114,868	130,312
1779	10,838	161,215	172,053
1789	7,364	143,339	150,703
1797	8,497	n.a.	n.a.

Source: Raben 1996: Appendix.

For these totals Raben also provides a subdivision into ethnic groups.

Table 8b. Total population of Batavia and its constituent population groups, 1673-1789

Year	Slaves	Europeans	Mestizos	Mardijkers	Chinese	Other	Total
1673	13,281	2,024	726	5,362	2,727	2,931	27,051
1679	15,995	2,134	619	6,204	3,006	3,595	31,553
1689	26,168	2,162	965	7,638	5,169	23,499	65,601
1699	25,721	2,258	1,177	7,922	8,074	26,447	71,599
1709	25,748	2,083	970	8,949	10,245	28,130	76,125
1719	25,974	1,849	1,270	8,407	11,641	38,316	87,457
1729	30,489	1,755	1,050	8,026	12,319	49,019	102,658
1739	24,322	1,548	925	6,286	14,773	38,677	86,531
1749	23,963	1,859	1,190	6,859	11,632	46,653	91,156
1759	27,157	1,899	1,073	6,624	26,034	65,299	128,086
1769	30,798	1,659	1,224	5,204	28,284	63,143	130,312
1779	40,654	1,143	447	4,425	32,463	92,921	172,053
1789	36,942	1,037	513	2,986	34,134	75,091	150,703

Source: Raben 1996: Appendix.

Table 8c. Population in Indonesian residencies*, 1812-1840

Year	European	Chinese	Other Asians	Indigenous
1812	7,672	62,244	18,872	4,527,767 (1815)
1820	8,935	64,372	26,870	(564,1000)
1830	9,897	77,675	19,526	7,148,912 (1831)
1840	13,726	101,109	24,848	8,481,260

Source: Boomgaard and Gooszen 1991:124, 127, 130 and 105-6.

For explanations and comments on numbers, definitions and categories regarding the European, Chinese and other Asian population in the residencies, please refer to Boomgaard and Gooszen 1991:67-9.

The indigenous population figures until 1880 are generally underestimated, because a. certain areas were so desolate and inaccessible that no administrator had ever set foot in them; b. migration is an important factor which administrators and historians tend not to take into account; c. the existence of vague dividing lines for defining those officially registered and those who were not, naturally allowed village chiefs a great deal of leeway with regard to withholding information on village populations; and d. Javanese society incorporated an oscillating population of itinerant workers staying for one or two years and travelling between districts because of the seasonal rice harvests (Boomgaard and Gooszen 1991:14).

*   Residencies:
Western Java (Banten, Batavia, Buitenzorg, Krawang, Priangan, Cirebon)
North Central Java (Tegal, Pekalongan, Semarang, Jepara, Rembang, Surabaya)
South Central Java (Banyumas, Bagelen, Kedu, Madiun, Pacitan, Kediri)
Principalities (Yogyakarta, Solo)
Eastern Java (Pasuruan, Probolinggo, Besuki, Banyuwangi, Madura)

Table 8d. Population of the Netherlands Indies, 1850-1930

Year	Region	Europeans and those equal*	Chinese	Arabs	Other Asians **	Indigenous	Slaves	Total
1850	Java and Madura	16,172	123,934		28,522	9,391,749	9,636	9,570,023
1860	Java and Madura	22,663	149,424	6,133	26,235	12,514,262		12,716,717
1870	Java and Madura	27,585	174,540	7,804	9,139	16,233,100		16,452,168
1880	Java and Madura	33,708	206,931	10,506	2,547	19,540,813		19,794,503
1890	Java and Madura	45,967	242,111	14,293	2,881	23,609,312		23,914,564
1900	Java and Madura	62,477	277,265	18,051	3,114	28,386,121		28,746,638
	Outer regions	13,356	260,051	9,348	13,536			
1905	Java and Madura	64,917	295,193	19,148	2,842	29,715,908		30,098,008
	Outer regions	15,993	268,256	10,440	20,128	7,304,552		7,717,377
1917	Java and Madura	111,430			395,723	33,652,230		34,157,383
	Outer regions	27,415			438,944	12,579,897		13,046,256
1920	Java and Madura	135,288			415,407	34,433,476		34,984,171
	Outer regions	34,420			460,490	13,871,144		14,366,663
1930	Java and Madura	192,571	582,431	41,730	10,539	40,891,093		41,718,364
	Outer regions	47,591	607,583	29,605	32,763	18,246,974		19,008,869

Sources: Demographic figures for the year 1860 can be found in KV 1860, those for 1870 in KV 1871, for 1880 in KV 1882, for 1890 in KV 1892, for 1900 in KV 1902, for 1905 in KV 1907, for 1917 in KV 1918, for 1920 in KV 1923 and the final results of the census of 1930 in *Indisch Verslag* 1933.

*   The category 'Europeans and those equal' contained Europeans born in Europe and in the Netherlands Indies, as well as foreigners born in other parts of the world, for instance North and South America, Armenia, Persia, Africa and Australia. They were Christians and do not qualify for the category 'Indigenous'.

**   In 1917 and 1920 the Chinese and Arabs were allocated to the category 'other Asians'.

Hanneke Lommerse

Table 8e. Batavia

Year	Europeans and those equal	Chinese	Arabs	Other Asians	Indigenous	Slaves	Total
1850	3,774	40,587		n.a.	296,417	7,556	348,325
1860	5,107	45,275	800	148	418,076		469,406
1870	6,386	68,360	952	88	876,497		948,283
1880	7,211	73,224	1,003	127	859,782		941,347
1890	10,793	78,925	2,410	162	978,466		1,070,756
1900	13,653	89,064	3,062	252	1,831,974		1,938,006
1905	13,805	92,520	2,772	277	1,999,978		2,109,352
1920	37,128			122,065	2,628,142		2,787,345
1930	38,561	149,225		9,121	2,440,128		2,637,035

Table 8f. Surabaya

Year	Europeans and those equal	Chinese	Arabs	Other Asians	Indigenous	Slaves	Total
1850	1,881	5,327		3,018	928,314	547	93,9087
1860	4,105	7,250	1,438	4,698	1,169,546		1,187,037
1870	4,950	9,214	1,626	710	1,419,207		1,435,707
1880	5,941	13,185	1,955	483	1,035,013		1,052,348
1890	8,164	17,623	2,652	485	2,025,279		2,054,203
1900	11,217	24,433	4,014	376	2,320,869		2,360,909
1905	10,600	26,646	3,732	367	2,395,618		2,436,963
1920	21,579			42,081	2,396,520		2,460,180
1930	30,519	53,675		7,197	1,813,259		1,904,650

Table 8g. Yogyakarta

Year	Europeans and those equal	Chinese	Arabs	Other Asians	Indigenous	Slaves	Total
1850	707	1,362		85	361,856	35	364,045
1860	870	1,800	13	144	349,973		349,890
1870	1301	1,759	77		393,983		397,120
1880	1,510	1,846	169	17	703,477		709,650
1890	2,097	4,417	84	146	778,729		785,473
1900	2,145	4,974	113	102	1,076,993		1,084,327
1905	2,342	5,366	97	86	1,110,814		1,118,705
1920	4,885			7,336	1,270,594		1,282,815
1930	7,317	12,637		202	1,538,868		1,559,024

Table 8h. Semarang

Year	Europeans and those equal	Chinese	Arabs	Other Asians	Indigenous	Slaves	Total
1852	3,031	9,211		2,218	666,613	483	681,556
1860	3,765	10,730	509	1,999	953,198		970,201
1870	4,018	12,560	358	773	1,242,029		1,259,738
1880	5,159	15,921	717	1,006	1,252,086		1,274,889
1890	6,214	19,592	738	1,020	1,375,371		1,402,935
1900	8,402	32,701	916	1,316	2,641,680		2,685,015
1905	8,834	32,724	854	1,019	2,517,492		2,614,923
1920	15,144			42,064	2,680,208		2,737,416
1930	17,965	40,651		2,979	1,950,021		2,011,616

AFRICA

Cape Colony

Elphick and Giliomee (1979) provide the longest run of demographic figures for the Cape Colony. As not all figures are complete, however, they abstain from giving total population figures.

Table 9. Population of the Cape Colony, 1670-1820

Year	European *freeburghers*	Free Blacks	Burghers' slaves	Khoikhoi and *bastaards*	VOC slaves
1670	125	13	52		101 (1669)
1690	788	48	381		322 (1693)
1711	1,693	63	1,771		445 (1714)
1730	2,540	221	4,037		597 (1727)
1750	4,511	349	5,327		506 (1752)
1770	7,736	352	8,220		559 (1770)
1798	ca. 20,000	ca. 1,700	25,754	14,447	509 (1793)
1820	42,975	1,932	31,779	26,975	

Sources: Giliomee and Elphick 1979:360; Amstrong 1979:86.

Ghana

The European population at the Dutch settlements on the so-called 'Gold' and 'Slave' Coasts was low. Van IJken (2001:5) provides an estimate of 225 in 1645. Goslinga (1985:51, 57) gives an estimate of circa 210 in 1700 and 260 in 1736, while Enthoven (2005:158) provide an estimate of 350 around 1800. The total European population remained low during the entire Dutch colonial period, whereas the total population of the town of Elmina oscillated between 10,000 and 20,000 inhabitants. An unidentified proportion of this number were of part European descent (see articles by Everts and Doortmont).

THE AMERICAS

Dutch Brazil

Wätjen (1921:58) provides an estimate of 7,030 present in the Dutch part of Brazil in 1631, of whom circa 6,000 are military personnel and sailors against 576 freeburghers (including an estimation of the number of women and children). For the year 1645 more detailed figures are available.

Table 10. Population of Dutch Brazil, 1645

Military and naval personnel	3,050
Freeburghers (Vrijluyden)	ca. 2,739
Indigenous (Brazilians)	ca. 2,683
Africans (enslaved)	ca. 4,083
Total	12,543

Source: Gonsalves de Mello 2001:114-5.

While Gonsalves de Mello (2001) has transcribed the official document from the WIC archive, the figures clearly show that the officials have estimated certain population numbers by rounding them off. In addition, the total given by Gonsalves de Mello is 160 people more than the total given in the equation above.

New Netherlands (New Amsterdam)

Jacobs (1999) provides estimates for the first years on the coast of North America of no more than a dozen traders in Fort Nassau (Castle Island near Albany). In 1624 several dozen colonists arrived, as well as about thirty Walloon families. Jacobs estimates the population of New Amsterdam and Beverwijck in 1664 at 2,500 and 1,000, respectively. Adding to those numbers about twenty villages of 125-200 inhabitants each, he estimates the total population of New Netherland between 7-8,000 people. Rink (1986) provides detailed information of 174 immigrants to Renselaerwyck between 1630-1644 and 1,079 immigrants to New Netherland between 1657-1664 (the latter constitutes about 27 per cent of the estimated total immigrant figure). Rink (1986:144) estimates a total population of about 300 in 1630 for the Dutch colony, which he upgrades to 500 a few pages later (p.158). The author proceeds by giving estimates for the total population in 1645 of circa 2,500 and at the time of the English take-over of about 9,000. Venema (2003) provides detailed information on the population of Beverwijck. Before 1652 no more than 200 people were living in the settlement, but the figure rises to 1,050 in 1660. The author also provides estimates of between 800 to 1,000 inhabitants for New Amsterdam in 1653 and 1,000 in 1656.

New Netherland was a mixed colony where Dutch Reformed and Lutherans, along with a few Roman Catholics and Jews (23 in 1654) lived among Amerindians. Jacobs (1999) provides an estimate of around 10,000 Amerindians living there in the early period of European settlement. This number was halved by the 1640s and in 1655 about ten per cent of the original figure was estimated to still be living in the area. Slaves were not a prominent feature in New Netherland. Jacobs estimates a population of 100 Africans in 1639 and around 500 free and enslaved Africans living in the colony in 1664. Venema (2003) mentions the arrival of 400 slaves between 1660-1664.

Essequibo, Demerara and Berbice

Reliable demographic figures for these three colonies west of Suriname are hard to obtain. In the late seventeenth century the European population of Essequibo barely exceeded 100, while the number of enslaved Africans may have been in the order of 500. Van der Oest (2003) provides a table in which plantations, slaves and Europeans figure. The table below is an excerpt.

Table 11. Population of Essequibo, Demarara and Berbice, 1700-1817

| Year | Slaves | | | Europeans |
	Essequibo	Demarara	Total	
1700	426		426	60
1716	374		374	
1735	2,600		2,600	110
1766	2,978	2,569	5,547	
1769	4,543	5,967	10510	
1782	8,550	14,132	22,682	1,434
1796	8,000	20,000	28,000	2,700
1817			77,000	

Source: Van der Oest 2003.

In 1762 the number of Europeans in Berbice was estimated at around 345, while the number of enslaved Africans was about 3,800. Three years later, after the 1763 Slave Revolt in the colony, the number of slaves was estimated at 2,500. By the 1780s, the number had risen to 5,000 and would continue to increase (Van Langen 2004 and Netscher 1888).

Suriname

Up until the mid-nineteenth century population figures are sporadic. The following tables summarize the data. As of 1850, demographic figures were collected for the Koloniaal Verslag on a yearly basis.

Table 12a. Inhabitants of Suriname, 1684

	Gentiles	Jews	Total
Europeans			
Males	362	105	467
Females	127	58	185
Total	489	163	652

Slaves	Owned by Gentiles	Owned by Jews	Total
Black males	1,299	543	1,842
Black females	955	429	1,384
Total	2,254	972	3,226
Red males	23	10	39
Red females	54	13	67
Total	83	23	106
Grand total			3,984

Source: Enthoven 2005:160.

Table 12b. Population of Suriname, 1752-1862 (excluding Amerindians and Maroons)

Year	Total free population	Slave population
1752	ca. 2,062	37,835
1774	2,671	59,923
1795	4,953	48,155
1813	ca. 6,104	44,084
1836		46,879
1854	11,597	38,545
1862	16,479	36,484

Source: Van Stipriaan 1993:311, 314.

Table 12c. Population of Suriname, 1850-1862 (excluding Amerindians and Maroons)

Year	Free	Slaves	Total
1850	12,401	39,679	52,080
1860	16,016	37,001	53,017
1862	16,479	36,484	52,963

Source: The demographic figures for the year 1850 can be found in KV 1850, those for 1860 in KV 1860, for 1862 in KV 1862.

Table 12d. Population of Suriname, 1865-1929 (excluding Amerindians and Maroons)*

Year	Male	Female	Total
1865	24,712	25,866	50,578
1870	24,945	25,265	50,210
1875	26,074	25,255	51,329
1880	26,406	26,070	52,476
1885	29,431	27,701	57,132
1890	30,768	29,198	59,966
1895	34,254	31,285	65,539
1900	38,199	33,945	72,144
1905	42,963	37,161	80,024
1910	49,989	42,153	92,142[a]
1915	54,762	45,483	100,245[a]
1920	61,843	51,338	107,723[b]
1925	62,581	57,345	119,926
1929	68,111	63,576	131,687

Source: The demographic figures for the year 1865 can be found in KV 1865, those for 1870 in KV 1871, for 1875 in KV 1876, for 1880 in KV 1881, for 1885 in KV 1886, for 1890 in KV 1891, for 1895 in KV 1896, for 1900 in KV 1901, for 1905 in KV 1906, for 1910 in KV 1911, for 1915 in KV 1916, for 1920 in KV 1921, for 1925 in KV 1926 and for 1929 in KV 1930.

* For the first 45 years after the abolition of slavery (1863) only aggregate population figures are available.
[a] The total does not correspond with table 12e, because records on arrival at and departure from the country were either irregularly carried out or were not carried out at all.
[b] The total consists of temporary numbers as of KV 1921.

Table 12e. Population of Suriname according to ethnicity, 1906-1929*

Year	European	Of whom born in the Netherlands	Afro-Surinamese	Javanese	Born in British India	Chinese	Others	Total	Adding Amer-indians	Adding Maroons
1906	903	604	52,300	5,663	14,887		4,371	78,124[a]		
1910	913	633	52,369	7,894	19,683		5,374	86,233[a]		
1915	915	613	53,027	8,589	21,686	940	3,593	88,750[a]	1,445	8,888
1919	1,109	447	52,425	11,480	26,096	784	3,036	94,930	1,365	9,470
1920**	n.a.	n.a.	n.a.	n.a.	n.a.	n.a.	n.a.	n.a.	n.a.	n.a.
1922	1,396	717	55,138	18,529	30,530	1,313	4,027	110,933	2,645	18,454
1925	1,468	696	58,351	22,201	32,533	1,580	3,793	119,926	2,563	17,380
1929	1,671	910	58,991	30,336	35,379	1,769	3,541	131,687	2,421	17,242

Source: The demographic figures for the year 1906 can be found in KV 1907, those for 1910 in KV 1911, for 1915 in KV 1916, for 1920 in KV 1921, for 1925 in KV 1926 and for 1929 in KV 1930.

*   Numbers for Amerindians and Maroons are estimations until KV 1923 and are always given separately (never included in the total).

**   Figures for 1920 are not available: the registration was not completed when KV 1921 was published.

a   The total does not correspond with table 12d, because records on arrival at and departure from the country were either irregularly carried out or were not carried out at all.

Table 12f. Population of Suriname according to ethnicity, 1931-1945

Year	European	Of whom born in the Netherlands	Afro-Surinamese	Hindustani	Indonesian	Chinese	Other	Total*
1931	1,725	947	60,764	36,756	31,502	1,845	3,625	136,218
1935	1,938	953	65,186	40,777	33,386	2,076	3,480	146,843
1940	2,042	1,027	70,209	46,984	34,365	2,255	3,541	159,396
1945	1,134	722	77,658	55,976	34,272	2,312	2,602	173,954

Source: Economische Stichting West-Indië-Nederland 1956.

* The totals need to be supplemented with the numbers of Maroons and Amerindians. These numbers are estimates ranging from 17,000 Maroons and 2,500 Amerindians in 1931 to 22,000 Maroons and 3,700 Amerindians in 1952.

Table 12g. Population of Suriname according to ethnicity, 31 October 1950

Year	Afro-Surinamese	Hindustani	Indonesian	Chinese (estimated)	European	Amerindian (not Black-Colored)	Other	Total
1950	94,098	63,770	35,949	2,468	2,626	3,546	2,104	204,561

Source: *Volkstelling 1950.*

Table 12h. Population of Suriname according to ethnicity, 1964 and 1974

	Afro-Surinamese	Hindustani	Indonesian	Chinese	European	Amerindian	Maroon	Other/unknown	total
1964	114,961	112,633	48,463	5,339	4,322	7,287	27,698	3,508	324,211
1971	118,483	142,349	58,896	6,400*	4,000*	10,234	39,450	5,100*	384,712

Sources: ABS 1967 and 1972.

* The total from this category is derived from table 5 in the Census of 1972. The other categories are derived from table 3 in the Census of 1972.

Table 12i. Population of Suriname, 1885-1925, Religions

Year	Protestant*	Roman Catholic	Jewish	Hindustani	Islamic	Unknown/ other
1885	32,904	8,024	1,348	5,784	1,270	4,184
1895	36,226	10,634	1,225	9,326	2,594	100
1905	39,144	14,812	1,131	11,148	7,374	1,856
1915	37,462	18,761	882	17,633	11,559	2,453
1925	41,540	24,565[a]	699	26,283	25,523	1,312

Sources: The demographic figures for the year 1885 can be found in KV 1886, those for 1895 in KV 1896, for 1905 in KV 1906, for 1915 in KV 1916 and for 1925 in KV 1926.

* The category 'Protestant' represents the worshippers of the Dutch Reformed, Evangelical Lutheran, Moravian, Evangelical Brother, Episcopal, Free Evangelical and Doopsgezinden. The majority of the Protestant category were worshippers of the Moravian school of thought (which around 1915 was classified as Evangelische Broeder Gemeente).
[a] This total does not contain the number of worshippers in the Maroon and Amerindian community.

The Netherlands Antilles and Aruba

Following the Second World War the six Dutch islands in the Caribbean were designated as the Netherlands Antilles. Aruba seceded from the Antilles in 1986. By 2010 the Antilles will cease to exist as a constitutional entity. All islands will have a direct constitutional relationship with the Netherlands. The tables below provide demographics per island and, later on for all six islands (The Antilles' combined). Until 1929 demographic figures were collected for the *Koloniaal Verslag* on a yearly basis.

Aruba

Table 13a. Population of Aruba on 1 January 1833

Year	White male	White female	Free Coloured male	Free Coloured female	Free Black male	Free Black female	Slave male	Slave female	total
1833	158	207	847	970	49	22	168	225	2,746

Source: Teenstra 1836: opposite 196.

All male and female numbers on the island include adults as well as children.

Bonaire

Table 13b. Population of Bonaire by status, 1806-1826

	Whites	Indians	Freedmen	Slaves	Government slaves
1806	72	284	225	92	272
1816	137	?	568	124	306
1828	90	?	839	137	410

Source: Goslinga 1990:130.

Table 13c. Population of Bonaire on 1 January 1833

Year	White male	White female	Free Coloured male	Free Coloured female	Free Black male	Free Black female	Slave male	Slave female	total
1833	57	55	412	448	110	99	72	85	1,348

Source: Teenstra 1836: opposite 190.

All male and female numbers on the island include adults as well as children.

Curaçao

The first reasonably reliable census for Curaçao dates from 1789. Prior to this, there are only rough estimates. Rupert (2006:147-8) provides an estimate for the population of Willemstad in 1709 of 687 whites, of whom 217 were Sephardic Jews. The first contemporary estimate of the total population on Curaçao dates from 1749. It is likely that these figures were highly inflated, with a total population figure of 70,000 including 44,000 slaves (Coomans-Eustatia, Coomans and Van der Lee 1998:82). Goslinga (1985) provides an estimate for the white population in 1750: 280 Jewish families, 265 Protestant families and 10 Roman Catholic families. All in all, according to his estimates there was an average of 5,35 people per family and a total white population of 2,969.

Table 13d. Population of Curaçao by status, 1789

White Protestants	2,469
Sephardic Jews	1,095
Free Blacks	3,714
Free white servants	846
Slaves	12,864
Total	20,988

Sources: Klooster 1994: table 2 and Rupert 2006:162.

Table 13e. Population of Curaçao by status, 1816-1840

Year	Whites	Free people	Slaves	Total
1816	2,780	4,549	6,741	14,070
1820	2,555	5,195	6,983	14,733
1825	2,884	5,203	5,781	13,868
1830	2,682	5,921	5,908	14,511
1835	2,402	6,176	4,949	13,527
1840	2,734	6,432	5,750	14,916

	Inhabitants	Slaves	Total
1845	5,569	9,451	15,020

Source: Renkema 1981:336.

St. Martin

Table 13f. Population of St. Martin 1699-1750

Year	Whites	Blacks	Total
1699			300
1705			251
1715	361	244	605
1736	599	1,382	1,961
1740	533	1,239	1,772
1745	540	1,284	1,824
1750	648	1,795	2,443

Source: Goslinga 1985:131,138.

Table 13g. Population of St. Martin by status, 1764-1816

Year	Whites	Free Coloured and Blacks	Slaves
1764	966		2,554
1768	1,048		3,142
1772	807		2,719
1774	751		2,593
1777	836		2,511
1790	1,151	194	4,226
1816	715	293	2,551

Source: Goslinga 1990:152, 154.

St. Eustatius

Table 13h. Population of St. Eustatius 1699-1747

Year	Whites	Blacks	Total
1699			784
1705			606
1715	524	750	1,274
1723	426	871	1,297
1729	431	944	1,375
1732	532	911	1,443
1738	627	1,191	1,181
1741	539	1,239	1,778
1747	1,002	1,513	2,515

Source: Goslinga 1985:131, 138.

Table 13i. Population of St. Eustatius by status, 1758-1816

Year	Whites	Free Coloured and Blacks	Slaves
1758	868		1,479
1762	778		1,339
1768	872		1,226
1779	1,574		1,631
1784	872	113	2,962
1789	2,375	511	4,944
1790	2,375	511	4,944
1816	507	336	1,748

Source: Goslinga 1990:152, 154.

Saba

Table 13j. Population of Saba, 1699-1715

Year	Whites	Blacks	Total
1699			453
1705			577
1715	336	176	512

Source: Goslinga 1985:131.

Table 13k. Population of Saba by status, 1790-1816

Year	Whites	Free Coloureds and Blacks	Slaves	Total
1790	730	7	564	1,301
1816	656	27	462	1,145

Source: Goslinga 1990:154.

Netherlands Antilles

Table 13l. Population of the Antilles by status, 1850-1862

Year		Bonaire	Curaçao	St. Martin	St. Eustatius	Saba	Aruba
1850	Free	1,478	11,225	1,227	782	1,014	2,443
	Slaves	143	5,453	1,612	1,150	649	596
	Gov. slaves	599	120				6
	Total	2,220	16,798	2,839	1,932	1,663	3,045
1860	Free	2,163	13,647	1,378	815	1,153	2,445
	Slaves	177	5,330	1,779	1,112	673	398
	Gov. slaves	691	68				6
	Total	3,031	19,045	3,157	1,927	1,826	2,849
1862	Free	2,440	13,629	1,441	832	1,159	2,802
	Slaves	159	5,431	1,883	1,145	708	450
	Gov. slaves	604	67				6
	Total	3,203	19,127	3,324	1,977	1,867	3,258

Table 13m. Population figures of the Antilles, 1870-2007

Year	Bonaire	Curaçao	St. Martin	St. Eustatius	Saba	Aruba
1870	3,750	21,089	2,850	2,049	1,863	3,881
1880	4,986	24,146	3,142	2,097	1,955	6,204
1890	3,821	26,045	3,882	1,588	1,883	7,743
1900	5,086	30,636	3,174	1,334	2,177	9,702
1910	6,353	32,585	2,871	1,325	1,948	9,357
1920	6,383	32,709	2,633	1,315	1,661	8,265
1929	7,119	44,344	2,180	965	1,408	13,450
1940	5,614	67,317	4,344*			30,614
1950	5,079	102,206	2,300	970	1,129	51,000
1960	5,812	125,094	2,728	1,014	980	56,910
1972	8,249	146,884	8,970	1,358	971	57,905
1981	8,753	147,884	13,156	1,708	965	60,312
1992	10,191	143,964	32,219	1,839	1,130	70,629
2001	10,790	130,822	30,444	2,293	1,359	92,676
2007	11,537	137,094	38,959	2,699	1,491	104,494

Sources: The population figures for the year 1870 can be found in KV 1871, those for 1880 in KV 1881, for 1890 in KV 1891, for 1900 in KV 1901, for 1910 in KV 1911, for 1920 in KV 1921 and for 1929 in KV 1930; Koulen and Oostindie 1987:4-5; Palm: 1985:71; CBS Antilles 2008; CBS Aruba 2008.

* Total for the three islands St. Martin, St. Eustatius and Saba.

Table 13n. Population of the Netherlands Antilles (without Aruba) according to place of birth in 1981

Nationality	Bonaire	Curaçao	St. Martin	St. Eustatius	Saba
Dutch:					
Born in the Antilles	5,599	99,901	1,472	842	931
Born in the Netherlands	143	8,429	66	40	10
Suriname		4,257	20		
Born elsewhere		1,865	107		
Portuguese		2,205			
Venezuelan		1,266			
Dominican Republic		428	25		
English or French, born in Caribbean		5,195	1,008		
European		394	2		
US and Canadian		183	28		
Other	70	1,058		132	39
	5,812	125,181	2,728	1,014	980

Source: CBS Antilles 1986.

Table 13o. Population of the Netherlands Antilles according to nationality and place of birth, 1972

Nationality	Bonaire	Curaçao	St. Martin	St. Eustatius	Saba	Aruba
Born in the Antilles	7,653	130,353	4,166	669	871	47,195
Other and unknown	434	16,531	3,269	672	78	7,953
Total	8,087	146,884	7,435	1,341	949	55,148

Sources: Bureau voor de Statistiek 1973; CBS Antilles 1981 and CBS Aruba 1981.

Table 13p. Population of the Netherlands Antilles and Aruba according to nationality, 1991

Nationality	Bonaire	Curaçao	St. Martin	St. Eustatius	Saba	Aruba 1992
The Netherlands	9,334	137,401	15,445	1,543	971	59,469
Dominican Republic	291	1,711	3,685	59	13	1,479
Colombia	102	513			10	1,345
China		251				
Venezuela	106	667				1,126
United States	140	319		93	64	503
United Kingdom		342	1,409	73		
Suriname	37	420				357
Haiti			4,508			277
India		356				
Philippines						236
Portugal		1,054				
Elsewhere	177	1,060	7,174	71	72	1,895
Total	10,187	144,094	32,221	1,839	1,130	66,687

Sources: CBS Antilles 1993; CBS Aruba 1993; Eelens 1994.

Table 13q. Population of Netherlands Antilles and Aruba according to nationality, 2000-2001

Nationality	Bonaire	Curaçao	St. Martin	St. Eustatius	Saba	Aruba 2000
China	52	307	96	21	1	
Colombia	233	1,458	178	-	27	5,769
Dominican Republic	411	2,139	3,098	94	52	2,139
Guyana	22	177	915	58	10	
Haiti	24	458	2,964	8	21	790
India	10	322	510	6	15	
Jamaica	3	418	1,516	10	3	663
The Netherlands	9,236	121,909	15,472	1,777	856	73,440
Portugal	13	493	5	-	1	
Suriname	103	421	273	25	-	450
United States	102	216	564	98	180	656
United Kingdom	13	107	625	16	26	
Venezuela	247	749	73	3	3	2,516
Others	250	789	4,003	150	128	4,083
Not reported	72	664	302	26	26	
Total	10,791	130,627	30,594	2,292	1,349	90,506

Sources: CBS Aruba 2000; CBS Antilles 2001, 2002.

Reference list

Asia

VOC
Lequin, Frank
2005   *Het personeel van de Verenigde Oost-Indische Compagnie in Azië in de achttiende eeuw, meer in het bijzonder in de vestiging Bengalen.* Alphen aan den Rijn: Canaletto.

Taiwan/Formosa
Lierop, Karin van
1983   'De porseleinhandel op Formosa 1624-1660'. MA thesis University of Amsterdam.
Oosterhoff, J.L.
1985   'Zeelandia; A Dutch colonial city on Formosa', in: Robert Ross and Gerard J. Telkamp (eds), *Colonial cities; Essays on urbanism in a colonial context*, pp. 51-63. Dordrecht/Boston/Lancaster: Nijhoff.
Veen, Ernst van
2003   'How the Dutch ran a seventeenth-century colony; The occupation and loss of Formosa 1624-1662', in: Leonard Blussé (ed.), *Around and about Formosa; Essays in honor of Professor Ts'ao Yung-ho*, pp. 141-60. Taipei: Ts'ao Yung-ho Foundation for Culture and Education.
Yao, Keisuke
2003   'Two rivals on an island of sugar; The sugar trade of the VOC and overseas Chinese in Formosa in the seventeenth century', in: Leonard Blussé (ed.), *Around and about Formosa; Essays in honor of Professor Ts'ao Yung-ho*, pp. 129-40. Taipei: Ts'ao Yung-ho Foundation for Culture and Education.

Malacca
Ketelaars, A.P.M.
1985   'Van inheemse stapelmarkt tot tweederangs koloniale stad; Een geschiedenis van Malakka van 1403 tot omstreeks 1690'. MA thesis University of Utrecht.

Cochin/Malabar
Singh, Anjana
2007   *Fort Cochin in Kerala 1750-1830; The social condition of a Dutch community in an Indian milieu.* PhD thesis University of Leiden.

Ceylon/Sri Lanka
Raben, Remco
1996   *Batavia and Colombo; The ethnic and spatial order of two colonial cities 1600-1800.* PhD thesis University of Leiden.

Mauritius
Moree, P.J.
1998   *A concise history of Dutch Mauritius 1598-1710; A fruitful and healthy land.*
            London/New York: Kegan Paul, Leiden: IIAS.

Indonesia/Amboina
Knaap, Gerrit
2004   *Kruidnagelen en christenen; De Verenigde Oost-Indische Compagnie en de*
            bevolking van Ambon, 1656-1697. Second revised edition. Leiden: KITLV
            Uitgeverij. [Verhandelingen 212; First edition 1987.]

Indonesia/ Batavia
Boomgaard, Peter and A.J. Gooszen
1991   *Changing economy in Indonesia; A selection of statistical source material*
            from the early 19th century up to 1940; Vol. 11: Population trends 1975-1942.
            Amsterdam: Royal Tropical Institute.
Raben, Remco
1996   *Batavia and Colombo; The ethnic and spatial order of two colonial cities 1600-*
            1800. PhD thesis University of Leiden.

Indonesia after 1850
Koloniaal verslag
1850-68   *Koloniaal verslag; Verslag van het beheer en den staat der koloniën.* 's-Graven-
            hage: n.n..
1868-1924   *Koloniaal verslag, Bijlage C van de Handelingen der Staten-Generaal.*
            's-Gravenhage: Algemeene Landsdrukkerij.
1924-30   *Koloniaal verslag; Verslag van bestuur en staat van Nederlandsch-Indië,*
            Suriname en Curaçao Bijlage C van de Handelingen der Staten-Generaal.
            's-Gravenhage: Algemeene Landsdrukkerij.
Centraal Kantoor voor de Statistiek van het Departement van Landbouw, Nijverheid
en Handel
1933   *Indisch verslag; II: Statistisch jaaroverzicht van Nederlandsch-Indië over het*
            jaar 1933. Batavia: Landsdrukkerij.

Africa

Cape Colony
Armstrong, James C.
1979   'The slaves, 1652-1795', in: Richard Elphick and Hermann Giliomee
            (eds), *The shaping of South African society, 1652-1820,* pp. 75-115. Cape
            Town: Longman.
Elphick, Richard and Hermann Giliomee (eds)
1979   *The shaping of South African society, 1652-1820.* Cape Town: Longman.

Ghana

Doortmont, Michel R., Natalie Everts and Jean Jacques Vrij
2000   'Tussen de Goudkust, Nederland en Suriname; De Euro-Afrikaanse
            families van Bakergem, Woortman, Rühle en Huydecoper', *De Neder-
            landsche Leeuw; Maandblad van het Koninklijk Nederlandsch Genootschap
            voor Geslacht- en Wapenkunde*117-5/6:170-212, 7/8:310-44, 11/12:490-577.

Doortmont, Michel R. and Natalie Everts
1996   'Onzichtbare Afrikanen; Euro-Afrikanen tussen de Goudkust en Ned-
            erland, 1750-1850', in: Marjolein 't Hart, Jan Lucassen, and Henk
            Schmal (eds), *Nieuwe Nederlanders; Vestiging van migranten door de
            eeuwen heen*, pp. 81-100. Amsterdam: Stichting Beheer IISG/ SISWO/
            Instituut voor Maatschappijwetenschappen.

Enthoven, Victor
2005   'Dutch crossings; Migration between the Netherlands and the New
            World, 1600-1800', *Atlantic studies* 2:153-76.

Everts, Natalie (N.C.)
1996   'Cherchez la Femme; Gender-related issues in eighteenth-century
            Elmina', *Itinerario* 20-1:45-57.
1998   '"Huwelijk naar 's lands wijze"; Relaties tussen Afrikaanse vrouwen
            en Europeanen aan de Goudkust (West Afrika) 1700-1781; Een aanpas-
            sing aan beeldvorming', *Tijdschrift voor Geschiedenis* 111:598-616.

Goslinga, C.Ch.
1985   *The Dutch in the Caribbean and in the Guianas 1680-1791.* Assen: Van
            Gorcum.

IJken, K. van
2001   *A brief history of the Dutch presence on the Gold Coast/in Ghana.* Den Haag:
            Ministerie van Buitenlandse Zaken.

The Americas

New Netherland
Jacobs, Jaap
1999   *Een zegenrijk gewest; Nieuw-Nederland in de zeventiende eeuw.* Amster-
            dam: Prometheus/Bert Bakker.

Rink, Oliver A.
1986   *Holland on the Hudson; An economic and social history of Dutch New York.*
            Ithaca/London: Cornell University Press.

Venema, Janny
2003   *Beverwijck; A Dutch village on the American frontier, 1652-1664.* Albany:
            State University of New York Press, Hilversum: Verloren.

Dutch Brazil
Gonsalves de Mello, J.A.
2001   *Nederlanders in Brazilië (1624-1654); De invloed van de Hollandse bezetting
            op het leven en de cultuur in Noord-Brazilië.* Zutphen: Walburg Pers.

Wätjen, Hermann
1921   *Das holländische Kolonialreich in Brasilien; Ein Kapitel aus der Kolonials-*
            geschichte des 17. Jahrhunderts. Haag: Nijhoff, Gotha: Perthes

Essequibo, Demerara and Berbice
Langen, J.C. van
2004   'De Britse overname van de Nederlandse koloniën Demerary, Esse-
            quebo en Berbice (Guyana); Van economische overvleugeling naar poli-
            tieke overheersing (1740-1814)'. MA thesis University of Amsterdam.
Netscher, P.M.
1888   *Geschiedenis van de koloniën Essequebo, Demerary en Berbice; Van de vesti-*
            ging der Nederlanders aldaar tot op onzen tijd. 's-Gravenhage: Nijhoff.
Oest, Eric van der
2003   'The forgotten colonies of Essequibo and Demerara, 1700-1814', in:
            Johannes Postma and Victor Enthoven (eds), *Riches from Atlantic com-*
            merce; Dutch transatlantic trade and shipping, 1585-1817, pp. 324-61. Lei-
            den/Boston: Brill.

Suriname
Enthoven, Victor
2005   'Dutch crossings; Migration between the Netherlands and the New
            World, 1600-1800', *Atlantic Studies* 2:153-76.
Stipriaan, Alex van
1993   *Surinaams contrast; Roofbouw en overleven in een Caraïbische plantage-*
            kolonie 1750-1863. Leiden: KITLV Uitgeverij. [Caribbean Series 13.]

Suriname after 1850
ABS
1967   *Surinaamse volkstelling 1964; Geheel Suriname, inclusief beperkte telling.*
            Paramaribo: Algemeen Bureau voor de Statistiek.
1972   *Voorlopig resultaat vierde algemene volkstelling; A preliminary report.* Para-
            maribo: Algemeen Bureau voor de Statistiek (ABS).
Economische Stichting West-Indië-Nederland
1956   *Suriname; Enige statistieken over de jaren 1931 t/m 1952.* 's-Gravenhage:
            Economische Stichting West-Indië-Nederland (ESWIN).
Koloniaal verslag (KV)
1850-68   *Koloniaal verslag; Verslag van het beheer en den staat der koloniën.* 's-Graven-
            hage: n.n.
1868-1924   *Koloniaal verslag; Bijlage C van de Handelingen der Staten-Generaal.*
            's-Gravenhage: Algemeene Landsdrukkerij.
1924-30   *Koloniaal verslag; Verslag van bestuur en staat van Nederlandsch-Indië,*
            Suriname en Curaçao Bijlage C van de Handelingen der Staten-Generaal.
            's-Gravenhage: Algemeene Landsdrukkerij.
Volkstelling 1950
1956   *Tweede algemeene volkstelling Suriname 1950; Deel 10; De eigenlijke volks-*
            telling. Paramaribo: Welvaartsfonds Suriname.

The Netherlands Antilles

Bonaire and Aruba
Goslinga, C.Ch.
1990   *The Dutch in the Caribbean and in Surinam 1791/5-1942.* Assen/Maastricht: Van Gorcum.
Teenstra, M.D.
1836-37   *De Nederlandse West-Indische eilanden in derzelver tegenwoordigen toestand.* Amsterdam: Sulpke. Two vols.

Curaçao
Coomans-Eustatia, Maritza, Henny E. Coomans and To van der Lee (eds)
1998   *Breekbare banden; Feiten en visies over Aruba, Bonaire en Curaçao na de Vrede van Munster 1648-1998.* Bloemendaal: Stichting Libri Antilliani.
Goslinga, C.Ch.
1985   *The Dutch in the Caribbean and in the Guineas 1680-1791.* Assen/Maastricht: Van Gorcum.
Klooster, Wim
1994   'Subordinate but proud; Curaçao's free blacks and mulattoes in the eighteenth century', *New West Indian Guide* 68:283-300.
Renkema, W.E.
1981   *Het Curaçaose plantagebedrijf in de negentiende eeuw.* Zutphen: Walburg Pers.
Rupert, Linda Marguerite
2006   *Inter-imperial trade and local identity; Curaçao in the colonial Atlantic world.* PhD thesis Duke University, Durham.

Sint Eustatius, Saba, Sint Maarten
Goslinga, C.Ch.
1985   *The Dutch in the Caribbean and in the Guineas 1680-1791.* Assen: Van Gorcum.
1990   *The Dutch in the Caribbean and in Surinam 1791/5-1942.* Assen: Van Gorcum.

The Netherlands Antilles after 1850
Koloniaal verslag
1850-68   *Koloniaal verslag; Verslag van het beheer en den staat der koloniën.* 's-Gravenhage: s.n.
1868-1924   *Koloniaal verslag, Bijlage C van de Handelingen der Staten-Generaal.* 's-Gravenhage : Algemeene Landsdrukkerij.
1924-30   *Koloniaal verslag; Verslag van bestuur en staat van Nederlandsch-Indië, Suriname en Curaçao Bijlage C van de Handelingen der Staten-Generaal.* 's-Gravenhage: Algemeene Landsdrukkerij.
Koulen, Ingrid and Gert Oostindie
1987   *The Netherlands Antilles and Aruba; A research guide.* Dordrecht: Foris Publications. [KITLV, Caribbean Series 7.]

Palm, J.Ph. de (ed.)
1985   *Encyclopedie van de Nederlandse Antillen*. Second revised edition. Zut-
                phen: Walburg Pers.

Antilles (without Aruba)
Bureau voor de Statistiek
1973?   *Eerste algemene volks- en woningtelling Nederlandse Antillen; Deel A: De
                uitkomsten van de volkstelling*. Willemstad: Departement Sociale en
                Economische Zaken, Bureau voor de Statistiek.
CBS Antilles
1986   *Enige kenmerken van de bevolking van de Nederlandse Antillen; Demografi-
                sche kenmerken, nationaliteit, taal, handicap, religie*. Willemstad: Centraal
                Bureau voor de Statistiek (CBS).
1993   *Third population and housing census Netherlands Antilles 1992*. Willem-
                stad: Centraal Bureau voor de Statistiek (CBS).
2001   'Population and housing census 2001', http://www.cbs.an/census/
                antde7.asp (accessed 2-6-2008).
2002   *Fourth population and housing census Netherlands Antilles 2001; Methodol-
                ogy, main results, concepts and definitions, code books and questionnaires*.
                Willemstad: Centraal Bureau voor de Statistiek (CBS).
2008   http://www.cbs.an/population/population_tables.asp (accessed 2-6-
                2008).
Volkstelling
1960   *Volkstelling 1960 Curaçao, Bonaire, St. Maarten, St. Eustatius en Saba*. Wil-
                lemstad: Statistiek- en Planbureau Nederlandse Antillen.

Aruba
CBS Aruba
1985   *Enige kenmerken van de bevolking van Aruba; Demografische kenmerken,
                nationaliteit en geboorteplaats, taal, handicap, religie*. Willemstad: Centraal
                Bureau voor de Statistiek (CBS).
2001   *Censo Aruba 2000*. Oranjestad: Centraal Bureau voor de Statistiek.
2008   Aa.1.1.1 Key Demographic Indicators, 1991-2006 on http://www.cbs.
                aw/cbs/getDocumentList.do?categoryId=103&categoryBranchId=103&
                firstItem=0&category=77 (accessed 2-6-2008).
Eelens, Frank
1994   *The population of Aruba; A demographic profile*. The Hague: Netherlands
                Interdisciplinary Demographic Institute (NIDI).

Index of geographical names

Index of personal names

General index

About the authors

Anouk Fienieg is project coordinator at the Dutch Centre for International Heritage Activities. She was trained as historian and graduated on the Dutch Mutual Cultural Heritage Policy.

Brittany Groot is an MA student in Archaeology at the University of Leiden. Her focus is on socio-political issues within archaeological heritage management.

Rivke Jaffe is a lecturer in the Department of Cultural Anthropology and Development Sociology, University of Leiden. She has done fieldwork in Curacao, Suriname and Jamaica and her research interests include urban studies, popular culture and the anthropology of the state.

Dr Gijs Kruijtzer is a historian of South and Southeast Asia and currently employed as researcher at the Institute of Netherlands History (ING).

Sjoerd van der Linde is a researcher and lecturer in the field of Archaeological Heritage Management at the Faculty of Archaeology at the University of Leiden. His research examines the socio-political and cultural contexts in which theory and practice of Dutch archaeological projects in postcolonial contexts are developed and utilized.

Hanneke Lommerse received her BA in History at the University of Amsterdam. Currently she is working on her thesis to complete her MA in History of European Expansion and Globalization at Leiden University.

Professor Gert Oostindie is director of the KITLV/Royal Netherlands Institute of Southeast Asian and Caribbean Studies and Professor of Caribbean History at the University of Leiden.

Robert Parthesius is director at the Dutch Centre for International Heritage Activities. His expertise and research focus on the cultural heritage of the European Expansion.

Pauline K.M. van Roosmalen is architectural historian, specialised in colonial and modern architecture and town planning in the Dutch East Indies and Indonesia.

Thio Termorshuizen studied history at the University of Leiden and has collaborated on several projects concerning social history in the Dutch colonial context.

Rik van Welie graduated from the the University of Leiden and is currently working on his dissertation at Emory University (Atlanta, Georgia) on the emergence of the Dutch slave trade in the early seventeenth century.